ORACLE® Reporting

Queries with SQL objects

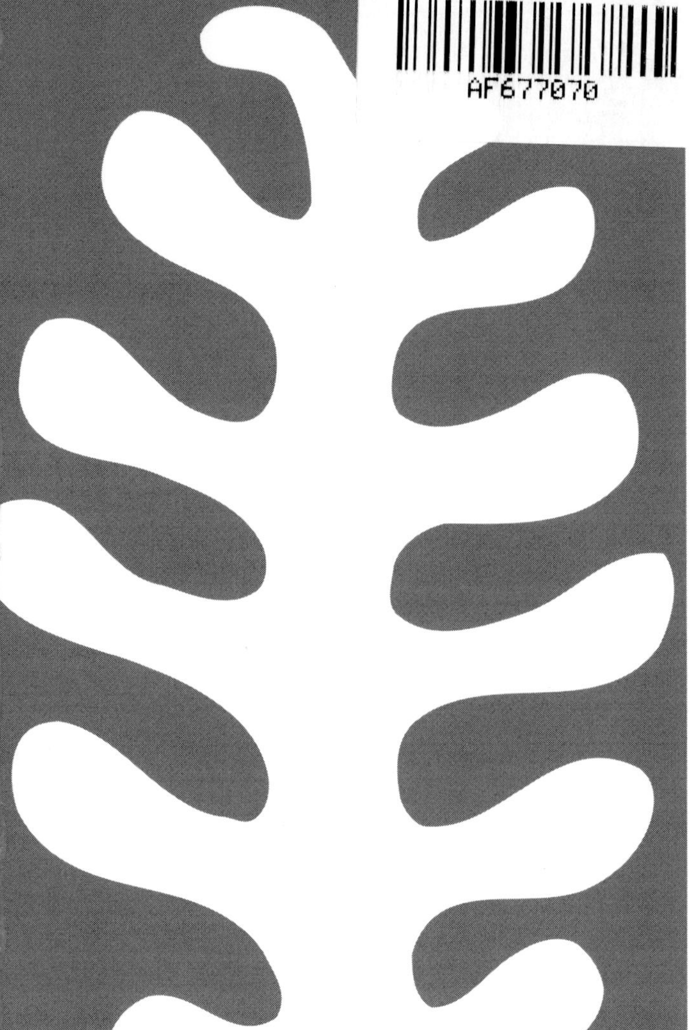

Gary M. Lewis

AF677070

SOLOMON R. BAKER LIBRARY
BENTLEY COLLEGE

Published by
Komenda Publishing Company
P.O. Box 38-1395
Cambridge, MA 02238-1395

Copyright © 1995 by Gary M. Lewis. All rights reserved.

No portion of this book may be reproduced or used in any form, or by any means, without prior written permission of the copyright owner. Requests for permission or more information should be addressed to Komenda Publishing Company. Program listings, however, may be entered, stored, and executed in a computer system, but they may not be reproduced for publication.

The following are trademarks or registered trademarks:
CorelDraw, Ventura Publisher—Corel Systems
LaserJet—Hewlett-Packard Company
Multi-Edit—American Cybernetics, Inc.
SQL*PLUS, SQL*FORMS, SQL*LOADER, ORACLE—Oracle Corporation
SQR—Management Information Technology, Inc.
VAX and VMS—Digital Equipment Corporation
Windows, MS-DOS, QuickBasic, Word, and Excel—Microsoft Corporation.
All other products and brand names are trademarks of their respective holders.

Considerable care was taken in the preparation of this book. Nevertheless, Komenda Publishing Company assumes no responsibility for any errors, omissions, or inaccuracies that remain in the book. Neither the publisher nor author assumes any responsibility for damages resulting from the use of information obtained in the book.

Library of Congress Catalog Card Number 95-94198
ISBN 0-9644912-3-0

First printing June 1995
10 9 8 7 6 5 4 3 2 1
Printed in the United States of America

Lewis, Gary M.
ORACLE reporting : queries with SQL objects / Gary M. Lewis.
p. cm.
Includes bibliographic references and index.
ISBN 0-9644912-3-0
1. ORACLE (Computer system). 2. SQL (Computer program language).
3. Relational databases. 4. Object oriented programming (Computer science). I. Title.
QA76.73.S67L484 1995 95-94198

To my wife

Dorothy Ekua Milligan

Contents Summary

Table of Contents

Preface

Structured Query Language (SQL) is the *lingua franca* of relational databases. Since relational systems dominate database markets today, SQL plays a particularly crucial role for anyone trying to wring information from data. SQL*PLUS is Oracle Corporation's extension of SQL. And since Oracle dominates the relational database market, SQL*PLUS plays a similarly important role. SQL and SQL*PLUS are simultaneously simple, complex, powerful, inept, exquisite, frustrating, and dangerous. They are, if nothing else, engaging; you cannot ignore them and expect to function as an information provider.

The message in *ORACLE Reporting* is simple—there is a way to simultaneously minimize the negative aspects of SQL and to accentuate its positives. The central idea is simplicity. It recognizes that experienced SQL query writers create building blocks that vastly improve their querying capability. These building blocks are just chunks of SQL or SQL*PLUS that they've written and then reuse in other queries. I call these chunks of code objects. Some of the objects define commonly requested report populations. Others serve as templates for specific types of reports, provide access to data columns appearing in a report, control the physical characteristics of the report, and massage data columns into useful report expressions.

SQL objects elevate the task of query writing. There is considerable parallel between an ad hoc query and a corresponding set of objects. Making the translation is comparable to parsing a written sentence. You identify the noun—the core population for the report—and any modifying adjectives that further define the report population. These get mapped to objects. You then identify the type of report requested and map it to an object. Requested data columns get mapped to objects that provide access to specific data tables. You proceed through the query, translating words or phrases into objects. You then assemble these objects into completed programs that produce a report. Object assembly can even be automated. Some day I believe that people will interact almost conversationally with organizational databases. While SQL is light years removed from that day, objects represent a definite step toward that future.

I came to this book through a curious route. My background is in higher education research; in providing decision-makers at colleges and universities with information to help them set institutional policy and direction. As such I use administrative databases extensively. Six years ago I worked at a college in Massachusetts doing research in admissions and financial aid. The college used an administrative database that was much maligned and reviled by nearly everyone. Yet it was quite simple to use. I wrote hundreds of queries that extracted data that I then imported into statistical packages for more detailed analysis. Other end users wrote queries that produced reports for day-to-day operations. The query language employed a simple syntax very similar to English. You needed only a single line to produce a report, but you could also string together many such lines to create more complex reports. Using this query tool, end users without any programming background routinely created "programs" that exceeded 100 lines. They just didn't know they were programming.

Then the college purchased an administrative database that used a relational database management system. The front-end was spectacular. Data input had a whole new pizzazz to it. And the functionality vastly exceeded what we could do with the previous system. For those of you who have ever converted from one database system to another, you know it's not a comfortable experience. So for many months after we purchased the new system, everybody focused on converting data from one system to another. But eventually a day arrived when people actually wanted to use the new database.

That's when the confusion began. SQL is not an end user query tool except in trivial situations; it is a programmer's tool. Staff people who wrote queries and supplied managers with reports suddenly found themselves disempowered. Reports got written using SQL, but they were frequently difficult and often wrong. Some things done with ease in the previous system could not be done at all without programming skills. Query writing previously occurred under the direction of managers running the various offices of the colleges. With the new relational database system, query writing became the responsibility of a central information systems staff. Managers resented the shift.

After several years we reached an equilibrium, made possible by considerable user training, by simplifying the database to use special data views and temporary tables constructed specifically for queries, and by purchasing an ad hoc query tool that distances end users from the underlying SQL. However, when people look back at this time I believe they'll see this as a modest plateau. Querying still occurs through translators, that is, people designated with responsibility for translating English into something the database can understand. Such a job description will surely disappear as databases become easier to use.

As the locus of query writing shifted from individual offices to a centralized information systems (IS) staff, I too made the shift. Today I work in IS, designing and developing what's typically called decision support or executive information systems. Whatever you call them, these systems are designed to help people make better informed operational and policy decisions. Over the past few years I've written several thousand ad hoc queries with SQL and SQL*PLUS. I've designed and written many data views for users so that they can run queries against live data. I've designed and developed extract tables that get refreshed regularly and whose sole function is to simplify ad hoc queries. I've also evaluated and used many of the graphical query tools that have become a small industry in the past few years as users clamor for easier ways to access relational databases. But, while I may work in information systems, my perspective remains that of an end user. I am most interested in converting data into information and using that information with some effect.

ORACLE Reporting reflects that interest. There are, I believe, six areas where the book differs significantly from others on SQL or SQL*PLUS. First, the book uses SQL objects as a meta-language. SQL is not an end-user query tool, but SQL objects come very close. And, unlike other solutions that strengthen end-user querying capability, SQL objects run against relational databases in all their complexity. You need not simplify the database to do ad hoc reporting with SQL objects.

Second, the book concentrates on reporting. SQL contains components that can be used for other purposes, such as database administration. I don't discuss these aspects of SQL. I'm interested in using SQL for analysis and this book only deals with SQL and SQL*PLUS as they relate to reporting. By focusing on one aspect of SQL, the book provides a depth not possible in more comprehensive texts.

Third, the book acknowledges that SQL is not a query language disembodied from some organizational context within which it is used. You cannot write accurate SQL without knowing organizational procedures, policies, and guidelines. In the book I introduce a fictitious college and simulate an administrative database for that college. This database is quite rich; it contains 30 tables, some with over 10,000 rows. It was simulated using probability distributions, conditional relationships, and random number generators. It provides the messiness and complexity of real databases without being overwhelming.

Fourth, the book provides many tools that will help you write your own queries. Some of these appear as utility programs that can be run on your own system to prepare data dictionaries, lists of unique indexes, or an inventory of data tables. Other tools appear as objects. For example, the objects that produce one-way frequency distributions or cross-tabulations are completely general to ORACLE version 6 and version 7. You need only incorporate them into your own work.

Fifth, the book reflects my belief that linearity in presentation is not always a good thing. What does that mean? Well, in many books the simple topics appear near the front and the difficult topics appear near the back. Unfortunately, the most innocuous sounding query can sometimes require quite complex SQL. The book makes no distinction between simple and difficult. Instead, it presents ideas when they're needed. And it only presents topics actually needed for reporting.

And finally, the book relies heavily on illustrations in the form of figures and tables. If you and I were working on a query together, much of that work would occur on a computer screen and be visual. We'd see the structure in a program, see the errors as we debugged the program, and see the final output. I've tried to incorporate that visual experience into the book by including numerous illustrations; they're as important as the words in the text.

For those of you familiar with ORACLE and SQL*PLUS, let me tell you about the versions represented in this book. Much of my experience with ORACLE has occurred with version 6 running on a VAX under VMS. I now use ORACLE v7.1.3 on the same platform. ORACLE made several significant changes between ORACLE v6 and v7, and the book discusses those changes when needed. From a reporting viewpoint, for example, the introduction of a VARCHAR2 datatype constitutes a substantial change. Chapter 4 discusses this and other version differences. I developed the database used throughout the book with ORACLE v6 running under DOS on a personal computer. As I write, ORACLE v7 is not yet available for personal computers, although I'm eagerly awaiting the arrival of a version for Microsoft Windows. In any event, the differences between ORACLE v6 and v7 don't affect the central argument of this book.

I've also tried to follow several conventions in the book. You'll find that SQL and SQL*PLUS commands are indicated in ***bold italic.*** Clauses of the SQL *select* command and options in SQL*PLUS commands appear in *italic.* As new terms appear, they too first appear in italic. I have generally ignored the convention of using uppercase letters for SQL and SQL*PLUS commands. ORACLE permits either upper or lowercase. When writing my own ad hoc queries, I exclusively use lowercase keywords because I find them easier to read. This book employs the same convention.

ORACLE Reporting presumes an audience of one—you, a writer of ad hoc queries. You may have no formal training in databases, but are still be expected to produce rosters so your office can function on a day-to-day basis. Or you may be a research analyst, trying to use your company's databases to improve the decisions made by policy makers. Or you may be a college student enrolled in a relational database course. Or you may be a programmer embedding SQL into procedural programs. Or you may be a database administrator gathering performance information. Or you may provide support to users whose ad hoc querying abilities are temporarily exceeded by a problem at hand. Or you may be a developer at a company that designs graphical query tools for relational databases. In short, you could be almost anyone who must translate an ad hoc request into SQL and SQL*PLUS.

While the audience is one of query writers, the skills that you bring to this book determine what portion will be most appropriate for you. End users with little formal programming background will find Parts I and III of the book most useful. Experienced query writers will find Parts II and III most useful and will want to use Part I as a smorgasbord from which they can sample items.

Part I assumes no prior knowledge about SQL or SQL*PLUS. It provides an introduction to SQL objects and also provides the necessary background in SQL and SQL*PLUS required by the remainder of the book. Chapter 1 discusses common reporting problems and identifies why SQL can, at times, be a frustrating query tool. Chapter 2 demonstrates how easy it is to construct queries by manipulating SQL objects. When you're freed from the need to write SQL and can assemble queries using higher order abstractions like objects, the query writing process improves considerably. Chapter 3 introduces Komenda College, a fictional college in upstate New York that serves as the basis for the queries in this book. The chapter documents Komenda's recruiting and admissions database. It also discusses how Komenda conducts its recruiting and admissions operations, because you can't write accurate SQL without reference to an organizational context.

Chapter 4 provides a primer on those portions of SQL most appropriate for ad hoc reporting. Appendix C supplements Chapter 4 and documents in one convenient location the material on SQL operators, functions, and formats. In Chapter 5 you'll discover a set of utility tools that should be assembled prior to writing queries. These tools vastly improve the ease with which you can write accurate and efficient SQL. Chapter 6 completes Part I by providing a primer of the SQL*PLUS commands most commonly used in ad hoc reporting. Appendix E supplements Chapter 6 and draws all the SQL*PLUS commands together in one place.

Part II puts you to work building objects. Chapters 7 through 11 each concentrate on one of the five major SQL object classes. The analogy to a construction site is warranted. You'll use indexes, dictionaries, database schematics, operators, functions, and formats; you'll join tables, construct subqueries, recode data columns, and perform date arithmetic; and in the process you'll build SQL objects that define populations, modify populations, provide access to data columns, create templates for reports, control report characteristics, and transform the data columns in a report. These chapters work through query after query, taking you from English to SQL and often passing through a pseudo-SQL intermediary. By the time you finish Part II, you'll have built nearly 50 objects for the simulated database that can be assembled into complete ad hoc queries.

I'd like to draw particular attention to Chapter 12, which concludes Part II. This chapter discusses the testing, debugging, and tuning of SQL objects. In ad hoc queries you should always count on one constant: things can go wrong, and they will go wrong. You need to know two things. First, how can you prevent problems from occurring? Second, what can you do about problems when they do occur? Chapter 12 addresses these questions. *Every* query should be tested. Chapter 12 shows you what to test, how to interpret the tests, and what to do about the results.

If Part II is a construction site, Part III is a good old-fashioned barn-raising. Query writers with all levels of experience should benefit from this part of the book. Chapter 13 uses the objects built in earlier chapters. It's based on a scenario involving you as the query writer and Komenda College's dean of enrollment planning, a very persistent woman who wants to know why the College of Arts & Sciences enjoys better admissions results than the College of Business. Chapter 14 discusses the automation of SQL objects. When used manually, SQL objects improve the ease with which ad hoc queries can be constructed. However, many end users do not want to assemble objects manually. Nor should they. Chapter 14 illustrates a menu driven system that automates the use of SQL objects. It concludes by speculating about alternative object systems that would be extremely powerful yet simple to use.

I wrote this book with a very definite image in my mind—you and I are seated in front of a computer screen, and we're working on an ad hoc request. I therefore deliberately use a conversational tone. This means that I use the first person occasionally and talk about my own experiences. I also use contractions and other devices more commonly found in verbal rather than written communication. When I use the word you, I mean you the reader of those words. When I use the word we, I mean you and me.

It is my hope that the book will serve a practical purpose, to improve the ease with which you can explore relational databases and convert data into information.

Gary Lewis
Cambridge, MA

Acknowledgments

Between the conception and publication of *ORACLE Reporting*, many people provided their support and encouragement—both indispensible ingredients that nurtured the book and the author. In particular, I'd like to thank Kate Anderson, Russ Davis, Peter Farago, Eileen Gentile, Margot Maley, Rebekah Mazzaferro, Dorothy Paradis, Anne Pugliese, Susan Schwab, Marty Tenney, Debbie Tomsho, my many friends at Bentley College in Management Information Systems and in Data Administration, the extended Milligan clan, and my family. Mike Corey, Paul Dorsey, Jim Foley, and Les Waguespack deserve special thanks for reading the manuscript in part or in full and offering their suggestions and comments. They should, however, be absolved of responsibility for any errors remaining in the book; that responsibility is mine alone. Lastly, but most importantly, I'd like to thank the people who provided the intellectual content for this book—the end-users at Bentley College who, over the years, have asked me for ad hoc reports. These include Kim Balkus, Andre Bell, Becky Brodigan, Dodie Daniell, Jane Ellis, Kent Ericson, Mary Flaherty, Janet Gardner, Ed Gillis, Maria Goodrich, Tanja Macaris, Nancy Marudzinski, Deirdre McGoldrick, Joann McKenna, Marilyn Molnar, Kathie Nolan, Rob O'Connor, Sharon Oliver, Pat Rogers, Mary Ryan, and Joyce Thaeler.

Part I
Introducing SQL Objects

Chapter 1

Common SQL Reporting Problems

Ad hoc reports vary tremendously, yet they all originate in the power and flexibility of a single SQL statement—the *select* command. This is an extraordinary achievement.

It is true that many other SQL commands exist. You can create or drop tables, insert or update data values, grant access rights to tables, and generally perform a variety of other housekeeping functions. For security reasons these privileges are usually reserved for database designers and administrators. Even programmers normally use the commands under restrictions. As a query writer you can forget about these commands. You won't have access rights to them, but you also won't need them. All you'll need is the SQL *select* statement to retrieve data and Oracle's SQL*PLUS to format the report.

The *Select* Command

If only one command is needed for ad hoc reporting, you'd think the command must be complex to be that powerful. But the contrary is true. The *select* command includes only six keywords, and four of the six are optional.

The six keywords function like clauses in a sentence. They each serve a specific purpose:

- *select*: Lists the data columns to appear in the report. Each query must include a *select* clause.
- *from:* Lists the tables that contain data for the report or that must be traversed to access the data. Each query must include a *from* clause.

- *where*: Places conditions on data to include in the report (e.g., where state = 'CA'), thereby defining the report population. The *where* clause also specifies how tables are related to each other.
- *order by*: Sorts the report data by some criteria (e.g., sorts a list of people by their last name).
- *group by*: Helps summarize subgroups of the report population with counts, averages, and other group functions.
- *having*: Restricts the report to only certain subgroups of the population based on a summary value. *Having* works in conjunction with *group by*.

Consider a data table called NAME that includes people's first, last, and middle names. The following is a legitimate SQL query that lists the first and last names of all people named Jones and orders the list by their first name:

```
select name_first, name_last from NAME
where name_last = 'Jones' order by name_first;
```

The query has syntax similar to an English sentence. Someone who knew nothing about SQL could read the query and make a decent guess about the report it produced.

To access data SQL uses only a single command containing, at most, six keywords arranged with a recognizable syntax. How much easier could a query tool get?

Relational Databases

The problem is the database. If all the data you need is stored in a single table, then SQL is an adequate tool for end-user ad hoc reports. But that's seldom the case; in fact, the other extreme is more likely. Databases with more than a thousand tables occur frequently.

To understand why databases queried with SQL are often complex, we should first dispense with some terminology. Data accessed through SQL is stored in *tables*. Each table is composed of *rows* and *columns*. Rows correspond to entities of some kind (e.g., people) and columns to pieces of information about the rows (e.g., first name). The intersection of a single row and a single column is a data *value*. Figure 1–1 shows a portion of the

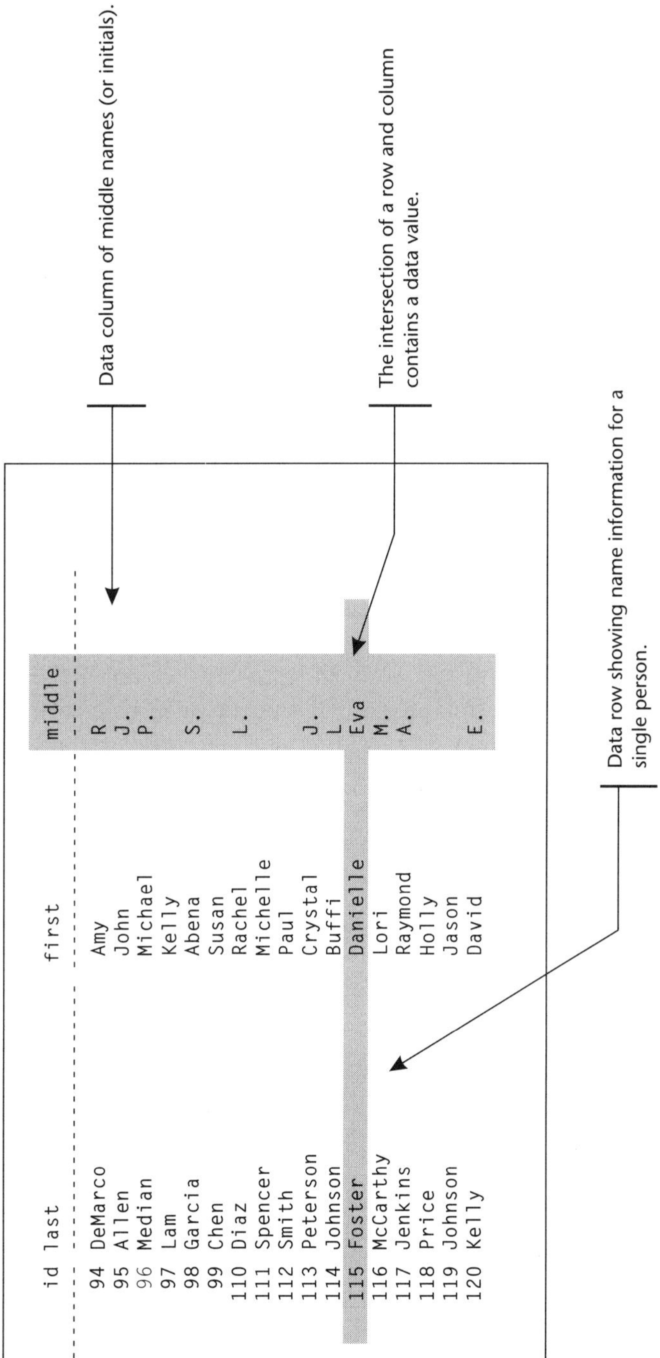

id	last	first	middle
94	DeMarco	Amy	R
95	Allen	John	J.
96	Median	Michael	P.
97	Lam	Kelly	
98	Garcia	Abena	S.
99	Chen	Susan	
110	Diaz	Rachel	L.
111	Spencer	Michelle	
112	Smith	Paul	
113	Peterson	Crystal	J.
114	Johnson	Buffi	L
115	Foster	Danielle	Eva
116	McCarthy	Lori	M.
117	Jenkins	Raymond	A.
118	Price	Holly	
119	Johnson	Jason	
120	Kelly	David	E.

Figure 1–1. Selected rows and columns in the NAME table.

NAME table described later in Chapter 3. The data value "Eva" occurs at the intersection of the highlighted row and the middle name column. Obviously, this person's middle name is Eva.

Designers of databases accessed through SQL use a procedure called *normalization* to identify the tables to include in a database. Essentially, normalization groups data columns into tables so that data for related columns gets stored in only one place. A person's name gets stored in a single name table, not in every table where information about the person may appear. This provides some real benefits. First, it eliminates the storage of redundant data and saves storage space. Second, it eliminates possible inconsistencies when updates occur. For example, a name must be updated in only one table.

Let's take a simple example and, without going through a formal normalization, speculate what the data tables might look like. Suppose we wanted to construct a database to store the following data on a group of college students: identification number, first name, middle name, last name, address and phone number, and sex and date of birth. We might start by placing all the data columns in a single "student" table.

Figure 1–2 shows this single table solution. But what assumptions are needed to make this design work? First, we limited ourselves to dormitory or permanent addresses and phone numbers. Suppose it later becomes important to store a billing address? Can new data columns be added easily?

STUDENT table

```
id
first_name
middle_name
last_name
sex
birthdate
dorm_street1
dorm_city
dorm_state
dorm_zip
dorm_phone
permanent_street1
permanent_city
permanent_state
permanent_zip
permanent_nation
permanent_phone
```

Figure 1–2. Single table of student data.

Second, we limited our options to update data as new information becomes available. What happens when a name changes, a student moves to a new dorm, or his or her phone number changes?

Two solutions exist for updating data. We could store only current data; or alternatively we could add another row to the table. This row would contain the updated data. Figure 1–3 on the following page shows both solutions. If current data is the only interest, the single table database in Figure 1–3(b) would work fine. It certainly makes reporting easy. All data appear in one place and there's only one row per person. But it might be important to confirm that Jen O'Brien in today's report is the same person as Eugenia Husarova in last year's report. In that case we have a few problems. Every time an update occurs, a new row appears in the table even if only one data value actually changes. What results is the storage of redundant data. Note in Figure 1–3(c) how much data is stored more than once when updates are made.

Normalization reduces this redundancy by splitting the data columns into multiple tables. Suppose it's important to document name changes but nothing else. We could minimize the storage of redundant data by storing names in a separate table and putting all other columns in a second table. Figure 1–4 on page 9 shows this solution. For this solution to work, however, some link between the two tables must exist; the two tables must share one or more data columns so the tables can be joined together for reporting. In Figure 1–4 this common data column is the identification number. Databases constructed through a normalization procedure, where tables are related through common data columns and accessed via SQL, are called *relational* databases.

Before discussing ad hoc report problems created by splitting data into multiple tables, let's pursue this normalization question a bit further. What happens if we want to store data on students' summer addresses or their billing addresses? Well, we could just add more columns to the "other" table in Figure 1–4. This might work briefly. But it makes more sense to simplify the table, as shown in Figure 1–5 on page 9, by including an ADDRESS table and a new data column that identifies the type of address (e.g., "P" identifies a permanent address). Using this technique you can add any new address type just by creating a new code.

Even this degree of normalization might not be enough. The address table assumes that phone numbers occur only for addresses. Certainly this is often the case, but how would you store a cellular phone number for a car? You could create a "C" code for a car address. But a cleaner database design occurs if you split the addresses and phone numbers into two separate tables.

(a) Original Data

id	first	middle	last	sex	birthdate	dorm street	dorm city	dorm state	dorm zip	dorm phone	perm street	perm city	perm state	perm zip	perm nation	perm phone
001	Helen		Benjamin	F	12-Aug-75	ARL310	Komenda	NY	12850	354-1175	RR 4	Crary Mills	NY	13310		555-430-9918
002	Bill	W.	Appleton	M	02-Sep-76						15 West St	Glen Falls	NY	12750		555-615-1902
003	Jessie	Ronald	Stillman	M		CAM223	Komenda	NY	12850	354-8390	Bayview Rd	Ipswich	MA	01938		
004	Kara		Nichols	F	28-Mar-75	MED115	Komenda	NY	12850	354-8718	1120 S 33rd St	Rochester	NY	14520		555-320-6470

(b) Updates storing current data only

id	first	middle	last	sex	birthdate	dorm street	dorm city	dorm state	dorm zip	dorm phone	perm street	perm city	perm state	perm zip	perm nation	perm phone
001	Helen		Benjamin	F	12-Aug-75	ARL310	Komenda	NY	12850	354-1175	RR 4	Crary Mills	NY	13310		555-430-9918
002	Bill	W.	Appleton	M	02-Sep-76	MED212	Komenda	NY	12850	354-8870	82 Jay St	Albany	NY	12205		555-614-3478
003	Jessie	Ronald	Stillman	M		CAM223	Komenda	NY	12850	354-8390	Bayview Rd	Ipswich	MA	01938		
004	Kara		Nichols	F	28-Mar-75	MED115	Komenda	NY	12850	354-8718	1120 S 33rd St	Rochester	NY	14520		555-320-6470

(c) Updates storing historical and current data

id	first	middle	last	sex	birthdate	dorm street	dorm city	dorm state	dorm zip	dorm phone	perm street	perm city	perm state	perm zip	perm nation	perm phone	seriesno
001	Helen		Benjamin	F	12-Aug-75	ARL310	Komenda	NY	12850	354-1175	RR 4	Crary Mills	NY	13310		555-430-9918	1
002	Bill	W.	Appleton	M	02-Sep-76						15 West St	Glen Falls	NY	12750		555-615-1902	1
002	Bill	W.	Appleton	M	02-Sep-76	MED212	Komenda	NY	12850	354-8870	82 Jay St	Albany	NY	12205		555-614-3478	2
003	Jessie	Ronald	Stillman	M		CAM223	Komenda	NY	12850	354-8390	Bayview Rd	Ipswich	MA	01938			1
004	Kara		Nichols	F	28-Mar-75	MED115	Komenda	NY	12850	354-8718	1120 S 33rd St	Rochester	NY	14520		555-320-6470	1

Figure 1–3. Update problems in flat files.

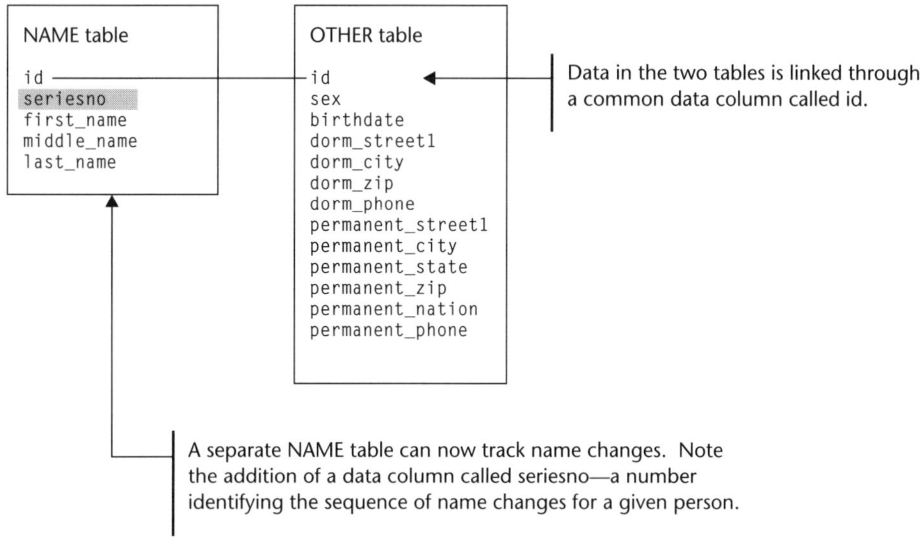

Figure 1–4. Normalization into a NAME and OTHER table.

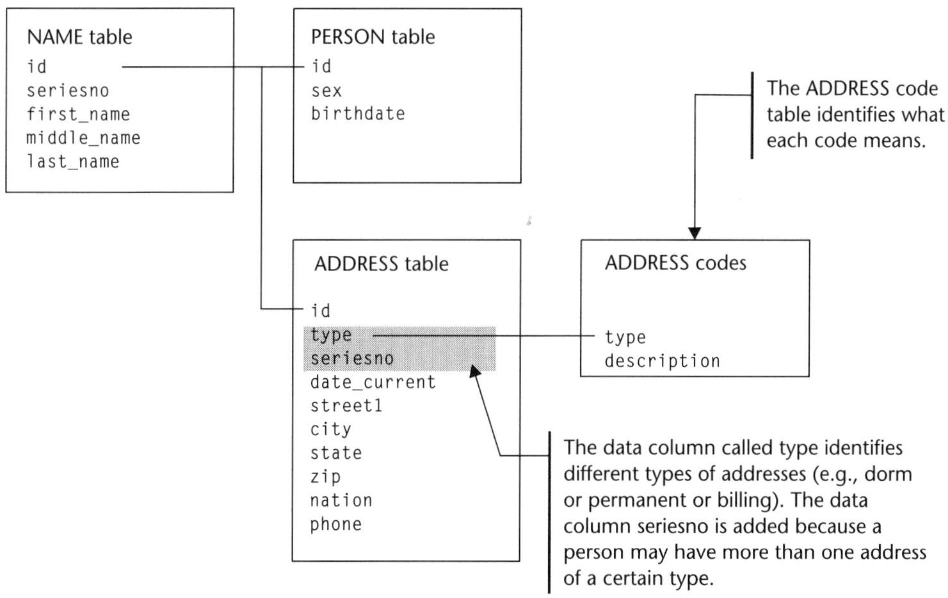

Figure 1–5. ADDRESS and PERSON tables included.

Figure 1–6 on the following page shows our simple database normalized into four tables: name, address, phone, and person, plus two supporting code tables for address type and phone type. Note that the phone and

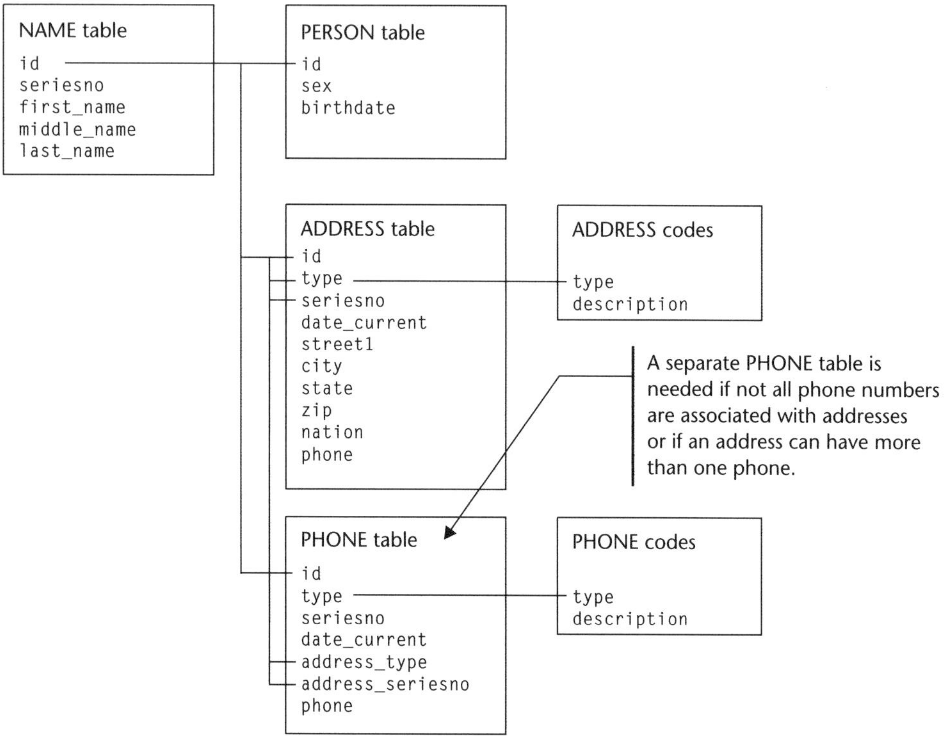

Figure 1–6. PHONE table included.

address tables are related through three data columns: the identification number, the address type, and the address series number. The series number distinguishes between two or more addresses of the same type; for example, if a person has two permanent addresses they are distinguished by a series number of 1 and 2. To find a person's permanent address and phone number, you must match the identification numbers, the address types, and the series numbers in the address and phone tables.

This simple example has gone from one table to six tables. This is typical of relational databases. Normalization does reduce storage of redundant data; it also reduces the number of updates needed when data changes. This improves consistency of data between tables. But the design of a relational database causes some major problems for those who only want to query the data.

Query Problems

While relational databases nicely solve a number of input, storage, and update issues, they create a variety of data retrieval problems. Let's pursue those problems through the simple example examined in the previous section.

Business Definitions Get Diluted

We began with a single data table, called students, that corresponded exactly with one of the major business definitions in colleges and universities (others being faculty, courses, etc.). Someone wishing to find out information about students need only access a single student table. Almost everything you might want to record about a student could be loaded into a single table: I.D. number, name, address, phone, sex, date of birth, social security number, ethnic status, class (freshman, etc.), entry term, major, degree, grade point average, SAT scores, and so on.

The relational design for our simple database created six tables, including two code tables. What disappears is the one-to-one correspondence between a business definition and a table. What is a student in a relational database? It's someone whose name is stored in one table, whose address is stored in a second table, whose phone information is in a third table, and whose personal characteristics appear in a fourth table. If we'd included information about courses taken, grades received, degree sought, major field of study, SAT scores, and other commonly collected information, the required relational tables would number in the dozens. The concept of a student disappears; it gets smeared over the various tables in which student information is collected.

Most businesses have dozens or hundreds of business concepts that mean something to the people who work there. If a person can't query a database in the language of the business, it means a foreign language must be learned—some process must translate the business terms into the language of the database. This typically requires a large investment in time, and most users simply refuse to make that investment.

Translating Business Definitions Is Difficult

Even for someone with the inclination or job-required motivation, mastering the translation of business questions into SQL queries is not easy. But how could this be true if only one query command must be learned?

NAME data

```
        id sort_name
---------- ------------------
         1 Allen, Frank
         2 Jackson, Andrew J.
         3 Thompson, Emily
         4 Lee, Kevin J.
         5 Lam, Ryan
         6 Silva, Scott
         7 Boucher, Richard
         8 Berger, Robin L
        84 Stephens, Phyllis
       368 Lee, Beth

10 rows selected.
```

ADDRESS data

```
           address
        id type    cszn
---------- ------- ------------------------------
         1 PR      Newark, NJ  07104
         2 PR      Bogota, COL
         3 PR      Destrehan, LA  70047
         4 PR      Fair Lawn, NJ  07410
         5 PR      Miami, FL  33032
         6 PR      Lansing, MI  48910
         7 PR      Staten Island, NY  10301
         8 PR      Raleigh, NC  27604
        84 LO      Lakeside, CT  06758
       368 LO      Saco, ME  04072

10 rows selected.
```

NAME and ADDRESS joined in query requesting PR addresses

```
                                         address
        id sort_name                     type    cszn
---------- ----------------------------- ------- ------------------------------
         1 Allen, Frank                  PR      Newark, NJ  07104
         2 Jackson, Andrew J.            PR      Bogota, COL
         3 Thompson, Emily               PR      Destrehan, LA  70047
         4 Lee, Kevin J.                 PR      Fair Lawn, NJ  07410
         5 Lam, Ryan                     PR      Miami, FL  33032
         6 Silva, Scott                  PR      Lansing, MI  48910
         7 Boucher, Richard              PR      Staten Island, NY  10301
         8 Berger, Robin L               PR      Raleigh, NC  27604

8 rows selected.
```

Note there are eight people in the report, not the ten that appear in both the NAME and ADDRESS tables. This happens because two people don't have a PR (permanent) address.

Figure 1–7. Falling through a join.

Falling Through a Report

Producing an ad hoc report from data distributed into many tables requires first joining those tables back together. Sometimes this is straightforward, but often it is not. Figure 1–7 shows what can happen when the name and address tables are joined in a simple query. Note that we started out with ten rows in the name table but finished with only eight rows after joining the name and address tables. This happened because two of the ten people did not have a permanent address.

This may or may not be a problem. If you want a report showing only those eight people who have permanent addresses, then the query works fine. But if you want a report showing ten people with their permanent address, if available, then you've experienced rows that "fall through a report." You've written a query that returns fewer people than in the population.

The danger is that users will write a syntactically acceptable yet logically incorrect query and not realize that rows have fallen through the report. Users often have only ballpark estimates for the size of their report population. If the number is within this range, they usually do not realize when they lose rows. Reports that inadvertently exclude items of the population usually come back to haunt you, with the seriousness of the problem ranging from mildly embarrassing to downright damaging. As we'll see in later chapters, there is a diagnostic test that signals when rows fall through a report. Correcting the problem can be easy under some circumstances or more difficult under others.

Multiplying Through a Report

Losing population items is one problem. The other extreme can also occur; that is, gaining rows when tables are joined. Figure 1–8 on the following page shows a situation where ten rows in the name table produce twelve rows when joined to the address table. This happens because two people in the report each had two permanent addresses. This may be exactly the desired report. If so, fine. But if you want a report showing ten people with their most current permanent address, you'll have to modify the query logic.

Users requesting rosters usually detect when unwanted multiple rows appear in a report. But if you're doing a report that returns only a count, you may not realize when some items are counted more than once. Only if the total count exceeds your ballpark estimate are you likely to suspect something went awry in the query.

Again there is a simple way to detect when undesired multiple rows enter a report. But users must first recognize that the potential for this error

NAME data

```
        id sort_name
---------- --------------------
         1 Allen, Frank
         2 Jackson, Andrew J.
         3 Thompson, Emily
         4 Lee, Kevin J.
         5 Lam, Ryan
         6 Silva, Scott
         7 Boucher, Richard
         8 Berger, Robin L
        23 Hill, Tara
        61 Boucher, Jason W.

10 rows selected.
```

ADDRESS table

```
           address
        id type    cszn
---------- ------- ------------------------------
         1 PR      Newark, NJ  07104
         2 PR      Bogota, COL
         3 PR      Destrehan, LA  70047
         4 PR      Fair Lawn, NJ  07410
         5 PR      Miami, FL  33032
         6 PR      Lansing, MI  48910
         7 PR      Staten Island, NY  10301
         8 PR      Raleigh, NC  27604
        23 PR      Memphis, TN  38107
        23 PR      Albuquerque, NM  87106
        61 PR      Hogansville, GA  30230
        61 PR      Fruita, CO  81521

12 rows selected.
```

NAME and ADDRESS joined in query requesting PR addresses

```
                                 address
        id sort_name             type    cszn
---------- -------------------- ------- ---------------------------
---
         1 Allen, Frank          PR      Newark, NJ  07104
         2 Jackson, Andrew J.    PR      Bogota, COL
         3 Thompson, Emily       PR      Destrehan, LA  70047
         4 Lee, Kevin J.         PR      Fair Lawn, NJ  07410
         5 Lam, Ryan             PR      Miami, FL  33032
         6 Silva, Scott          PR      Lansing, MI  48910
         7 Boucher, Richard      PR      Staten Island, NY  10301
         8 Berger, Robin L       PR      Raleigh, NC  27604
        23 Hill, Tara            PR      Memphis, TN  38107
        23 Hill, Tara            PR      Albuquerque, NM  87106
        61 Boucher, Jason W.     PR      Hogansville, GA  30230
        61 Boucher, Jason W.     PR      Fruita, CO  81521

12 rows selected.
```

Two people each have two permanent addresses. While the initial population consisted of ten people, the report shows twelve rows.

Figure 1–8. Multiple rows generated through a join.

exists in each query. They'll need to conduct a diagnostic test on each query to determine if the report population increases through the table joins. To most users testing is a complication. They want answers, not complications in their queries.

Simple Requests Can Require Complex SQL

All too frequently even a simple ad hoc question can require complex SQL for an answer. The example just discussed provides a hint of this problem. Suppose we wanted a listing of students with their current permanent residence. What exactly does "current permanent residence" mean? There's nothing in the data tables that flags such a residence, so you must create a definition. Something like this might work: "the current permanent address is the most recent address where the address type is P, with most recent being determined by the date at the time the address was input or updated." Operationally this means that for each student you must access the address table, find all records for that student with a P address type, and then find which of these records is the last one.

Without going into details, the procedure just described requires something called a correlated subquery in SQL. In most standard SQL texts the chapter on correlated subqueries appears near the end of the book. It's considered an advanced topic. Yet the question wasn't advanced in any way. We just wanted to list current permanent addresses; what could be more elementary? This gap between the simplicity of the question and the complexity of the SQL creates yet another hurdle too high for most end users.

Easy-to-Read Reports Are Not Always Easy to Prepare

The structure of SQL varies considerably across report types. For example, the SQL required for a simple listing of data columns differs from the SQL used to count a population by some characteristic like age. Yet SQL and SQL*PLUS include no templates to guide users when they want reports of a certain type. Without a clear understanding of report types, how to control characteristics of the printed output (e.g., linesize), how to create column headings, how to insert report titles, how to coordinate SQL*PLUS and SQL commands to include totals or subtotals, or a variety of other aesthetic considerations, users commonly produce reports where the message gets buried in ugly output.

Someone who is willing to invest the time will find that SQL*PLUS offers a variety of ways to make intelligible and pleasing reports. But most end users do not want to write programs where they must set printer escape sequences, restrict output from scrolling to the monitor while the report runs, and control whether the page pause is set on or off. Users need a way to manipulate these factors easily, by choosing default settings for a given report type and then modifying these settings if needed. No such default templates exist now in SQL*PLUS.

Solutions to Query Problems

It has been clear for many years that end users find it difficult to query complex relational databases. Several strategies now attempt to make queries easier. I'll discuss these options as if they were distinctly different, but in fact they are often combined in practice.

Option 1: Create Data Views

A data *view* is a virtual table; it's a table without any physical reality since no data is actually stored in a view. But to a user a view looks like a single table created by combining several (real) tables. In the example above, we might create a view that combined the address table and the phone table. Data columns would include identification number, address type, address, and phone for that address type. The availability of such a view means the user need not include in his or her SQL query the logic joining the phone and address tables. The view already joins the two tables.

This has several advantages. First, views can be created by information systems staff who can test and verify that the joins return accurate information. Leaving the join option to user discretion creates opportunities to get the logic wrong. So report accuracy improves with views. Second, views improve ease of use because more data columns are located in a single place. Instead of getting an address from one table and a phone from a second table, now you can get both from a single view.

Unfortunately, views also have limitations. Views are fine for specific, narrow functions. Creating a view of address and phone numbers is fine. But users would still need to join the name table to the new view and to the person table to produce a report with name, sex, and current permanent address. How about a view that combines all these columns? That also can be done; but now the view contains a four table join. In practice, the pressure from users expands the content of data views: "such-and-such a view has everything in it for this report except for column x; can you add that?" Again the answer is yes. If the data column exists in a table already joined in the view, then this is a trivial change. However, if the data column appears in another table, then an additional join is required.

Why is this a problem? The answer is system performance and query response time. Complex joins can seriously degrade both. Every time an ad hoc query uses a view, each table join occurs whether or not data from the table is requested. For example, suppose a view exists that joins the name, address, phone, and person tables. By combining all the data about students in one place, this view nicely restores the business concept of a student. But it also requires a four table join for each query. If you use this view to produce a report that just lists name and sex, then the joins to address and phone aren't needed. Unfortunately, they still occur. So processing time increases.

At best, views represent only a partial answer to ad hoc query problems. A view is most effective when the reports frequently request data from many of the tables joined in the view. Consequently effective views have specialized functions; rather than restore business concepts they restore pieces of those concepts. Once views get beyond a certain size, the performance penalty can become steep. So while views do improve ease of use somewhat, they exact a cost.

Option 2: Use Graphical Query Tools

The difficulty of querying relational databases has spawned a good-sized industry of businesses trying to fill a niche. Many of these products now build on the graphical interfaces in personal computers. The products, which range from query tools to full-fledged report writers, typically use a mouse and point-and-click operation. Users click on a table name to select a table, then click on data column names to select columns, and click open a window to add limiting criteria (which can be entered with additional mouse clicks). The sort order can be selected, expressions built, and summary statistics computed. A screen painter often allows the user to lay out the appearance of the report. In some products the joins needed for a report occur automatically—if information systems staff have first defined how tables are related and how they should be joined.

These products are very nice. For an end user they represent a major improvement over the bare SQL prompt one stares at when logging into SQL*PLUS. The interface is friendlier; formatting reports is easier; worries about joins are reduced.

Did you hear a "but" coming? Well here it is. Most graphical tools are fine for simple databases but lack the power to handle complex databases. Since complexity is reached fairly quickly with normalized relational databases, the present array of graphical query tools have limited range. To understand why, let's go back to the simple name, address, and phone example again. Suppose we have a group of ten students and we want a report that shows their names and their permanent addresses. Eight of the ten people have well-behaved data; that is, they each have one permanent address. But suppose the data for two students look different. One has no address information, so doesn't appear in the address table at all; the second has only a business address. As we'll see in later chapters, the type of join required between the name and address tables depends upon the type of report desired. If you only want a report with the eight students who do have permanent addresses, one type of join will do. But if you want to include the students without a permanent address, a different type of join is needed. So you can't divorce the join from either the data (and its variability) or from the type of report needed.

In some of the graphical query tools, information systems staff can create rules for joining two tables like the name and address table in this example. What isn't easy, however, is to foresee the conditions under which the join will be used. So you can't build rules that will fit all situations. In simple databases, this limitation is less a problem. But in databases where tables number in the hundreds or thousands, the number of permutations is just too great for graphical query tools.

In other words, two factors act to limit the usefulness of graphical query tools: you need to know too much about a user's intentions for the report and you need to know too much about the data itself. Later chapters make this abundantly clear.

Option 3: Build Extract Tables

There is a third strategy frequently used to simplify ad hoc queries. This strategy says, "Okay, we'll store data in relational tables but they're too complex to query so we'll build separate tables that users can query." Information systems staff write programs that extract data from the relational tables and store it in temporary tables that get refreshed periodically. Sometimes you hear these tables described as temporary tables, or extract tables, or a data warehouse. Whatever the name, they exist to simplify data retrieval and use.

Here's how these extract tables work. Suppose we know that most queries against student data request name, current dorm address and phone, current business address and phone, or gender. If all these data columns existed in a single table, queries would be greatly simplified. This is accomplished by writing a program to copy the data from several relational tables into one extract table. In this case we end up with a single student table instead of name, address, phone, and person tables.

Extract tables have several advantages. First, they are much easier to query. Almost everything a user needs is in one place. Second, there is often good correspondence between extract tables and business definitions. By building a single student extract table we reestablish the one-to-one relationship between a table and one of the key populations in a college. This is no small feat.

But extract tables aren't the perfect solution either. Data in extract tables is not "live" data; that is, it's never current data. It is current only at the time of extraction. Reports run against extract data never represent the most recent information. In many situations this may not be an issue. But for time critical information, extract tables must be refreshed frequently.

Extract tables can also grow out of control. When many extracts get built they require coordination to avoid inconsistencies. They also require system resources to construct, accessing the universe of data that users may want but may not use. An extract table may contain two dozen data columns, but on a given day users may run queries that use only one-half of the available columns. You need to put all the data out there on the chance that users will request it, but if they don't use it then system resources were wasted that day. With many large tables to extract daily, these inefficiencies can add up.

And finally, of course, there's the ironic twist to extract tables. They are a throwback to the old flat file design that relational databases replaced. Extract tables are still relational; they still have rows and columns. But they are often denormalized. The normalization of student data in our example split apart name, address, phone, and person data. Building our extract student table put all this back together, in effect undoing the normalization. In large part the existence of extract tables signal the failure of relational database design to accommodate easy end-user queries.

What's the Answer to the Query Problem?

There isn't really a complete answer to the problems users face when querying relational databases. Sometimes combining strategies provides an adequate way for users to get the reports they need. For example, using graphical query tools against extract tables makes a lot of sense with small or moderately sized databases.

This book proposes a different strategy from those discussed above. It preserves basic business definitions, shields users from programming, and accesses real-time data. It's based on the concept of SQL and SQL*PLUS objects.

Chapter 2

Introduction to SQL Objects

There is nothing fancy about how I use the terms "SQL objects" or "SQL*PLUS objects." They are just chunks of SQL or SQL*PLUS that are stored and reused. Instead of writing new programs for each ad hoc query, users manipulate objects created and tested in previous queries. I use five major categories or classes of objects. Each object class performs a different function. One class identifies the type of report, another defines report populations, a third creates joins to tables containing data for the report, a fourth constructs report display columns, and a fifth controls the physical characteristics of the report.

There is almost a one-to-one mapping between objects and how an ad hoc query is requested in English. So generating an output report only requires selecting the necessary objects, putting them together, answering a few questions that might be embedded in the objects, and running the program. This chapter identifies the five object classes and then works through a simple example using several objects to generate a SQL program and report. In this chapter and in most of those that follow, manipulation of the objects will be done manually with the use of an editor. However, objects can also be used with a graphical interface as illustrated in Chapter 14.

Classes of Objects

There are five major categories of objects. Subsequent chapters describe how to build and use objects in each of these classes. For now it's enough to know generally what each class does.

Report Objects

Different types of reports utilize different SQL and SQL*PLUS structures. For example, if you want to list several data columns for a report population, you use one kind of SQL program. This program differs in structure from that required if you want a frequency distribution showing counts. The latter uses a special *group by* clause coordinated with ***break*** and ***compute*** commands. None of these appear in a standard roster listing. Other types of reports use still different structures. Cross-tabulations use a variation on the structure found in frequency distributions. If a roster lists too much information to display across the page, you'll need to block it down a page one row per data value. This requires still another type of SQL program. And the list could go on.

Report objects define the broad report type. They establish the structure of the SQL required to produce a report of a certain type. They also provide a framework within which other objects can be embedded and assembled.

Population Objects

You can think of a *population* object as the subject of a sentence. In some cases the objects are just nouns; for example, in a college they might be students, employees, alumni, or faculty. Often, however, *population* objects are a combination of adjective and noun. These are business definitions that get used so frequently that it's helpful to think of the adjective and noun together, for example, accepted applicants, registered students, full-time faculty, or present employees.

Population objects define the principal business populations. What constitutes a principal business population is open to question. But in practical terms these are populations that appear frequently in ad hoc reports. The population of "registered students" may appear frequently in reports at a college, while the population of "international registered students" may appear only occasionally in report requests. In this situation it makes sense to create a *population* object for registered students and a modifying *where* object to define international.

Where Objects

Where objects serve two functions. As mentioned, they can act as adjectives and modify a *population* object. However, they also provide access to data tables containing columns that the user wishes to display in the report. Here's the distinction. Suppose you want to list the names and home phone numbers of present male employees. Unless this is a commonly requested population, it's unlikely you'd have a *population* object already prepared. So you'd start with a *population* object for "present employees" and then select a *where* object that defined "male." This is a *where* object used as an adjective. It qualifies the population.

To list names and home phone numbers in the report, you'll need to access the tables that contain this data. One *where* object will access a NAME table; a second *where* object will access a PHONE table. Used in this manner, *where* objects serve as gateways to data columns.

The two types of *where* objects are quite similar. In one case the *where* object modifies the population and the data column does not usually appear in the report; in the second case, it accesses a table so that a data column can appear in the report.

Select Objects

By comparison to other objects, *select* objects are often very small. But they perform useful functions in the *select* clause of a SQL program. It's easiest to illustrate by example what function *select* objects perform. The name table in relational databases will contain one column for last name, one for first name, and one for middle name. For reporting purposes, however, you might want to see a "sort name" constructed by concatenating last, first, and middle names (with appropriate commas and spaces). Instead of reports listing the three columns separately, you need only use the sort name. This is, as the name implies, particularly useful when the report is sorted alphabetically.

Sort name is an example of a *select* object. These are objects that get used in the *select* clause of a SQL program. They are most often used to modify existing data columns for display in a report.

Shell Objects

Choosing and combining *report*, *population*, *where*, and *select* objects produce a completed SQL program. The program could be run and you'd get the information requested. But it might not look inviting or be easy to read. That's the purpose of *shell* objects. These objects contain a number of useful utilities that activate default column headings, add titles to reports, stamp reports with dates and times, insert page numbers, control printer setups, and perform a variety of other functions.

Shell objects get their name from the way they interact with the other classes of objects. Objects from other classes get combined into a completed SQL program that is then started from the shell program. You can think of the shell program as the main program and the SQL program as a subprogram.

Embedded Messages

Objects often contain embedded messages that serve to generalize their use. For example, suppose you construct an object of applicants accepted for admission to a college. Instead of creating a separate object for each semester that students are admitted to the college (e.g., Fall 1995, Spring 1996), it's simpler to create a single object with a placeholder for the semester. This placeholder is just an embedded message that requires insertion of a specific value before using the object at runtime.

Documentation of objects is important if they're shared among users. Object creators may differ from object users. In these cases users must understand the function of an object and how to complete any embedded messages. Separate documentation files should be created for each object. Then users need only access the help files when they encounter a new object or they're unsure how to use an object.

How Do Objects Work?

Let's look at an example. Suppose you wanted to determine the anticipated academic majors of applicants accepted for admission; that is, you want to know how many students expect to major in music, how many in accountancy, and so on. This query can be easily accomplished using objects. In the figures below, don't worry about the content of the objects. You'll have considerable opportunity in later chapters to actually build objects. For now just think of the objects as building blocks that get assembled into an ad hoc query. At this point, only pay attention to the manipulation of objects.

As discussed, you'll need to complete two programs from a set of objects. One program will be a shell that calls a second program that actually retrieves the data. Let's start with the shell. Figure 2–1 shows a *shell* object and its documentation or help file. If you use objects repeatedly, it's usually unnecessary to refer to the help file. But if the object is new or if it's used infrequently, the help file guides you through the steps required to use the object. The *shell* object is used with each ad hoc query. So completing a *shell* object quickly becomes routine.

Figure 2–2 on page 26 shows a completed *shell* object. Note that the object is saved under a new name (in this case as fig2-2.sql). This preserves the *shell* object for use in later queries. In addition to the SQL program

OBJECT

```
/*
     sql:      <shell_name>
     date:     <date>
     author:   <author>
     purpose:  <purpose>
*/
set termout off
start &&object_dir.\clears
start &&object_dir.\hpprintr
start &&object_dir.\date
start &&object_dir.\time
start &&object_dir.\owncol
start &&object_dir.\escape

ttitle left xEscape skip 1-
     '<report_title>' -
     right 'Report name: <report_name>' skip 1 -
     left 'Date: ' xDate '      Time: ' xTime -
     right 'SQL name:    <shell_name>' skip 1 -
     right 'Page: ' format 999 sql.pno skip 2;

spool <report_name>
     start <SQL_program>
     start &&object_dir.\reset
spool off

start &&object_dir.\clears
start &&object_dir.\screen
```

To use an object in an ad hoc query, each item in brackets (<>) must be replaced.

HELP

```
help file:     shell.hlp
date created:  09-may-1994
author:        glewis
revisions:

Purpose:       Provides a shell for each ad hoc report from which the
               SQL program is started.  Controls printer and screen
               characteristics, report titles, column headers, and other
               features of the finished report

Usage:         <shell_name>: Replace with name for SQL shell (eg,
               exmple1.sql).
               <date>: Replace with date report was created.
               <author>: Replace with author of report.
               <purpose>: Replace with a brief statement of why the
               report was created.
               <report_title>: Replace with the text to appear at the top
               of each page of the report.
               <report_name>: Replace with the name of file that will
               contain the output report.
               <SQL_program>: Replace with the name of the SQL program
               that will actually retrieve the data for the report.

Hints:         None
```

Figure 2–1. *Shell* object and help file.

name, you need to enter today's date, your name (if you're creating the query), and a brief statement of why the report was done. You'll also need to enter a title to appear at the top of each page of the report, the name of the second (SQL) program, and the name of the output report.

I've found it helpful to use a simple naming convention for SQL programs and reports. If I call the completed shell program "example.sql," then I'll call the output report "example.lis" and the data retrieval program something like "xexample.sql." In Figure 2–2 the names are fig2-2.sql for the shell, fig2-2.lis for the output report, and xfig2-2.sql for the SQL program that retrieves the data. I have tried using a naming convention that indicates the content of the query, but found this awkward after months of writing similar queries. Instead I'll now concatenate the requester's initials with

Highlighted areas show the entries made to complete the object. Note that it was saved under the file name fig2-2.sql. The SQL program it starts is called xfig2-2.sql (see Figure 2–5).

SHELL

```
/*
        sql:      fig2-2.sql
        date:     01-jan-1995
        author:   glewis
        purpose:  Shell program for Figure 2-2
*/
set termout off
start &&object_dir.\clears
start &&object_dir.\hpprintr
start &&object_dir.\date
start &&object_dir.\time
start &&object_dir.\owncol
start &&object_dir.\escape

ttitle left xEscape skip 1-
        'Accepted applicants in Arts and Sciences by academic major: Fall 1995' -
        right 'Report name: fig2-2.lis' skip 1 -
        left 'Date: ' xDate '      Time: ' xTime -
        right 'SQL name:     fig2-2.sql' skip 1 -
        right 'Page: ' format 999 sql.pno skip 2;

spool fig2-2.lis
        start xfig2-2
        start &&object_dir.\reset
spool off

start &&object_dir.\clears
start &&object_dir.\screen
```

Figure 2–2. Completed shell.

today's date. So the shell program might be mr060195.sql, the output report mr060195.lis, and the SQL program xmr061095.sql.

Let's move to the second program that needs completion, the one that actually retrieves the data. Each of these SQL programs is constructed from at least two objects. You must choose a *report* object that matches the type of report you want. You must also choose one of the *population* objects that defines the basic set of people, places, or things in your query. Later chapters go into considerable detail about the various *report* and *population* objects and how to construct them. But for now, let's think a moment about the query. We were asked to provide a report showing counts of accepted applicants by their anticipated academic major. The population, then, is "accepted applicants." The report should show a column of majors and a second column of associated counts. As you'll see in Chapter 10, the object that produces this type of frequency distribution report is called count1.obj.

Figure 2–3 on the following page shows the *population* object for accepted applicants. To use it you must insert the academic term when applicants hope to enroll, their level (e.g., undergraduate or graduate), and the college if appropriate (e.g., Arts & Sciences or Business). Take a good look at Figure 2–3. Two items stand out. First, it's pretty clear why SQL is such a difficult end-user query tool. You don't want users entering ten or fifteen lines of SQL every time they want to access a simple population. Second, *population* objects are specific to a given database. They depend upon database design and, as you'll see later, they also depend on the business rules that control data entry, updates, and deletes.

Figure 2–4 on page 29 shows the count1 *report* object. *Report* objects possess greater generality than *population* objects and are not specific to a single database design. *Report* objects provide the foundation for assembly of other object classes. To make the count1 object operational, you need to insert a *population* object and, optionally, a *where* object. In this case the *population* object from Figure 2–3 gets inserted into count1. Since the report population needs no modification and since no new table must be accessed to provide data for the report, no *where* object is necessary. Figure 2–5 on page 29 shows the completed SQL program. Note that it's called xfig2-2.sql to be consistent with the completed shell program.

That's it. You completed a shell program and a SQL data retrieval program. At the SQL prompt you simply start the shell program. It sets up the report environment and calls the data retrieval program. The output report appears in Figure 2–6 on page 30.

This example is typical of reporting with SQL*PLUS objects. A user asks a question. That question gets clarified and then mapped into SQL

OBJECT

```
from
     applicant
where
     applicant_term = '<term>'
             and applicant_level = '<level>'
             and applicant_college = '<college>'
     and exists
     (select 'x'
     from
             cdecision,
             decision
     where
             decision_id = applicant_id
                     and decision_applicant_term = app
                     and decision_applicant_seriesno =
             and cdecision_code = decision_code
                     and cdecision_accept_ind = 'Y')
```

COMPLETED OBJECT

```
from
     applicant
where
     applicant_term = '199509'
             and applicant_level = 'UG'
             and applicant_college = 'AS'
     and exists
     (select 'x'
     from
             cdecision,
             decision
     where
             decision_id = applicant_id
                     and decision_applicant_term = applicant_term
                     and decision_applicant_seriesno = applicant_seriesno
             and cdecision_code = decision_code
                     and cdecision_accept_ind = 'Y')
```

HELP

```
object:        popacapp.obj
date created:  09-may-1994
author:        glewis
revisions:

Purpose:       Defines the population of applicants accepted for admissions
               for a specified term, level and college

Usage:         <term>: replace with term (eg, 199409 for Fall 1994)
               <level>: replace with level (eg, UG for Undergrad)
               <college>: replace with college code (eg, BU for Business)

Hints:         none
```

Figure 2–3. *Population* object defining applicants accepted for admission.

```
OBJECT

break on report
compute sum of count on report
select
     <col1>,
     count(*) "count"
<<population>>
<<where>>
group by
     <col1>
/
```

Items in double brackets mark places where other objects should be inserted.

```
HELP

object:        count1.obj
date created:  09-may-1994
author:        glewis
revisions:

Purpose:       A report object for frequency distributions of
               character data columns.

Usage:         <col1>: Replace with the name of the data column upon
               which the frequency counts will be done (eg,
               applicant_degree).
               <<population>>: Replace with a population object.
               <<where>>: Replace with one or more class 1 or class
               2u where objects. Remove if none is required.

Hints:         None
```

Figure 2–4. *Report* object and help file for a frequency distribution report.

```
SQL PROGRAM

break on report
compute sum of count on report
select
       applicant_major,
       count(*) "count"
from
       applicant
where
       applicant_term = '199509'
              and applicant_level = 'UG'
              and applicant_college = 'AS'
       and exists
       (select 'x'
       from
              cdecision,
              decision
       where
              decision_id = applicant_id
                     and decision_applicant_term = applicant_term
                     and decision_applicant_seriesno = applicant_seriesno
              and cdecision_code = decision_code
                     and cdecision_accept_ind = 'Y')
group by
       applicant_major
/
```

This is the *population* object from Figure 2–3 embedded in the *report* object.

Figure 2–5. Completed *report* object (saved as xfig2-2.sql).

```
REPORT

Accepted applicants in Arts and Sciences by academic major: Fall 1995        Report name: fig2-2.lis
Date: 01-JAN-1995     Time: 15:35                                             SQL name:    fig2-2.sql
                                                                                     Page:     1

appl
major      count
----- ----------
ART            9
BIOL          46
CHEM          14
ECON          31
ENGL          21
GOV           26
HIST          24
LANG          22
MATH          11
MUSC          13
PEDC          10
PHIL           3
PHYS           8
PSYC          22
RELG           4
SOC           21
UN           139
              26
      ----------
sum          450

18 rows selected.
```

Figure 2–6. Completed report.

objects. The objects get assembled into a shell program and a retrieval program. You then run the shell program to produce the final report. The utility of objects occurs in the mapping stage. Instead of translating from English into SQL code, you translate to the higher order abstraction of objects.

Before actually building objects, let's ensure a common background of knowledge.

Chapter 3

The Simulated Database

SQL objects return their greatest benefits in complex databases. When the number of tables is small and the relationships between tables simple, there is less need for these query objects. This chapter introduces a simulated database that maintains a delicate balancing act, with enough complexity to make evident the usefulness of SQL objects yet not overwhelm the reader with so much complexity that more time is spent learning the database than learning how to build and use objects. The database introduced here is a step removed from the complexity of large databases, but it doesn't lose touch with that reality.

The simulated database also has one other unique feature: it is presented within a business setting. Databases you will query are not disembodied from the larger institution; they exist for a purpose, whether it's to process insurance claims, register motor vehicles, or give course grades to students. Whatever the purpose of the database, there are an associated set of day-to-day operational procedures and longer term policies that interact with it. Even though some of these procedures and policies are reflected in the design of the database (particularly if the design and development were done in-house), you cannot write accurate SQL queries unless you understand these policies and procedures. In otherwords, there's an interaction between database design, the data itself, and the business context within which the database exists. In order to write ad hoc queries that will return meaningful results, you need to understand all three aspects. The importance of this fact is often overlooked or underappreciated. The simulated database used throughout this text provides the opportunity to see how this works.

The business described below is a fictitious small college. With one exception, none of the data used throughout this book is real. It has all been simulated using probability distributions, conditional relationships, and random number generators. Street addresses, for example, were simulated based on probabilities of certain types of addresses occurring— whether the address had an apartment number attached, whether it was a street or rural delivery address, whether it was in the United States or another country, and so on. The simulation was based on real data; the data here will look real (including some messiness deliberately retained), but it is not. Appendix A contains complete data dictionaries for the tables in the simulated database. Appendix B describes in detail how the simulation was done. The only data not simulated occurs in one of the code tables, where the publicly available names and addresses of high schools and colleges are real.

Let's set the fictional stage.

The Business Setting

Komenda College is a small college in the Adirondack region of upstate New York. Situated on a hill overlooking Lake George, it was founded in 1908 by Dutch businessmen whose ancestors had emigrated from West Africa when the Dutch West Indies Company stopped its gold trade. The college was intended for "young men who desired training in business skills," and for two decades Komenda concentrated in accountancy.

In the early 1930s, however, the college briefly discontinued operations when student enrollments fell and faculty were paid with vouchers. But in 1936 Komenda reopened under the leadership of William Vrendenburg and in the course of his twenty-three year presidency the college experienced sustained, if modest, growth. It was Vrendenburg who realized the danger of basing Komenda's financial security on young men intending careers as accountants. He diversified the business curriculum to include management, marketing, and finance programs, opened admissions to women in 1943, and finally convinced a reluctant faculty to create new majors in English and history.

When Vrendenburg retired, Komenda College was poised to catch the rising wave of baby boomers approaching college age. Throughout the 1960s and 1970s, college enrollment grew from 900 to 3000. Five new red-brick residential dormitories contrasted nicely with the gray limestone of older buildings. Komenda also added new buildings for administration, faculty offices, classrooms, and a computer center. A major renovation and expansion of the library occurred when Henry Voorhees donated $1 million.

Much of Komenda's growth occurred in the liberal arts; faculty and majors were added in the sciences, government, music, mathematics, philosophy, and psychology. Tensions existed between the business and liberal arts faculty but abated somewhat when Komenda created separate undergraduate colleges of business and liberal studies. This truce lasted into the 1980s when interest in undergraduate business programs doubled throughout the country. Komenda's business faculty and programs expanded in response. Internally the business faculty began exerting more influence over college policies, even though student enrollments in the colleges of business and liberal studies were roughly equal. It was during this period that Komenda opened a graduate school of business administration.

This burst of growth in business programs lasted only a decade. In the mid-1980s, Komenda absorbed two blows. As the baby boomers passed college age, the demographic pressure switched from growth to decline. Almost simultaneously, interest in business as a field of study began to decrease sharply across the United States.

Komenda responded aggressively. They hired a new dean of enrollment management and consolidated all undergraduate recruiting, admissions, financial aid, and student registration under her control. The college also hired a director of new student market research; conducted focus groups to determine what students liked and disliked about the college; added three staff to the admissions office with regional recruiting responsibilities; hired external consultants to design a new series of publications for prospective students; doubled the amount of institutional funds devoted to financial aid; and invested in a new integrated administrative database system that included modules for recruiting and admissions.

These efforts succeeded in stemming the decline in liberal arts enrollment, but the business programs continued to suffer enrollment decline. Komenda started using retirement and attrition to reduce business faculty and has relied more heavily on part-time adjunct faculty hired from nearby Glens Falls.

And that is the situation Komenda faces today. The college would like to stabilize overall enrollment at its present level. That means stopping the hemorrhaging in the business programs, but doing so without an infusion of new funds. It means working more productively with existing resources, and in part it means getting a lot of mileage from the recruiting and admissions database.

Introduction to the Database

The Specific Business Function

The financial health of Komenda College depends heavily on student tuition. The success or failure of new student recruiting and admissions translates directly into resources available for educational programs, faculty and staff salaries, and general expenses. Because of this, Komenda's president and her cabinet closely follow recruiting and admissions reports—often on a daily basis.

When the dean of enrollment management was hired in 1984, the separate admissions offices in the business college and the college of liberal studies were consolidated under one person responsible for all undergraduate recruiting and admissions. Komenda now uses sophisticated strategies in an effort to attract and enroll new students. These include:

- Use of an external enrollment planning service to identify geographic areas where college-bound high school students reside, especially students interested in liberal arts or business studies. A specific recruiting plan is developed for each target market.
- Direct marketing to students who have taken the ACT or SAT examinations and whose academic interests and potential correspond closely with the type of student Komenda hopes to enroll. Initial mailings are segmented by geographic area, high school academic performance levels, and anticipated college major. Respondents have a chance to express interest in a number of areas (e.g., athletic programs, receiving financial assistance, etc.) and later mailings are made more individual based on these interests. For example, students who express an interest in music all receive a letter and a brochure from the department chairperson describing course offerings and performance facilities.
- Assignment of in-house recruiters to primary geographic regions, with responsibility for personal contact with all students from those regions who express an interest in Komenda. Most students enroll from upstate New York, but substantial numbers also come from Massachusetts, Pennsylvania, Connecticut, and New Jersey. These recruiters also arrange and host special on- and off-campus functions for students from Komenda's primary feeder schools.
- Assignment of regional recruiters to geographic areas of secondary interest, where the potential for new students is significant but

largely untapped. Komenda now employs a regional recruiter in northern New England, another in Ohio and Michigan, and a third in Florida. These recruiters represent Komenda at college day programs hosted by high schools, visit high schools and speak with guidance counselors and students, and make personal contact with students who've already indicated an interest in the college.

- Use of specialty recruiters for selected groups of students that Komenda would like more highly represented. This includes international students, business students, and students of color. It also includes students transferring from two-year community colleges or other four-year colleges and universities.

Some potential students self-initiate contact with Komenda. For example, they may phone and request a catalog of courses and an admissions packet. Others respond to direct mailings; still others are first contacted during staff travel to schools. However the contact is made, this group of students constitutes Komenda's "recruits." For the past few years the college has obtained about 9000 recruits for each new fall class. Only one in nine of these recruits actually submits an application for admission. This conversion ratio is highest among self-initiated contacts and lowest among direct mail contacts. One goal of Komenda's director of admissions is to increase the overall conversion ratio.

Komenda now uses a two-part application process. On part 1, applicants fill out biographical information. They return this single form with an application fee of $25 and are officially considered an applicant for admission. Before an admission decision can be made, however, a number of other documents are required. Part 2 of the application must be received. This contains a written essay, a record of high school activities and leadership positions, and letters of recommendations. For freshmen Komenda also requires standardized achievement test scores and transcripts from the last high school attended. For transfer students the college requires that applicants submit transcripts from all colleges attended.

Once an applicant's file is complete, a committee composed of faculty and admissions staff review the material and recommend an admissions decision to the director of admissions. Separate committees process applications to the Business College and the Arts & Sciences College. In clear cases the application for admission is either accepted or denied. Where uncertainty exists, the application is held for a second review at a later date. Komenda also "wait-lists" some applicants, meaning they're accepted for admission conditional on there being sufficient space in the new entering class. The college uses the wait-list as a buffer to ensure that enrollment targets are met should a larger than anticipated number of regularly accepted students decide not to enroll.

Housing and financial aid decisions occur after the admissions decision. In fact, Komenda takes great pride that their admission is "need-blind"; that is, made without considering a student's need for financial assistance. Each applicant for admission then receives a decision letter; if the student was accepted, that letter will also contain a financial aid award if aid was sought. A student accepted for admission may guarantee a place in the new entering class by paying an enrollment deposit of $100. Over time Komenda has found that about 5% of the students who pay an enrollment deposit will later change their mind and decide not to enroll.

The Data Tables

The integrated administrative database that Komenda purchased several years ago contains modules for recruiting and admissions. The vendor just released a major upgrade that provides stronger letter-writing support and management of marketing materials. The principal tables that get used for ad hoc recruiting and admissions queries include:

PERSON: contains information, including sex, date of birth, and ethnic status, on each individual in the database. These individuals include faculty, employees, alumni, recruits, applicants, and students.

RECRUIT: contains information on each individual who requested admissions materials, including their anticipated term of entry, degree program, and academic major.

APPLICANT: contains information on each applicant for admission, including their student type (freshman or transfer), the type of application submitted (regular or international), intended major and degree, and whether they expect to apply for financial aid.

NAME: contains first, middle, and last names of individuals.

ADDRESS: contains street, city, state, zip, and nation addresses for individuals, with codes to indicate the type of address (e.g., permanent or billing).

PHONE: contains area code and phone number for individuals, with a link to the ADDRESS table.

VISA: contains current visa data for international recruits and applicants.

MAIL: contains a record of what letters and literature were sent to recruits and applicants and when they were sent.

ACADEMIC: contains the prior academic record of recruits and applicants, including the high schools or colleges attended, dates of graduation, and rank in class.

TEST: contains information on all standardized aptitude and achievement test scores submitted by recruits and applicants.

DECISION: contains each admissions decision made by the college and by applicants, including the type of decision and its date.

DOCUMENT: contains a checklist of admissions materials required for each applicant and the date they were received.

The full data dictionaries for tables in the recruiting and admissions modules are shown in Appendix A. These include a description of what each data column means. Some of these data columns are merely codes. For example, in the APPLICANT table codes are used to identify the type of application submitted, whether the applicant is a freshman or transfer, and his or her anticipated degree and major. Associated with each coded data column is a table that describes the meaning of the codes. For example, there is a CMAJOR table that contains all codes for academic major and a fuller description of each code. All code tables are also included in Appendix A.

Figure 3–1 shows the relationships among the various recruiting and admissions tables. First a bit of nomenclature on the various symbols in Figure 3–1. The connections between tables in this module are all "one-to-many," indicated in the figure with the lines that end in the crow's foot. For example, the PERSON and the RECRUIT table are connected with such a line. It is possible for a single individual in the PERSON table to appear several times in the RECRUIT table. This could happen if he or she was a recruit in several different terms or was a recruit at the undergraduate level and then later at the graduate level. The circles appearing on some connecting lines indicate that an individual appearing in one table need not appear in the second table. Again consider the PERSON and RECRUIT relationship. The symbols show that a single person may appear zero, one, or many times as a recruit.

The names inside the table boxes in Figure 3–1 refer to data column names. Except for the PHONE table the data column names identify the primary key for each table. For example, the data columns called applicant_id, applicant_term, applicant_level, and applicant_seriesno uniquely identify a single row in the APPLICANT table. The PHONE table also includes two data columns (phone_address_type and phone_address_seriesno) that are foreign keys linked to the ADDRESS table. Chapter 4 discusses primary and foreign keys in more detail.

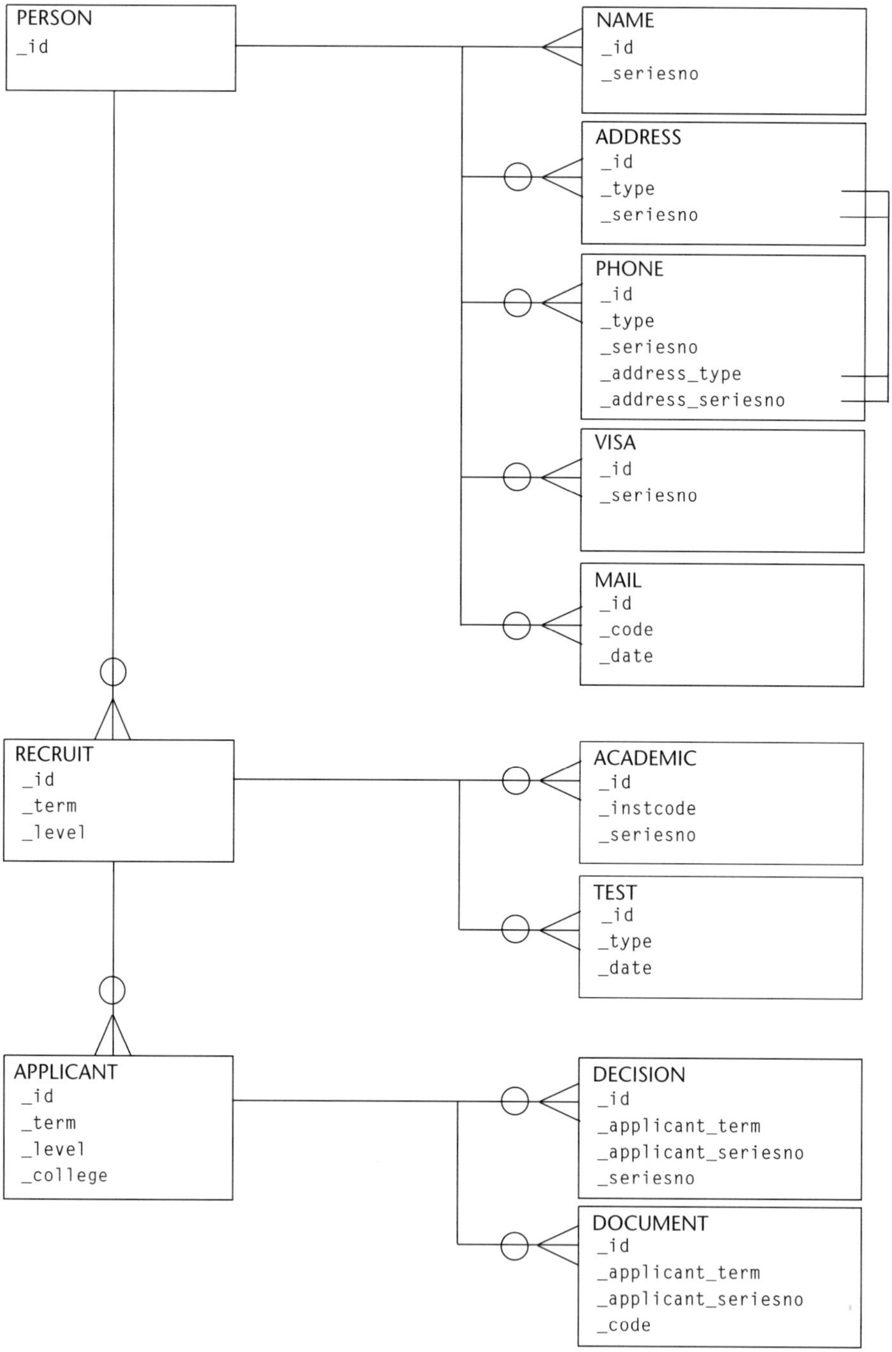

Figure 3–1. Database schematic of simulated recruiting and admissions data.

Business Rules

Some operational procedures may be inferred directly from the table relationships in Figure 3–1. For example, the figure shows that a person must have a name. It also implies that the college tracks name changes. What you might suspect, but isn't stated explicitly in the figure, is that the latest name information is contained in the row with the maximum name_seriesno. This is an example of a business rule. In this case it's a simple rule that is most likely embedded in the database software. However, other rules result from data input standards, policy internal to a specific office, college-wide policy, and requirements of govenment or external groups.

Some of the business rules that apply to Komenda's recruiting and admissions database include:

- All data columns that end with "_seriesno" represent sequential numbers and may be used to find the latest information about a given item. For example, the latest name data for a person is found by locating the maximum name_seriesno for that person.
- Recruits can submit test scores and academic transcripts before an application. This data is entered into the database.
- Recruits and applicants may take the SAT, ACT, or Achievement tests multiple times. All scores are input but only the maximum score of a particular type is used in the admissions decision.
- Documents required of an applicant are determined automatically by the database software based on a set of rules supplied by the admissions office. When an applicant record is created, the appropriate rows are automatically generated in the DOCUMENT table. When the applicant submits the various materials, these rows are updated with the date of receipt.
- A recruit may apply to both the college of business and the college of liberal studies in the same term, but must do so on separate applications.
- Freshman rank in class and transfer grade point averages are considered in the admissions decision. Only the high school rank or grade point average in the last school attended is considered.
- An admissions decision cannot be made unless all required documents have been received.
- Database software prevents sending the same mailing more than once to the same person on the same day. In fact, a warning is is-

sued to the user if the same mailing has been sent within a predetermined period of time.

- An applicant may cancel an admissions application at any time. Any cancellation decision inactivates the application. No further action is taken on inactive applications.
- International students whose first language is not English must submit a TOEFL examination. While standardized aptitude or achievement tests are required of international students, the English test scores are not used in the official averages reported to external agencies.
- Transfer students must submit high school transcripts unless they have completed two or more years of college.

Some college policies that affect recruiting and admissions at Komenda include:

- Quantity and quality considerations coexist uneasily in admissions decisions. Meeting enrollment targets pays Komenda's bills. But on occasion Komenda has deliberately downsized to stabilize what it perceived as eroding academic quality among its applicants.
- Student diversity is encouraged and actively sought. International applicants, applicants of color, and women business applicants receive particular attention.
- Academic excellence is particularly encouraged. Komenda actively seeks applicants with records of academic achievement.
- Some highly recruited applicants receive merit financial aid awards unrelated to actual need.
- All applicants with financial need receive aid awards matching their need. However, Komenda varies the type of aid awards it makes. Highly sought applicants receive a greater proportion of their aid award as grants and scholarships than do other applicants, where the loan and student work components are higher.
- Two sets of admissions standards are used at Komenda. To encourage increased enrollment of business students, applicants at the Business College stand a better chance of being accepted than applicants at the Arts & Sciences College.

It is in this context that ad hoc queries against the recruiting and admissions database occur.

Chapter 4

An SQL Primer

Before it's possible to construct and use objects for ad hoc reports, you must have a minimal understanding of the SQL *select* command. This chapter provides a foundation for the rest of the book. Many readers already familiar with SQL can safely skim this chapter. However, I urge everyone to read the section on structured queries; it's a lot easier to debug and maintain well-structured ad hoc queries than syntactically identical but structurally messy queries.

This chapter discusses the six SQL *select* clauses; various arithmetic, character, comparison and logical operators; and many useful number, date, and character functions. A few commonly used SQL*PLUS commands will sneak into the discussion also, although the SQL*PLUS primer occurs in Chapter 6.

I introduce SQL in a somewhat unconventional manner through a series of examples, based on the belief that it's easier to understand something if you actually see it used. The drawback is that things can become a jumble after a few examples. Appendix C provides a more conventional and linear introduction to SQL.

SQL *Select* Command

The *select* command is the only SQL command available for ad hoc reporting. Nonetheless it is an exquisite tool, deceptively simple and yet extremely powerful.

The foundation of the ***select*** command is its six language elements or clauses. From these six clauses queries from one line to several hundred lines can be constructed. Table 4–1 shows these six clauses: *select*, *from*, *where*, *group by*, *having*, and *order by*. Only the *select* and *from* clauses must be used in each query; the others are optional. Of the six, the *group by* and *having* clauses present the most difficulty to new SQL users. *Group by* must sometimes be coordinated with other clauses to produce a desired effect, such as report totals or subtotals, and *having* looks suspiciously like the *where* clause. Examples using these two clauses appear later in this chapter.

Table 4–1. SQL ***select*** command clauses.

Clause	Action
select	lists the data columns to appear in the report (required)
from	lists the tables needed in the query (required)
where	defines the population for the report and also defines how to join the tables in the *from* clause
group by	used to group data before performing summaries such as average, count, minimum, maximum, etc.
having	used only with *group by* to limit the groups appearing in the report
order by	sorts the report results

Figure 4–1 shows the use of four common ***select*** clauses. Like many figures in this chapter, it shows a final ad hoc report, the SQL used to produce the report, a translation of the SQL into English, and several notes that highlight key points in the figure. Figure 4–1 illustrates that:

- The *select* clause lists the data columns to appear in the report.
- Data column names in the *select* clause are separated by commas.
- The order of the data column names in the *select* clause determines the order of the columns in the report.
- Table names, column names, and the six clause names may be uppercase or lowercase.
- Tables defining the report population, or containing the data columns for the report, or providing access to the data columns appear in the *from* clause.
- The *order by* clause sorts the rows of the report into ascending or descending order, the default being ascending order.

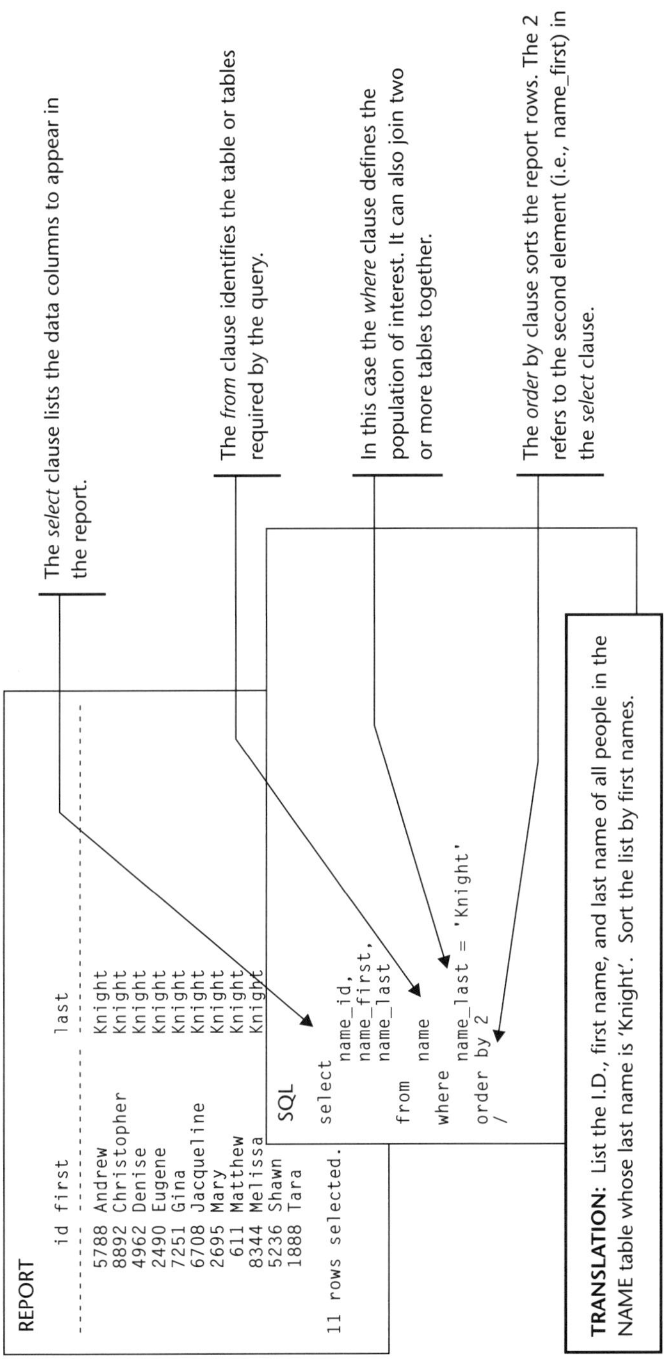

Figure 4–1. SQL *select, from, where,* and *order by* clauses.

- The *order by* clause may use column names or numbers referring to the position of column names in the *select* clause.
- Only the *select* and *from* clauses are required.
- The *where* clause defines the population of interest and specifies how the tables in the *from* clause should be joined together.
- The SQL ***select*** command ends with "/" or ";".

SQL operators

Figure 4–1 also illustrates the use of the "=" sign to specify that the last name of people appearing in the report must be equal to Knight. The "=" is an example of an operator, one of many special SQL characters that perform operations on data values.

Operators come in different flavors depending on the type of the data values on which they work. For our purposes, we need only be concerned with three general data types: numeric, date, and character.

Character data columns may contain all forms of text. The specific datatype name given to character data differs between ORACLE v6 and v7. In ORACLE v6 if the text contains less than 256 characters, the column has a CHAR or CHARACTER datatype. If the length of the text string is between 256 and 65,535, the column datatype is specified as LONG. In version 7 ORACLE introduced a new character datatype called VARCHAR2. It is equivalent to the CHAR datatype in version 6 except that its maximum length is 2000. ORACLE also increased the maximum length of a LONG datatype to 2 gigabytes. In version 7 ORACLE changed the CHAR datatype from variable length to fixed length. This affects the way that CHAR data values are compared. For example, suppose that a data column called last_name is CHAR(15) in a version 6 data table. A query requesting last_name = 'Knight' returns all people whose last name is Knight. In version 7, however, this same query returns no rows because the comparison is actually last_name = 'Knight   '; the name is padded with blanks to fill out the 15 characters. The important thing to remember is that CHAR in version 6 and VARCHAR2 in version 7 are equivalent except that VARCHAR2 values have a larger maximum length. In this book you'll see CHAR used for character datatypes because the examples were done using ORACLE v6 running under DOS. Just substitute VARCHAR2 for CHAR if you're using version 7.

Date data columns contain valid dates in the range from January 1, 4712 BC to December 31, 4712 AD. The datatype is called DATE.

Numeric data columns contain numbers, most commonly in the datatype called NUMBER. This datatype also supports characteristics called precision and scale. Precision identifies the maximum number of digits that may appear in the number; scale identifies the maximum number of digits that may appear to the right of the decimal place. So a datatype of NUMBER(5,2) may contain five or fewer digits, two of them to the right of any decimal point.

Table 4–2 shows the most common SQL operators. Table C–1 in Appendix C provides a complete list of operators. Note that there are four types of operators:

- Arithmetic operators work on numeric data values to perform addition, subtraction, multiplication, and division.
- Character operators work on character data values; for example, to concatenate two character strings into one longer string.
- Comparison operators work with both numeric and character data values. The "=" is an example of a comparison operator. In Figure 4–1 the "=" operator compared last names with the character string 'Knight'. It can also compare numeric values; for example, to compare age with the number 21.
- Logical operators work when multiple conditions appear in the *where* clause. They affect how the conditions must be met. Use of "and" means both conditions must be true; use of "or" means at least one of the two conditions must be true; and use of "not" negates the condition (e.g., "is not null" is the reverse of "is null").

Table 4–2. Common SQL operators.

Operator	Action	General form
ARITHMETIC		
*	Multiplication	a * b
/	Division	a / b
+	Addition	a + b
–	Subtraction	a + b
CHARACTER		
||	Concatenate strings	a || b

(Continued)

Table 4–2. Common SQL operators.

Operator	Action	General form
COMPARISON		
=	Equal	a = b
!= or <>	Not equal	a != b
>	Greater than	a > b
<	Less than	a < b
>=	Greater than or equal to	a >= b
<=	Less than or equal to	a <= b
COMPARISON		
in	Equals any member	in (list); e.g. in (a,b,c)
not in	Not equal any member	not in (list); e.g. not in (a,b,c,d)
between	Equal to or between	between a and b means >= a and <= b
not between	Less than or greater than	not between a and b means < a or > b
like	Match pattern	like 'a%' matches any string beginning with 'a'
not like	Does not match pattern	not like 'a%' returns any string not beginning with 'a'
is null	Data value does not exist	y is null means a row contains no data in column y
is not null	Data value does exist	data value does exist in column y for selected row
LOGICAL		
and	Expression true if both conditions are true	a and b
or	Expression true if either condition is true	a or b
not	Reverses result	see examples under comparison operators

Figure 4–2, Figure 4–3, and Figure 4–4 on pages 47, 48, and 49 illustrate the use of several SQL operators. The figures demonstrate the versatility of several operators, including the concatenation character operator; comparison operators for *greater than, between, in,* and *like;* and the logical operators *or* and *and.* Of special note in these figures are the following:

- Constructed or computed data columns may appear in the *select* clause (as when a sort name is constructed from last, first, and middle name). These are called *expressions.*

REPORT

```
        id sort_name
---------- ----------------------------------
      2695 Knight, Mary S.
       611 Knight, Matthew M.
      8344 Knight, Melissa
      5236 Knight, Shawn
      1888 Knight, Tara E.

5 rows selected.
```

The concatenation operator combines last, first, and middle names into a new report column given the alias "sort_name."

SQL

```
select
      name_id,
      name_last||', '||name_first||' '||name_middle "sort_name"
from
      name
where
      name_last = 'Knight'
      and name_first > 'L'
order by 2
/
```

Note the use of the greater than operator (>). This is an example of a comparison operator. Others include = (equals), != (not equals), < (less than), >= (greater than or equal to) and <= (less than or equal to).

TRANSLATION: List the I.D. and a sort name constructed by concatenating last, first and middle name, for each person in the NAME table whose last name is Knight and whose first name begins with a letter after L in the alphabet. Order the list by the sort name.

Figure 4–2. *Concatenation* and *greater than* operators.

REPORT

```
        id sort_name
---------- ----------------------------------
      2695 Knight, Mary S.
       611 Knight, Matthew M.

2 rows selected.
```

SQL

```
select
     name_id,
     name_last||', '||name_first||' '||name_middle "sort_name"
from
     name
where
     name_last = 'Knight'
            and name_first between 'L' and 'N'
            and name_middle is not null
order by 2
/
```

The two end values are included in a *between* selection; in this case the first name must begin with L, M, or N.

In this case the logical operator *not*, when used with *is null*, will only include people for whom a middle name exists.

TRANSLATION: List the I.D. and sort name for all people in the NAME table whose last name is Knight and whose first name begins with the letters L, M, or N and for whom a middle name exists. Order the list by their sort name.

Figure 4–3. Comparison operators *between* and *is null* and logical operator *not*.

REPORT

```
        id sort_name
---------- --------------------------------
      4962 Knight, Denise
      2695 Knight, Mary S.
       611 Knight, Matthew M.
      8344 Knight, Melissa
      1086 Plante, Danielle
      2158 Plante, Mathew
      2927 Plante, Matthew
      5316 Plante, Michelle M.

8 rows selected.
```

SQL

```
select
       name_id,
       name_last||', '||name_first||' '||name_middle "sort_name"
from
       name
where
       name_last in ('Knight','Plante')
               and (name_first like 'M%'
               or name_first like 'D%')
order by 2
/
```

In lists the items for selection; in this case people whose last name is Knight or Plante.

Like matches character patterns; in this case a first name beginning with M. The wildcard "%" means that zero or more additional characters may follow the M.

Note the use of parentheses to make the meaning of the phrase clearer. In this case the first name must begin with M or D.

TRANSLATION: List the I.D. and sort name for all people in the NAME table whose last name is either Knight or Plante and whose first name begins with M or D. Order the list by the sort name.

Figure 4–4. Comparison operators *in* and *like* and logical operator *or.*

- Items in the *select* clause may be given alias names—nicknames if you will—that can then be used in SQL*PLUS commands when referring to the item (in v7.1 ORACLE plans to allow column aliases to be used in the *order by* clause to sort the report rows).
- A data value is "null" when it does not exist (the corollary being that a data value does exist if it is not null).
- Wildcard matching can occur when the *like* comparison operator is used, with "%" matching zero or more characters and "_" matching any single character.
- Parentheses are highly recommended to clarify the order of operations in complex *where* conditions.
- The comparison operator *between* includes the end values (e.g., integers between 1 and 3 means 1, 2, and 3).

Joining Tables

So far the SQL examples have been trivial, involving only a single data table. Unless you're working with specially constructed snapshot (extract) data tables, this happens infrequently. Most queries require that two or more tables be joined. Joins are needed in either of the following situations: (1) the data columns specified in the *select* clause come from two or more tables, or (2) the data columns needed in the *where* clause to define the population come from two or more tables.

Figure 4–5 shows an SQL query with only one modification from those in earlier figures. Columns appearing in the report now include the previous high school attended in addition to the I.D. and name. Name information occurs in the NAME table; previous academic information occurs in the ACADEMIC table. Both tables must appear in the *from* clause and the *where* clause must explicitly join the two tables. Actually the last statement is not quite true. You can forget to join two tables in a *where* clause and no error message will be generated. But the result, something called a Cartesian product between the two tables, will return gibberish and take forever to complete—not a desirable result.

Two tables are joined on data columns common to both. To understand exactly how this happens, it's useful to identify two special kinds of data columns. If one or more data columns uniquely identifies each table

REPORT

```
                                     inst
    id sort_name                     code
------ ------------------------- ------
  4169 Ahearn, Allison               2219
  2611 Ahearn, Ashley                2219
  3542 Ahearn, Denise                0517
  3542 Ahearn, Denise                1424
  3614 Ahearn, Gina                  0609
   115 Ahearn, Jennifer              3004
  7053 Ahearn, Karen                 4001
  5541 Ahearn, Sarah                 2816
  6489 Ahearn, Timothy R.            0123
  6489 Ahearn, Timothy R.            1406
  4550 Ahearn, Wei                   0000

11 rows selected.
```

Two people each attended two prior schools. Their I.D. and name information is reported twice in this report, once for each school.

SQL

```
select
      name_id,
      name_last||', '||name_first||' '||name_middle "sort_name",
      academic_instcode
from
      academic,
      name
where
      name_last = 'Ahearn'
      and academic_id = name_id
order by 2
/
```

Information on prior academic history is stored in the ACADEMIC table and must appear in the *from* phrase.

The ACADEMIC and NAME tables are joined by matching I.D. in the NAME table to I.D. in the ACADEMIC table.

TRANSLATION: List the I.D., sort name, and code of the previous schools attended for people in the NAME table whose last name is Ahearn. Order the list by the sort name.

Figure 4–5. Table joins when data columns are selected from more than one table.

row from all other rows in the table, those columns are called the *primary key* for the table. Figure 3–1 in Chapter 3 identifies all primary keys for tables in the simulated database.

Tables may also contain *foreign keys*. These are one or more data columns derived from the values in the primary key of another table. For example, look at the ADDRESS and PHONE tables in Figure 3–1. The PHONE table has the foreign key of phone_address_type and phone_address_seriesno—columns in the primary key in the ADDRESS table that appear in the PHONE table so that phone numbers and addresses properly match. Tables may contain more than one foreign key.

Joins between tables occur through primary and foreign keys. Examine Figure 4–5 again. The primary key in the NAME and ACADEMIC tables each contain the I.D. number. The *where* clause specifies that NAME and ACADEMIC are joined by matching I.D. numbers. So, for example, the name data for the person with I.D. = 010 in NAME can be linked to academic information in ACADEMIC for the same I.D. That sounds simple enough.

However, all the fun of SQL begins with table joins. Three things can happen when tables are joined. To illustrate, suppose that you join table A with table B and table A has 10 rows in it, each for a different person. How many rows will result from the simple join between A and B? The answer, of course, depends on table B. The join might have 10 rows if all 10 people are in table B and each appears there only once. But the join may also return fewer than 10 (even zero) if some or all of the people are not in B. A third possibility occurs if some or all of the people appear more than once in B. In this case the number of rows in the join may be larger than 10.

Figure 4–5 illustrates this third case, where two people named Ahearn each attended two previous schools. They each appear twice in the report, once for each school. If you want a report showing all previous schools attended, then the report in Figure 4–5 works nicely. But if you want a report that shows only the most recent school attended, then you'd need to modify the SQL that generated the report. Or if we objected to the printing of redundant information on I.D. and name, you'd also need to modify the program. Figure 4–6 shows such a modification and introduces the first of many SQL*PLUS commands that will be used in the next several chapters. This command, the ***break*** command, can be used to suppress the printing of redundant information. Note that like all SQL*PLUS commands, the ***break*** command does not end with ";" or "/" as the SQL *select* command does.

Let's think a bit more deeply about the three results that can occur when two tables are joined. The first possibility never, in my experience,

REPORT

```
                                  inst
    id sort_name                  code   school
------ ------------------------- ------ ------------------------------
  4169 Ahearn, Allison            2219   Somerville High School
  2611 Ahearn, Ashley             2219   Somerville High School
  3542 Ahearn, Denise             0517   Manual Arts Sr HS
                                  1424   Nazareth Academy
  3614 Ahearn, Gina               0609   Arapahoe High School
   115 Ahearn, Jennifer           3004   Nashua High School
  7053 Ahearn, Karen              4001   Classical High School
  5541 Ahearn, Sarah              2816   Norfolk Senior HS
  6489 Ahearn, Timothy R.         0123   Scottsboro High School
                                  1406   Lane Technical High School

10 rows select
```

Using the SQL*PLUS ***break*** command eliminates the problem of redundant I.D. and name information found in Figure 4–5.

SQL

```
break on name_id on sort_name
select
      name_id,
      name_last||', '||name_first||' '||name_middle "sort_name",
      academic_instcode,
      cinst_name
from
      cinst,
      academic,
      name
where
      name_last = 'Ahearn'
      and academic_id = name_id
      and cinst_code = academic_instcode
order by 2
/
```

A third table (CINST) appears in this SQL, to retrieve the school name. The join occurs through the institution code column common to CINST and ACADEMIC.

TRANSLATION: List id, sort name, and the code and name of prior schools attended for each person in the NAME table whose last name is Ahearn. Order the report by sort name.

Figure 4–6. Use of ***break*** to eliminate redundant information.

produces a problem for ad hoc queries. Joining table A with 10 people to table B that contains the same 10 people, but only once, never creates a reporting problem. However, each of the other two possibilities can produce problems. Starting out with 10 people and getting a report with only 8 is a problem if you wanted all 10 to appear. I call this problem "falling through" a join.

Conversely, starting out with 10 people and getting a report with 12 rows is a problem if all the report data is redundant for one or more rows. I call this problem "loss of singularity." Inexplicably the report contains some rows that appear more than once. How can this happen? It's actually a variation of the situation in Figure 4–5. Imagine the data columns appearing in a report come from table A and table C, but that in order to get to table C we need to pass through table B (that is, tables A and C are related indirectly through B). Suppose the person with I.D. = 010 appears once in A, but twice in table B. Then unless we take special precautions the joins A = B and B = C will produce two rows for this person. Picking report columns from only table A and C will produce a report with two rows for the person, and the two rows may be identical! This frustrates the person writing an SQL query and baffles the report user; if it happens often enough the report user grows wary about the accuracy of reports.

Solutions exist for both the loss of singularity and falling through a join. However each solution exacts a performance (i.e., response time) penalty. Various options will be discussed in later chapters. For now it's enough to know that joining tables can produce unintended consequences. One of the main benefits from building SQL objects is that they eliminate or make explicit the join consequences.

SQL Functions

In addition to operators there are many SQL functions that perform useful actions. Like operators, SQL functions come in different flavors:

- Character functions act on character data values.
- Number functions act on numeric data values.
- Date functions act on data values that are dates.
- Conversion functions act to convert one type of data value to another, for example, to convert a number to a character.
- Miscellaneous functions provide a number of different actions and are not limited to a specific data type.

- Group functions provide summaries such as averages for data values that have been grouped on some characteristic.

Table 4–3 shows the most common functions used with character and numeric data. Table C-2 in Appendix C provides a complete listing of these SQL functions. Note the range of possibilities. Character strings can be capitalized or forced to lowercase; the length of a character string can be determined; repeating characters can be trimmed from or added to the left and right sides of a string; and substrings can be returned from a longer string. Number functions can compute an absolute value, raise a number to a given power, round a number to a certain number of decimal places, or truncate a number. For example, if the data value = 12.56 then round(12.56,1) = 12.6 and trunc(12.56,1) = 12.5.

Table 4–3. Common SQL character and numeric functions.

Function	Action	General form	Example
CHARACTER			
initcap	Capitalizes initial letter	init(string)	init('ok') = 'Ok'
length	Number of characters	length(string)	length('ok') = 2
lower	All letters lowercase	lower(string)	lower('OK') = 'ok'
lpad	Left pads a string	lpad(string1,n,string2) left pads string1 to length n with characters in string2	lpad('ok',5,'*') = '***ok'
ltrim	Trims characters from left	ltrim(string1, string2) trims string2 from the left side of string1	ltrim(' ok',' ') = 'ok'
rpad	Right pads a string	rpad(string1,n,string2) right pads string 1 to length n with characters in string2	rpad('ok',5,'*') = 'ok***'
rtrim	Trims characters from right	rtrim(string1,string2) trims string2 from right side of string1	rtrim('ok ', ' ') = 'ok'
substr	Returns a substring	substr(string,m,n) returns a substring of length n beginning at character m	substr('***ok',4,2) = 'ok'
upper	All letters uppercase	upper(string)	upper('ok') = 'OK'
NUMBER			
abs	Absolute value	abs(n)	abs(-1) = 1
power	Raise number to nth power	power(m,n); in Oracle v7, n need not be an integer	power(2,4) = 16

(Continued)

Table 4–3. Common SQL character and numeric functions.

Function	Action	General form	Example
round	Round number m places from decimal	round(n,m)	round(12.56,1) = 12.6 round(12.56,0) = 13
sign	Distinguish negative from positive	sign(n)	sign(7) = 1; sign(-7) = -1; sign(0) = 0
trunc	Truncate a number to m decimal places	trunc(m,n)	trunc(12.56,1) = 12.5 trunc(12.56,0) = 12

Table 4–4 shows the most common date, conversion, group, and miscellaneous SQL functions. Tables C–3 and C–4 in Appendix C provide a complete list of these functions. Date functions can return today's date and time; determine the number of months between two dates; find the date of the last day in a month; and return the date a specified number of months in the future. Table 4–4 shows, for example, that months_between('19-APR-95','31-DEC-94') is 4.129 months. Group functions can produce averages, counts, minimums, maximums, and summations. In all cases except one (i.e., count(*)), null values are ignored in group functions. Conversion functions convert a number to a character, a date to a character, a character to a date, or a character to a number. Conversions between datatypes usually occur according to a specified format. For example, converting the number 12000 to a character value using the format of $99,999 will yield $12,000 — a dollar sign gets added at the left of the string and a comma is inserted to more easily distinguish thousands of dollars. The most common conversion formats for dates and numbers are shown in Table 4–5 on page 58 while Tables C–5 and C–6 in Appendix C provide a complete list. Again, the range of possible formats is impressive. For example, if a data value is the date 15-DEC-94 then using to_char(date, 'Mon DD "of" YYYY') results in Dec 15 of 1994.

Table 4–4. Common SQL date, conversion, group, and miscellaneous functions.

Function	Action	General form	Example
DATE			
add_months	Returns date plus n months	add_months (date, n)	add_months('15-DEC-94',2)='15-FEB-95'
last_day	Last day of month	last_day(date)	last_day('15-DEC-94') = '31-DEC-94'
months_between	Number of months between two dates	months_between (date1, date2)	months_between('19-APR-95', '15-DEC-94')=4.129

Table 4–4. Common SQL date, conversion, group, and miscellaneous functions.

Function	Action	General form	Example
DATE *continued*			
next_day	Date of next week day after specified date	next_day(date1,day)	next_day('15-DEC-94', 'SATURDAY') = '17-DEC-94'
sysdate	Current date and time	sysdate	
CONVERSION			
to_char	Convert number to character	to_char(n,format)	to_char(12000,'$99,999') = $12,000
to_char	Convert date to character	to_char(date,format)	if d = 15-DEC-94 to_char(d,'MM/DD/YY') = 12/15/94
to_date	Convert character date to date	to_date(char,format)	if c='2/9/95' to_date(c,'DD-MON-YY') = 02-FEB-95
to_number	Convert character to number	to_number(char)	if char = '15' then 2*(to_number(char)) = 30
OTHER ROW			
decode	Compare two values and return a third	decode(val,comp1, result1, comp2, result2,default)	if val = 'OK' then decode (val,'ok',1,'OK',2,'Ok',3,9) = 2 if val = 'oK' then decode (val,'ok',1','OK',2','Ok',3,9) = 9
greatest	Returns greatest in a list of values	greatest(val1, val2, ...)	greatest('first','last') = 'last' greatest(10,1) = 10
least	Returns least in a list of values	least(val1, val2, ...)	least('first','last') = 'first'
nvl	If value is null, return a replacement	nvl(data column, replacement)	if age is null, then nvl(age, 'unknown') = 'unknown'
GROUP			assume 4 ages = 15, 20, 25, and unknown
avg	Group average ignoring nulls	avg(data column)	avg(age) = 20
count	Count of rows ignoring nulls	count(data column)	count(age) = 3
count(*)	Count of rows including nulls	count(*)	count(*) = 4
min	Group minimum ignoring nulls	min(data column)	min(age) = 15
max	Group maximum ignoring nulls	max(data column)	max(age) = 25
sum	Sum of values for group, ignoring nulls	sum(data column)	sum(age) = 60

Table 4–5. Common formats in *to_char(number,fmt), to_char(date,fmt)* and *to_date(char,fmt).*

Element	Action	Result
NUMBER		
9	Display width determined by number of 9s	123 if n=123 and fmt = 9999
0	Leading zeroes displayed	0123 if n=123 and fmt = 0999
$	Dollar signed prefixed to number	$123 if n=123 and fmt = $999
E	Scientific notation (use four Es)	1.23E+02 if n=123, fmt=9.99EEEE
MI	Minus (–) displayed after negative numbers	123– if n = -123 and fmt=999MI
PR	Negative numbers in <> brackets	<123> if n = -123 and fmt=999PR
comma	Place comma	1,234 if n=1234 and fmt = 9,999
period	Place decimal point	123.00 if n=123 and fmt=999.99
DATE (assume 2:15 pm 15-DEC-94)		
DDD	Day of year	349
DD	Day of month	15
D	Day of week	5
DAY	Name of day (9 characters with blanks)	THURSDAY
DY	Name of day (3 character abbreviation)	THU
MM	Number of month	12
MONTH	Name of month (9 characters with blanks)	DECEMBER
MON	Name of month (3 character abbreviation)	DEC
YYYY	Year in 4–digits	1994
YY	Last 2 digits of year	94
YEAR	Year spelled out	NINETEEN-NINETY-FOUR
WW	Week of year (week 1 = days 1–7 of year)	50
W	Week of month (week 1 = days 1–7)	3
Q	Quarter of year	4
J (J)	Julian date (days since Jan 1, 4712 BC)	2449702
/ or : or etc	Punctuation included in result	12/15/94 if 'MM/DD/YY'
"..."	String included in result	Dec 15 of 1994 if 'Mon DD "of" YYYY'
HH or HH12	Hour of day (1–12)	02
HH24	Hour of day (0–23)	14
MI	Minutes	14:15 if 'hh24:mi'
SS	Seconds	14:15:00 if 'hh24:mi:ss'
AM,PM,A.M., P.M.	AM, PM, A.M. or P.M. indicator	02:15 p.m. if 'hh:mi a.m.'

Note: Capitalization can be changed on some formats by using variations of the elements listed above. For example, if the month is December then 'MON' = 'DEC', 'Mon' = 'Dec', and 'mon' = 'dec'.

Figures 4–7 through 4–11 on the following five pages illustrate the use of two additional SQL*PLUS commands and several SQL functions, including *round*, *upper*, *initcap*, *substr*, *length*, *decode*, *to_char*, *sysdate*, *trunc*, *months_between*, *count*, and *nvl*. It's worth noting several items:

- Functions take the general form of fn(arg1, arg2, ...) where fn is the function name, arg1 is the first argument, and so on. Some function arguments are optional or may be omitted with a default value assumed.
- When functions are used to construct new report columns, it's often useful to give the new column an alias and define column characteristics using the SQL*PLUS ***column*** command. Figures 4–7 and 4–8 provide examples where the ***column*** command is used.
- The default format for dates is 'DD-MON-YY'. Many additional date and time formats exist. Uppercase formats differ from lower case formats; for example, a 'dd-Mon-yyyy' format for December 15, 1994 results in 15-Dec-1994 while a 'DD-MON-YYYY' format yields 15-DEC-1994.
- The *decode* function provides if ... then ... else functionality and is quite powerful if somewhat obtuse to decipher. Figure 4–9 and Figure 4–10 both illustrate uses of the *decode* function. The general form is decode(a,b,c,d,e,...x), which reads "if a=b then do c, else if a=d then do e, etc., else do x." In Figure 4–10, for example, the *decode* function determines whether an age should be computed; if the date of birth does not exist, an age is not computed.
- Functions can be nested within other functions.

SQL *Select* Command Continued

Earlier figures demonstrated the use of four components of the ***select*** command: the *select*, *from*, *where*, and *order by* clauses. As mentioned previously there are two additional clauses that get used when group functions like *avg*, *sum*, *count*, *min*, or *max* are needed.

Figure 4–11 shows the first departure from a standard roster or listing, showing instead counts of people by their gender. Figure 4–12 on page 65 provides another variation, showing applicants for admission who submitted more than one application in the same term. It is the *having* clause in

REPORT

```
                                      inst        size      rank  pct
    id sort_name                      code        class     class rank
------ ------------------------- ------ ---------- ---------- -----
  4290 Davis, Amy                      7968         588       482   82
  8629 Davis, Danielle                 3604         739       222   30
   307 Davis, Laura R                  0704           7         4   57
  4628 Davis, Lori                     4000          63        28   44
  8442 Davis, Michelle                 1923         761       137   18
  3967 Davis, Rebecca                  1431        1287       309   24
  5899 Davis, Thomas                   3303        1197       694   58

7 rows select
```

SQL

```
column pctrank heading 'pct|rank' format 9999
break on name_id on sort_name
select
      name_id,
      name_last||', '||name_first||' '||name_middle "sort_name",
      academic_instcode,
      academic_sizeclass,
      academic_rankclass,
      round((academic_rankclass/academic_sizeclass)*100,0) "pctrank"
from
      academic,
      name
where
      name_last = 'Davis'
      and academic_id = name_id
             and academic_sizeclass is not null
order by 2
/
```

Column is a SQL*PLUS command used to format report columns and headers. See Chapter 6 for details.

The SQL*PLUS ***column*** and ***break*** commands can use column aliases.

Round will round a numeric data value to a specified number of decimal places; in this case to zero decimal places.

TRANSLATION: List I.D., sort name, code of prior schools attended, the size of the graduating class, the person's rank in that class, and a computed percentile class rank for each person in the NAME table whose last name is Davis. Order the report by sort name.

Figure 4–7. Use of the ***column*** command and the *round* number function.

REPORT

```
id     name                         first           middle
-----  ---------------------------  --------------  --------------
 6179  ALLEN, Angela A              Angela          Ann
 3905  ALLEN, Christine M           Christine       Marie
 8267  ALLEN, John H                John            Hon
   23  ALLEN, Melissa C             melissa         Cheryll
 5887  ALLEN, Sang D                Sang            Dustin
  535  ALLEN, Yulannda D            Yulannda        David

  6 rows selected.
```

SQL

```
column name format a25
select
       name_id,
       upper(name_last)||', '||initcap(name_first)||' '||
              substr(name_middle,1,1) "name",
       name_first,
       name_middle
from
       name
where
       name_last = 'Allen'
              and length(name_middle) > 2
order by 2
```

Upper converts character data values to uppercase and *initcap* capitalizes the first character (see report at left). The *substr*(str1,m,n) returns a substring from the string 'str1' beginning at character m and extending for n characters.

Length computes how many characters appear in a character data value. In this case the selection requires that middle name has more than 2 characters.

TRANSLATION: List I.D. and a modified sort name for each person in the NAME table whose last name is Allen and whose middle name has more than two characters. Order the report by the sort name. The sort name is modified by capitalizing the last name, ensuring the first letter of the first name is a capital letter, and by only using the first letter of the middle name.

Figure 4–8. Several character functions: *upper, initcap, substr,* and *length.*

REPORT

```
                                          char
                  inst   size   rank  pct pct
  id sort_name    code   class  class rank rank
------ ------------------------ ------ ------ ------ ----- ----
  4290 Davis, Amy          7968    588    482    82 82%
  8629 Davis, Danielle     3604    739    222    30 30%
  .307 Davis, Laura R      0704      7      4    57 57%
  4628 Davis, Lori         4000     63     28    44 44%
  8442 Davis, Michelle     1923    761    137    18 18%
  3967 Davis, R
  5899 Davis, T

7 rows selected.
```

SQL

```
column pctrank heading 'pct|rank' format 9999
column pctrank2 heading 'char|pct|rank' format a4
select
     name_id,
     name_last||', '||name_first||' '||name_middle "sort_name",
     academic_instcode,
     academic_sizeclass,
     academic_rankclass,
     round((academic_rankclass/academic_sizeclass)*100,0) "pctrank",
     to_char(round((academic_rankclass/academic_sizeclass)*100,0))||
            decode(academic_rankclass,null,null,'%') "pctrank2"
from
      academic,
      name
where
      name_last = 'Davis'
      and academic_id = name_id
             and academic_sizeclass is not null
order by 2
/
```

The "a" in "a4" identifies the format as a character; the "4" determines the width of the column.

The *decode* function provides if ... then ... else logic. In this case if rank in class is null, don't concatenate a % sign (otherwise it would produce a report cell value with only %).

TRANSLATION: List the I.D., sort name, prior school, size of graduating class, rank in class, computed percentile rank in class, and the same percentile rank expressed as a character value. Order the report by sort name.

The *to_char* function converts the numeric percentile rank into a character string. Then concatenate % to produce the last column in the report.

Figure 4–9. *Decode* and *to_char* functions.

REPORT

```
                                    birth     report
   id sort_name                 sex date      date      age
------ ------------------------ --- --------- --------- ---
  2186 Byrne, Matthew           M   25-JAN-75 10-AUG-94 19
  2567 Byrne, Melissa           F   20-NOV-73 10-AUG-94 20
  6388 Byrne, Patricia B        F   17-JUN-75 10-AUG-94 19
  4788 Byrne, William           M   23-MAY-75 10-AUG-94 19

4 rows selected.
```

SQL

```
column age format a3
column sex format a3
column today heading 'report|date'
select
       person_id,
       name_last||', '||name_first||' '||name_middle "sort_name",
       person_gender "sex",
       person_birthdate,
       sysdate "today",
       decode(person_birthdate,null,null,
              trunc((months_between(sysdate,person_birthdate)/12),0)) "age"
from
       name,
       person
where
       name_last = 'Byrne'
       and person_id = name_id
              and person_birthdate is not null
order by 2
/
```

Months_between returns the number of months between two dates.

Trunc will truncate a numeric value to a specified number of decimal places; in this case the years of age are truncated to zero decimal places.

Sysdate returns the current date and time.

TRANSLATION: List the I.D., sort name, sex, date of birth, today's date, and the age of people in the NAME table whose last name is Byrne and whose birthdate is not null in the table. Age is computed using birthdate and the date the report was run. Order the report by sort name.

Figure 4–10. Use of the *sysdate, trunc,* and *months_between* functions.

REPORT

```
sex      count
--- ----------
             4
F           14
M            5
    ----------
sum         23

3 rows selected.
```

SQL

```
break on report
compute sum of count on report
column sex format a3
select
      nvl(person_gender, ' ') "sex",
      count(person_id) "count"
from
      name,
      person
where
      name_last = 'Byrne'
      and person_id = name_id
group by
      nvl(person_gender, ' ')
/
```

The ***break*** and ***compute*** commands coordinate to calculate the total count at the end of the report.

The null value function (*nvl*) temporarily replaces null with a specified value. In this case everybody whose gender is unknown gets counted as a blank (' ').

Count is a group function. In this case people are grouped by their gender and then counted.

Group by is another SQL phrase, like *select, from, where,* and *order by*. *Group by* occurs in conjunction with group functions like *count*.

TRANSLATION: For people in the NAME table whose last name is Byrne, get a count by gender. If gender is unknown, include that in the report as well. Also provide a total count.

Figure 4–11. ***Compute*** command, *group by* clause and *nvl* and *count* functions.

REPORT

```
        id sort_name                            COUNT(*)
---------- ---------------------------------- ----------
      3163 Adams, Amy                                  2
      3004 Allen, Alicia                               2
      5898 Allen, Karen                                2
      4846 Allen, Kristen                              2
      1798 Baker, Evelyn                               2
      4656 Baker, Samuel                               2
      7133 Berger, Kimberly                            2
      8023 Burke, Paula                                2
       833
       786
       727
        32
```

SQL

```
select
     applicant_id,
     n.name_last||', '||n.name_first "sort_name",
     count(*)
from
     name n,
     applicant
where
     applicant_term = '199409'
           and applicant_level = 'UG'
     and n.name_id = applicant_id
           and n.name_seriesno =
           (select max(m.name_seriesno)
           from name m
           where m.name_id = n.name_id)
group by
     applicant_id,
     n.name_last||', '||n.name_first
having count(*) > 1
order by 2
/
```

TRANSLATION: List the I.D. and sort name of undergraduate applicants for Fall 1994 who applied more than once that term. Order the report by sort name.

This subquery returns the most recent name if people have more than one row in the NAME table. Note the use of aliases for the NAME table (n and m) that distinguish the use of NAME in the main query from its use in the subquery.

Having limits the groups that appear in a report. In this case the grouping was done by applicant; only those applicants who applied more than once will be included in the report. *Having* can only be used in conjunction with a *group by*.

Figure 4–12. The *having* SQL clause and illustration of a subquery.

Figure 4–12 that limits the report to applicants with two or more applications. There are four important points made in these figures:

- Whenever a group function is used in the *select* clause along with columns that do not include group functions, a *group by* clause is mandatory. The effect of this structure in Figure 4–11 is to group people by gender before counting them.
- Columns in the *group by* clause must match all columns in the *select* clause that don't include the group function. In Figure 4–11 there is one such column; in Figure 4–12 there are two. Note in each case how the *select* clause and the *group by* clause are coordinated.
- Report totals require another coordinated effort, but this time between the two SQL*PLUS commands ***break*** and ***compute.*** Chapter 6 discusses this in more detail.
- SQL ***select*** commands can be nested within each other. Nested queries are called subqueries. Again several different kinds of subqueries exist. The one shown in Figure 4–12 is a particularly useful type called a correlated subquery. Features that distinguish types of subqueries will be discussed in later chapters. For now, it's enough to know that subqueries are possible.

Structured SQL Queries

The impression this chapter should leave is one of hidden power and complexity within the SQL ***select*** command. Only one command: that's all you need for ad hoc queries. And only six clauses within this single command. Ad hoc reports sound simple.

But throw in operators, functions, formats, joins, and subqueries and things begin to look different. The examples in this chapter went from trivial to simple. In fact much more complex SQL programs will be constructed in later chapters. This complexity is one of the main reasons that SQL objects serve such a useful purpose. Instead of writing dozens of lines of SQL code, it's only necessary to choose and coordinate the use of previously stored chunks of code. By moving up a level of abstraction, where objects get manipulated instead of individual SQL elements, ad hoc queries simplify considerably.

However, it's still necessary to write the SQL in the objects. This should be done so the code is easy to read, test, debug, and maintain. Structuring the SQL makes these tasks considerably easier. What does structure mean? Take another look at the SQL portion of the figures in this chapter. There is a definite structure in each program. For example, each of the six clauses begins in the left-hand margin of the program; each of the *select* clause columns is listed on a separate line; each table name appears on a separate line; each table join in the *where* clause is made prominent with indents; and each column appearing in a *group by* or *order by* clause also appears on a line by itself. This structure makes writing, reading, and understanding an SQL program much easier.

Physical structure to an SQL program is not required. It is perfectly legitimate to string everything together. For example, the SQL in Figure 4–12 could begin:

```
select applicant_id, n.name_last||', '||n.name_first
"sort_name", count(*) from name n,
applicant where applicant_term = '199409' and
applicant_level = 'UG' and n.name_id =
applicant_id and n.name_seriesno = etc.
```

Unstructured SQL that is syntactically identical to physically structured SQL will produce the same report. Unless the query is a one- or two-line program, however, writing unstructured SQL only invites problems. Everything may seem clear at the time, but come back a week later and try to understand what the SQL does. It's tough. It's also tough to debug unstructured SQL; it's difficult sometimes to even identify the table joins. For example, if two tables are joined through more than one column, it is not necessary to place the join conditions near each other in the program. You can write legitimate SQL that starts the join between tables A and B on one line, then does the join between tables A and C on several lines, and then comes back to finish the A to B join. Visually it's mess, but it's valid (or can be valid) SQL.

Throughout this book, I'll use physically structured SQL. The structure you'll see is my own preference developed over time. It is not necessary to use the structure you see here, but I do urge you to structure your SQL code in some fashion.

Chapter 5

Reporting Tools

Writing robust SQL queries takes effort when the database is complex. Users think of their data in business terms, not in the relational terms of tables and columns and rows. SQL objects make the translation from business definitions to relational definitions far easier. But constructing objects requires a firm understanding of both sides of this gap—the business definitions and the relational landscape of the database. Before constructing SQL objects, several tools must be assembled. These tools simplify the task of translating business concepts into relational definitions. All too often users writing their own ad hoc queries don't even know that these tools exist.

This chapter introduces tools useful for constructing SQL objects. The tools are arranged hierarchically based on breadth, each tool adding detail to the previous tools. Appendix D provides the SQL and SQL*PLUS programs that produced most of the tools discussed in this chapter. These programs also provide the foundation for the SQL*PLUS primer in Chapter 6.

Owners

Most users of complex databases only deal with a small portion of that database. Staff in a college admissions office only concern themselves with the admissions and recruiting tables; those in the registrar's office with enrollment-related tables; and so on. Within these module areas, staff may specialize and deal with an even smaller part of the data.

This specialization may work fine. But it's the interstices between areas of specialization, or between broader modular areas, that often create the most interesting ad hoc queries. So it's important to first locate areas of specialization within the broader context of the database. Otherwise, it's a bit like a person knowing he or she is from Colorado without having an internal map of the world that first locates Colorado in the United States, then within the North American continent, and so on. The first tool gives you a very broad overview of the database.

In ORACLE databases, tables have owners. There is often a structure to table owners, much like the geographic structure of states. This is particularly true if the database application software was purchased rather than developed internally. Vendors develop database applications in broad modules that can be sold separately (a human resource module separate from a financial module, and so on). These modules will likely have different table owners, so knowing what owners exist serves to distinguish broad modular areas in the database. Database designers are not required to differentiate modular areas with different table owners, but identifying owners is always a good place to start examining the structure of a database.

Figure 5–1 shows a count of tables by owners for the simulated database introduced in Chapter 3. In this case the landscape is particularly simple. There are only three table owners and two of them exist in all ORACLE databases. SYS and SYSTEM are both ORACLE user names with database administrator (DBA) privileges. Both are installed in every ORACLE system. SYS and SYSTEM own tables used to maintain information about the database. Some of these tables provide database housekeeping and won't concern users writing ad hoc queries. But other tables and views contain useful documentation about the database—critical items such as the names of the data columns and what they mean. Many of the reporting tools discussed here and in Chapter 6 are based on these SYS or SYSTEM tables and views.

```
Database tables and views by owner                          Report name: overview.lis
Date: 14-SEP-1994     Time: 05:21                                          Page:    1

OWNER                               count
------------------------------ ----------
KOMENDA                                32
SYS                                   122
SYSTEM                                  9
                               ----------
                                      163

3 rows selected.
```

Figure 5–1. Database overview of table owners.

Note in Figure 5–1 that one owner is KOMENDA. Tables in the simulated database have only a single owner. Since the database is restricted to admissions and recruiting, this is not unreasonable. But if more functional areas existed, such as financial aid or accounts receivable, it's likely that these functional areas would be distinguished by different table owners. There might also be a separate owner of tables shared across several modules.

Tables

Identifying table owners paints a broad picture of the database. Identifying individual tables for a specified owner paints a more detailed picture; a bit like adding county lines into a map of the United States that only showed state boundaries.

Figure 5–2 on the following page identifies the tables owned by KOMENDA. The figure shows an alphabetical list of all table names and a column describing the tables. Many of the tables, such as RECRUIT or DECISION, were discussed when Chapter 3 introduced the simulated database. But interestingly, there are many other tables that were not mentioned in Chapter 3. These are all code tables, like CDEGREE, which lists the codes for each type of degree (BA, BS, MS, etc.) and gives a descriptive translation of what each code means (e.g., BA is Bachelor of Arts).

Usually a database will contain a separate code table for each coded data column. Figure 5–2 shows that the simulated database uses codes to distinguish different types of addresses, applicants, admissions decisions, degrees, dormitories, required admissions documents, ethnic statuses, sex, prior high school or college codes, academic majors, nations, states, phones, standardized tests, and visas.

There is no requirement that databases contain codes. But codes offer distinct data input and storage advantages. It's far easier, for example, to input BA than Bachelor of Arts. It also takes up less space in the data tables. So codes and code tables proliferate. Complex databases will contain hundreds of code tables.

The presence of code tables complicates modestly the work required in ad hoc queries. I once provided a college director of public relations a count of degree recipients by nation of citizenship. It only included the nation codes and an associated count. About 15 minutes after I e-mailed the report, I got a call to ask what country the code SUI represented. I'd neglected to join the nation code table into the SQL, so that I could report counts by the nation name instead of by the nation code. Joins to code tables are usually not difficult, although they do introduce another opportunity for an item in

```
Tables for owner: KOMENDA                                                      Page:    1
Date: 09-OCT-1994     Time: 10:05                                Report name: komenda.lis
                                                                 SQL name:     tables.sql
Name                      Type        Owner                      Comments
------------------------- ----------- -------------------------- ----------------------------------------------------
ACADEMIC                  TABLE       KOMENDA                    High School and Previous College Academic Records
ADDRESS                   TABLE       KOMENDA                    Address Information
APPLICANT                 TABLE       KOMENDA                    Applicant Information
CADDRESS                  TABLE       KOMENDA                    Address Type Code Translation Table
CAPPLICANT                TABLE       KOMENDA                    Application Type Code Translation Table
CCOLLEGE                  TABLE       KOMENDA                    College Code Translation Table
CDECISION                 TABLE       KOMENDA                    Admissions Decision Code Translation Table
CDEGREE                   TABLE       KOMENDA                    Degree Code Translation Table
CDOCUMENT                 TABLE       KOMENDA                    Document Code Translation Table
CDORM                     TABLE       KOMENDA                    Residence Code Translation Table
CETHN                     TABLE       KOMENDA                    Ethnic Code Translation Table
CGENDER                   TABLE       KOMENDA                    Gender Code Translation Table
CINST                     TABLE       KOMENDA                    Institutions Code Translation Table
CLEVEL                    TABLE       KOMENDA                    Level Code Translation Table
CMAIL                     TABLE       KOMENDA                    Document Code Translation Table
CMAJOR                    TABLE       KOMENDA                    Major Code Translation Table
CNATION                   TABLE       KOMENDA                    Nation Code Translation Table
CPHONE                    TABLE       KOMENDA                    Phone Type Code Translation Table
CSTATE                    TABLE       KOMENDA                    State Code Translation Table
CSTYPE                    TABLE       KOMENDA                    Student Type Code Translation Table
CTERM                     TABLE       KOMENDA                    Term Code Translation Table
CTEST                     TABLE       KOMENDA                    Test Code Translation Table
CVISA                     TABLE       KOMENDA                    Visa Code Translation Table
DECISION                  TABLE       KOMENDA                    Admissions Decision Information
DOCUMENT                  TABLE       KOMENDA                    Admissions documents received
MAIL                      TABLE       KOMENDA                    Recruit and Applicant Correspondence
NAME                      TABLE       KOMENDA                    Table of Name Information
PERSON                    TABLE       KOMENDA                    Person Specific Information
PHONE                     TABLE       KOMENDA                    Telephone Information
RECRUIT                   TABLE       KOMENDA                    Prospects for Admission
TEST                      TABLE       KOMENDA                    Test Score Information
VISA                      TABLE       KOMENDA                    Visa Information for Internationals
```

Figure 5–2. Tables for owner KOMENDA.

the report population to fall through a join. But if the report recipient isn't familiar with the codes being used, the person writing the ad hoc query should include a join to the code table so that the report contains descriptive translations of the codes instead of the codes themselves.

Note in Figure 5–2 that the database designer tried to provide an easy way to distinguish code tables. They all begin with the letter C for Code, followed by a word that identifies what type of codes the tables contain (e.g., CMAJOR contains codes and descriptions for academic major codes). Designers are not required to logically name data tables, and some names can be extremely cryptic, but there is often a logic to table names in databases. If so, you need to get the documentation that reveals the logic. Table naming conventions act a bit like zip codes; they help place a given table within owners, broad module areas, or subspecialty, much like zip codes help place an address within a state, county, and city.

One final note about Figure 5–2: all tables have an associated comment column that describes in general terms the contents of the table. Database designers are required to name tables and owners; they are not required, however, to provide descriptive comments about the tables. If you run the script in Appendix D to list the tables for a specific owner in your database, and you get a report with blank comments, then it's time to chide the designer and insist that these comment data columns be added. The absence of comments indicates sloppy database documentation.

Data Columns and Data Dictionaries

At the risk of overextending the geographic analogy, identifying the data columns for a specific table and owner is a bit like identifying the towns in a specific county and state. Lists of data columns in a table are called data dictionaries. Data dictionaries function just like word dictionaries. You look up a data column name to find out basic definitions for that column. Is it numeric or character? If numeric, is it integer or can it contain a decimal? How many characters or number digits may it contain? Must the data column contain data for each row, or can it contain null values for some or all rows? And, perhaps most importantly, what data gets stored in the data column?

Figure 5–3 on the following page shows the data dictionary for the APPLICANT table. Dictionaries for all the tables in the simulated database, including the code tables, appear in Appendix A. The SQL and SQL*PLUS program used to produce data dictionaries appears in Appendix D. If your database doesn't already have a convenient way to generate data dictionaries for each data table, then you can run the script in Appendix D against your

```
Date: 07-JAN-1995     Time: 07:00              TABLE: APPLICANT                          Page:    1
Report name: applicant.dic                      Owner: KOMENDA                      SQL name: dic.sql
                                             Applicant_Information

Column name                 Type    Width  Scale Nulls     Column comments
==========================================================================================================
APPLICANT_ID                NUMBER      4        NOT NULL  ID number of applicant
APPLICANT_TERM              CHAR        6        NOT NULL  Anticipated term of enrollment
APPLICANT_LEVEL             CHAR        2        NOT NULL  Level (Undergrad, Grad) of applicant
APPLICANT_SERIESNO          NUMBER      2        NOT NULL  Sequential number if more than one application in single term
APPLICANT_RECRUIT_TERM      CHAR        6        NOT NULL  Anticipated enrollment term from recruit record
APPLICANT_COLLEGE           CHAR        2        NULL      College (Arts and Sciences, Business)
APPLICANT_DORM_INTENT       CHAR        1        NULL      Anticipated residence status (commuter or dorm)
APPLICANT_AID_INTENT        CHAR        1        NULL      Anticipated need for financial aid
APPLICANT_TYPE              CHAR        2        NULL      Type of application
APPLICANT_STUDENT_TYPE      CHAR        1        NULL      Type of student (freshman, transfer)
APPLICANT_DATESTAMP         DATE        7        NULL      Last date record was updated
APPLICANT_DEGREE            CHAR        6        NULL      Anticipated degree
APPLICANT_MAJOR             CHAR        4        NULL      Anticipated major
APPLICANT_APPLDATE          DATE        7        NULL      Date application received
```

Figure 5–3. Example of a data table dictionary.

database. Writers of ad hoc queries should keep a current dictionary for each data table that they write queries against. At each database upgrade, the dictionaries should be rerun to catch any column deletions, additions, or changes.

Figure 5–3 provides some interesting information about the APPLICANT table. Let's look first at the column names. Despite the best intentions of database designers, data column names often appear as obtuse abbreviations to new users or even experienced users new to a table. The data column names for the simulated database do provide some help. For example, the data column names are divided into distinct parts separated by an underline. The first part of each column name is the name of the table. This can be convenient if you reuse a query months after it was written. The appearance of applicant_id in the *select* clause immediately makes clear which table the I.D. column is being taken from.

But some level of obtuseness will likely remain in data column names of all databases. Consider the column called applicant_student_type. What exactly does this mean and how does it differ from the column applicant_type? When naming columns, the designer must compromise between complete but lengthy descriptive column names and shorter, but easier to use, names. The data dictionary for the applicant table shows that applicant_student_type distinguishes freshman applicants from transfer applicants. A more descriptive name for this column might have been applicant_freshman_or_transfer. In actual use, however, descriptive names become burdensome; the longer the name, the longer it takes to type. The other extreme assumes only experienced users will write ad hoc queries; little effort is made to make column names descriptive. Then applicant_student_type merely becomes stype. The important point is that naming columns involves trade-offs between ease of use and complete description. You'll rarely find completely descriptive column names.

That's one purpose of data dictionaries. Figure 5–3 includes a comments column that explains the meaning of each data column name. If you run the script in Appendix D for a table dictionary in your database and you get blank comments, it indicates incomplete database documentation. Time to again chide the database designer or your information systems staff.

Data dictionaries also provide important information about the type of data that a table contains. Figure 5–3 shows that the APPLICANT table contains three date columns and several character data columns. The width of a column indicates the maximum number of bytes it can contain; for example, a CHAR data column with a width of 6 may contain strings of 6 or fewer characters (in ORACLE v7 this is true of VARCHAR2 datatypes). The APPLICANT table also contains two numeric columns. In Figure 5–3 and other data dictionaries in Appendix A, the report column called Scale indicates if the number can contain decimal points. The absence of a scale number for applicant_id and applicant_seriesno means that both columns are integers. The APPLICANT table has no numeric data columns containing decimal data values, but consider Table A–3 (in Appendix A), showing the dictionary for the ACADEMIC table. The column of grade point averages from prior colleges, named academic_gpa, has a width of 3 and a scale of 2. This means that grade point averages can contain three or fewer digits and two of these may appear to the right of the decimal point.

Data dictionaries often contain important clues about primary and foreign keys. Recall from Chapter 4 that primary and foreign keys help join tables accurately. The primary key in a table uniquely identifies each row from all other rows in the table. Columns labeled Not Null in data dictionaries are often good candidates for primary keys, because they must contain data for each row in the table.

Database Architecture

So we know the table owners, the table names, and the data column names. Now what we need is a map that shows how the tables are related, much as a map of the United States shows states in relationship to surrounding or distant states. If you're in Colorado it helps to know that you can go directly to Kansas, but that if you want to go to Missouri you must first pass through Kansas. Similarly, in a database it helps to know that you can go directly from the PERSON table to the ADDRESS table, but that if you want to go from PERSON to PHONE you must first traverse the ADDRESS table.

Database schematics provide the roadmaps that relate tables. Figure 3–1 showed a schematic for the simulated database. It identified the major tables, the primary keys in each table, any foreign keys that link a table to another, and whether the relationship between rows in any two tables is one-to-one, one-to-many, or many-to-one. A database schematic also shows if two tables are related directly or indirectly through one or more intermediate tables.

Database schematics often come with the documentation a vendor supplies. Make sure you get a copy; they're invaluable. In a complex database, the schematics will fill many pages.

Indexes and Primary Keys

The time needed to access data in large tables can often be significantly reduced with indexes. These are physical structures separate from the data itself, but describing where in the data files a given row is located. Sometimes this location is known exactly; other times the location is only known approximately. In either case, access time to retrieve a row frequently improves compared to a sequential search beginning with row one and proceeding row after row until the desired row is found.

Writers of ad hoc queries have no control over which indexes get created. That's a database design and administration issue. But query writers should understand what indexes exist. There are two reasons for this:

- Proper use of available indexes can significantly improve query performance. This topic is discussed in Chapter 12 when testing and debugging objects. If a query takes a long time to complete, it's time to worry about what indexes are being used.
- Indexes help identify the primary key in a table and, in so doing, provide information useful for joining tables and eliminating one of the two primary sources of end-user query error.

It's this latter issue that's important here. There are two types of indexes: unique and non-unique. As their name implies, unique indexes uniquely identify the location of each row in a table. Indexes get built on one or more data columns in a table. To say that an index built on column A and column B, for example, is unique means that no two rows in the table can have the same combination of data values in A and B.

But this is just the definition of a primary key—one or more data columns in a table that uniquely identify each row in the table. While indexes and primary keys are different concepts, unique indexes identify the primary key in a table.

Figure 5–4 on the following two pages shows the indexes built for tables in the simulated database. Consider the two indexes on the NAME table. One is a unique index; the other non-unique. The unique index, given the name NAME_KEY, is composed of the two data columns name_id and name_seriesno. This means that no two rows in the NAME table may have the same name_id and name_seriesno. In fact, building a unique index prevents the creation or update of a row that would contradict the uniqueness criteria. On the other hand, the non-unique index called name_last only

```
Indexes on tables owned by: KOMENDA                                                              Page:     1
Date: 07-JAN-1995     Time: 06:51                                                        Report name: indexes.lis
                                                                                         SQL name:    indexes.sql

table                      index                          uniqueness column                           position
-------------------------- ------------------------------ ---------- ------------------------------ ----------
ACADEMIC                   ACADEMIC_KEY                   UNIQUE     ACADEMIC_ID                             1
                                                                     ACADEMIC_INSTCODE                       2
                                                                     ACADEMIC_SERIESNO                       3

ADDRESS                    ADDRESS_KEY                    UNIQUE     ADDRESS_ID                              1
                                                                     ADDRESS_TYPE                            2
                                                                     ADDRESS_SERIESNO                        3

APPLICANT                  APPLICANT_KEY1                 UNIQUE     APPLICANT_ID                            1
                                                                     APPLICANT_TERM                          2
                                                                     APPLICANT_SERIESNO                      3

                           APPLICANT_KEY2                 UNIQUE     APPLICANT_ID                            1
                                                                     APPLICANT_TERM                          2
                                                                     APPLICANT_LEVEL                         3
                                                                     APPLICANT_COLLEGE                       4

CDECISION                  CDECISION_KEY                  UNIQUE     CDECISION_CODE                          1

CINST                      CINST_KEY                      UNIQUE     CINST_CODE                              1

DECISION                   DECISION_KEY                   UNIQUE     DECISION_ID                             1
                                                                     DECISION_APPLICANT_TERM                 2
                                                                     DECISION_APPLICANT_SERIESNO             3
                                                                     DECISION_SERIESNO                       4

DOCUMENT                   DOCUMENT_KEY                   UNIQUE     DOCUMENT_ID                             1
                                                                     DOCUMENT_APPLICANT_TERM                 2
                                                                     DOCUMENT_APPLICANT_SERIESNO             3
                                                                     DOCUMENT_CODE                           4

MAIL                       MAIL_KEY                       NONUNIQUE  MAIL_ID                                 1
                                                                     MAIL_CODE                               2
                                                                     MAIL_DATE                               3

NAME                       NAME_KEY                       UNIQUE     NAME_ID                                 1
                                                                     NAME_SERIESNO                           2
```

Figure 5–4. Indexes for tables owned by KOMENDA.

```
Indexes on tables owned by: KOMENDA                                                        Page:    2
Date: 07-JAN-1995     Time: 06:51                                            Report name: indexes.lis
                                                                             SQL name:    indexes.sql

table                     index                         uniqueness column                         position
------------------------- ----------------------------- ---------- ------------------------------ ----------

NAME                      NAME_LAST                     NONUNIQUE  NAME_LAST                               1

PERSON                    PERSON_KEY                    UNIQUE     PERSON_ID                               1

PHONE                     PHONE_KEY                     UNIQUE     PHONE_ID                                1
                                                                   PHONE_TYPE                              2
                                                                   PHONE_SERIESNO                          3

RECRUIT                   RECRUIT_KEY                   UNIQUE     RECRUIT_ID                              1
                                                                   RECRUIT_TERM                            2
                                                                   RECRUIT_LEVEL                           3

SAVELIST                  SAVELIST_KEY                  UNIQUE     SAVELIST_ID                             1

TEST                      TEST_KEY                      UNIQUE     TEST_ID                                 1
                                                                   TEST_TYPE                               2
                                                                   TEST_DATE                               3

VISA                      VISA_KEY                      UNIQUE     VISA_ID                                 1
                                                                   VISA_SERIESNO                           2
```

Figure 5–4. Indexes for tables owned by KOMENDA .

approximately locates each row in a table. Many people may have the same last name; this is why the index is non-unique and why the location address is only approximate.

Knowing the primary key helps eliminate the problem of multiplying through a join discussed earlier. Consider the NAME table again. A single person (name_id) can have more than one row in the NAME table (more than one name_seriesno). But by writing the query so that only the latest name_seriesno row is retrieved for each name_id, we can ensure that each person only appears once in the report.

The SQL and SQL*PLUS script used to run the report in Figure 5–4 is provided in Appendix D. If you don't already have a program that produces a listing of indexes for the data tables you use, run the program in Appendix D.

Other Sources

If you've run the scripts in Appendix D against your own database, then at this point you've accumulated an impressive encyclopedia of information useful for writing ad hoc queries. You have reports on table owners, on table names and definitions, on column names and definitions, on indexes and primary keys, and a schematic showing table relationships. Keep this material in a large binder. It will serve as an ad hoc query reference book.

However useful, the query reference book will not provide sufficient documentation for some queries. This is particularly true when tables number in the hundreds or even thousands. There's some point when a database reaches a critical size and becomes almost a living entity, too large and too complex for any single person to understand. When this happens, you need to treat the database as a neuroscientist treats the brain. You're up against something which you, in your lifetime, won't ever understand; something with interrelating parts waiting to be discovered. The reference encyclopedia helps by pointing you in the right direction. But beyond that it's a matter of discovery.

The ad hoc query writer as scientist is a useful analogy. When a scientist works at the fringes of her knowledge, she consults colleagues and their written work. This is precisely what the query writer should do. Find someone who knows something about the part of the database you're beginning to explore. That person might be a programmer, so ask to see relevant sections of existing programs. The person might be a departmental analyst, someone already writing queries against the tables you need to understand. Ask to see existing queries. The person might also be a data entry clerk.

Nobody understands the data protocols and procedures better than data entry staff. If they have a written procedures manual, get a copy. Otherwise, ask questions and document what you find out.

Another good source of information is the logic existing behind data entry and display-only screens. Take, for example, a data column called family income in a financial aid module. Operationally it's a commonly used piece of information. But in all likelihood, family income is actually a computation based upon the actual values existing in several other data columns. If you want to write queries that display family income, you'll need to discover the algorithm used for the computation. You can get the algorithm from the logic existing in the display screen. If SQL*FORMS, for example, was used to construct the screen containing family income, there will be a trigger or series of triggers controlling the screen operation that will also reveal the algorithm for computing family income. Ask to see the programming logic used to develop user screens.

The reference encyclopedia tells you a lot about how the database was designed. But you also need to understand how it's really being used. The two can be quite different and writing accurate queries depends on knowing its actual use, not its intended use. This is the information you gather from programmers, writers of queries, data entry staff, and the logic behind user display screens.

Chapter 6

An SQL*PLUS Primer

One other skill is necessary before we can actually build SQL objects. Both *shell* objects and *report* objects utilize SQL*PLUS commands. SQL*PLUS is Oracle's extension of SQL. Many SQL*PLUS commands make writing ad hoc queries and reports much easier than is possible with SQL alone. It's the SQL*PLUS commands that allow you to:

- Enter and exit the SQL environment.
- Edit, save, and run commands entered interactively at the SQL prompt.
- Retrieve and rerun stored command files.
- List and change many characteristics of the current SQL environment.
- Create titles to appear at the top or bottom of each report page.
- Define headings and formats for report columns.
- Direct report output to a printer or a file.
- Prompt the user for input and store that input in a user-defined variable.
- Compute summary values such as report totals or subtotals.
- Determine what actions occur when grouping data (e.g., skipping to a new page for each group).
- List the data columns that appear in a table.
- Reset previous commands to their default conditions.

Table 6–1 provides a brief overview of the most common SQL*PLUS commands used for ad hoc reporting. Table E–1 in Appendix E provides a complete list of SQL*PLUS commands. This chapter discusses each of the common reporting commands. It does so, however, in a somewhat unconventional manner. Rather than discussing each SQL*PLUS command in succession, the chapter relies upon the actual use of the commands in functional programs. The previous chapter introduced a number of useful reporting tools without showing the programs that produced those tools. This chapter examines the programs for two of the tools—the overviews of owners and tables—and uses these programs to discuss common SQL*PLUS commands. The chapter begins, however, with several general navigational SQL*PLUS commands.

Table 6–1. Common SQL*PLUS commands.

Command	General form	Effect
@	@filename	Runs the command file "filename"
/	/	Runs the SQL command currently in the buffer
ACCEPT	ACCEPT variable options	Stores input in a user-defined variable
APPEND	APPEND text	Adds "text" to end of current buffer line
BREAK	BREAK ON element actions	Determines report formatting when "element" changes
BTITLE	BTITLE print_specs options	Specifies title appearing at bottom of each report page
CHANGE	CHANGE /old/new	Changes "old" text to "new" text in current buffer line
CLEAR	CLEAR options	Resets current value for options (breaks, columns, etc.)
COLUMN	COLUMN name options	Specifies report column characteristics
COMPUTE	COMPUTE function OF element1 ON element2	Computes summary (e.g., average) of "element1" breaking on "element2"
DEFINE	DEFINE variable = text	Creates a user-defined variable with a CHAR value of "text"
DEL	DEL	Deletes current buffer line
DESCRIBE	DESCRIBE owner.name	Lists data columns in table or view called "name" and owned by "owner"
EDIT	EDIT filename	Calls default operating system editor and loads "filename"
EXIT	EXIT	Exits from SQL*PLUS environment
GET	GET filename	Loads a file called "filename" into the SQL buffer
INPUT	INPUT text	Adds one or more lines of "text" after the current buffer line
LIST	LIST [n m]	Lists buffer lines n to m. Lists all lines if n and m are omitted
PROMPT	PROMPT text	Sends "text" to user's screen
REMARK	REMARK text	Denotes a comment line in a command file
RUN	RUN	Executes the SQL command in the buffer

Table 6–1. Common SQL*PLUS commands.

Command	General form	Effect
SAVE	SAVE filename options	Saves SQL command in the buffer to a file called "filename"
SET	SET system_variable value	Changes SQL*PLUS environment characteristics
SHOW	SHOW option	Lists the setting of an SQL*PLUS environment variable
SPOOL	SPOOL filename options	Stores report output in a file called "filename"
SQLPLUS	SQLPLUS options	Starts SQL*PLUS from the operating system
START	START filename arguments	Executes a command file, passing data values to parameters in the file
TTITLE	TTITLE print_specs options	Specifies title appearing at top of each report page
UNDEFINE	UNDEFINE variable	Deletes a user-defined variable created with DEFINE

General SQL*PLUS Commands

Entering, exiting, and generally navigating in the SQL environment occur through several simple SQL*PLUS commands. You can:

- enter the SQL environment by issuing the ***sqlplus*** command at the host operating system prompt, and
- leave the SQL environment and return to the host operating system with the ***exit*** command.

While in the SQL environment you can enter SQL or SQL*PLUS commands at the SQL prompt. The latest SQL commands get stored in a buffer. You can:

- ***save*** the buffer as a command file for later reuse,
- ***run*** the command stored in the buffer, and
- ***get*** an existing file and store it in the buffer.

The contents of the buffer appear as numbered lines, with the current line indicated by an asterisk (*). You can move from the current buffer line to another line by typing in that buffer line number at the SQL prompt. To revise the contents of the buffer, you can:

- ***list*** the buffer contents,
- ***del*** (delete) the current buffer line,
- ***append*** text to the end of the current buffer line,

- *input* one or more new lines after the current buffer line, and
- *change* existing text in the current buffer line to new text.

Figure 6–1 shows a typical SQL session in which a simple ad hoc query is constructed and run. It demonstrates many of the SQL*PLUS editing and navigational commands. After logging into SQL, the query writer:

1. Entered an ad hoc query (i.e., ***select*** command) and ran this initial query.
2. Examined the query by listing it from the SQL buffer.
3. Moved to buffer line 1 containing the data column names and appended an additional data column.
4. Ran the query again, this time receiving an error message because the additional data column name was incorrect.
5. Changed the incorrect column name.
6. Moved to the last buffer line, input an additional query line, and ran the query again.
7. Saved this query in a file.
8. Reloaded the query into the SQL buffer by retrieving the file.
9. Inserted another new line between two existing buffer lines and ran the query again.
10. Saved the query using the replace option in the ***save*** command (see Table 6–2).
11. Started the query from the saved file.

Table 6–2. Options available in the ***save*** command.

General form: SAVE filename options

Option	Values	Effect
CREATE/REPLACE/APPEND	CREATE	Creates a file with buffer contents
	REPLACE	Replaces an existing file with buffer contents
	APPEND	Appends buffer contents to end of existing file

These actions are fairly typical of how a simple SQL ad hoc query gets constructed. Most complex queries, however, get completed another way. The sheer size of larger programs makes working in an editor easier than working in the buffer. Use the ***edit*** command to invoke the default editor. With the editor you can assemble SQL objects into complete programs. You

```
SQL> select name_id, name_last, name_first
  2  from name                                                   1
  3  where name_last = 'Atkinson';
ENTER to continue ...
   NAME_ID NAME_LAST                NAME_FIRST
--------- --------------------- --------------
      513 Atkinson                 Julie
     1465 Atkinson                 Angela
     1575 Atkinson                 Mathew
     4980 Atkinson                 Kristen
     7656 Atkinson                 Michelle
     7727 Atkinson                 Tina
     2771 Atkinson                 Adam
     3068 Atkinson                 Elizabeth
     3658 Atkinson                 Kevin

9 rows selected.

SQL> list
  1  select name_id, name_last, name_first                      2
  2  from name
  3* where name_last = 'Atkinson'
SQL> 1
  1* select name_id, name_last, name_first                      3
SQL> append, name_mi
  1* select name_id, name_last, name_first, name_mi
SQL> run
  1  select name_id, name_last, name_first, name_mi
  2  from name
  3* where name_last = 'Atkinson'
select name_id, name_last, name_first, name_mi
                                       *
ERROR at line 1:
ORA-00904: invalid column name                                   4

SQL> 1
  1* select name_id, name_last, name_first, name_mi
SQL> change/name_mi/name_middle                                  5
  1* select name_id, name_last, name_first, name_middle
SQL> run
  1* select name_id, name_last, name_first, name_middle
  2  from name
  3* where name_last = 'Atkinson'
```

```
ENTER to continue ...
   NAME_ID NAME_LAST                NAME_FIRST      NAME_MIDDLE
--------- --------------------- -------------- ----------
      513 Atkinson                 Julie           A.
     1465 Atkinson                 Angela
     1575 Atkinson                 Mathew
     4980 Atkinson                 Kristen
     7656 Atkinson                 Michelle
     7727 Atkinson                 Tina
     2771 Atkinson                 Adam            A.
     3068 Atkinson                 Elizabeth
     3658 Atkinson                 Kevin

9 rows selected.

SQL> list
  1  select name_id, name_last, name_first, name_middle
  2  from name
  3* where name_last = 'Atkinson'
SQL> input                                                       6
  4  order by name_first;
ENTER to continue ...
   NAME_ID NAME_LAST                NAME_FIRST      NAME_MIDDLE
--------- --------------------- -------------- ----------
     2771 Atkinson                 Adam            A.
     1465 Atkinson                 Angela
     3068 Atkinson                 Elizabeth
      513 Atkinson                 Julie           A.
     3658 Atkinson                 Kevin
     4980 Atkinson                 Kristen
     1575 Atkinson                 Mathew
     7656 Atkinson                 Michelle
     7727 Atkinson                 Tina

9 rows selected.

SQL> save fig6-2.sql                                             7
Created file fig6-2.sql
```

Figure 6–1. A typical SQL session for a simple ad hoc query.

(Continued)

8

```
SQL> get fig6-2
  1  select name_id, name_last, name_middle
  2  from name
  3  where name_last = 'Atkinson'
  4* order by name_first
SQL> 3
  3* where name_last = 'Atkinson'
```

9

```
SQL> input
  4i and name_first < 'M'
  5i
SQL> list
  1  select name_id, name_last, name_middle
  2  from name
  3  where name_last = 'Atkinson'
  4  and name_first < 'M'
  5  order by name_first
SQL> /
ENTER to continue ...
   NAME_ID NAME_LAST            NAME_FIRST   NAME_MIDDLE
---------- -------------------- ------------ -----------
      2771 Atkinson             Adam         A.
      1465 Atkinson             Angela
      3068 Atkinson             Elizabeth
       513 Atkinson             Julie        A.
      3658 Atkinson             Kevin
      4980 Atkinson             Kristen

6 rows selected
```

10

```
SQL> save figg6-2.sql replace
Wrote file fig6-2.sql
```

11

```
SQL> start fig6-2
SQL> select name_id, name_last, name_middle
  2  from name
  3  where name_last = 'Atkinson'
  4  and name_first < 'M'
  5  order by name_first
  6  /
ENTER to continue ...
   NAME_ID NAME_LAST            NAME_FIRST   NAME_MIDDLE
---------- -------------------- ------------ -----------
      2771 Atkinson             Adam         A.
      1465 Atkinson             Angela
      3068 Atkinson             Elizabeth
       513 Atkinson             Julie        A.
      3658 Atkinson             Kevin
      4980 Atkinson             Kristen

SQL>
```

Figure 6–1. A typical SQL session for a simple ad hoc query.

can also save and revise programs. After you've created a program in the editor, save it and exit to the SQL prompt. Then use the ***start*** or @ command to run the stored program.

Command Files Used for Owners Report

Figure 5–1 in Chapter 5 provided an overview of the simulated database by showing counts of tables by owners. Figure 6–2 on the following page shows the shell program that produced the report, and Figure 6–3 on page 91 shows the SQL sub-program started from the shell. Both these figures contain SQL*PLUS commands. Let's start with Figure 6–2 and peel it apart, layer by layer, to discover how the various parts function and interact.

On the surface the shell program in Figure 6–2 appears to use only four SQL*PLUS commands, shown highlighted in the figure. These are as follows:

- The ***set*** command controls characteristics of the SQL environment. In this case the command "set termout off" prevents the program and its output from scrolling to the screen. This is especially convenient for long reports that will be printed, where no purpose is served by endlessly watching a report scroll to the screen.
- The ***start*** command executes other SQL and SQL*PLUS programs. In Figure 6–2 the ***start*** command executes programs called clears.sql, hpprinter.sql, date.sql, time.sql, owncol.sql, escape.sql, xover.sql, reset.sql, and screen.sql. Later in this chapter we'll examine each of these programs to see what they do. The strange looking "&&object_dir" that appears in many of these ***start*** commands is actually a subdirectory name that physically locates the files. I'll demonstrate how this happens later in the chapter.
- The ***ttitle*** command places a title at the top of the report, including date and time stamps, page numbers, documentation, and a description of the report contents.
- The ***spool*** command directs output to a file or a printer. In this case the destination is a file called overview.lis.

```
/*
      sql:    overview.sql
      date:   22-mar-1994
      author: glewis
      purpose: database tables by owner
*/
set termout off

start &&object_dir.\clears
start &&object_dir.\hpprintr
start &&object_dir.\date
start &&object_dir.\time
start &&object_dir.\owncol
start &&object_dir.\escape

ttitle left xEscape skip 1-
      'Database tables and views by owner' -
      right 'Report name: overview.lis' skip 1 -
      left 'Date: ' xDate '      Time: ' xTime -
      right 'Page: ' format 999 sql.pno skip 2;

spool overview.lis
      start xover
      start &&object_dir.\reset
spool off

start &&object_dir.\clears
start &&object_dir.\screen
```

Prevents program from scrolling to terminal screen.

Each of these is a separate SQL*PLUS program that performs a specific setup function and is run with the SQL*PLUS ***start*** command. See text for details.

The SQL*PLUS ***ttitle*** command determines the title that appears at the top of each report page.

The SQL*PLUS ***spool*** command defines the report name as overview.lis. The SQL program xover.sql then retrieves the report information.

These two SQL*PLUS programs clean up after the report and reset the SQL environment.

Figure 6-2. Shell program for overview of table owners.

```
/*
        sql:     xover.sql
        date:    17-apr-1994
        author:  glewis
        purpose: SQL subprogram for overview.sql
*/
break on report
compute sum of count on report
select
        owner,
        count(*) "count"
from
        all_catalog
where
        table_type in ('TABLE','VIEW')
group by owner
order by 1
/
```

The SQL*PLUS ***break*** and ***compute*** commands coordinate to produce report totals, and the SQL *group by* clause works with the *count (*)* function to produce counts of tables and views by owner name.

Figure 6–3. SQL program xover.sql started from shell in Figure 6–2.

Set *and* Show *Command*

The *set* command is wonderful; it finds wide use when constructing *shell* objects. The general form for ***set*** is "***set*** system_variable value," where "system_variable" is a characteristic of the SQL environment and "value" is the setting specified. All system variables have default values that operate until the setting is changed.

Table 6–3 shows the most common system variables, their default values, and the optional values that may be set. For example, the *termout* variable defaults to "on"; output will ordinarily be displayed at the screen. To prevent the scrolling of lengthy reports, the *termout* variable can be set to "off" as occurred in the shell program shown in Figure 6–2.

Table 6–3. Common system variables used in the ***set*** command.

General form: SET system_variable value

System variable	Default	Optional values	Effect
CONCAT	on .	on/off, ./c	Defines end of substitution variable in a string (e.g., &y is substitution var in "&y.more")
DEFINE	on &	on/off, &/c	Character prefixing substitution variables
ECHO	off	on/off	Lists commands in ***start*** file as executed
EMBEDDED	off	on/off	"Off" forces each report to start on a new page
ESCAPE	off \	on/off, \ or c	Used in front of a substitution character if it validly appears as an ordinary character in a string

(Continued)

Table 6–3. Common system variables used in the ***set*** command.

General form: SET system_variable value

System variable	Default	Optional values	Effect
FEEDBACK	on	on/off	Displays number of rows returned in a query
HEADING	on	on/off	"On" prints column headings in a report
HEADSEP	on |	on/off, | or c	Divides column headings into two or more lines
LINESIZE	80	n	Maximum display characters on a line
NEWPAGE	1	n	Blank lines printed before top title on each page ("0" sends a formfeed between pages)
NULL	"" (blank)	text	Display when ***select*** returns null value
NUMFORMAT	""	format	Default format for displaying numbers
NUMWIDTH	10	n	Width for displaying numbers
PAGESIZE	14	n	Number of lines from top title to page bottom
PAUSE	off none	on/off, text/none	Controls scrolling of terminal
RECSEP	wrap	wrap/each/off	Displays a line of RECSEPCHAR ("wrap" displays only after wrapped lines)
RECSEPCHAR	' ' (space)	space/c	Character used with RECSEP
SHOWMODE	on	on/off	"Off" suppresses display of ***set*** changes
SPACE	1	n	Number of spaces between report columns
SQLCASE	mixed	mix/lower/upper	Converts case of commands before execution
SQLPROMPT	SQL>	text	SQL*PLUS command prompt
SQLTERMINATOR	on ;	on/off, ;/c	Character used to end and execute SQL
SUFFIX	sql	sql/text	Default file suffix
TAB		on/off	"On" uses the TAB character (default is system dependent)
TERMOUT	on	on/off	"Off" suppresses output display from ***start*** file
TIME	off	on/off	"On" displays current time at SQL prompt
TIMING	off	on/off	Controls display of timing statistics
TRIMOUT	on	on/off	"On" if trailing blanks allowed on display line
UNDERLINE	on -	on/off, -/c	Character used to underline column headings
VERIFY	on	on/off	"On" shows command with substitution variable replaced with a value
WRAP	on	on/off	"On" wraps data value to next line if too large for display column

Note:
"/" means "or" (e.g., "on/off" means "on or off"), "c" means a character, and "n" a number.

Here are some of the things that the *set* command controls:

- The dimensions of a report page
- Whether column headings appear in a report

- How many spaces occur between report columns
- What character is used to underline report columns
- Whether data values that are too long for a report column will wrap to the next line or be truncated
- If reports sent to the screen will pause or scroll continuously
- The default column width for displaying numbers in reports

We'll come back to the ***set*** command options shown in Table 6–3 as we peel back more layers of the program overview.sql.

The ***show*** command acts as companion to the ***set*** command. It lists the current system variable settings and a few other variables that are system maintained. The latter variables include the current page and line numbers, the current user name, and whether output is presently being spooled. Table 6–4 shows the options available with the ***show*** command. A simple "***show*** all" will list all settings presently in effect.

Table 6–4. Options available in the ***show*** command.

General form: SHOW options

Option	Values	Effect
Any combination of values	system_var	Current value of system variable set with ***set*** command
	ALL	Lists all settings
	BTITLE	Current ***btitle*** definition
	LNO	Current line number in display or spooled output
	PNO	Current page number
	RELEASE	Release number of ORACLE RDMS
	SPOOL	Shows if output is being spooled
	TTITLE	Current ***ttitle*** definition
	USER	Current username used to access SQL*PLUS

Start *Command*

The ***start*** command provides a convenient way to modularize programs. Each of the ***start*** commands shown in Figure 6–2 executes another SQL or SQL*PLUS command file. For example, the command "***start*** clears" executes a program called clears.sql that ensures any preexisting ***column, compute,*** and ***break*** definitions are cleared before beginning the new report. The program hpprintr.sql establishes characteristics for printed reports. The program date.sql captures today's date for use in report titles. And so on. Each of these programs serves a specific function. Each of them consists of several additional SQL*PLUS command statements.

It's perfectly acceptable to put all these command statements together in a single program. The program would function identically. The effect, however, is a program that's harder to understand and harder to debug. Don't do this; it's preferable to take advantage of the ***start*** command.

Ttitle *and* Btitle *Commands*

Placing titles on ad hoc reports should be mandatory; without them a report is meaningless to everyone but its creator. Even then, a report without titles is only useful at the time it's produced. Items that should appear in every report include:

- A description of the population upon which the report is based.
- The date and time the report was run.
- Documentation that identifies the name of the output file containing the report and/or the SQL program that produced the report.
- Page numbers if the report exceeds a single page.
- The name of the user who ran the report.

With the ***ttitle*** and ***btitle*** commands, top and bottom titles can be constructed that include all these features and more. Table 6–5 shows the general form for title commands and lists the various options available in the commands. The ***ttitle*** command shown in overview.sql (i.e., Figure 6–2) includes several of the options. Let's take that command apart to find out what it does.

Table 6–5. Options available with the ***btitle*** and ***ttitle*** command.

General form: TTITLE/BTITLE print_specs text/variable OFF/ON

Option	Values	Effect
print_specs (one or more)	COL n	Indents to print at position n
	SKIP n	Skips to the start of a new line n times
	TAB n	Skips forward or backward n spaces
	LEFT	Left align in current line of title
	CENTER	Center in current line of title
	RIGHT	Right align in current line of title

Table 6–5. Options available with the ***btitle*** and ***ttitle*** command.

General form: TTITLE/BTITLE print_specs text/variable OFF/ON

Option	Values	Effect
	BOLD	Bold print
	FORMAT format	Sets a format model for title elements (e.g., page numbers)
text	text	Text of title, in single quotes
variable	user	Displays user-defined variable in title
	SQL.LNO	Displays current line number
	SQL.PNO	Displays current page number
	SQL.USER	Displays current username
ON/OFF	ON	Turns on display of title (the default)
	OFF	Suppresses display of title

The *ttitle* command in Figure 6–2 is:

```
ttitle left xEscape skip 1 -
     'Database tables and views by owner' -
     right 'Report name: overview.lis' skip 1 -
     left 'Date: ' xDate ' Time: ' xTime -
     right 'Page: ' format 999 sql.pno skip 2;
```

Here's what's happening in this command:

- A user-defined variable called xEscape is left-justified in line 1 of the title. As you'll see shortly, xEscape is defined as the escape sequence that places a Hewlett-Packard LaserJet printer in landscape compressed mode. This escape sequence will appear in the output file, but won't appear on the actual printed report. The same technique can be used to control other characteristics of printers accepting escape sequences.
- The "-" at the end of line 1 is a continuation marker, indicating that the title definition continues on another line.
- The report description "Database tables and views by owner" will appear on line 2 of the title, placed there by the "skip 1" option which means "skip to the next line." By default the report description is left-justified. It could also have been centered or forced to start in a specific position. By default the report description appears as normal text, but it also could have been printed bold.
- The report name (overview.lis) is right-justified on line 2 of the title and serves as documentation for someone reading the report long after it was created. Including the user name and the SQL

program name also makes sense, although neither appears in this title.

- On line 3 of the title, a user-defined variable called xDate is left-justified and followed by another user-defined variable called xTime. These variables contain the date and time the report was run. Later sections describe how to capture a date and time so they can appear in the title.
- The page number from the system-maintained variable sql.pno is right-justified on line 3 of the title. It's given a format of 999.
- The "skip 2" at the end of the ***ttitle*** command causes one blank line to appear between the title and the body of the report.

Spool *Command*

The final command utilized in Figure 6–2 is ***spool.*** This command writes report output to a file with a user-specified name. Spooling is started with "***spool*** filename"; it is stopped with "***spool*** off" or "***spool*** out" (see Table 6–6). The out option stops spooling and prints the file at a default printer. Simple, but effective.

Table 6–6. Options available in the ***spool*** command.

General form: SPOOL filename options

Option	Values	Effect
OFF/OUT	OFF	Stops spooling
	OUT	Stops spooling and prints output at default printer

Column *Command*

At this point we've looked at the surface of overview.sql. Let's now go a layer deeper and examine some of the other command files executed from overview.sql. A good place to begin is the command file called owncol.sql shown in Figure 6–4. It's this command file that creates headers and formats for report columns.

For a column with character datatype, the width of its default report heading is the width defined in the database. For example, the data column containing gender in the simulated database appears in the PERSON table as person_gender. It's a CHAR datatype of length 1, meaning that the default width appearing in reports will be 1. The default report header

OWNCOL.SQL

```
/* ACADEMIC */
column academic_id heading 'id' format 99999
column academic_instcode heading 'inst|code'
column academic_degree heading 'degree'
column academic_degreedate heading 'degree|date'
column academic_sizeclass heading 'size|class' format 99999
column academic_rankclass heading 'rank|class' format 99999
column academic_gpa heading 'gpa'

/* ADDRESS */
column address_id heading 'id' format 99999
column address_type heading 'type' format a4
column address_begindate heading 'begin|date'
column address_enddate heading 'end|date'
column address_city heading 'city'
column address_state heading 'state' format a5
column address_zip heading 'zip'
column address_nation heading 'nation' format a6
column address_street1 heading 'street1'
column address_street2 heading 'street2'

/* APPLICANT */
column applicant_id heading 'id' format 99999
column applicant_term heading 'term'
column applicant_level heading 'level' format a5
column applicant_recruit_term heading 'recruit|term' format a7
column applicant_college heading coll format a4
column applicant_dorm_intent heading 'dorm|intent' format a6
column applicant_aid_intent heading 'aid|intent' format a6
column applicant_type heading 'appl|type' format a4
column applicant_student_type heading 'student|type' format a7
column applicant_degree heading 'appl|degree'
column applicant_major heading 'appl|major'
column applicant_appldate heading 'appl|date'
column applicant_housingdate heading 'housing|date'

.
.
.
```

OWNCOL.SQL specifies report column headings and formats for commonly used data columns.

The heading separator character '|' places a heading on two or more lines.

In the ADDRESS table address_state is CHAR(2), but the heading "state" is 5 characters long. Use a format of 'a5' to ensure that the entire heading appears above the report column.

Figure 6–4. Control of report column headings.

will be the first character in the data column name ('p'). In a report, a column of width 1 with a heading of 'p' won't be very meaningful except perhaps to the person who wrote the query.

With the ***column*** command you can define formats and headers for data columns that appear in a report. The general form for this command is "***column*** name options," where "name" specifies a database column name, an expression created from one or more data column names, or an alias given to a data column or expression. Optional settings create different effects. Table 6–7 shows the available options. Using these it is possible to:

- Specify column headings, spreading these over multiple lines if desired.
- Center, left-justify, or right-justify the column heading.
- Suppress the printing of a column.
- Determine if lengthy character strings will wrap to another report line, keeping words intact if desired.
- Set the report column width and format the data appearing in that column.
- Create report layouts that are not matrix (rows and columns) in format.
- Capture data values for use in report titles.

Table 6–7. Options available in the ***column*** command.

General form: COLUMN name options

Option	Values	Effect
name	column_name	Specifies the data column
	expression	Specifies the expression
	alias	Specifies an alias
Any combination of values	ALIAS alias	Assigns the column an alias named "alias"
	CLEAR	Resets column display attributes to the default values
	FOLD_AFTER n	Inserts a carriage return after each row in the column
	FOLD_BEFORE n	Inserts a carriage return before each row in the column
	FORMAT format	Determines the display format for the column
	HEADING text	Specifies the column heading. Enclose in single quotes
	NEWLINE	Identical to FOLD_BEFORE n

Table 6–7. Options available in the ***column*** command.

General form: COLUMN name options

Option	Values	Effect
	NEW_VALUE var	Specifies a variable containing the data column value. Useful for displaying column values in top title
	NULL char	Specifies text to print when null values occur
	OLD_VALUE var	Specifies a variable containing the data column value. Useful for displaying column values in bottom title
JUSTIFY L/C/R	LEFT	Left align column heading
	CENTER	Center column heading
	RIGHT	Right align column heading
PRINT/NOPRINT	PRINT	Print the column. This is the default
	NOPRINT	Suppresses printing the column
ON/OFF	ON	Sets column display attributes on. This is the default
	OFF	Turns off the column display attributes without resetting
WRAP/WORD/TRUN	WRAPPED	Wraps CHAR string to next line if longer than column width
	WORD	Wraps CHAR string at word breaks
	TRUNCATED	Truncates a CHAR string at end of the column width

NOTES:

1. Format specifications for number datatypes are shown in Table 4–5. Numbers are right-justified and never truncated. Formats for character datatypes use the form An, where n specifies the column width. Character data is left-justified by default. Dates can be formatted by using the *to_char* function and a ***column*** format of An.
2. Column display attributes remain in effect for an entire SQL*PLUS session unless they are changed, thus controling column attributes for any reports run during that session.
3. Variables specified in the NEW_VALUE or OLD_VALUE must also occur in the ***break*** command using the SKIP PAGE option if they are to appear in top or bottom titles.

Examine owncol.sql in Figure 6–4 again. What's happening in this command file? Each user typically works with just a portion of a large complex database. They repeatedly use certain data columns in a subset of database tables; they also seldom or never use other data columns or other tables. The command file owncol.sql recognizes that a user typically works with a well-defined set of data columns. Each of these data columns appears in owncol.sql in a ***column*** command that sets a header and format for that column. This command file can be built over a period of time. Whenever a user writes an ad hoc query containing a new table or a new data column, then she adds the appropriate ***column*** commands to owncol.sql. The next time her query accesses one of these new data columns, it will already be formatted and appear in the report with an appropriate heading.

Using a command file like owncol.sql eliminates the need to repeatedly specify report column characteristics for the same data columns. It saves considerable time; it also improves the consistency of reports since you don't use two different column headers to identify the same data column.

There are a few items that are worth extra attention:

- In Figure 6–4 the column academic_degreedate is given a heading called "degree|date." The character "|" is a heading separator. Its effect is to break the heading into two (or more) lines. In this case, "degree" will appear on line 1 of the header and "date" will appear on line 2. It's possible to get quite creative with this feature. For example, a report might contain many data columns. Fitting the columns across the report page then becomes an issue. Suppose that person_gender was one of the report columns. Rather than make the heading "gender," which takes up 6 positions, you could make the header "s|e|x" which only takes up 1 position. The character used for the heading separator can be changed from the default value of "|" to another value using the ***set*** headsep command.
- Character formats appear in the general form "A#" or "a#," where "#" is the desired column width. Specifying report column width becomes especially important when the heading you specify is longer than the database column width. Consider person_gender again. In the database, this column has the datatype CHAR with width 1. To label the report column "sex," use the command "column person_gender heading 'sex' format a3." Otherwise the heading "sex" will be truncated to 1 position and appear as "s."
- Column headings and formats remain in effect until explicitly changed or until you exit the SQL environment. This can be convenient when running several reports in a single session, each of which uses the same column formats and headings. But sometimes it can be a nuisance. Suppose you normally define person_gender to have the heading "sex" and this gets set in owncol.sql. If you override that heading by choosing "s|e|x", the new heading remains in effect for all subsequent reports during the current SQL session unless you change it. To achieve consistency in appearance from report to report, I prefer to clear column settings before (and after) each report and then use owncol.sql to reset them to my default settings.

Define *Command and Substitution Variables*

Whenever you enter thc SQL environment, a special file called login.sql gets run if it exists. This happens automatically, so login.sql is a convenient site for those commands that customize the SQL environment to your way of working. Figure 6–5 shows one variation of a login.sql command file.

Pay particular attention in Figure 6–5 to the two ***define*** commands. ***Define*** creates a user-defined variable; its general form is "***define*** variable_name = text." Note that one user variable called object_dir is defined as "c:\oracle6\metasql\objects." This is the name of the DOS subdirectory on my computer that contains the SQL objects created in this book. The same technique could be used to specify an object location in any operating system. For example, suppose that users on a DEC VAX share a central repository of objects in a directory called users:[shared.objects]. You could define object_dir as users:[shared.objects] and then use the variable object_dir to refer to this physical location.

The second ***define*** in Figure 6–5 uses a special user-defined variable called _editor (or _EDITOR). As mentioned previously, SQL command files can be created and revised with an editor. Unless _editor is specified, the host operating system's default editor gets used. If you prefer to use another editor, then place a ***define*** in login.sql so that your own choice of editors will be available each time you enter the SQL environment. Note in Figure 6–5 that the specified editor is one called me.exe (I use the editor Multi-Edit from American Cybernetics). Use whatever editor you feel most comfortable with.

Also note in Figure 6–5 the use of the command "***start*** &&object_dir.\ screen." The strange looking double ampersands (&&)

LOGIN.SQL

```
set termout off
define object_dir = c:\oracle6\metasql\objects
define _editor = me
start &&object_dir\screen
set termout on
```

The program login.sql runs each time you enter the SQL environment. It's a convenient place to customize SQL for your own work requirements. In this case a default editor is specified and an object subdirectory identified.

Figure 6–5. Login program for customizing the SQL environment.

also appeared in Figure 6–2 in other ***start*** commands. Whenever double ampersands appear in SQL or SQL*PLUS, it's a signal that what follows is a *substitution* variable. Substitution variables get replaced at runtime. If the variable is currently defined, that definition replaces the substitution variable. If the variable is currently undefined, then the user is prompted for a replacement value. The period (.) in "***start*** &&object_dir.\screen" identifies where in the string the substitution variable ends. In this case the substitution variable is &&object_dir and not &&object_dir\screen. Since object_dir was previously defined as c:\oracle6\metasql\objects, the command that actually gets executed is "***start*** c:\oracle6\metasql\objects\screen.sql."

Defining the subdirectory location of objects and referring to this location with a substitution variable serves two purposes. First, it's easier to maintain the programs. If the physical location of the objects changes, you need only make that change in the login.sql program rather than in each individual SQL query. Second, it ensures that only the latest version of an object will be used. For example, if you execute the command "***start*** screen.sql," the command file screen.sql gets run from the local subdirectory. This may or may not be the most recent version of the program. By placing all current versions of objects in a central repository and then accessing them via defined substitution variables, you'll always use the most recent objects.

User-defined variables can be listed by issuing a ***define*** command. They can be undefined by using the ***undefine*** variable_name command.

Break *and* Compute *Commands*

Probably more confusion surrounds the ***break*** and ***compute*** commands than any other SQL*PLUS commands. The confusion stems from the need to coordinate ***break*** and ***compute*** with each other and with the *select* and *order by* clauses of the SQL ***select*** command. These two commands, however, prove extremely useful. This section demonstrates how to use the commands to achieve certain effects and then describes a set of rules for their general use.

Double-Spacing

Users who expect to use a lengthy or complicated roster over a considerable time often request that the report rows be double- or triple-spaced. Use the ***break*** command to skip 1 or more lines between rows, as shown in Figure 6–6. The command "***break*** on row skip 1" double-spaces the report;

REPORT

```
Applicants for admission to arts and sciences college: Fall 1995

id sort_name
------ -------------------------
  2574 Abraham, Alicia

  3163 Adams, Amy

  2687 Adams, Samuel

  8584 Adams, Thomas P.

  1897 Affsa, Rita A.

  6287 Agnew, Angela

  6260 Allen, Adam
         .
         .
701 rows selected.
```

SQL

```
break on row skip 1
select
       name_id,
       name1.name_last||', '||name1.name_first||' '||name1.name_middle "sort_name"
from
       name name1,
       applicant
where
       applicant_term = '199509'
                and applicant_college = 'AS'
       and name1.name_id = applicant_id
                and name1.name_seriesno =
                (select max(name2.name_seriesno)
                from name name2
                where name2.name_id = name1.name_id)
order by 2
/
```

This ***break*** command skips 1 line between each row of the report. You can triple-space a report with skip 2.

Figure 6–6. Double-spacing a report with the ***break*** command.

Note that I.D. and name are repeated for each row of decisions. The command "break on id on sort_name" suppresses the printing of this duplicate information.

REPORT 1

```
Decisions of applicants for admission to arts and sciences college: Fall 1995
    id sort_name                          code  decision                          date
------ ---------------------------------- ----- --------------------------------- ---------
  2574 Abraham, Alicia                    AC    Accept regular                    07-JAN-95
  2574 Abraham, Alicia                    PD    Paid enrollment deposit           15-JUN-95
  2574 Abraham, Alicia                    CP    Canceled after paid               22-JUN-95

  3163 Adams, Amy
  3163 Adams, Amy

  2687 Adams, Samuel

  8584 Adams, Thomas P.
  8584 Adams, Thomas P.
  8584 Adams, Thomas P.

  1897 Affsa, Rita A.
  1897 Affsa, Rita A.

  6287 Agnew, Angela

  6260 Allen, Adam
  6260 Allen, Adam
     .
     .
     .
29 rows selected.
```

REPORT 2

```
Decisions of applicants for admission to arts and sciences college: Fall 1995
    id sort_name                          code  decision                          date
------ ---------------------------------- ----- --------------------------------- ---------
  2574 Abraham, Alicia                    AC    Accept regular                    07-JAN-95
                                          PD    Paid enrollment deposit           15-JUN-95
                                          CP    Canceled after paid               22-JUN-95

  3163 Adams, Amy

  2687 Adams, Samuel

  8584 Adams, Thomas


  1897 Affsa, Rita A.


  6287 Agnew, Angela

  6260 Allen, Adam
     .
     .
     .
29 rows selected.
```

SQL for REPORT 2

```
break on id on sort_name skip 1
column id format 99999
select
     name_id "id",
     name1.name_last||', '||name1.name_first||' '||name1.name_middle "sort_name",
     decision_code,
     cdecision_translation,
     decision_date
from
     cdecision, decision, name name1, applicant
where
     applicant_term = '199509'
           and applicant_college = 'AS'
     and name1.name_id = applicant_id
           and name1.name_last <= 'Allen'
           and name1.name_seriesno =
           (select max(name2.name_seriesno)
           from name name2
           where name2.name_id = name1.name_id)
     and decision_id = applicant_id
           and decision_applicant_term = applicant_term
           and decision_applicant_seriesno = applicant_seriesno
     and cdecision_code = decision_code
order by 1, 2, 5/
```

The *order by* clause must coordinate with the ***break*** command as it does here.

Figure 6–7. Suppressing duplicate data with the ***break*** command.

PACKING SLIP

1 4 3 0 5 1 5

Via

Ship To

ABE TP Orders
0000000000
help@textbookrush.com
800 AVONDALE AVE
COLUMBUS, OH 43212, US

Market ID: 738041333
Order ID: 1430515
Order Date: 09/10/2026
Shipping Method:

SKU	QTY	TITLE	TOTAL
BSM.1CFLZ	1	Oracle Reporting: Queries With SQL Objects	0.00

Order Total: $50.17

Your order has been packaged and created with great care. Enjoy! Bay State Books

#1430515

"***break*** on row skip 2" triple-spaces; and so on. Used in this fashion, the ***break*** command needs no coordination with the ***select*** command.

Suppressing Duplicate Information

Figure 6–7 shows a roster of admissions applicants and the decisions made by Komenda College about their application. Note that many applicants have multiple decisions. Each decision appears in a new report row, but the identification number and name get repeated on each row. Use the ***break*** command to suppress the printing of duplicate information.

To suppress duplicate information, the ***break*** command and *order by* clause must work together; in fact, the *order by* must mirror the break. For example, if the ***break*** command is "***break*** on x on y on z," then the *order by* must be "*order by* x, y, z." Think about the command "***break*** on name_id." It works by checking a name_id against the previous name_id. If they are the same, nothing happens. If the two values of name_id differ, then a break occurs and an action is triggered. For breaks to be meaningful, the rows must first be sorted by the break data column. That's why the ***break*** and *order by* must be coordinated.

Whenever a break occurs, several actions are possible—including "skip" used to double-space. But the default action suppresses duplicate information. You don't need to include any special keywords to achieve this effect; "***break*** on name_id" will automatically suppress duplicate name_id information.

Report Totals

With quantitative data, it's often important to provide an overall summary at the end of the report. For example, financial reports often include the sum or average of monetary data columns. With the SQL*PLUS ***compute*** command, you can calculate averages, maximums, minimums, sums, counts, and statistical measures for variance and standard deviation.

But to work properly, you must coordinate the ***compute*** with the ***break*** command and the *select* clause. Figure 6–8 on the following page shows how to do this. There are two requirements. First, the data columns being summarized in the ***compute*** must appear in the *select.* Second, the "on report" option must appear in both the ***compute*** and ***break*** commands. When you think about it, both these requirements make sense. You shouldn't be allowed to summarize a data column that doesn't appear in the report. And the break action occurring at the end of the report triggers the computation and display of the summary value.

REPORT

```
Expected majors of applicants for admission to arts and sciences college: Fall 1995

appl
major major                               count
----- ------------------------------ ----------
ART   Art                                    15
BIOL  Biology                                65
CHEM  Chemistry                              31
ECON  Economics                              56
ENGL  English                                30
GOV   Government                             40
HIST  History                                36
LANG  Modern Languages                       31
MATH  Mathematics                            18
MUSC  Music                                  26
PEDC  Physical Education                     17
PHIL  Philosophy                              4
PHYS  Physics                                12
PSYC  Psychology                             34
RELG  Religion                                5
SOC   Sociology                              31
UN    Unknown                               211
                                             39
                                     ----------
sum                                         701

18 rows selected.
```

Note that the ***break*** and ***compute*** commands both contain "on report." The ***compute*** and *select* clause are similarly coordinated; any data column, expression, or alias referenced in a ***compute*** must also appear in the *select* clause.

SQL

```
break on report
compute sum of count on report
select
      applicant_major,
      cmajor_translation,
      count(*) "count"
from
      cmajor,
      applicant
where
      applicant_term = '199509'
              and applicant_college = 'AS'
      and cmajor_code(+) = nvl(applicant_major, ' ')
group by
      applicant_major,
      cmajor_translation
/
```

Figure 6–8. Using ***break*** and ***compute*** to display grand totals.

Report Subtotals

It's a seemingly small jump from report totals to subtotals, but producing subtotals requires another level of command coordination. Figure 6–9 on page 109 shows the SQL used to generate a report containing subtotals. In addition to the coordination required to produce totals, Figure 6–9 shows that the ***break*** command and *order by* clause are also coordinated. This happens because the break producing subtotals occurs on a data column, and for this break to be meaningful the data must first be ordered by that column. Also note that any data columns appearing in the ***compute*** must also appear in the *select* clause.

General Rules

Table 6–8 shows the options available with the ***break*** command; Table 6–9 on the following page shows options for ***compute.*** Note that breaks and computes may occur on expressions and aliases as well as data columns, rows, or the end of report. Also note that a break action can produce a formfeed in a printed report. This is convenient if the report consists of subreports, each of which should start on a new page.

Finally, note that the syntax of the "on" clause differs between ***break*** and ***compute.*** For example, suppose you wanted a report showing a grand total of employee salaries as well as subtotals for each different department. The ***break*** command would read: "***break*** on report on department." The corresponding compute statement is "***compute*** sum of salary on report department." You only use one "on" in the ***compute;*** "on report department" in ***compute*** equates with "on report on department" in ***break.***

Table 6–8. Options available with the ***break*** command

General form: BREAK ON element actions

Option	Values	Effect
element	column_name	Performs action whenever value of the data column changes
	expression	Performs action whenever the value of a user-defined *select* expression changes. Most conveniently used by giving the expression an alias in the *select* clause
	ROW	Performs an action after each report row; "break on row skip 1" double-spaces a report
	REPORT	Used with the ***compute*** command to print summaries at the end of a report

(Continued)

Table 6–8. Options available with the ***break*** command

General form: BREAK ON element actions

Option	Values	Effect
SKIP n/PAGE	n	Skip n lines before printing
	PAGE	Skip to a new page before printing
NODUP/DUP	NODUP	Does not print break column value if it is identical to the value in the preceeding row. This is the default
	DUP	Prints the break column value for each report row

Table 6–9. Options available with the ***compute*** command.

General form: COMPUTE function OF element1 ON element2

Option	Values	Effect
One or more function	AVG	Average of non-null NUMBER values
	COUNT	Counts non-null values of all datatypes
	MAXIMUM	Maximum of non-null NUMBER or CHAR values
	MINIMUM	Minimum of non-null NUMBER or CHAR values
	NUMBER	Count of rows, including null values, for all datatypes
	STD	Standard deviation of non-null NUMBER values
	SUM	Sum of non-null NUMBER values
	VARIANCE	Variance of non-null NUMBER values
OF elements	column_name	Specifies the data column to use in the computation. The data column must appear in the *select* clause
	expression	Specifies an expression to use in the computation. Most conveniently referenced with an alias given to the expression in the *select* clause
ON elements	column_name	The computation is printed whenever the value of the specified data column changes
	expression	Prints the computation whenever the expression breaks
	alias	Prints the computation whenever an alias breaks
	ROW	Prints the computation for each row
	REPORT	Prints the computation at the end of the report

NOTES:

1. A data column, expression, or alias referenced in the OF clause must appear in the ***select*** command.
2. If more than one function is selected, they must be separated with a space.
3. If more than one element in the OF or ON clause is selected, they must be separated with a space.
4. The elements referenced in the ON clause must appear in a ***break*** command.

REPORT

```
Student type of applicants for admission to arts and sciences college, by gender: Fall 1995

      student
sex   type     student_type                          count
----- -------  ------------------------------  ----------
F     F        New Freshman                           273
      T        New Transfer                            43
*****                                          ----------
sum                                                   316

M     F        New Freshman                           224
      T        New Transfer                            36
*****                                          ----------
sum                                                   260

na    F        New Freshman                           111
      T        New Transfer                            14
*****                                          ----------
sum                                                   125

                                               ----------
sum                                                   701

6 rows selected.
```

SQL

```
break on report on sex skip 1
compute sum of count on report sex
column sex format a5
set null 'na'
select
       person_gender "sex",
       applicant_student_type,
       cstype_translation,
       count(*) "count"
from
       person,
       cstype,
       applicant
where
       applicant_term = '199509'
               and applicant_college = 'AS'
       and cstype_code(+) = nvl(applicant_student_type, ' ')
       and person_id = applicant_id
group by
       person_gender,
       applicant_student_type,
       cstype_translation
order by 1
/
```

Note how the ***break*** and ***compute*** commands are coordinated. The two columns appearing in ***compute*** must also appear in the *select* clause.

Any column referenced in the ***break*** command must appear in the *order by* clause.

Figure 6–9. Using ***break*** and ***compute*** to display totals and subtotals.

The permutations possible with ***break*** and ***compute*** often create confusion with users. Table 6–10 tries to cut through that confusion by summarizing some general rules for creating certain effects in a report. You can see the nice progression from simple to the more complex in the figure; double-spacing requires only one command while totals and subtotals require the coordination of several. Keep in mind that:

- A ***compute*** may never be used independently of a ***break,*** but the reverse is not true.
- Each data column appearing in the "on" clause of the ***compute*** command must also appear in the ***break*** command.
- Any data columns or expressions in the ***break*** must appear in the *order by* clause.
- The data columns in the "on" and "of" clauses of ***compute*** must appear in the *select* clause.
- Never use a comma in a ***break*** or a ***compute.***
- An alias name for a data column or expression may be used in either a ***break*** or a ***compute.***
- If the data columns in the ***break*** command are logically related, they must be entered from largest to smallest to give meaningful results (e.g., "break on state on county on city").
- Only one ***break*** command may be in effect; issuing another ***break*** overrides the previous one.
- Multiple ***compute*** commands may be in effect simultaneously, but if more than one ***compute*** references the same data column in the "on" clause, only the latest of these commands actually works.
- A ***break*** or ***compute*** issued at the SQL prompt without any qualifying options will list the current settings.

These rules are logical, but complicated. Unless I use something repeatedly, I'm likely to forget something that's complicated no matter how logical it may be. Consequently I prefer to capture the effects of ***break*** and ***compute*** commands in objects. For example, when I want a report showing totals and subtotals, I just pick out an appropriate *report* object. The object already contains the proper syntax for ***break*** and ***compute***; it frees me to think about the content of the report rather than worrying about how to coordinate SQL*PLUS commands. When building *report* objects in Chapter 10, you'll use ***break*** and ***compute*** several times and gain more experience with them.

Table 6–10. Summary of ***break*** and ***compute*** syntax needed in common report situations.

Command or clause	Double-space	Suppress duplicates	Totals	Totals and subtotals
break	break on row skip 1	break on col1 on col2 on ...	break on report	break on report on colx on coly ...
compute			compute fn of col1 col2 ... on report	compute fn of col1 col2 ... on report colx coly...
select			select col1, col2 ...	select col1, col2, ... colx, coly, ...
order by		order by col1, col2, ...		order by colx, coly, ...

Clear *Command*

Any option set with the ***column***, ***compute***, or ***break*** commands can be reset with the ***clear*** command. This feature makes ***clear*** useful in shell programs. You can use it to create a tabula rasa before running the query and then use it again at the end to exit cleanly without retaining any breaks, computes, or column settings.

The general form of the ***clear*** command is "***clear*** option," where "option" can take any combination of values shown in Table 6–11. Note that you can also clear the monitor or the SQL buffer with this command.

Table 6–11. Options available with the ***clear*** command.

General form: CLEAR option

Option	Values	Effect
Any combination of values	BREAKS	Clears breaks set with the ***break*** command
	BUFFER	Clears the SQL buffer
	COLUMNS	Resets column display characteristics set with ***column***
	COMPUTES	Clears all computes set with the ***compute*** command
	SCREEN	Clears the monitor screen
	SQL	Clears the SQL buffer
	TIMING	Deletes timing areas set with the ***timing*** command

Actions of Other Command Files

Let's return again to overview.sql in Figure 6–2 and peel back another layer of SQL*PLUS by examining the remaining command files executed with ***start***. Figure 6–10 shows the contents of these command files. Let's go over what each command file accomplishes.

Screen Preferences

The screen is your home base in SQL. From it you'll enter the editor and write queries, debug these stored queries, and run simple queries created on-the-fly. You'll only configure the SQL environment for a printed report when you've fully tested and debugged your query and are ready to run it a final time.

The command file screen.sql sets several SQL system variables appropriate for working from the screen. It turns on the pause option so reports sent to the screen don't scroll continuously. Instead, a page at a time appears on the screen with an "ENTER to continue ..." message. Pressing the ENTER key brings up the next page. The page is set at 80 characters wide by 24 lines high. Reports wider than 80 characters wrap to the next line. Top titles are turned off, commands in stored files get echoed to the screen as they execute, and termout is set to "on" to ensure that the query results appear on the screen.

Any or all of these options may be changed. Much of it is personal preference. It's not the contents of screen.sql that's important; it's the existence of a command file that explicitly sets screen characteristics. Note where screen.sql gets used. It's executed from login.sql (see Figure 6–5) whenever you log into SQL. It's also executed at the conclusion of each shell program. In both cases, screen.sql ensures that when you enter or reenter your home base—the screen—it will have a consistent look and feel to it.

Housekeeping

The command file clears.sql serves a housekeeping function. It's executed early in shell programs to clear out any breaks, computes, or columns that may have been set from the screen while creating or testing a query. Then it's executed again at the end of the shell program to clear out any breaks, computes, or columns set while running your query. You clean house before starting the query and then you tidy up afterwards.

SCREEN.SQL

```
set pause "ENTER to continue ..."
set pause on
set linesize 80
set pagesize 24
set newpage 1
ttitle off
set escape off
set termout on
set echo on
```

SCREEN.SQL sets a user's screen preferences.

CLEARS.SQL

```
clear breaks
clear computes
clear columns
```

CLEARS.SQL clears any previously set ***column*** definitions, ***compute*** statements, or ***break*** statements.

HPPRINTR.SQL

```
set pause off
set pagesize 45
set linesize 160
set echo off
set timing off
set escape #
set feedback on
```

HPPRINTER.SQL sets a user's printer preferences.

DATE.SQL

```
break on today
column today new_value xDate
select to_char(sysdate, 'dd-MON-yyyy') today from dual;
clear breaks
```

DATE.SQL captures today's date for use in the report title.

TIME.SQL

```
break on now
column now new_value xTime
select to_char(sysdate, 'hh24:mi') now from dual;
clear breaks
```

TIME.SQL captures the present time for use in the report title

ESCAPE.SQL

```
define xEscape = EcEEc#&110Ec(s16.66HEc#&a101176M
define xReset =  EcE
```

ESCAPE.SQL creates two user-defined variables, xEscape and xReset, both consisting of escape sequences that control a Hewlett-Packard LaserJet printer.

RESET.SQL

```
ttitle left xReset;
column xCol noprint
set feedback off
select 'x' "xCol" from dual;
```

RESET.SQL starts a nonprinting ***select*** whose purpose is to activate the ***ttitle*** command that sends the xReset escape sequence to the printer.

Figure 6–10. SQL*PLUS utility programs started from overview.sql (Figure 6–2).

Printer Preferences

While the screen is your home base, the product you share with other people is the printed report. After you've written and tested a query, the SQL environment must be reconfigured to produce a printed report. This occurs in the command file hpprintr.sql.

Note in Figure 6–10 that pausing is turned off; you want the report to run from start to finish rather than pause at each page. I also prefer not to overwhelm the person requesting the report by including the SQL and SQL*PLUS commands used to produce the report, so I turn off echoing of commands. You might choose otherwise to provide the user with more complete documentation. The version of hpprintr.sql shown in Figure 6–10 sets the pagesize as 45 lines by 160 characters. These settings are appropriate for a laser printer in landscape compressed mode. If you're printing to a line printer the dimensions would be different (e.g., pagesize 60 and linesize 132). If you're printing on continuous feed paper, you'll also want to include the command "set newpage 0" which will send a formfeed between pages and ensure that the report starts at the top of each page.

There are two commands in hpprintr.sql which may not be obvious. The first, "set feedback on," will print the number of rows returned by the query. This is useful for rosters and listings because it provides a convenient count of the items in the report. With feedback set on, for example, a name and address roster might say "167 rows selected."

The second command that's not obvious is the escape setting "set escape #." This command is necessary because the printer I use for reports is a Hewlett-Packard LaserJet. The escape sequence to put the printer in landscape compressed mode includes some ampersands (&). But recall from an earlier section that the ampersand identifies a substitution variable. The ampersands in the LaserJet escape sequence would get read as substitution variables. To prevent this you must precede the ampersand with an escape character; in this case the escape character is set as #. So & or && starts a substitution variable; but #& means & and does not start a substitution variable.

Again, the content of hpprintr.sql is not the important feature; rather, it's the existence of a single command file that customizes the printer environment for your own work. Modify hpprintr.sql to suit yourself.

Date Stamp and Time Stamp

Both date.sql and time.sql function identically. One captures the present time into a variable called xTime; the other captures the present date into a variable called xDate. These user-defined variables can then be used in report titles to conveniently datestamp and timestamp a report. Let's take a look at how they work.

Consider date.sql. The ***select*** command formats sysdate using the *to_char* function and gives this expression the alias "today." The ***column*** and ***break*** commands work together to define the variable xDate as the value in "today." This seems convoluted, but it works. If you execute a ***define*** command at the SQL prompt, you'll see that xDate is defined as today's date.

Printer Communications

In Figure 6–2 the top title included a user-defined variable called xEscape. The command file escape.sql defines this variable and another one called xReset. Both contain escape sequences recognized by Hewlett-Packard laser printers. The first, xEscape, sends the sequence to place the printer in landscape compressed mode and use a right margin of 176. The second, xReset, sends the sequence that restores the default printer settings.

Note that xReset gets used in the command file called reset.sql. This program sets up a dummy query that never gets printed. The sole purpose of the query, in fact, is to use xReset in the top title of this unprinted report so that the reset escape sequence gets embedded in the output file and read by the printer when the output file is printed.

This method of changing printer settings is a hybrid of sorts, using the *ttitle* command to send the escape sequence at the top of each page and then using a second (dummy) report to send a single reset. I've experimented with two alternatives. Each contains more internal symmetry than the hybrid approach, and in that sense they're more aesthetically pleasing, but neither is as effective as the hybrid.

One alternative creates a dummy query that sends the escape sequence settings just once. The structure here would be (1) dummy query to send the escape sequence, (2) main query, and (3) dummy query to send the reset. The second alternative doesn't use dummy queries at all, but rather puts the xReset variable in a btitle command for the main query. The effect is to set and reset the printer on each printed page. Both alternatives create problems, either with the placement of titles or the effect on the feedback line at the end of a report. The hybrid approach solves both these problems.

Command Files Used for Tables Report

The second tool discussed in Chapter 5 was a report of tables for a single owner. Figures 6–11 and 6–12 show the shell and subprograms used to construct the tables report. Much of it already looks familiar. The command files clears.sql, hpprintr.sql, date.sql, time.sql, owncol.sql, escape.sql, and screen.sql that appear in tables.sql (Figure 6–11) are identical to those in Figure 6–2.

However, tables.sql contains two new command files: getowner.sql and definvar.sql. Let's take a closer look at each of these command files. One introduces a useful new SQL command; the other demonstrates the powerful technique of building SQL or SQL*PLUS programs at runtime.

TABLES.SQL

```
set termout off
start &&object_dir.\clears
start &&object_dir.\hpprintr
start &&object_dir.\date
start &&object_dir.\time
start &&object_dir.\owncol
start &&object_dir.\escape

start getowner
start definvar

ttitle left xEscape skip 1 -
      'Tables for owner: ' xOwner -
      right 'Page: ' format 999 sql.pno skip 1 -
      left 'Date: ' xDate '     Time: ' xTime -
      right 'Report name: ' xReport skip 1 -
      right 'SQL name:     tables.sql' skip 2;

spool &&xReport
      start xtables
      start &&object_dir.\reset
spool off

start &&object_dir.\clears
start &&object_dir.\screen
```

The two command files started here prompt the user for a table owner and then use the response to define variables that appear in the ***ttitle*** and ***spool*** commands.

Figure 6–11. Shell program for report showing tables for a specific owner.

The ***accept*** command requests a table owner from the user.

GETOWNER.SQL

```
set verify off
set termout on
accept Owner prompt 'Enter owner of tables (eg, KOMENDA): '
set termout off
```

Note the use of SQL to create another SQL program at runtime. The program created, called defines.sql, actually defines xOwner and xReport.

DEFINVAR.SQL

```
set feedback off
set heading off
column NextLine newline
ttitle off
set linesize 300
spool defines.sql
       select 'define xOwner =', upper('&&Owner'),
               'define xReport =' NextLine, '&&Owner'||'.lis'
       from dual;
spool off
start defines
set linesize 160
ttitle on
set heading on
set feedback on
```

The user-defined variable xOwner gets used in the SQL program that retrieves the data for the report.

XTABLES.SQL

```
column comments format a85 word_wrap
select
       t.table_name "name",
       t.table_type "type",
       t.owner "owner",
       c.comments "comments"
from
       all_tab_comments c,
       all_catalog t
where
       t.owner = '&&xOwner'
       and c.owner = t.owner
               and c.table_name = t.table_name
               and c.table_type = t.table_type
order by 1
/
```

Figure 6–12. Programs started from the tables.sql shell in Figure 6–11.

Accept *Command*

Many queries require interaction with the user before they can be run. This is particularly true of reports that get run multiple times. For example, a financial report may contain information on the current fiscal year. The year can be hard-coded into the SQL, but then when a new fiscal year begins or the user wants to run the report against a previous fiscal year, the SQL must be changed. It would be cleaner if the user could be prompted for the fiscal year at the time the query gets executed.

This capability becomes even more important if there are several runtime parameters the user would like to control and each has several values. The user might want to specify the fiscal year, a quarter or month in the year, and only a few income categories. The more permutations possible, the greater the need for input from the user at runtime.

The SQL ***accept*** command provides this function. With this command you can prompt a user for information and then store the user's response in a variable that can appear in an SQL program (see Table 6–12 for options available in ***accept***). Note in Figures 6–11 and 6–12 that when you run tables.sql, you'll be asked to identify the table owner. The response to this prompt gets stored in the variable called Owner.

Table 6–12. Options available in the ***accept*** command

General form: ACCEPT variable options

Option	Values	Effect
NUMBER/CHAR	NUMBER	Variable must be a number
	CHAR	Variable must be a character datatype
PROMPT text/NOPROMPT	PROMPT text	Displays text before accepting user input for variable
	NOPROMPT	No prompting message displayed (the default)
HIDE	HIDE	User input for variable not displayed on screen

The ***accept*** command allows you to build an SQL query with considerable generality. Don't hard-code parameters into the SQL unless you know the report will only be run once or unless the parameters will never change from query to query. Use ***accept*** instead.

Runtime SQL

Accepting runtime parameters from the user generalizes ad hoc queries, but it's possible to further improve the ease with which users can run tables.sql. It's a small improvement but it nicely demonstrates a procedure in which a SQL subprogram gets built at runtime and then is executed as part of the main program.

ORACLE owner names are all uppercase. This means that when users supply an owner's name in tables.sql it is case sensitive. Entering the name in lowercase or initial capitals will return no rows. Transforming the user's response to an uppercase owner name eliminates a source of potential error. That's one purpose of the subprogram called definvar.sql shown in Figure 6–11 and Figure 6–12.

The most important elements of definvar.sql appear in the ***spool*** and ***start*** commands (see Figure 6–12). The ***spool*** command creates an output file called defines.sql that contains two SQL*PLUS ***define*** commands. This is a command file being built at runtime. The ***start*** command then executes this new command file. The two variables created, xOwner and xReport, are then available for use as substitution variables or in report titles.

The important point is that an SQL *select* (from the utility table DUAL) actually built another SQL command file. This command file, defines.sql, could not have been executed prior to runtime because it required user input to define the table owner. In this case the runtime generation of SQL performed two relatively minor functions, but it's a general technique that can be used in a variety of situations.

With this as background, we can begin building and using SQL objects for reporting.

Part II
Building SQL Objects

Chapter 7

Building *Population* Objects

Three steps occur as an ad hoc query gets built. First and most importantly, you identify in words the population on which the report will be based. Second, you identify in words what pieces of information you want to see about that population and how the information should appear. And third, you translate each of these descriptions into SQL and SQL*PLUS. This chapter concentrates on identifying report populations and translating the population definitions into SQL. In the process we'll construct several *population* objects based on the simulated admissions and recruiting database for Komenda College.

Every ad hoc query includes a population. It may be a population of people or automobiles or inventory items or purchase orders, but there's always some population. Populations provide the starting point for queries. If you don't specify the population clearly or don't accurately translate the specification into SQL, then the report will be worthless or misleading.

The number of possible populations used in an organization might seem infinite. But, surprisingly, populations occur in hierarchies based on frequency of use. And at the most fundamental level, the number of populations in a specific unit within even large organizations is usually quite small. Consider Komenda College's database of admissions and recruiting. Recruits and applicants are the two primary populations; all other populations are merely variations of these two.

Let's start with these populations—recruits and applicants—and build objects for each. Put on your hard hat; this is a construction site. We'll be working on the foundation for several chapters. You won't see the finished product until Chapter 13.

Populations from a Single Table

Suppose you are asked the question "How many undergraduate recruits are there for the Fall 1995 term?" Start by specifying the population in words. If you can't identify the population for a query, you need to ask more questions to find out what the person making the request actually meant. In this case the population is "undergraduate recruits for Fall 1995." How should we translate these words into SQL? It's not exactly clear. So let's start with our database tools–the database schematic, data dictionaries, and indexes provided in Appendix A.

Recruits are found in the RECRUIT table. By examining the RECRUIT data dictionary, you can see that the adjective "undergraduate" can be specified with recruit_level, while the Fall term can be specified with recruit_term. At this point a pseudo-SQL translation looks like "select ... from recruit where recruit_term = <code for Fall 1995> and recruit_level = <code for undergraduate>."

Let's fill in the SQL ***select*** by identifying the appropriate codes to use for Fall 1995 and undergraduate. You get this information from code tables. Appendix A shows the appropriate code tables are CLEVEL and CTERM. Figure 7–1 shows the actual codes available in these tables. Fall 1995 translates to "199509" and undergraduate translates to "UG." The ***select*** now reads "select ... from recruit where recruit_term = '199509' and recruit_level = 'UG'." We've successfully translated an English definition of the report population into its SQL equivalent. Pretty simple so far.

Figure 7–2 shows the completed SQL query and the report results. Note that the two counts included in the query are identical. I'll discuss the importance of these counts shortly.

Recruit Population *Object*

Admissions and recruiting staff will request many reports on various populations of recruits. "What's the gender breakdown of our recruits for the fall?" "Can you get me a listing of fall recruits from the Buffalo area?" "How many recruits in my geographical area of responsibility actually applied for admission?" All these requests and many more start from the population we just translated to SQL.

Populations that get used repeatedly in queries are good candidates for conversion into *population* objects. Making the conversion requires two considerations. First, the objects should be generalized as much as possible. Second, documentation should be created for each object. Let's build an object for the population of recruits.

TERM REPORT

```
SQL> select * from cterm order by 1;
ENTER to continue ...
term
code   term                               datestamp
------ ---------------------------------- ---------
198909 Fall 1989                          11-MAR-94
199001 Spring 1990                        11-MAR-94
199009 Fall 1990                          11-MAR-94
199101 Spring 1991                        11-MAR-94
199109 Fall 1991                          11-MAR-94
199201 Spring 1992                        11-MAR-94
199209 Fall 1992                          11-MAR-94
199301 Spring 1993                        11-MAR-94
199309 Fall 1993                          11-MAR-94
199401 Spring 1994                        11-MAR-94
199409 Fall 1994                          11-MAR-94
199501 Spring 1995                        11-MAR-94
199509 Fall 1995                          11-MAR-94
199601 Spring 1996                        11-MAR-94
199609 Fall 1996                          11-MAR-94
199701 Spring 1997                        11-MAR-94
199709 Fall 1997                          11-MAR-94
199801 Spring 1998                        11-MAR-94
199809 Fall 1998                          11-MAR-94
199901 Spring 1999                        11-MAR-94

20 rows selected.
```

LEVEL REPORT

```
SQL> select * from clevel order by 1;
ENTER to continue ...
level
code   level                              datestamp
------ ---------------------------------- ---------
GR     Graduate                           11-MAR-94
UG     Undergraduate                      11-MAR-94
```

Figure 7–1. Codes for term and level.

REPORT

```
SQL> select count(*), count(distinct recruit_id)
     from
          recruit
     where
          recruit_term = '199509'
                 and recruit_level = 'UG'
     /
ENTER to continue ...
  COUNT(*) COUNT(DISTINCTRECRUIT_ID)
---------- -------------------------
      8587                      8587
```

Figure 7–2. Report of undergraduate recruits for Fall 1995.

Our SQL population is "... from recruit where recruit_term = '199509' and recruit_level = 'UG'." This chunk of SQL could be a *population* object; it will work fine for many queries. But what happens if you want a report of graduate level recruits or recruits for Spring 1996? You could create other objects to cover these permutations. But doing this just proliferates objects, all of which differ only slightly from each other. It's far better to build a single object that generalizes the term and level.

Figure 7–3 shows one way to do this. Note that the object itself does not include a term or level. Rather it contains placeholders for term and level that can be edited whenever the object gets used. Alternatively, you could create a generalized object that required the user to enter the level and term at runtime. Figure 7–4 shows such an object. For myself I generally use the objects that require explicit editing, just so I'm forced to look at the SQL again. Sometimes I'll find something that needs revision this way. But prompting users is particularly effective when objects get automated. Chapter 14 discusses this more fully.

Note the help file in Figure 7–3 that accompanies the object. Each object that you create should have a corresponding help file. The more frequently you use an object, the less important help files become. But for objects that are used infrequently, having help available is reassuring. And help is absolutely essential when objects get shared among many users.

HELP

```
object:        poprecr.obj
date created:  13-oct-1994
author:        glewis
revisions:

Purpose:       Defines the population of recruits
               for a specified term and level

Usage:         <term>: replace with term (eg, 199509 for Fall 1995)
               <level>: replace with level (eg, UG for Undergrad)

Hints:         none
```

OBJECT

```
from
      recruit
where
      recruit_term = '<term>'
            and recruit_level = '<level>'
```

The object can be used by specifying term and level.

Figure 7–3. Recruit *population* object and help file.

```
REPORT

SQL> select count(*), count(distinct recruit_id)
  2  from
  3        recruit
  4  where
  5        recruit_term = '&term'
  6                and recruit_level = '&level'
  7  /

Enter value for term: 199509
Enter value for level: UG

ENTER to continue ...
  COUNT(*) COUNT(DISTINCTRECRUIT_ID)
---------- -------------------------
      8587                      8587
```

Using a single "&" in a substitution variable results in a prompt whenever the variable is encountered in an SQL query. This provides a convenient way to generalize objects so the user supplies the necessary values at runtime.

Figure 7–4. Recruit population with embedded prompts.

Applicant Population *Objects*

Without going through quite the detail of the previous example, let's build another object that depends only on a single table. Suppose you're asked "How many undergraduate Arts & Sciences applicants do we have for Fall 1995?" The population here is "Fall 1995 undergraduate Arts & Sciences applicants"; the information requested is a count.

Applicants appear in the APPLICANT table. Use the APPLICANT data dictionary in Appendix A to find that:

- applicant_term specifies the term,
- applicant_level specifies the level as undergraduate or graduate,
- applicant_college specifies the college as Business or Arts & Sciences.

The code table CCOLLEGE contains codes for the two colleges at Komenda; BU means Business and AS means Arts & Sciences (not shown).

Translating the population into SQL is easy; it's just "... from applicant where applicant_term = '199509' and applicant_level = 'UG' and applicant_college = 'AS'." Figure 7–5 on the following page shows the completed query and the report. Note that again the two counts in the report are identical (at 700). Figure 7–6 on the following page shows the generalization into a *population* object and its associated help file.

```
REPORT

SQL> select count(*), count(distinct applicant_id)
  2  from
  3        applicant
  4  where
  5        applicant_term = '199509'
  6                 and applicant_level = 'UG'
  7                 and applicant_college = 'AS'
  8  /

ENTER to continue ...
  COUNT(*) COUNT(DISTINCTAPPLICANT_ID)
---------- ---------------------------
       700                         700
```

Figure 7–5. Report of undergraduate Arts & Sciences applicants for Fall 1995.

```
HELP

object:        popapp.obj
date created:  13-oct-1994
author:        glewis
revisions:


Purpose:       Defines the population of applicants for a specified
               term, level, and college (Arts & Sciences, Business)

Usage:         <term>: replace with term (eg, 199509 for Fall 1995)
               <level>: replace with level (eg, UG for Undergrad)
               <College>: replace with college (eg, AS or BU)

Hints:         none
```

```
OBJECT

from
     applicant
where
     applicant_term = '<term>'
          and applicant_level = '<level>'
          and applicant_college = '<college>'
```

The object can be used by specifying the term, level, and college.

Figure 7–6. Applicant *population* object and help file.

The Nature of Populations

Constructing the applicant *population* object was nearly identical to the recruit object. In that respect it wasn't very interesting. But suppose the ad hoc query was just slightly different: "How many undergraduate applicants do we have for Fall 1995?" Note that no college is specified in this query.

The SQL population here is "... from applicant where applicant_term = '199509' and applicant_level = 'UG'." Figure 7–7 shows the query and report results.

Note that now the two counts in the report differ. The report returns 928 rows for 859 distinct people. There are apparently some students who applied to both the Business and the Arts & Sciences colleges in the same term. They may be uncertain about their intended majors or they may simply want to maximize their chances of being accepted for admission.

Whatever the reason for multiple applications, their existence raises an important question about populations. What exactly is a population? How do you recognize a population? In Figure 7–5, where a term, level, and college were specified, the answer seems clear. The population consists of distinct people who applied. But in Figure 7–7, where only a term and level get specified, the answer is less clear. The query was asked as if the population consisted of people (i.e., "how many undergraduate applicants ..."). But the differing counts in Figure 7–7 indicate the population actually consists of distinct applications and not distinct people.

This is fine; applications make a perfectly acceptable population. But you, as the query writer, must make the distinction between applications and people. In fact, whenever a population count(*) differs from a count(distinct ...) it's best to pause a moment and consider what really constitutes the report population. The answer is important. Consider the simple situation of two applicants, one residing in Massachusetts and the other in New York. If the person from New York submits two applications and the person from Massachusetts submits only one, then 67% of the applications

REPORT

```
SQL> select count(*), count(distinct applicant_id)
  2  from
  3         applicant
  4  where
  5         applicant_term = '199509'
  6                and applicant_level = 'UG'
  7  /
ENTER to continue ...
  COUNT(*) COUNT(DISTINCTAPPLICANT_ID)
---------- ---------------------------
       928                         859
```

Apparently some applicants apply for admission to both the undergraduate college of Business and the college of Arts & Sciences.

Figure 7–7. Report of applicants for Fall 1995 at all Komenda undergraduate colleges.

come from New York even though only 50% of the applicants reside in that state. Sometimes you'll want to report the 67% and other times the 50%. Knowing the difference keeps you out of trouble.

Populations from Multiple Tables

Populations from single tables won't take you very far. Even the most innocuous sounding ad hoc queries often involve multiple tables requiring table joins and more complex SQL. This complexity presents a hurdle that prevents SQL from being an end-user tool. But if the SQL is already embedded in objects, end users can simply manipulate the objects and need not worry about joins and complicated SQL.

Recruits Without Applications

Suppose the director of admissions approaches you and says "I'd like to mail applications to all undergraduate recruits for Fall 1995 who haven't already applied. Can you tell me how many there are?" That sounds like a fair question. You've got part of the population already built. The object poprecr.obj built in the previous section (see Figure 7–3) covers the "undergraduate recruits for Fall 1995." Now we just need to attach some SQL that translates to "who haven't already applied."

Let's work on this last phrase. Sometimes recasting the language suggests the SQL. How would you know if a recruit hadn't already applied? If you had a single recruit record, you'd go to the APPLICANT table and see if he or she had an undergraduate applicant record for Fall 1995. If an applicant record did not exist, then the recruit is part of the population. This suggests that we use the SQL comparison operator *not exists* (see Table C-1 in Appendix C). We can then define the report population in pseudo-SQL as "recruits (poprecr.obj) where not exists (an applicant record)." Figure 7–8 shows the final step into SQL.

The structure shown in Figure 7–8 uses a main query (poprecr.obj) and a *subquery* that checks the APPLICANT table. The subquery works because it's hooked to the main query through the line in Figure 7–8 that reads "where applicant_id = recruit_id." The RECRUIT table does not appear in the subquery, so when recruit_id is mentioned in the subquery it's the recruit_id from the main query that's inferred. Here's how to think about what's happening. The main query takes a recruit that meets our undergraduate Fall 1995 criteria, and then uses that recruit_id to search the APPLICANT table trying to locate a record. If a record does not exist,

REPORT

```
SQL> column distinct heading 'distinct|count'
SQL> select
          count(*),
          count(distinct recruit_id) "distinct"
     from
          recruit
     where
          recruit_term = '199509'
               and recruit_level = 'UG'
          and not exists
          (select 'x'
          from applicant
          where applicant_id = recruit_id
          and applicant_term = recruit_term
          and applicant_level = recruit_level)
     /

ENTER to continue ...
             distinct
  COUNT(*)      count
---------- ----------
      7762       7762
```

An example of a correlated subquery, used to exclude from the report population anyone who applied for admission. Correlated subqueries prove very useful in ad hoc reporting. See text for details of their operation.

Figure 7–8. Report of undergraduate recruits for Fall 1995 who did not apply for admission.

the recruit appears in the population and the next recruit_id in the main query is processed. The subquery is checked again and the record retained or discarded based on whether an APPLICANT record exists. This process gets repeated for each recruit record in the main query.

When a table in a subquery is joined to a table from the main query through common data columns, the subquery is called a *correlated subquery*. This just means that the subquery is executed for each row in the main query. We'll use correlated subqueries often; they are extremely useful.

Note how the SQL and the English population definition match item for item. Examine the SQL in Figure 7–8 and read it in English. The SQL population is "recruits for the undergraduate level and the Fall 1995 term where an applicant record does not exist for that term and level." In other words, it's a population of recruits who haven't applied. Figure 7–9 on the following page shows a *population* object and help file for this population.

Accepted Applicants

Using the *exists* comparison operator and correlated subqueries is so important in ad hoc queries it warrants repetition with another example. Suppose the director of admissions asks "Can you give me a count of the undergraduate Arts & Sciences applicants accepted for admission in Fall 1995?"

HELP

```
object:         poprecwo.obj
date created:   13-oct-1994
author:         glewis
revisions:

Purpose:        Defines the population of recruits for a specified
                term and level who have not submitted applications for
                that term and level

Usage:          <term>: replace with term (eg, 199509 for Fall 1995)
                <level>: replace with level (eg, UG for Undergrad)

Hints:          Exclude anyone who submitted an application to either
                college (AS or BU) for the specified term and level.
```

OBJECT

```
from
    recruit
where
    recruit_term = '<term>'
         and recruit_level = '<level>'
    and not exists
    (select 'x'
    from applicant
    where applicant_id = recruit_id
         and applicant_term = recruit_term
         and applicant_level = recruit_level)
```

The object can be used by specifying the term and level.

Figure 7–9 *Population* object and help file for recruits who did not apply for admission.

Again, we have much of this request already covered by an existing object. The object popapp.obj takes care of "undergraduate Arts & Sciences applicants in Fall 1995." All that remains is to translate the word "accepted" into SQL.

Code Tables and Robust Objects

An applicant is accepted during the admissions decision process. The DECISION table stores these decisions. You could determine if an applicant was accepted by examining the DECISION table to see if an accept decision existed. Figure 7–10 shows the admissions decision codes used by Komenda College. Note there are four codes (AC, AD, AE, and WA) for different kinds of accept decisions.

At this point you can write a pseudo-SQL for "accepted" as: "where exists a row in the DECISION table with decision_code in ('AC', 'AD', 'AE', 'WA')." In other words, we would construct a correlated subquery linking the APPLICANT table in the main query to the DECISION table in the subquery. Before doing this, however, let's linger on the issue of codes.

```
REPORT

SQL> select * from cdecision order by 1;
ENTER to continue ...
decision                                accept  cancel enrl
code     decision                       ind     ind    ind    datestamp
-------- ------------------------------ ------- ------ ------ ---------
AC       Accept regular                 Y                     20-MAR-94
AD       Accept deferred                Y       Y             20-MAR-94
AE       Accept early                   Y                     20-MAR-94
CI       Cancel, incomplete                     Y             20-MAR-94
CO       Cancel by office                       Y             20-MAR-94
CP       Canceled after paid                    Y             20-MAR-94
CS       Canceled before decision               Y             20-MAR-94
CZ       Canceled after accept                  Y             20-MAR-94
DR       Deferred to regular                                  20-MAR-94
HL       Decision pending                                     20-MAR-94
PD       Paid enrollment deposit                       Y      20-MAR-94
RJ       Rejected                               Y             20-MAR-94
SR       Second reading                                       20-MAR-94
WA       Wait-list accept               Y                     20-MAR-94
WC       Wait-list cancel by appl               Y             20-MAR-94
WL       Wait-listed                                          20-MAR-94
WR       Rejected from wait-list                Y             20-MAR-94

17 rows selected.
```

Decision codes that indicate an applicant was accepted for admission all have a "Y" in this column.

Figure 7–10. Admission decision codes.

When you convert chunks of queries into objects, there's no way to tell when the object will be used. What if the admissions office adds a fifth accept code? Unless this change gets reflected in the object, any queries using the object will return incorrect results. Explicitly entering codes into objects should be avoided whenever possible.

There are two options available. You could create an object in which you deliberately left the accept decision codes blank, forcing the user to enter them each time the object was used. In some cases, this might be the only option. But note in Figure 7–10 that the CDECISION table contains several data columns that identify the type of decision. If cdecision_accept_ind = 'Y' then the decision code is one of the accepted codes. This makes it possible to build a more robust object using the pseudo-SQL: "where exists a row in the DECISION table where the decision_code has a cdecision_accept_ind = 'Y'." Now the admissions office can add as many new accept decisions as they wish and the object will never be obsolete (assuming, of course, that the person who sets up the new codes in CDECISION remembers to enter a 'Y' in cdecision_accept_ind).

Now, let's continue building the population of accepted applicants.

Table Joins

At this point we've got two portions of the SQL for our population. One is the main query represented by the population of applicants (popapp.obj). The second is a pseudo-SQL defining "accepted" and suggesting a correlated subquery structure. How should we hook the DECISION table in the subquery to the APPLICANT table in the main query? More generally, how should two tables be joined? Once again, let's turn to the reporting tools developed in Chapter 5—the database schematic, data dictionaries, and table of indexes assembled in Appendix A.

As previously mentioned, joins occur through data columns that appear in both tables. But which ones? The database schematic (Figure A–1 in Appendix A) shows the APPLICANT and DECISION tables directly related through I.D. number and term. Examining the data dictionaries for both tables supports this link. The database schematic also shows the two tables related through a column called decision_applicant_seriesno. The DECISION data dictionary for this column says it's a "sequential number of application in APPLICANT table for a given term." The corresponding data column in the APPLICANT table is called applicant_seriesno.

The database schematic implies that specifying an applicant_id, applicant_term, and applicant_seriesno uniquely identifies a row in the APPLICANT table. Examining the indexes for the APPLICANT table shows two unique indexes exist. One consists of applicant_id, applicant_term, applicant_level, and applicant_college. The second consists of applicant_id, applicant_term, and applicant_seriesno (see Table A–2 in Appendix A). Consider the implications of this. Specifying a level and college for a given I.D. and term uniquely identifies an applicant; merely specifying the applicant_seriesno for a given I.D. and term does the same job. Apparently applicant_seriesno is equivalent to the combination of applicant_level and applicant_college. What we have here is a database design issue. From a user's perspective, specifying the term, level, and college makes sense. But the forms used to input applicant information apparently contain a sequential counter (i.e., applicant_seriesno) for a given I.D. and term.

Figure 7–11 shows an object for accepted applicants. Note the correlated subquery defining "accepted." The DECISION table in the subquery is

```
OBJECT

from
      applicant
where
      applicant_term = '<term>'
               and applicant_level = '<level>'
               and applicant_college = "<college>'
      and exists
      (select 'x'
      from
               cdecision,
               decision
      where
               decision_id = applicant_id
                         and decision_applicant_term =
                                    applicant_term
                         and decision_applicant_seriesno =
                                    applicant_seriesno
               and cdecision_code = decision_code
                         and cdecision_accept_ind = 'Y')
```

This correlated subquery checks to see if an applicant has an "accept" decision code.

```
HELP

object:        popacapp.obj
date created:09-may-1994
author:        glewis
revisions:

Purpose:       Defines the population of applicants accepted for
               admissions for a specified term, level, and college

Usage:         <term>: replace with term (eg, 199509 for Fall 1995)
               <level>: replace with level (eg, UG for Undergrad)
               <college>: replace with (eg, BU for Business)

Hints:         none
```

Figure 7–11. *Population* object and help file of applicants accepted for admission.

linked to the APPLICANT table in the main query through the three data columns for I.D., term, and application seriesno. Figure 7–12 on the following page uses this object in a report.

It may not be obvious but the object of accepted applicants in Figure 7–11 makes some assumptions about business operations at Komenda. The subquery assumes, for example, that the presence of ANY accept decision code means an applicant has been accepted for admission. But recall that Komenda College has a two-step review process; an application is first considered by a committee of faculty and admissions staff and then their recommendation is considered by the director of admissions. If accept decision

```
REPORT

SQL> select
        count(*), count(distinct applicant_id)
  from
        applicant
  where
        applicant_term = '199509'
                and applicant_level = 'UG'
                and applicant_college = 'AS'
        and exists
        (select 'x'
        from
                cdecision,
                decision
        where
                decision_id = applicant_id
                        and decision_applicant_term =
applicant_term
                        and decision_applicant_seriesno =
applicant_seriesno
                and cdecision_code = decision_code
                        and cdecision_accept_ind = 'Y'
        /
ENTER to continue ...
   COUNT(*) COUNT(DISTINCTAPPLICANT_ID)
----------- ---------------------------
        450                         450
```

Figure 7–12. Report of undergraduate Arts & Sciences applicants accepted for admission in Fall 1995.

codes were required at each step, the object in Figure 7–11 is incorrect. We'd need to look for two accept codes for an applicant. Apparently that is not the case at Komenda.

This point is important. Writing accurate *population* objects certainly depends upon technical issues like joins, but it also depends on the business context. You can't write objects in a vacuum. This is what makes it difficult to write objects that can be shared across similar institutions (e.g., colleges) using the identical database software application.

Alternative SQL Structures

SQL often provides several ways to accomplish the same task. The SQL object for accepted applicants in Figure 7–11 used a correlated subquery and the *exists* comparison operator. Figure 7–13 shows an alternative that uses no subquery. Instead, the joins to DECISION and CDECISION occur in the main query. Both queries return the same result. Which one is better?

REPORT

```
SQL> column distinct heading 'distinct|count'
SQL> select
         count(*),
         count(distinct applicant_id) "distinct"
  from
         cdecision,
         decision,
         applicant
  where
         applicant_term = '199509'
                and applicant_level = 'UG'
                and applicant_college = 'AS'
         and decision_id = applicant_id
                and decision_applicant_term =
                    applicant_term
                and decision_applicant_seriesno =
                    applicant_seriesno
         and cdecision_code = decision_code
                and cdecision_accept_ind = 'Y'
  /
ENTER to continue ...
             distinct
   COUNT(*)     count
----------- ---------
        450       450
```

Both the DECISION and CDECISION tables appear in the main query. In Figure 7–12 they appear in the correlated subquery. Both queries return identical results.

Figure 7–13. Alternative SQL structure for population of accepted applicants shown in Figure 7–12.

You can use several criteria to help decide between alternative structures that define the same population. These are as follows:

- Performance: how fast do the queries run?
- Robustness: how resistant are the queries to data errors?
- Intent: what data columns appear in the report?

Any one of these three criteria may be the determining factor when choosing between alternative SQL structures. Let's discuss each briefly and then return to the topic again in Chapter 12 when testing and tuning queries.

Performance

All other things being equal, a faster query is preferable to a slower one. Fewer system resources get used, and less time is spent waiting for a report. Everybody seems to gain. When the query gets run against an enormous database or when the query is particularly complex, time spent on performance issues brings real benefits. The drawback can occur if performance issues are taken too seriously, when query writers try to wring every last second of CPU time from their queries. This increases developing, testing, and debugging time considerably. Optimizing queries just for the sake of optimizing them can actually result in more system resource use, not less. And it makes the end user wait longer for the report.

I prefer a satisficing strategy with performance. If a query is a resource hog, fix it. Otherwise just apply the general performance guidelines discussed in Chapter 12 and decide between alternative population structures based on robustness or the intent of the query.

Robustness

All other things being equal, a query less resistant to data problems is preferable to one that relies on data being clean. Consider the alternative SQL definitions of accepted applicants shown in Figures 7–12 and 7–13. The structure in Figure 7–13, in which the DECISION join occurs in the main query, assumes that each accepted applicant has only one accept decision. If not, then this structure returns as many rows for a single applicant as he or she has accept decisions. An applicant with two accept decisions gets double-counted, triple-counted with three, and so on. If your report should count people, the numbers will be inaccurate. Data errors translate into report errors using the structure in Figure 7–13.

In my experience the subquery structure generally provides greater defense against data errors. In Figure 7–12, the DECISION table gets searched for each applicant. If that applicant has one, two, or ten accept decisions it doesn't matter. The subquery merely looks to see if such a decision exists; the number of such decisions is irrelevant.

I tend to use *exists* (or *not exists*) subquery structures frequently when writing SQL objects. It's particularly useful when checking for the presence or absence of an adjective (e.g., "accepted") and when the value of that adjective (e.g., "AC" or "AW") does not need to appear in the report.

Intent

All other things being equal, a query that provides easier access to the requested data columns is preferable to one taking a more convoluted route to those columns. Again, consider the alternative definitions of accepted applicants. A report can only display data columns from tables that appear in the main query. The subquery structure of Figure 7–12 precludes displaying the admissions decision in the report because the DECISION table does not appear in the main query. So if the person requesting a report of accepted applicants wished to include the accept decision, the structure in Figure 7–13 is preferable. This, of course, means sacrificing some robustness for more direct column access.

Balancing Decision Factors

Very seldom are all other things equal. Obviously you'd prefer one population structure that was simultaneously the most direct, the most robust, and the fastest. But sometimes there are trade-offs to be made and often the choice of a population structure depends on juggling the relative importance placed on performance, robustness, and query intent. The weights to apply to each factor can vary from query to query. Chapter 12, on testing and tuning queries, discusses these issues in more detail.

Practice Building *Population* Objects

Let's pull all this together by building another *population* object. Suppose the director of admissions requests a count of the number of accepted freshman applicants for Fall 1995 who expect to enroll in the undergraduate college of Arts & Sciences.

You've already got an object that serves as a building block for this report population. The object popacapp.obj defines "accepted applicants for a specified term, level, and college." This leaves only the adjective "freshman" and the clause "who expect to enroll." Freshman or transfer status is an attribute of applicants, so you'd look in the logical place and consult the APPLICANT data dictionary. Sure enough the data column called applicant_student_type captures the freshman or transfer distinction. Specifying the applicant as a freshman then becomes a one-line addition to our accepted applicant object.

But what about the clause "who expect to enroll?" This one's tougher. If you were a new analyst in the admissions office, you'd ask the director of admissions how she defined "applicants who expect to enroll." She'd reply "oh, that's someone we accepted for admission who paid an enrollment deposit and who hasn't canceled that deposit." This is a business definition; it's the type of definition discussed as business rules in Chapter 3. You must know these rules and definitions to write accurate SQL.

Keep asking questions until you have the definition cast into data columns. How do you know if someone's paid an enrollment deposit? "Well, that information gets entered as an admissions decision, because it's the student deciding about us." And how about cancellation of a deposit? "Again, that's an admissions decision made by the applicant." Now you've got enough to work with; you know the tables and columns that you'll need to translate the clause "who expect to enroll."

How then should we translate the verbal population definition into SQL? You may have noticed in Figure 7–10 that the CDECISION table includes two data columns that prove useful in the present query. One is cdecision_cancel_ind, which flags those decision codes when the application is canceled. The second data column is cdecision_enrl_ind, which flags those decisions when an accepted applicant pays an enrollment deposit. In an entirely analogous manner to the previous example of accepted applicants, correlated subqueries can be used to define the phrase "who expect to enroll." It's just that this time two subqueries are necessary, one to see if an applicant has paid an enrollment deposit and a second to see if the applicant has made any cancellation decisions.

The pseudo-SQL translation bridging English words and true SQL looks like this: "select ... from (popacapp.obj) where applicant_student_type = 'F' and exists (a row in DECISION where the decision code has a cdecision_enrol_ind = 'Y') and not exists (a row in DECISION where the decision code has a cdecision_cancel_ind = 'Y')." Figure 7–14 shows an object that completes the translation to SQL and defines the population of accepted applicants expected to enroll. Figure 7–15 on page 142 uses the object in a report.

Again, consider the way that business rules affected the SQL defining accepted applicants who expect to enroll. Two organizations in the same industry may use completely different definitions for the same concept. When asked for clarification a director of admissions at another college might have responded, "that's an accepted applicant whose last admissions decision is a PD indicating an enrollment deposit was paid." Another director might respond "that's someone who's paid an enrollment deposit and who doesn't have a cancellation *after* the enrollment deposit date." The SQL for these definitions differ, even though the report populations are conceptually identical.

OBJECT

```
from
     applicant
where
     applicant_term = '<term>'
            and applicant_level = '<level>'
            and applicant_college = '<college>'
     and exists                                          [1]
     (select 'x'
     from
            cdecision cd0,
            decision d0
     where
            d0.decision_id = applicant_id
                    and d0.decision_applicant_term =
                    applicant_term
                    and d0.decision_applicant_seriesno =
                    applicant_seriesno
            and cd0.cdecision_code = decision_code
                    and cd0.cdecision_accept_ind = 'Y')
     and exists                                          [2]
     (select 'x'
     from
            cdecision cd1,
            decision d1
     where
            d1.decision_id = applicant_id
                    and d1.decision_applicant_term = applicant_term
                    and d1.decision_applicant_seriesno =
                    applicant seriesno
            and cd1.cdecision_code = decision_code
                    and cd1.cdecision_enrl_ind = 'Y')
     and not exists                                      [3]
     (select 'x'
     from
            cdecision cd2,
            decision d2
     where
            d2.decision_id = applicant_id
                    and d2.decision_applicant_term =
                    applicant_term
                    and d2.decision_applicant_seriesno =
                    applicant_seriesno
            and cd2.cdecision_code = decision_code
                    and cd2.cdecision_cancel_ind = 'Y')
```

HELP

```
object:        popenrl.obj
date created:  13-oct-1994
author:        glewis
revisions:

Purpose:       Defines the population of applicants accepted for
               admissions for a specified term, level, and college who
               are expected to enroll.  That is, they have paid an
               enrollment deposit and they have not canceled their
               application.

Usage:         <term>: replace with term (eg, 199509 for Fall 1995)
               <level>: replace with level (eg, UG for Undergrad)
               <college>: replace with college code (eg, BU for Business)

Hints:         none
```

Key:

1. Has the applicant been accepted for admissions?
2. Has the applicant paid an enrollment deposit?
3. Is the application still active (i.e., not canceled)?

Figure 7–14. *Population* object and help file of accepted applicants who expect to enroll.

REPORT

```
SQL> select
        count(*), count(distinct applicant_id)
     from
        applicant
     where
        applicant_term = '199509'
                and applicant_level = 'UG'
                and applicant_college = 'AS"
                and applicant_student_type = 'F'
        and [rest of popenrl.obj object from Figure 7-14]
 /
ENTER to continue ...
   COUNT(*) COUNT(DISTINCTAPPLICANT_ID)
----------- ---------------------------
        141                         141
```

The correlated subqueries from the *population* object in Figure 7–14 would appear here.

Figure 7–15. Report of undergraduate Arts & Sciences accepted applicants who expect to enroll in Fall 1995.

Which Objects to Build

Objects would quickly become unmanageable if you created one for each report you completed. The number of possible permutations is just too large. It's better to have a small core of *population* objects that get used repeatedly and can be modified when necessary. When identifying these core populations, I've found it helpful to listen to people while they work.

If you get a chance, immerse yourself in a work environment for some time. You quickly find that people use a language that may not mean anything to the uninitiated. They invent words or they redefine common words and use them differently than in normal language. These invented words are often the populations you want to capture as objects. For example, consider the object just built—the population of accepted applicants who expect to enroll. People who work in an admissions office are not going to say "accepted applicants who expect to enroll" every time they talk about this population. They'll invent a name for this group. It might, for example, be called "net paids." That actually makes some sense; a "net paid" is someone who has paid an enrollment deposit who has not canceled the deposit—in other words an accepted applicant who expects to enroll. Create a lexicon of these words. When you identify the language that people invent to do their work, you've located starting points for building objects.

There's one other reason for keeping the number of population objects to a minimum. That concerns the nature of *where* objects. There are two subclasses of *where* objects: one that provides the join logic required to access data columns requested in the *select* clause, and one that acts as adjectives to basic *population* objects. It's this second subclass of *where* objects that also allows you to maintain only a core of *population* objects. For example, rather than create an object for "international accepted applicants" you create a *population* object of "accepted applicants" and a *where* object of "international." This provides greater flexibility because you can apply the adjectives against many different core populations.

Primacy of Population

The concept of a report population is critical in ad hoc queries. You first define your population. You then go after the data columns. It's true that the structure of the SQL gets influenced by the choice of data columns to appear in the report. But the primacy of a report population is very important and underappreciated by end users and by vendors of ad hoc query tools.

Recall from earlier discussions that two types of errors can creep into SQL. One is "falling through a join," where the population decreases; the other is "multiplying through a join," where the population increases. To identify these errors you absolutely must nail down your population. You must determine its size and whether any population items appear more than once.

It's easy to understand why end users place secondary importance on report populations. The structure of the SQL ***select*** command starts with the *select* clause and then proceeds to the *from* and *where* clauses. It seems logical to build a query by starting at the top and moving down. I'm arguing instead that you should:

- start in the middle with the *from* and *where* clauses and define the population as if only a count had been requested;
- move to the top and choose the data columns in the *select* clause;
- return to the middle and examine and adjust, if necessary, the population SQL to provide more direct access to any requested data columns (again testing the population counts after any SQL alterations);
- add any additional *where* clauses required to access the data columns; and
- end it with the *group by*, *having*, and *order by* clauses.

This route through the SQL is less linear, but it improves the likelihood of accurate reports because it forces you to explicitly identify and define the population for the report. If you start with 100 distinct population items, you want a report on those 100 distinct items and not a report with 98 items or one with 102 items. You eliminate these errors by placing primary emphasis on the report population.

Table 7–1 provides an inventory of objects built in this chapter. It's helpful to organize objects in inventories. Later chapters add objects to this list, and also provide additional opportunities to build *population* objects.

Table 7–1. Inventory of SQL objects.

Class	Name	Purpose
POPULATION	popacapp	Applicants accepted for admissions for a specified term, level, and college
	popapp	Applicants for admissions for a specified term, level, college
	popenrl	Accepted applicants for a specified term, level, and college who are expected to enroll
	poprecr	Recruits for a specified term and level

Chapter 8

Building *Where* Objects

Where objects accomplish two tasks: They modify *population* objects to further define the report population; or they access tables that are not part of the population definition, thereby making the data available for display in the report. The first class of *where* objects serve as adjectives to the nouns of *population* objects. The second class of *where* objects serve as gateways to other data tables.

This chapter describes how to build objects from each of the two *where* classes. Class 2 gateway objects receive most of the attention because many ad hoc reports fail when users improperly join tables needed to access columns required in their report. The chapter discusses sources of these problems, and several objects demonstrate how to construct robust joins.

First, a word of caution. Prepare yourself to ponder; some sections of the chapter require considerable thought. But fortunately everything in later chapters appears easy by comparison.

Class 1 Objects: Modifying Populations

You begin writing ad hoc queries by defining the report population. This first requires specifying the population in words and then translating that verbal definition into SQL. *Population* objects allow you to get close to the SQL translation without writing any original code. But if you're parsimonious and only build core *population* objects, there will be many situations when an existing object doesn't fully define the report population. What you'll be missing are the modifying conditions, the adjectives that further define a population.

Sometimes these modifying conditions are extremely specific and occur infrequently in report requests. For example, the director of market research might ask for a report on recruits from the Chicago area who expressed an interest in athletics. Other times the modifying conditions apply more generally to many different types of populations and occur more frequently in report requests (e.g., reports on recruits, applicants, or accepts who are women). Commonly requested adjectives become good candidates for *where* objects, particularly if there is any complexity involved in translating the adjective into SQL.

Detailed Example

In college admissions offices the word diversity now occurs frequently. In a world increasingly international and multicultural, many colleges stress the importance of representing this diversity in their students. It becomes the goal of the admissions office to improve student diversity, to enroll more international students, students of color, or other groups that might be underrepresented on campus. These priorities generate many report requests concerning specially targeted groups of recruits or applicants. The same set of adjectives appear repeatedly in report requests.

Let's start by building an object for one such adjective—"international." You always start by trying to understand what people mean when they use a term and then determine how the meaning can be represented in SQL. This may or may not be hard to do. Sometimes the definition is obvious; a "male" is someone whose person_gender = M. Other times the definition is determined by law or external authority; a "new freshman" means something very specific in the federal enrollment reports. Other times, however, you'll be surprised to find competing definitions. Consider international students. Certainly citizens of foreign countries should be included. But what about permanent residents in the United States? Or students with dual citizenship, one of which is the United States? Or U.S. students residing in foreign countries? In a college you'll likely find that several definitions of international students exist; one in admissions, one in the international student office, another perhaps in the English as a Second Language program. So nail down the definition.

At Komenda College, Chapter 3 identified an international student as someone with foreign citizenship who is not a permanent resident of the United States. With that as a basis, it's easy to develop an object for "international." Two data columns in the VISA table look promising (see the VISA dictionary, Table A–14 in Appendix A). One is visa_type, a NOT NULL column containing a code identifying the type of visa; the other is visa_citizen, a column that identifies the country of citizenship. The unique index (see Table A–2 in Appendix A) is visa_id and visa_seriesno, indicating that the last visa for a student is the one with the maximum visa_seriesno.

Armed with this information we can examine the data. Figure 8–1 lists the visa codes from the code table CVISA. Note that "PR" is a permanent resident. It seems likely that permanent residents of the United States receive a PR in the visa_type data column. Verify this by asking staff in the office responsible for maintaining visa codes. At Komenda that is the case; a permanent resident does have a visa_code of PR. This helps with part of the definition of an international student.

But what does "someone with foreign citizenship" mean? Figure 8–2 on the following page shows a count of Fall 1995 undergraduate recruits at Komenda by the country of citizenship. The results are interesting. First, there are 23 recruits in the VISA table who have a visa_type but no country of citizenship. Second, many of the visa_type values show UN for Unknown. Apparently at the recruit stage, the college has less than complete information about international students. If we translate "someone with foreign citizenship" to mean someone whose visa_citizen is not null and not USA then we'll undercount the actual number of international students.

```
SQL> select * from cvisa order by 1;
ENTER to continue ...
visa
code visa                            datestamp
---- ------------------------------- ---------
B1   Tourist/business                17-MAR-94
B2   Tourist/pleasure                17-MAR-94
F1   Student visa                    17-MAR-94
F2   Dependent on student visa       17-MAR-94
J1   Exchange visitor                17-MAR-94
PR   Permanent resident              17-MAR-94
UN   Unknown                         17-MAR-94

7 rows selected.
```

Figure 8–1. Visa codes.

```
citizen                                         visa
code    nation                                  type        count
------- -----------------------------           ----   ----------
                                                F1              5
                                                J1              1
                                                UN             17
ARG     Argentina                               B2              1
ARG     Argentina                               F1              1
BRA     Brazil                                  F1              1
BRA     Brazil                                  UN              3
CAN     Canada                                  J1              1
COL     Colombia                                B1              1
COL     Colombia                                UN              2
DOM     Dominican Republic                      F1              2
DOM     Dominican Republic                      UN              3
ECU     Ecuador                                 UN              3
ENG     England                                 F1              1
ENG     England                                 UN              2
ESA     El Salvador                             F1              1
ESA     El Salvador                             UN              2
GRE     Greece                                  UN              3
HAI     Haiti                                   F1              1
HAI     Haiti                                   UN              1
HKG     Hong Kong                               B2              1
HKG     Hong Kong                               F1              1
HKG     Hong Kong                               UN              5
INA     Indonesia                               F1              1
INA     Indonesia                               UN              1
IND     India                                   F1              4
IND     India                                   UN              1
ISR     Israel                                  F1              1
ITA     Italy                                   F1              1
ITA     Italy                                   UN              1
JPN     Japan                                   F1              1
JPN     Japan                                   J1              1
KOR     Korea                                   UN              1
KUW     Kuwait                                  UN              2
LUX     Luxembourg                              UN              1
NGR     Nigeria                                 B1              1
PAK     Pakistan                                B2              1
PAK     Pakistan                                F1              2
PAN     Panama                                  UN              6
PER     Peru                                    F1              2
PER     Peru                                    UN              2
POL     Poland                                  UN              1
PRC     People Republic of China                F1              1
PRC     People Republic of China                UN              1
RUS     Russia                                  UN              1
SKO     South Korea                             F1              2
                                                       ----------
sum                                                            95

46 rows selected.
```

These 23 recruits have visa codes and appear to be internationals, but Komenda has no citizenship information for them.

Figure 8–2. Country of citizenship and visa types for Fall 1995 international recruits.

It seems likely that as recruits become applicants and as applicants become students, Komenda would know progressively more information about international students. If true, it may not be possible to write one "international" object that works equally well for all populations. Figure 8–3 shows the count of citizenship for Fall 1995 applicants. It does appear that our reasoning was correct. All applicants in this report have citizenship data; all of them also have known visa types. The numbers in the report are small, so you'd want to verify the results against past years as well. But it does appear that at the applicant stage "someone with foreign citizenship" translates most directly into "someone with a visa_citizen that is not null and not USA."

We're left with two options: (1) build two international objects, one for recruits and one that could be used for applicants, students, and other populations where Komenda has detailed citizenship information; or (2) search for a way to build one general object that would work for all populations. Here's my advice: go for the generality first, then fall back to multiple objects only when you can't write a general object. In this situation we need to retranslate "someone with foreign citizenship." The essential feature of international students is that they have a VISA row. For their VISA row, check country of citizenship to make sure it's not the United States. Also check visa_type to make sure the person is not a permanent resident. But let's then assume that the presence of a VISA record identifies someone with foreign citizenship, even if visa_citizen is null.

Figure 8–4 on the following page shows a *where* object developed using this definition. It also shows two reports using the object. One counts international applicants and the other international recruits. Both counts

```
citizen                                visa
code     nation                        type       count
-------  --------------------------   ----  ----------
DOM      Dominican Republic            F1             1
ESA      El Salvador                   F1             1
GRE      Greece                        F1             1
HAI      Haiti                         F1             1
IND      India                         F1             1
PER      Peru                          F1             1
                                            ----------
sum                                                   6

6 rows selected.
```

Figure 8–3. Citizenship and visa types of undergraduate international applicants: Fall 1995.

```
HELP
object:         whrintl.obj
date created:   24-oct-1994
author:         glewis
revisions:

Purpose:        Defines the term "international."

Usage:          Need to include the VISA table with an alias of 'v1'
                in the main query (i.e., from visa v1, ...)
                <driving_table>: replace with name of table driving
                the query (e.g., APPLICANT).

Hints:          Provides access to other data columns in the VISA table
                also.
```

```
OBJECT
     and v1.visa_id = <driving_table>_id
              and v1.visa_type != 'PR'
              and v1.visa_seriesno =
              (select max(v2.visa_seriesno)
              from visa v2
              where v2.visa_id = v1.visa_id)
```

In each query, one table drives the data retrieval strategy. Normally it's the principal table in the *population* object.

Report 1: International recruits

```
SQL> select
  2         count(*),
  3         count(distinct recruit_id)
  4  from
  5         visa v1,
  6         recruit
  7  where
  8         recruit_term = '199509'
  9              and recruit_level = 'UG'
 10         and v1.visa_id = recruit_id
 11              and v1.visa_type != 'PR'
 12              and v1.visa_seriesno =
 13              (select max(v2.visa_seriesno)
 14              from visa v2
 15              where v2.visa_id = v1.visa_id)
 16  /
ENTER to continue ...
  COUNT(*) COUNT(DISTINCTRECRUIT_ID)
---------- -------------------------
        95                        95
```

Report 2: International applicants

```
SQL> select
  2         count(*),
  3         count(distinct applicant_id)
  4  from
  5         visa v1,
  6         applicant
  7  where
  8         applicant_term = '199509'
  9              and applicant_level = 'UG'
 10              and applicant_college = 'AS"
 11         and v1.visa_id = applicant_id
 12              and v1.visa_type != 'PR'
 13              and v1.visa_seriesno =
 14              (select max(v2.visa_seriesno)
 15              from visa v2
 16              where v2.visa_id = v1.visa_id)
 17  /
ENTER to continue ...
  COUNT(*) COUNT(DISTINCTAPPLICANT_ID)
---------- ---------------------------
         6                           6
```

Figure 8–4. Class 1 *where* object and help file defining "international".

match the counts shown in Figures 8–2 and 8–3. Our general object, even though it didn't directly translate from the verbal definition into an SQL definition, appears to work.

This example nicely illustrates two important points:

1. You can't write objects in the abstract. They evolve from interactions between database design, programming logic built into the input screens, institutional standards and definitions, and day-to-day operational procedures. Examining the data is just as important as determining the data column definitions, the unique index, and the join relationships. In this case we only discovered the complexity of defining "international" after running two reports that looked at visa and citizenship data for recruits and for applicants. Writing the object without examining the data would not have worked.
2. You can't write objects of unlimited generality. If offices use different definitions for the same concept, one object won't apply across these offices. You'll have to write multiple objects. But in the international example, the problem was actually more subtle. The recruiting and admissions offices used the same definition, yet the recruiting office had less complete visa and citizenship data than the admissions office. We got around this only by recasting the SQL definition into a lowest common denominator that applied to both recruits and applicants. Alternatively we could have built two separate objects to utilize the different data that existed in the two offices.

Practice Example

The previous example explored in considerable detail the thinking involved when constructing class 1 *where* objects. The example here keeps the diversity theme, but has a much more direct solution than the international object.

Komenda College hopes to diversify its student composition by recruiting, admitting, and enrolling more students of color. In the vernacular of Komenda, these students are called "minority" students. Staff frequently request reports on minority recruits and applicants, making the word minority a prime candidate for a *where* object.

As always, you start the process of building an object by getting clarification. According to Chapter 3, a minority student at Komenda is someone

```
SQL> select * from cethn order by 1;
ENTER to continue ...
ethnic
code   ethnic status                  datestamp
------ ------------------------------ ---------
A      Asian-American                 17-MAR-94
B      Black                          17-MAR-94
C      Caucasian                      17-MAR-94
H      Hispanic                       17-MAR-94
I      American Indian                17-MAR-94
N      Non-resident                   17-MAR-94
X      Unknown                        17-MAR-94

7 rows selected.
```

Figure 8–5. Ethnic codes.

whose ethnic status is Asian-American, Black, Hispanic, or Native American. The PERSON table includes a data column called person_ethnic (see Table A–10 in Appendix A). Figure 8–5 shows the codes used to identify a person's ethnic status. It's clear from this figure that our working definition of minority translates directly into an SQL statement where "person_ethnic in ('A','B','H','I')."

Figure 8–6 shows the *where* object defining minority. It's constructed with a straight join between the PERSON table and the driving table of the query (e.g., RECRUIT or APPLICANT). We could also have constructed the object with a correlated subquery and *exists*. Using the straight join structure, however, allows any data column from the PERSON table to appear in the report. In that sense it's more flexible than the subquery structure. Also, the unique index on PERSON is person_id. This means that an individual can only appear once in the PERSON table. Multiplying through a join will not be a problem, thereby negating the main advantage a subquery structure holds over a straight join.

Class 2 Objects: Accessing New Tables

Population objects and class 1 *where* objects define report populations. Each of these objects uses one or more tables. As long as the tables don't appear in subqueries, the data columns in these tables become available for reporting. For example, using the international object (i.e., whrintl.obj) provides access to any of the data columns in the VISA table. Similarly, the minority object whrmnrty.obj provides access to the PERSON table.

Many reports, however, require data columns that do not appear in the tables used to define report populations. Suppose the director of admissions

HELP

```
object:        whrmnrty.obj
date created:  24-oct-1994
author:        glewis
revisions:
Purpose:       Defines the term "minority."

Usage:         Need to include the PERSON table in the main query.
               <driving_table>: replace with name of table driving
               the query (e.g., APPLICANT).

Hints:         Provides access to other data columns in the PERSON
               table also.
```

OBJECT

```
   and person_id = <driving_table>_id
           and person_ethnic in ('A','B','H','I')
```

REPORT

```
SQL> select count(*), count(distinct applicant_id)
  2  from
  3        person,
  4        applicant
  5  where
  6        applicant_term = '199509'
  7                 and applicant_level = 'UG'
  8                 and applicant_college = 'AS'
  9        and person_id = applicant_id
 10                 and person_ethnic in ('A','B','H','I')
 11  /
ENTER to continue ...
  COUNT(*) COUNT(DISTINCTAPPLICANT_ID)
---------- ---------------------------
        38                          38
```

Figure 8–6. Class 1 *where* object and help file defining "minority".

requests a roster of international applicants showing their I.D. number, name, and country of citizenship. The two objects popapp.obj and whrintl.obj define the report population and provide access to the APPLICANT and VISA tables but not the NAME table. To complete the SQL we need a join to the NAME table.

Class 2 *where* objects provide access to tables not used to define the report population. In structure they must appear as straight joins rather than subqueries because data columns from these tables will appear in the *select* clause. Class 2 *where* objects themselves contain two sub-classes, which I distinguish as class 2u and class 2m. They differ in how they maintain something I call *population singularity*. This is a simple concept. Reports maintain population singularity when each population item gets included once and only once in the report. If a population has 100 items, a roster report will show 100 rows when population singularity is maintained. When singularity is relaxed, the report will show all 100 population items but any individual item may appear more than once. At Komenda this could happen, for example, when listing addresses, test scores, prior schools attended, or admissions decisions. For example, applicants might have multiple SAT math scores. Similarly they might have two permanent addresses. Class 2u *where* objects maintain population singularity; class 2m objects relax the singularity restriction. The "u" of class 2u was chosen to reflect "uni"; the "m" of class 2m to reflect "multi."

Class 2u Objects: Maintaining Singularity

Objects intended to maintain singularity must not permit population items to fall through or to multiply through a join. They generally require rigorous construction, testing, and attention to the data itself. Let's start off easy and then examine progressively more difficult situations.

The Basic Idea

Let's build an object providing access to the NAME table. We'll start by asking two questions that should be asked with minor variation whenever building any class 2 *where* object: (1) Can anyone appear multiple times in the NAME table? and (2) Does everyone in the report population appear at least once in the NAME table? The database schematic (Figure A–1 in Appendix A) provides the answers. Note the connection between PERSON and NAME. It's a one-to-many relationship meaning that any one person could have multiple NAME rows. Komenda does track name changes, so this seems reasonable. The schematic also implies that everybody must have a least one NAME row, because the relationship between PERSON and NAME does not include the symbol (a circle) that indicates zero rows are possible. Apparently the input screen used to enter new PERSON records ensures that a NAME record is created at the same time.

This means that of the two potential problems, we need only worry about multiplying through the NAME join. The table of indexes shows the unique index on NAME composed of name_id and name_seriesno. Chapter 3 identifies the most recent name as the name with the highest name_seriesno. Selecting the maximum name_seriesno for an individual returns his or her latest name information; it prevents multiplying through a join.

Figure 8–7 on the next page shows the class 2u *where* object accessing NAME. It also shows a report based on this object. Note the object uses a correlated subquery to select the max(name_seriesno) if an applicant appears more than once in the NAME table.

Practice Example

Komenda maintains sex, birthdate, and other personal characteristics of people in the PERSON table. For this information to appear in a report, you must join the PERSON table in the main query. Figure 8–8 on page 157 shows this join in a query. It also shows the object constructed to generalize the join. Note how simple this object is. It hardly seems worthwhile to construct a one-line object, but even these objects become useful when automating objects for end users who know nothing about SQL and don't care to learn more.

How Data Can Complicate Object Construction

The join into the PERSON table was simple. Everybody has a PERSON record and they only have one. The NAME join was somewhat complicated by the fact that people may have NAME changes and appear more than once in the table. But everybody appeared at least once in NAME. Now let's consider joins to other tables where people may not appear at all.

Detailed Example

Suppose the director of admissions requests a report of all undergraduate applicants to the college of Arts & Sciences for Fall 1995, with the report displaying their highest SAT math score. If there are 100 such applicants, she expects to see a report with 100 rows. Let's use this request to build an object accessing the TEST table. In the process we'll explore the interactions between data and SQL objects.

HELP

```
object:         whrname.obj
date created: 24-oct-1994
author:         glewis
revisions:

Purpose:        Provides access to the NAME table.

Usage:          1. Need to include the NAME table with an alias
                of 'n1' in the main query (i.e., from name n1, ...)
                2. <driving_table>: replace with name of table
                driving the query (e.g., APPLICANT)

Hints:          none
```

OBJECT

```
and n1.name_id = <driving_table>_id
     and n1.name_seriesno =
     (select max(n2.name_seriesno)
     from name n2
     where n2.name_id = n1.name_id)
```

Note the use of the correlated subquery that returns the last known NAME row for each person in the report population.

REPORT

```
SQL> select
  2         name_id,
  3         name_last,
  4         name_first
  5  from
  6         name n1,
  7         applicant
  8  where
  9         applicant_term = '199509'
 10              and applicant_level = 'UG'
 11              and applicant_college = 'AS'
 12         and n1.name_id = applicant_id
 13              and n1.name_seriesno =
 14              (select max(n2.name_seriesno)
 15              from name n2
 16              where n2.name_id = n1.name_id)
 17  order by 2, 3
 18  /
ENTER to continue ...
   NAME_ID NAME_LAST                       NAME_FIRST
---------- ------------------------------ ---------------
      2574 Abraham                         Alicia
      3163 Adams                           Amy
      2687 Adams                           Samuel
      8584 Adams                           Thomas
      1897 Affsa                           Rita
      6287 Agnew                           Angela
       ...
```

Objects used:
1. popapp.obj
2. whrname.obj

Figure 8–7. Class 2u *where* object and help file accessing the NAME table.

HELP

```
object:         whrpersn.obj
date created:   07-nov-1994
author:         glewis
revisions:

Purpose:        Provides access to the PERSON table.

Usage:          1. Need to include the PERSON table in the main query.
                2. <driving>_table>: replace with name of table driving
                the query (e.g., APPLICANT)

Hints:          none
```

OBJECT

```
    and person_id =<driving_table>_id
```

REPORT

```
SQL> select
  2        count(*), count(distinct applicant_id)
  3   from
  4        person,
  5        applicant
  6   where
  7        applicant_term = '199509'
  8                 and applicant_level = 'UG'
  9                 and applicant_college = 'AS'
 10        and person_id = applicant_id
 11   /
ENTER to continue ...
  COUNT(*) COUNT(DISTINCTAPPLICANT_ID)
---------- ---------------------------
       700                         700
```

Figure 8–8. Class 2u *where* object and help file accessing the PERSON table.

The database schematic (Figure A–1 in Appendix A) shows a single applicant may have zero, one, or several tests of a specified type. The unique index (Table A–2) shows that multiple tests of a specified type must occur on separate days. This means there are four distinct data configurations possible:

1. An applicant may have no test scores and thus have no rows in TEST.
2. An applicant may have test scores but not of the type we want.
3. An applicant may have one test score of the type we want.
4. An applicant may have several test scores of the type we want.

We can dismiss data of type 3; this never presents a problem. But applicants with data of types 1 and 2 will fall through improperly constructed joins, while applicants with data of type 4 will multiply through a join. Figure 8–9 on the following page shows TEST data for three applicants.

```
ENTER to continue ...
       test                                                   test test
    id type   test                                           score date
------ ------ ------------------------------ ---------- ---------
   265 ACHES  English Essay Achievement                        400 18-JUN-94
   265 ACHES  English Essay Achievement                        460 10-NOV-94
   265 ACHIT  Italian Achievement                              450 10-NOV-94
   265 ACHM1  Math Level 1 Achievement                         600 10-NOV-94
   279 SATM   SAT Mathematics                                  680 28-APR-94
   279 SATM   SAT Mathematics                                  680 15-FEB-95
   279 SATM   SAT Mathematics                                  670 10-MAR-95
   279 SATV   SAT Verbal                                       520 28-APR-94
   279 SATV   SAT Verbal                                       510 15-FEB-95
   279 SATV   SAT Verbal                                       530 10-MAR-95
   181

11 rows selected.
```

Note that applicant 279 has two SAT math scores that qualify as maximum. Applicant 181 has no test scores of any kind, while applicant 265 has several scores but no SAT scores.

Figure 8–9. TEST data for three applicants.

Each applicant represents one of the three types of potential problems; applicant 265 has test scores but no SATM scores, applicant 181 has no test scores at all, and applicant 279 has three SATM scores. To make matters worse, two SATM scores of applicant 279 tie for being the highest (680). The task then is to write a join to TEST that prevents applicants 181 and 265 from falling through the join and simultaneously returns only one row for applicant 279.

Figure 8–10 shows an initial join to the TEST table based on the logic provided in the database schematic, but without considering data problems. It returned three rows, which is what we want, but they all belong to applicant 279. Two applicants fell through the join and one multiplied through the join. The join is wrong; the query is wrong; the query writer is chagrined; and the user is frustrated.

Let's deal first with the problem presented by applicant 279, who has multiple SATM scores. The unique index on TEST indicates that specifying an I.D. number, a test score, and a test date will return one row. To ensure that applicant 279 appears only once in the report, we should find the maxi-

```
SQL> select
        applicant_id,
        test_type,
        ctest_translation,
        test_score,
        test_date,
 from
        ctest,
        test,
        applicant
 where
        applicant_term = '199509'
               and applicant_level = 'UG'
               and applicant_college = 'AS'
               and applicant_id in (181, 265, 279)
        and test_id = applicant_id
               and test_type = 'SATM'
        and ctest_code = test_type
 /
ENTER to continue ...
     test                                           test test
  id type   test                                   score date
------ ------ ------------------------- ---------- ---------
   279 SATM   SAT Mathematics                        680 28-APR-94
   279 SATM   SAT Mathematics                        680 15-FEB-95
   279 SATM   SAT Mathematics                        670 10-MAR-95
```

Almost nothing works correctly in this query. Applicants 181 and 256 both fall through the TEST join. Applicant 279 appears multiple times even though only a single maximun SAT math score is sought.

Figure 8–10. First attempt to return maximum SAT math scores for three applicants.

mum SAT math score and break any ties by selecting the data from the latest test date. Figure 8–11 on the following page and Figure 8–12 on page 161 show two ways to do this. The first method uses one subquery to find the maximum SATM score and a second subquery to find the maximum test date for this score. The second method converts test scores and test dates into character strings, with test_date formatted as YYYYMMDD, and then finds the maximum value of these concatenated strings. This requires only a single subquery. Either method returns the same data.

Before selecting a join structure, let's deal with the applicants who fell through the join. The best structure to eliminate multiplying through the join may be suggested by solutions to the problem of falling through the join.

METHOD 1

```
SQL> select
        applicant_id,
        test_type,
        ctest_translation,
        test_score,
        test_date,
  from
        ctest
        test t1,
        applicant
  where
        applicant_term = '199509'
                and applicant_level = 'UG'
                and applicant_college = 'AS'
                and applicant_id in (181, 265, 279)
        and t1.test_id = applicant_id
                and t1.test_type = 'SATM'
                and t1.test_score =
                        (select max(t2.test_score)
                        from test t2
                        where t2.test_id = t1.test_id
                        and t2.test_type = t1.test_type)
                and t1.test_date =
                        (select max(t3.test_date)
                        from test t3
                        where t3.test_id = t1.test_id
                        and t3.test_type = t1.test_type
                        and t3.test_score = t1.test_score)
        and ctest_code = t1.test_type
  /
ENTER to continue ...
       test                                     test test
    id type   test                             score date
------ ------ ----------------------- ---------- ---------
   279 SATM   SAT Mathematics                    680 15-FEB-95
```

This correlated subquery identifies the maximum test score.

If two or more test scores tie as the maximum, this correlated subquery breaks the tie by returning the maximum score with the latest test date. Note only one score for applicant 279 appears in the report.

Figure 8–11. One method for returning a maximum SAT math score.

Applicant 181 has no test scores and falls through the join at the line reading "and test_id = applicant_id." Without any test data, there is no test_id = 181 and the join criteria fails. We can nicely solve this problem using a special kind of join called an *outer join*. Outer joins use the symbol "(+)" as in "test_id(+) = applicant_id." Used in this way, the outer join adds a null row for each applicant_id that does not appear in the TEST table;

```
METHOD 2

SQL> select
        applicant_id,
        test_type,
        ctest_translation,
        test_score,
        test_date,
 from
        ctest
        test t1,
        applicant
 where
        applicant_term = '199509'
                and applicant_level = 'UG'
                and applicant_college = 'AS'
                and applicant_id in (181, 265, 279)
        and t1.test_id = applicant_id
                and t1.test_type = 'SATM'
                and to_char(t1.test_score)||to_char(t1.test_date,'YYYYMMDD') =
                        (select max(to_char(t2.test_score)||
                                to_char(t2.test_date,'YYYYMMDD'))
                        from test t2
                        where t2.test_id = t1.test_id
                        and t2.test_type = t1.test_type)
        and ctest_code = t1.test_type
 /
ENTER to continue ...
      test                                          test test
   id type   test                                  score date
------ ------ ---------------------- ---------- ---------
   279 SATM   SAT Mathematics                        680 15-FEB-95
```

This structure requires only a single correlated subquery to return the maximum test score. Note that the test date is converted into a format 'YYYYMMDD' so that the maximum returns the latest date.

Figure 8–12. Second method for returning a maximum SAT math score.

applicant 181 would be retained with a null TEST row. An outer join may appear on either side of the equals sign, but the two joins mean entirely different things. For example, the join "test_id = applicant_id(+)" would add a null row for each test_id that did not appear in the APPLICANT table. Making the correct placement of the (+) symbol is important. It may help to think of it this way: place the (+) symbol with the table that population items fall through. In our case, applicants fall through the TEST table so that test_id(+) = applicant_id is the correct syntax.

Let's deal next with the problem presented by applicant 265, who has test scores in TEST but no SATM scores. This applicant falls through the join on the line that reads "and test_type = 'SATM'." Without any SATM scores the applicant does not meet the criteria and is omitted from the query. Applicant 181 would also fail the criteria that test_type = SATM, because the null row created with the outer join will contain no test_type data. The solution is a second outer join, this time as "test_type(+) = 'SATM'." This statement now returns every row where the test type is SAT math. It also temporarily (for the duration of the query) creates a dummy row with null columns for any applicant who has test data but no SATM data. It also retains the null row for any applicant who has no TEST data at all.

Figure 8–13 shows the effect of using the two outer joins. Both applicant 181 and 265 now appear in the report. All their test data is null, of course, but at least they no longer disappear from the report.

At this point we've separately solved the two problems of falling and multiplying through joins. Figure 8–11 or Figure 8–12 solved the population increase problem and returned only a single row for applicant 279; Figure 8–13 solved the population decrease problem and returned null rows for applicants 181 and 265. But an interesting thing happens when the two solutions are combined in an effort to return all three rows in the same query (see Figure 8–14). Applicants 181 and 265 again fall through the join, obviously at the subquery criteria returning a maximum SATM score.

It turns out that the subquery created two problems. One concerns null values; the second concerns the interaction of correlated subqueries and outer joins. The solution to the first problem requires only a simple trick. The second problem is more fundamental and requires discussion. Let's start with the easy problem.

Since the outer joins created dummy rows consisting entirely of null values for applicants 181 and 265, these applicants don't have SATM scores or test dates. Consequently the join criteria that selects a maximum SATM score fails. The *nvl* (null value) function solves this problem. You can use *nvl* to set null SATM scores and null test dates to whatever values you like. Suppose we set null test scores to 800 and null test dates to '01-JAN-50'. The join criteria then becomes:

```
... and to_char(nvl(t1.test_score, 800))||
     to_char(nvl(t1.test_date, '01-JAN-50'), 'YYYYMMDD') =
(select max(to_char(nvl(t2.test_score, 800))||
     to_char(nvl(t2.test_date, '01-JAN-50'), 'YYYYMMDD')
from test t2 ...
```

This structure prevents the two applicants from falling through this part of the join.

Now let's tackle the more fundamental problem. Examine Figure 8–14 again. The main query contains an outer join between the TEST and

```
SQL> select applicant_id, test_type, test_score, test_date
  2  from
  3      test,
  4     applicant
  5  where
  6        applicant_term = '199509'
  7                and applicant_level = 'UG'
  8                and applicant_college = 'AS'
  9                and applicant_id in (181, 265, 279)
 10        and test_id(+) = applicant_id
 11                and test_type(+) = 'SATM'
 12  /
ENTER to continue ...
       test        test test
    id type        score date
------ ------ ---------- ---------
   181
   265
   279 SATM          680 28-APR-94
   279 SATM          680 15-FEB-95
   279 SATM          670 10-MAR-95
```

This outer join creates a null row for applicants like 181 who don't appear in the TEST table.

In conjunction with the first outer join, this outer join creates a null row for applicants like 265 who appear in the TEST table but not with SATM data. It also retains the null row created for applicants like 181 who don't have any TEST data.

Figure 8–13. An outer join to the TEST table.

```
SQL> select applicant_id, test_type, test_score, test_date
  2  from
  3          test t1,
  4          applicant
  5  where
  6          applicant_term = '199509'
  7                  and applicant_level = 'UG'
  8                  and applicant_college = 'AS'
  9                  and applicant_id in (181, 265, 279)
 10          and t1.test_id(+) = applicant_id
 11                  and t1.test_type(+) = 'SATM'
 12                  and to_char(t1.test_score)||
 13                          to_char(t1.test_date, 'YYYYMMDD') =
 14                  (select max(to_char(t2.test_score)||
 15                          to_char(t2.test_date,'YYYYMMDD'))
 16                  from
 17                          test t2
 18                  where t2.test_id = applicant_id
 19                          and t2.test_type = 'SATM')
 20  /
ENTER to continue ...
       test        test test
    id type        score date
------ ------ ---------- ---------
   279 SATM          680 15-FEB-95
```

The null rows created in the outer joins don't make it through this portion of the SQL because null rows contain no test scores

Applicants 181 and 265 again fall through the join.

Figure 8–14. Combining outer joins to the TEST table with a subquery returning the maximum score.

APPLICANT tables, but the correlated subquery does not. It's logical to suppose that this is the source of the problem; that applicants 181 and 265 fall through the subquery because there is no outer join. However, Figure 8–15 shows that outer joins linking a main query to a subquery in a correlated fashion don't work.

Figure 8–16 and Figure 8–17 on page 166 illustrate two solutions to the problem. One involves using a NOT NULL data column and an OR (see Solution 1 in Figure 8–16). Since test_score is NOT NULL, the only rows that meet the criteria "and t1.test_score is null" are the two null rows created with the outer joins; applicants 181 and 265 would be retained by this line, while applicant 279 meets the criteria in the subquery. The second solution utilizes the base table PERSON in the correlated subquery (see Solution 2 in Figure 8–17). Since each applicant has a PERSON record, the join "where person_id = applicant_id" will link the main query to the subquery for all three applicants. Then the outer join within the subquery works fine. Either solution returns all three rows. I generally use the more compact structure shown in Solution 2. Both solutions exact a performance penalty, one because of the OR and the other because it requires a second outer join.

Figure 8–18 on page 167 shows a *where* object for joins to the TEST table. The figure also shows the help file associated with the object. We arrived at the object through a fairly complex process that involved analyzing the database schematics and unique indexes, but which also required analysis of the data. The resulting object is much more robust than if we only considered the schematics and indexes.

```
SQL> select count(*),count(distinct applicant_id)
     from applicant
     where applicant_id in (181, 265, 279)
            and applicant_term = '199509'
            and applicant_level = 'UG'
            and applicant_college = 'AS'
            and exists
            (select 'x'
            from test
            where test_id(+) = applicant_id
                    and test_type(+) = 'SATM')
     /
ENTER to continue ...
  COUNT(*) COUNT(DISTINCTAPPLICANT_ID)
---------- --------------------------
         1                          1
```

The main query includes three applicants. Using an outer join in the subquery to correlate TEST data with the APPLICANT table fails to return rows for the two applicants who don't have SATM scores.

Figure 8–15. Outer joins cannot directly correlate subqueries and main queries.

SOLUTION 1

```
SQL> select
        applicant_id,
        test_type,
        test_score,
        test_date
  from
        test t1,
        applicant
  where
        applicant_term = '199509'
                and applicant_level = 'UG'
                and applicant_college = 'AS'
                and applicant_id in (181, 265, 279)
        and t1.test_id(+) = applicant_id
                and t1.test_type(+) = 'SATM'
                and
                (
                (t1.test_score is null)
                or
                (to_char(t1.test_score)||
                        to_char(t1.test_date,'YYYYMMDD') =
                        (select max(to_char(t2.test_score)||
                                to_char(t2.test_date,'YYYYMMDD'))
                        from
                                test t2
                        where t2.test_id = t1.test_id
                                and t2.test_type = t1.test_type))
                )
  /
ENTER to continue ...
       test          test test
    id type          score date
------ ------ ---------- ---------
   181
   265
   279 SATM          680 15-FEB-95
```

This retains null rows created for applicants 181 and 265 in the outer joins.

This correlated subquery returns the maximum test score data for applicants like 279 who do have SAT math scores.

All three applicants appear in the report.

Figure 8–16. First solution that returns the maximum SAT math score for three applicants.

Practice Example

The previous example demonstrated many principles for writing robust *where* objects. Let's nail these concepts down with a second example. Suppose the director of admissions requests a report of applicants to the college of Arts & Sciences for Fall 1995, showing their last known permanent address. If there are 100 applicants, she expects to see a report with 100 rows.

The database schematic shows that a person may have zero, one, or many addresses of a particular type. The data dictionary shows that address_seriesno tracks addresses of a specified type, so that the maximum

SOLUTION 2

```
SQL> select
        applicant_id,
        test_type,
        test_score,
        test_date
    from
        test t1,
        applicant
    where
        applicant_term = '199509'
                and applicant_level = 'UG'
        and applicant_college = 'AS'
        and applicant_id in (181, 265, 279)
        and t1.test_id(+) = applicant_id
                and t1.test_type(+) = 'SATM'
                and to_char(nvl(t1.test_score,800))||
                        to_char(nvl(t1.test_date,'01-JAN-50'),'YYYYMMDD') =
                        (select max(to_char(nvl(t2.test_score,800))||
                                to_char(nvl(t2.test_date,'01-JAN-50'),'YYYYMMDD'))
                        from
                                test t2,
                                person
                        where person_id = applicant_id
                                and t2.test_id(+) = person_id
                                and t2.test_type(+) = 'SATM')
    /
ENTER to continue ...
       test          test test
    id type         score date
------ ------ ---------- ---------
   181
   265
   279 SATM          680 15-FEB-95
```

The null rows created in the outer joins get carried through this spot by using the *nvl* function to specify test scores and test dates.

The correlated subquery uses a base table (PERSON) that includes all applicants. An outer join into this base table then retains all three applicants (two of whom will have null rows).

Figure 8–17. Second solution that returns the maximum SAT math score for three applicants.

```
HELP

object:         whrtest.obj
date created:   26-oct-1994
author:         glewis
revisions:

Purpose:        Provides access to the TEST table for the highest test
                score of a specific type.

Usage:          1. Need to include the TEST table with an alias of 't1' in
                the main query (i.e., from test t1, ...)
                2. <driving_table>: replace with name of table driving the
                query (e.g., APPLICANT)
                3. <test_type>: replace with code for type of test (e.g.,
                'SATM')

Hints:          Written so 1 row returned for each person in the population,
                regardless of whether they have any tests of the specified
                type.
```

To use the object, fill in the name of the driving table and the type of test. Note these also appear in the subquery.

```
OBJECT

    and t1.test_id(+) = <driving_table>_id
            and t1.test_type(+) = '<test_type>'
            and to_char(nvl(t1.test_score,800))||
                    to_char(nvl(t1.test_date,'01-JAN-50'),'YYYYMMDD') =
                    (select max(to_char(nvl(t2.test_score,800))||
                            to_char(nvl(t1.test_date,'01-JAN-50'),'YYYYMMDD'))
                    from
                            test t2,
                            person
                    where person_id = <driving_table>_id
                            and t2.test_id(+) = person_id
                            and t2.test_type(+) = '<test_type>')
```

Figure 8–18. Class 2u *where* object and help file accessing the TEST table.

value in this column identifies the last known address of that type. The unique index combines I.D. number, address type, and seriesno. Figure 8–19 lists the various codes that identify types of addresses. We're interested in the permanent (PR) addresses.

Figure 8–20 shows address data for three applicants. One (I.D. 455) has no data in the ADDRESS table; a second (I.D. 413) has only a local address; and the third (I.D. 408) has two permanent addresses. The *where* object we write must accommodate all three data situations and return three rows, one for each applicant.

Each of the three problems can be solved individually. The applicant without any address data is easy; just use the outer join logic "... and address_id(+) = applicant_id." The applicant who has only a local address also presents an easy problem; just use the outer join logic "... and address_type(+) = 'PR'." The applicant with two permanent addresses also presents a problem we've solved previously; just use a correlated subquery to return the maximum address_seriesno.

Getting these three solutions to work together requires the same reasoning discussed in the previous section. To prevent the rows created in the outer join from falling through the correlated subquery, we'll need to adjust the structure of the subquery. Either of the two solutions used in the TEST object will work. Figure 8–21 shows the final report and the SQL used

```
SQL> select * from caddress order by 1;

ENTER to continue ...
address
code    address                        datestamp
------- ------------------------------ ---------
AR      Accounts Receivable            17-MAR-94
LO      Local                          17-MAR-94
PR      Permanent                      17-MAR-94
SU      Summer                         17-MAR-94
```

Figure 8–19. Address type codes.

```
ENTER to continue ...
       addr    address begin      end
    id type   seriesno date       date
------ ---- ---------- --------- ---------
   408 PR            1 18-JUN-92
   408 PR            2 01-MAR-94
   413 LO            1 03-JUN-92
   455

4 rows selected.
```

Note that applicant 408 has two permanent addresses. Applicant 455 has no known addresses, while applicant 413 has only a local address.

Figure 8–20. ADDRESS data for three applicants.

```
SQL> select
        applicant_id,
        address_type,
        address_seriesno,
        address_begindate,
        address_enddate
  from
        acdress d1,
        applicant
  where
        applicant_term = '199509'
                and applicant_level = 'UG'
                and applicant_college = 'AS'
                and applicant_id in (408, 413, 455)
        and d1.address_id(+) = applicant_id
                and d1.address_type(+) = 'PR'
                and nvl(d1.address_seriesno, 1) =
                (select max(nvl(d2.address_seriesno, 1))
                from
                        address d2,
                        person
                where
                        person_id = applicant_id
                        and d2.address_id(+) = person_id
                                and d2.address_type(+) = 'PR')
  /
ENTER to continue ...
       addr    address begin      end
    id type   seriesno date       date
------ ---- ---------- --------- --------
   408 PR            2 01-MAR-94
   413
   455
```

These lines create null rows for applicants without addresses (e.g., 455) and applicants without permanent addresses (e.g., 413)

Using the *nvl* function in these lines preserves the null rows created in the outer join.

The correlated subquery returns the last permanent address and uses a base table (PERSON) to connect the main query to the subquery.

The query returns report rows for all three applicants.

Figure 8–21. A join to the ADDRESS table providing access to latest permanent address data.

to produce the results. Figure 8–22 shows the *where* object accessing ADDRESS. Note that the *nvl* function links the main query and the subquery so that dummy rows created with the outer join don't fall through the subquery. Also note that the subquery correlates to the main query through the PERSON table, which contains all three applicants. This solution is exactly analogous to the solution for the TEST join discussed in the previous section.

More Complex Where *Objects*

By now the real benefit from using objects to construct ad hoc queries should be apparent. There is no way that most end users would do what we just did to construct joins to the TEST and ADDRESS tables. Having *where* objects available makes the job of writing queries much easier. But surprisingly simple user requests can require even more complex joins. In this section we'll look at two common situations.

```
HELP
object:          whraddr.obj
date created:    26-oct-1994
author:          glewis
revisions:

Purpose:         Provides access to the ADDRESS table for the most recent
                 address of a specified type.

Usage:           1. Need to include the ADDRESS table with an alias of 'd1' in
                 the main query (i.e., from address d1, ...)
                 2. <driving_table>: replace with name of table driving the
                 query (e.g., APPLICANT)
                 3. <address_type>: replace with code for type of address (e.g.,
                 'PR')

Hints:           Written so 1 row returned for each person in the population,
                 regardless of whether they have any addresses of the
                 specified type.
```

```
OBJECT
    and d1.address_id(+) = <driving_table>_id
            and d1.address_type(+) = '<address_type>'
            and nvl(d1.address_seriesno, 1) =
            (select max(nvl(d2.address_seriesno, 1))
            from
                    address d2,
                    person
            where
                    person_id = <driving_table>_id
                    and d2.address_id(+) = person_id
                            and d2.address_type(+) = '<address_type>')
```

Figure 8–22. Class 2u *where* object and help file accessing the ADDRESS table.

Report Column Hierarchies

Suppose the director of admissions requests a report of applicants to the college of Arts & Sciences for Fall 1995. She would like to see address information showing their local address if available or, if not, their permanent address. If there are 100 applicants, she expects to see 100 rows in the report.

The director of admissions is actually asking for a data column of addresses arranged in a hierarchy. At the top, her first choice, are local addresses. If an applicant has a local address, this should appear on the report. If the applicant does not have a local address, the report should display the director's second choice—the permanent address. If an applicant has neither a local or permanent address, then the report should display the director's last choice and list the applicant without any address information.

Let's first identify the data situations the object must handle properly:

1. An applicant may have no address information.
2. An applicant may have address information but no local or permanent address.
3. An applicant may have one or more local addresses and no permanent addresses.
4. An applicant may have one or more permanent addresses and no local address.
5. An applicant may have one or more local and one or more permanent addresses.

Item 3 above doesn't present a problem; this is the well-behaved data situation that even a sloppily written join will handle correctly. The other data situations each require attention. Figure 8–23 shows address

```
ENTER to continue ...
       addr      address begin      end
    id type     seriesno date       date
------ ---- ---------- --------- ---------
   352 SU              1 25-MAR-93
   387 LO              1 01-JUN-94
   387 PR              1 10-JUN-92
   408 PR              1 18-JUN-92
   408 PR              2 01-MAR-94
   455

 6 rows selected.
```

In an LO/PR address hierarchy, the ADDRESS join should return a current local address if available. Otherwise it should return a current permanent address.

Figure 8–23. ADDRESS data for four applicants to test an LO/PR address hierarchy.

information for four individuals who represent these different data configurations. Applicant 455 has no address data; applicant 352 has only a summer address; applicant 408 has permanent addresses but no local address; and applicant 387 has both a local and a permanent address.

Figure 8–24 shows SQL that correctly returns one row for each of the four applicants. Different parts of the SQL solve different problems. These solutions are as follows:

- Applicants without any address data (e.g., applicant 455) and applicants without a local or permanent address (e.g., applicant 352) get included because of the outer joins "and d1.address_id(+) = applicant_id and d1.address_type(+) in ('LO','PR')." The line that reads "and (d1.address_seriesno is null)" prevents these null rows from falling through the rest of the join.
- Applicants with a local address (e.g., applicant 387) get their address row returned in the correlated subquery that begins "d1.address_type = 'LO' and d1.address_seriesno = (select max(d2.address_seriesno) ...."
- Applicants with a permanent address but no local address (e.g., applicant 408) get their permanent address row returned in the series of two correlated subqueries at the end of the SQL. The first correlated subquery says "return the last permanent address." The second correlated subquery says "for anyone who does not have a local address."

Figure 8–25 on page 174 shows an address object based on the hierarchical SQL just developed. Note that it can be used for any combination of addresses: business first and permanent second, billing first and local second, and so on. Occasionally users request hierarchies that require even more than two choices. For anyone interested, try to modify the object in Figure 8–25 to accommodate a three-level hierarchy (e.g., local address first, permanent second, and summer third).

Traversing Joins

The most subtle SQL errors occur when traversing through one table to access data in a second table. By traversing I mean joining to one table solely for the purpose of joining to a second table. And the longer the traverse, the greater the likelihood of error; passing through one intermediary table entails less risk than passing through two intermediary tables.

Consider the simple situation shown in Figure 8–26. There are three tables A, B, and C; table A contains information on students, table B on

```
SQL> select applicant_id, address_type, address_seriesno, address_begindate,
            address_enddate
     from
            address d1,
            applicant
     where
            applicant_term = '199509'
                   and applicant_level = 'UG'
                   and applicant_college = 'AS'
                   and applicant_id in (352, 387, 408, 455)
            and d1.address_id(+) = applicant_id
                   and d1.address_type(+) in ('LO','PR')
                   and
                   (
                   (d1.address_seriesno is null)
                   or
                   (d1.address_type = 'LO'
                   and d1.address_seriesno =
                   (select max(d2.address_seriesno)
                   from address d2
                   where d2.address_id = d1.address_id
                           and d2.address_type = d1.address_type))
                   or
                   (d1.address_type = 'PR'
                   and d1.address_seriesno =
                   (select max(d3.address_seriesno)
                   from address d3
                   where d3.address_id = d1.address_id
                           and d3.address_type = d1.address_type)
                   and not exists
                   (select 'x'
                   from address d4
                   where d4.address_id = d1.address_id
                   and d4.address_type = 'LO'))
                   )
     /
ENTER to continue ...
       addr    address begin     end
    id type   seriesno date      date
------ ---- ---------- --------- ---------
   352
   387 LO            1 01-JUN-94
   408 PR            2 01-MAR-94
   455
```

Sections of the query perform specific functions:

1. Creates null rows if no LO or PR addresses exist.
2. Retains the null rows created in the outer joins.
3. Returns the latest LO address.
4. Returns the latest PR address IF ...
5. ... no LO address exists.

All four applicants appear in the report.

Figure 8–24. A join to the ADDRESS table accessing addresses in a hierarchy.

OBJECT
```
      and d1.address_id(+) = <driving_table>_id
            and d1.address_type(+) in ('LO','PR')
            and
            (
            (d1.address_seriesno is null)
            or
            (d1.address_type = '<address_type1>'
            and d1.address_seriesno =
            (select max(d2.address_seriesno)
            from address d2
            where d2.address_id = d1.address_id
                 and d2.address_type = d1.address_type))
            or
            (d1.address_type = '<address_type2>'
            and d1.address_seriesno =
            (select max(d3.address_seriesno)
            from address d3
            where d3.address_id = d1.address_id
                 and d3.address_type = d1.address_type)
            and not exists
            (select 'x'
            from address d4
            where d4.address_id = d1.address_id
                 and d4.address_type = '<address_type1>'))
            )
```

HELP
```
object:         whraddr.obj
date created:   26-oct-1994
author:         glewis
revisions:

Purpose:        Provides access to the ADDRESS table in a hierarchical
                fashion. Returns an address of specified type (e.g., local).
                If this type of address is not available, it returns an
                address of a second specified type (e.g., permanent).

Usage:          1. Need to include the ADDRESS table with an alias of 'd1' in
                the main query (i.e., from address d1, ...)
                2. <driving_table>: replace with name of table driving the
                query (e.g., APPLICANT)
                3. <address_type1>: replace with code for type of address
                returned first if available.
                4. <address_type2>: replace with code for type of address
                returned if <address_type1> is unavailable.

Hints:          Written so 1 row returned for each person in the population,
                regardless of whether they have any addresses of the
                specified types.
```

Figure 8–25. Class 2u *where* object and help file accessing the ADDRESS table in a hierarchy.

their academic advisors, and table C on the academic departments of each advisor (e.g., Art, Biology, etc.). Table A just contains an I.D. number and last name of the student. Table B contains the student I.D. and the I.D. of the advisor. If a student has two academic advisors, two rows appear in table

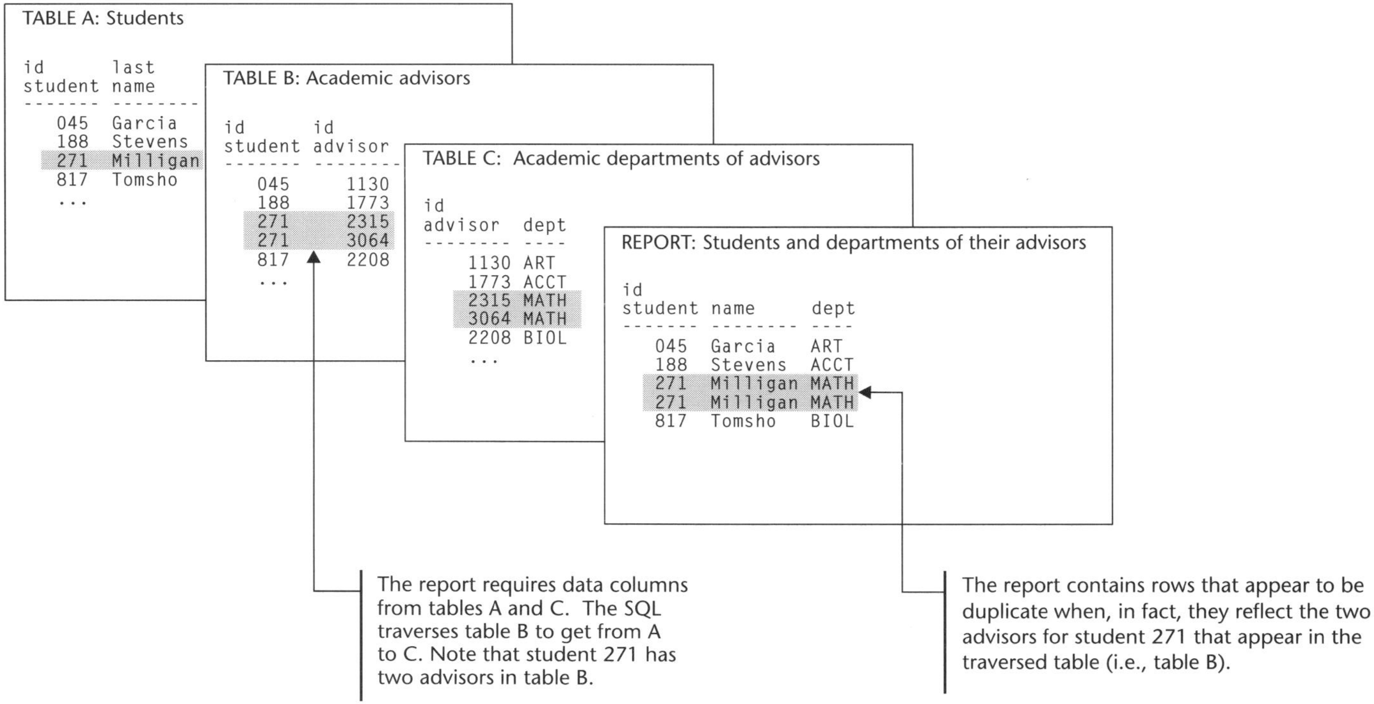

Figure 8–26. Illustration of problems that can occur when traversing one table to access a second table.

B for that student. Table C contains the I.D. of the academic advisor and the code of his or her academic department.

Suppose a user requests a report showing the student I.D., last name, and the advisor's department. In other words, she wants report columns that appear only in tables A and C. Tables A and C, however, are related indirectly through table B. You'll need to join table A to table B and then join table B to table C. Figure 8–26 shows the results for a few data rows. Note that the student with I.D. 271 appears in the report twice, with what appears to be completely duplicate information. Nothing on the report makes the user aware that table B was traversed to yield the results; table B is completely transparent in the report.

This example is somewhat contrived. Most users in a college would realize that a student might have more than one advisor and then deduce from this that the duplicate information in Figure 8–26 is not really duplicate; it's rather reporting information for two different advisors of the same student. But other queries may not be this apparent, particularly if the query was constructed using a graphical query tool. Many of these tools shield the user from making table joins by incorporating an auto-join feature. For two tables related indirectly, the query tool chooses the best path between the tables. The user may be completely unaware that one or more intermediary tables get traversed. These tables are truly transparent, befuddling users with reports that appear to contain inconsistencies.

Let's examine a specific example. Suppose you're asked to provide a listing of applicants to the college of Arts & Sciences for Fall 1995, showing the applicant's phone number at his or her permanent address. This sounds fairly simple; what could be more basic than a name, address, and phone report?

Let's begin as always, by consulting the various reporting tools available. The database schematic (Figure A–1 in Appendix A) shows the PHONE table related to the ADDRESS table through the foreign key composed of phone_address_type and phone_address_seriesno. The table of indexes (Table A–2) shows that an I.D. number, type of phone, and a seriesno uniquely determine a row in the PHONE table. Apparently people may have one or more phones of a certain type; the last one of each type can be found by selecting the maximum phone_seriesno. The data dictionary for PHONE shows that phone_address_type and phone_address_seriesno— the foreign keys providing the link to the ADDRESS table—may be null. This means it's possible to have phone information without corresponding address information. For example, cellular car phones don't have an associated address. Accommodating this type of phone in the database design, however, means it's also possible to have a residential phone without the corresponding permanent address.

ORACLE version 7 provides a mechanism for enforcing something called *referential integrity* in the database. Referential integrity ensures that meaningful relationships exist between the primary and foreign keys in tables. Consider the PHONE table again. It includes the two foreign keys called phone_address_type and phone_address_seriesno. It doesn't make sense to have a phone_address_type = XX if XX is not a valid address_type. Referential integrity constraints require that foreign keys contain valid information. Valid information means that the data values in the foreign keys must exist as primary keys elsewhere, in this case in the ADDRESS table. It is perfectly acceptable, however, to have null foreign keys. As discussed previously, the PHONE table could have null foreign keys for cellular phones or residential phones where the address is not known. So referential integrity helps eliminate data errors, but still leaves considerable room for various data permutations.

Figure 8–27 on the following page shows ADDRESS and PHONE data for 16 applicants. An applicant could have no known addresses, an address but not a permanent one, one permanent address, or several permanent addresses. The same set of four situations could also exist in the PHONE table. Traversing the ADDRESS table to get to the PHONE table creates 4 * 4 = 16 different data combinations (no known addresses or phones, no known addresses but a residential phone, etc.). The 16 applicants in Figure 8–27 were selected to represent each of these 16 possible combinations of address and phone data. In actual practice you probably wouldn't see this extreme a case. But nevertheless the SQL objects must be robust enough to handle all of the possible data combinations.

ADDRESS

```
ENTER to continue ...
             address
   id type   seriesno
------ ---- ----------
   309 PR            1
   320 PR            1
   323 PR            1
   323 PR            2
   324 LO            1
   351 LO            1
   352
   379
   387 LO            1
   387 PR            1
   408 PR            1
   408 PR            2
   413 LO            1
   455
   459
   460 PR            1
   460 PR            2
   494 PR            1
   494 PR            2
   504 LO            1
   506 PR            1

21 rows selected.
```

PHONE

```
ENTER to continue ...
                                      phone        phone
       phone      phone               address    address
    id type    seriesno status type     seriesno
------ ----- ---------- ------ ------- ----------
   309 LO             1
   320
   323 PR             2        PR               2
   324
   351 PR             1
   352
   379 LO             1
   387 PR             1        PR               1
   408
   413 LO             1        LO               1
   455 PR             1
   459 PR             1
   459 PR             2
   460 LO             1
   494 PR             1        PR               2
   494 PR             2        PR               2
   504 PR             1
   504 PR             2
   506 PR             1        PR               1
   506 PR             2        PR               1

20 rows selected.
```

SUMMARY

```
                  PHONE
ADDRESS      0    1      2      null
-----------------------------------------------
      0    413    351    504    324
      1    309    387    506    320
      2    460    323    494    408
   null    379    455    459    352
```

The 16 applicants each represents a different combination of ADDRESS and PHONE data. For example, applicant 323 has two PR addresses and one phone.

Figure 8–27. ADDRESS and PHONE data for sixteen applicants.

Figure 8–28 shows a logical SQL query accessing PHONE through the ADDRESS table. Note the query started with 16 applicants but ended with only four of them! In fact the join works fine for any applicant with both a permanent address and a phone at the address. But apparently 12, and possibly 14, of the 16 applicants don't have well-behaved data. The

```
SQL> select
        count(*), count(distinct applicant_id)
     from
        phone p1,
        address d1,
        applicant
     where
        applicant_term = '199509'
               and applicant_level = 'UG'
               and applicant_college = 'AS'
               and applicant_id in (309, 320, 323, 324, 351, 352, 379, 387,
                      408, 413, 455, 459, 460, 494, 504, 506)
        and address_id = applicant_id
               and address_type = 'PR'
        and phone_id = applicant_id
               and phone_type = 'PR'
               and phone_address_type = address_type
               and phone_address_seriesno = address_seriesno
     /
ENTER to continue ...
  COUNT(*) COUNT(DISTINCTAPPLICANT_ID)
---------- ---------------------------
         6                           4
```

Only 4 of the 16 applicants made it through the join criteria.

This SQL uses the foreign address key that appears in PHONE (phone_address_type and phone_address_seriesno) to join with the ADDRESS table.

Figure 8–28. Accessing PHONE data by traversing through the ADDRESS table.

standard SQL traversing ADDRESS to access PHONE is riddled with holes; holes that permit individuals with ill-behaved but valid data to fall through the join. We need something better.

It's clear that the SQL must include joins to both the ADDRESS and PHONE tables. Let's discard Figure 8–28 and start by using the *where* object developed previously to access ADDRESS. Figure 8–29 on the following page shows the results. This helped considerably. We started with 16 applicants and carried all 16 through the ADDRESS join using whraddr.obj. Now it's just a matter of adding the join to PHONE.

Figure 8–30 on page 181 provides one solution, returning 16 rows with the correct address and phone information. Outer joins temporarily create null records for anyone without phone data or anyone without a PR phone type. A correlated subquery returns the maximum phone_seriesno in case someone has more than one permanent phone. Figure 8–30 differs from similar objects discussed earlier because of the traverse through the ADDRESS table. This linkage occurs on phone_address_type and

SQL

```
SQL> select
        applicant_id,
        d1.address_type,
        d1.address_seriesno
 from
        address d1,
        applicant
 where
        applicant_term = '199509'
              and applicant_level = 'UG'
              and applicant_college = 'AS'
              and applicant_id in (309, 320, 323, 324, 351, 352, 379, 387,
                     408, 413, 455, 459, 460, 494, 504, 506)
        and d1.address_id(+) = applicant_id
              and d1.address_type(+) = 'PR'
              and nvl(d1.address_seriesno, 1) =
              (select max(nvl(d2.address_seriesno, 1))
              from
                     address d2,
                     person
              where
                     person_id = applicant_id
                     and d2.address_id(+) = person_id
                            and d2.address_type(+) = 'PR')
 order by 1
 /
```

Objects used:
1. popapp.obj
2. whraddr.obj

REPORT

```
ENTER to continue ...
           addr    address
     id type   seriesno
------ ---- ----------
   309 PR            1
   320 PR            1
   323 PR            2
   324
   351
   352
   379
   387 PR            1
   408 PR            2
   413
   455
   459
   460 PR            2
   494 PR            2
   504
   506 PR            1

16 rows selected.
```

Figure 8–29. Using the *where* object whraddr.obj to access addresses of 16 applicants.

phone_address_seriesno. Note in Figure 8–30 the extensive use of the *nvl* function and the symmetry of *nvl* functions required at one point. This structure prevents applicants from falling through the join if they don't have address data or if they don't have phone data linked to addresses. Figure 8–31 on page 182 shows a *where* object and help file providing access to the PHONE table.

SQL

```
SQL> select
       applicant_id, d1.address_type, d1.address_seriesno,
       p1.phone_type, p1.phone_seriesno,
       p1.phone_address_type, p1.phone_address_seriesno
  from
       phone p1, address d1, applicant
  where
       applicant_term = '199509'
            and applicant_level = 'UG'
            and applicant_college = 'AS'
            and applicant_id in (309, 320, 323, 324, 351, 352, 379,
                  387, 408, 413, 455, 459, 460, 494, 504, 506)
       and d1.address_id(+) = applicant_id
            and d1.address_type(+) = 'PR'
            and nvl(d1.address_seriesno, 1) =
            (select max(nvl(d2.address_seriesno, 1))
            from
                  address d2,
                  person
            where
                  person_id = applicant_id
                  and d2.address_id(+) = person_id
                        and d2.address_type(+) = 'PR')
       and p1.phone_id(+) = applicant_id
            and p1.phone_type(+) = 'PR'
            and nvl(p1.phone_address_type, 'PR') = 'PR'
            and nvl(p1.phone_address_seriesno, nvl(d1.address_seriesno, 99)) =
                  nvl(d1.address_seriesno, nvl(p1.phone_address_seriesno, 99))
            and nvl(p1.phone_seriesno, 99) =
            (select max(nvl(p2.phone_seriesno, 99))
            from
                  phone p2, person
            where person_id = applicant_id
                  and p2.phone_id(+) = person_id
                  and p2.phone_type(+) = 'PR')
  order by 1
  /
```

REPORT

```
ENTER to continue ...
                                                       phone     phone
       addr   address phone      phone        address   address
    id type  seriesno type    seriesno status type     seriesno
------ ---- ---------- ----- ---------- ------ ------- ----------
   309 PR           1
   320 PR           1
   323 PR           2 PR             1        PR               2
   324
   351                PR             1
   352
   379
   387 PR           1 PR             1        PR               1
   408 PR           2
   413
   455                PR             1
   459                PR             2
   460 PR           2
   494 PR           2 PR             2        PR               2
   504                PR             2
   506 PR           1 PR             2        PR               1

16 rows selected.
```

Note the symmetrical nature of this SQL that retains rows when either phone_address_seriesno or address_seriesno is null.

Figure 8–30. Adding a class 2u join to access PHONE data of the 16 applicants.

HELP

```
object:        whrphon.obj
date created:  27-oct-1994
author:        glewis
revisions:

Purpose:       Provides access to the PHONE table for the most
               recent phone of a specified type and associated
               with an address of a specified type.

Usage:         1. Must be used with the object whraddr.obj to
               access the ADDRESS table.  Include ADDRESS with
               alias d1 in the from clause.
               2. <driving_table>: replace with name of table
               driving the query (e.g., APPLICANT).
               3. <phone_type>: replace with code for the type
               of phone (e.g., 'PR').
               4. <phone_address>: replace with code for the
               address (e.g., 'PR' for permanent).

Hints:         Written so 1 row returned for each person in the
               population, regardless of whether they have any
               phones of the specified type.
```

OBJECT

```
  and p1.phone_id(+) = <driving_table>_id
        and p1.phone_type(+) = '<phone_type>'
        and nvl(p1.phone_address_type, '<phone_address_type>') =
               '<phone_address_type>'
        and nvl(p1.phone_address_seriesno, nvl(d1.address_seriesno, 99)) =
               nvl(d1.address_seriesno, nvl(p1.phone_address_seriesno, 99))
        and nvl(p1.phone_seriesno, 99) =
        (select max(nvl(p2.phone_seriesno, 99))
        from
               phone p2,
               person
        where person_id = <driving_table>_id
               and p2.phone_id(+) = person_id
               and p2.phone_type(+) = '<phone_type>')
```

Figure 8–31. Class 2u *where* object and help file accessing the PHONE table.

Class 2m Objects: Relaxing Singularity

Class 1 *where* objects modify populations. Class 2u *where* objects provide access to data about the population. Both classes adhere rigorously to the property of population singularity. Class 2m *where* objects operate differently. They relax the singularity restriction. Like class 2u objects they also provide access to data about the population, but they return one or more rows per population item. If a population has 100 items, the report should show at least 100 rows (one for each) but may show many more.

Consider applicants and their addresses. A user might want to receive a roster that lists all permanent addresses for each applicant; if two addresses exist then two should appear on the report. Figure 8–32 on the following page shows a report for several applicants. Note that four applicants have multiple permanent addresses. The SQL for this report is straightforward. Outer joins prevent applicants from falling through the join, but no correlated subquery is necessary to return only the last known address. Figure 8–33 on page 185 shows a where object and help file derived from this SQL.

Let's do an example in a table we've not yet used. The admissions office at Komenda tracks the documents required of applicants because an application is not considered complete and ready for review until all supporting documents are received. In the database this tracking occurs in the DOCUMENT table. The database schematic shows the DOCUMENT and APPLICANT tables related through I.D., term, and seriesno. An applicant may have one, many, or no items in the DOCUMENT table. The data columns document_id, document_applicant_term, document_applicant_seriesno, and document_code make up the unique index.

Figure 8–34 on page 186 shows that the 700 applicants to the undergraduate Arts & Sciences college for Fall 1995 submitted a total of 2808 documents. The outer joins ensure that an applicant without any documents does not fall through the join. But the join makes no attempt to preserve population singularity. If an applicant has five rows in the DOCUMENT table, he or she will appear five times in the report. Figure 8–35 on page 186 shows a class 2m *where* object accessing the DOCUMENT table.

This class of *where* objects raises an issue of semantics. What really is the population in a report of applicants and their admissions documents? Is it a population of applicants or a population of applicants' documents? If 100 applicants have 1000 total documents, is the population size 100 or 1000? Based on the previous chapter about *population* objects, you could strongly argue the case for 1000. A population gets defined when no more

SQL

```
SQL> select
        applicant_id,
        d1.address_type,
        d1.address_seriesno,
        d1.address_city,
        d1.address_state
from
        address d1,
        applicant
where
        applicant_term = '199509'
                and applicant_level = 'UG'
                and applicant_college = 'AS'
                and applicant_id in (309, 320, 323, 324, 351, 352, 379,
                    387, 408, 413, 455, 459, 460, 494, 504, 506)
        and d1.address_id(+) = applicant_id
                and d1.address_type(+) = 'PR'
order by 1
/
```

REPORT

```
ENTER to continue ...
       addr     address
    id type    seriesno city              state
------ ---- ---------- ----------------- -----
   309 PR             1 San Diego         CA
   320 PR             1 Coral Gables      FL
   323 PR             1 Philadelphia      PA
   323 PR             2 Glen Falls        NY
   324
   351
   352
   379
   387 PR             1 Troy              NY
   408 PR             1 Newton            MA
   408 PR             2 Newton            MA
   413
   455
   459
   460 PR             1 Houston           TX
   460 PR             2 Glen Falls        NY
   494 PR             1 Los Angeles       CA
   494 PR             2 Glen Falls        NY
   504
   506 PR             1 Katy              TX

20 rows selected.
```

The join creates null rows for applicants without permanent addresses, but makes no attempt to return only one row by selecting the maximum address_seriesno. Note in the report that several applicants have two permanent addresses.

Figure 8–32. A class 2m join to the ADDRESS table.

```
HELP
object:          whraddrm.obj
date created:    07-nov-1994
author:          glewis
revisions:

Purpose:         Provides access to the ADDRESS table for all addresses
                 of a specified type.

Usage:           1. Need to include the ADDRESS table with an alias
                 of 'dl' in the main query (i.e., from address dl, ...)
                 2. <driving_table>: replace with name of table driving
                 the query (e.g., APPLICANT)
                 3. <address_type>: replace with code for type of
                 address (e.g., 'PR')

Hints:           Written so 1 or more rows returned for each person in
                 the population, regardless of whether they have any
                 addresses of the specified type.
```

```
OBJECT
    and dl.address_id(+) = <driving_table>_id
            and dl.address_type(+) = '<address_type>'
```

Figure 8–33. Class 2m *where* object and help file accessing the ADDRESS table.

items should fall through or multiply through joins. With class 2m *where* objects, however, I prefer to back off this strict interpretation of populations. When users request a report of applicants and their admissions documents, they think of the report population as applicants rather than documents. To them the population size is 100 and not 1000. I'd rather let popular usage drive population definitions even if I as a query writer may think of the population differently.

Extract Data and Graphical Query Tools

This chapter hammers home the lesson that table joins can be quite complex. Some of that complexity derives from the various uses that joins serve. They can qualify populations as adjectives do nouns, reducing the population but maintaining its singularity. They can provide access to data columns required in the report, while maintaining the population singularity. Or they can relax population singularity entirely. How two tables get joined depends on the intent of the report.

Even more ominously, how two tables get joined also depends on the data itself. Joins that work with well-behaved data may not work with valid but ill-behaved data. It's this data, the 1 percent or 2 percent, that requires

The outer joins prevent any applicant without DOCUMENT data for a specified term from falling through the report.

REPORT

```
SQL> select count(*), count(distinct applicant_id)
     from
            document,
            applicant
     where
            applicant_term = '199509'
                and applicant_level = 'UG'
                and applicant_college = 'AS'
            and document_id(+) = applicant_id
                and document_applicant_term(+) = applicant_term
                and document_applicant_seriesno(+) = applicant_seriesno
     /
ENTER to continue ...
  COUNT(*) COUNT(DISTINCTAPPLICANT_ID)
---------- ---------------------------
      2808                         700
```

The report includes 700 applicants who have a total of 2808 items in the DOCUMENT table.

Figure 8–34. A class 2m join to the DOCUMENT table.

HELP

```
object:        whrdcmnt.obj
date created:  24-oct-1994
author:        glewis
revisions:

Purpose:       Provides access to the DOCUMENT table.

Usage:         Requires that the APPLICANT and DOCUMENT
               tables appear in the main query.

Hints:         none
```

OBJECT

```
    and document_id(+) = applicant_id
        and document_applicant_term(+) = applicant_term
        and document_applicant_seriesno(+) = applicant_seriesno
```

Figure 8–35. Class 2m *where* object and help file accessing the DOCUMENT table.

extra care and work. If 98 percent report accuracy is acceptable, then your SQL job is much easier. But if users flinch when they find people falling through reports, you need to spend time on the joins to ensure this doesn't happen.

These two factors—report intent and data dependence—make it difficult to reduce table joins to an algorithm that works well in all situations. Many graphical query tools attempt to do this, however, in an effort to hide joins from users. These tools employ a variety of mechanisms to automatically join tables. I've not seen a tool that makes these automatic joins context-sensitive depending on report intent or data configurations. To do so would require an expert system built into the query tool. Rather, the tools rely heavily on database schematics, primary keys, and foreign keys to link tables. As this chapter demonstrates, database schematics and keys provide a starting point only. Graphical query tools are just not presently equipped to handle the complexity in moderate or large relational databases. They work best with extracted data tables that have been denormalized to make queries easy. Joins become less an issue with such tables and many graphical query tools handle this type of data nicely. Objects, on the other hand, eliminate or reduce the need to create data redundancy with extracted tables.

Table 8–1 provides a running inventory of the *population* and *where* objects developed for the simulated Komenda database.

Table 8–1. Inventory of SQL objects.

Class	Name	Purpose
POPULATION	popacapp	Applicants accepted for admissions for a specified term, level, and college
	popapp	Applicants for admissions for a specified term, level, college
	popenrl	Accepted applicants for a specified term, level, and college who are expected to enroll
	poprecr	Recruits for a specified term and level
WHERE 1	whrintl	Defines the term "international" and modifies a population so only internationals are included
	whrmnrty	Defines the term "minority" and modifies a population so only individuals of color are included

(Continued)

Table 8–1. Inventory of SQL objects.

Class	Name	Purpose
WHERE 2u	whraddr	Provides access to the ADDRESS table for the most recent address of a specified type
	whradhi	Provides access to the ADDRESS table in a hierarchical fashion. Returns an address of a specified type (e.g., local). If this type of address is not available, it returns an address of a second specified type (e.g., permanent)
	whrname	Provides access to the NAME table for the most recent name
	whrpersn	Provides access to the PERSON table
	whrphon	Provides access to the PHONE table for the most recent phone of a specified type and associated with an address of a specified type
	whrtest	Provides access to the TEST table for the highest test score of a specified type
WHERE 2m	whraddrm	Provides access to the ADDRESS table for all addresses of a specified type
	whrdcmnt	Provides access to all documents in the DOCUMENT table for a population of applicants

Chapter 9

Building *Select* Objects

Users frequently request reports where data columns must be reformulated in some fashion. For example, the report may require that numeric data appear in a calculation, that character data appear as a longer concatenated string, or that dates appear with special formatting. These revised data columns all appear in the *select* clause of the SQL ***select*** command; hence the name *select* objects when the reformulation is stored for later reuse.

Select objects are best created when one or more conditions occur:

- The object will be used often.
- The object contains institutional definitions that should be standardized across offices.
- The object utilizes codes or formats that are difficult to remember.
- The logic in the object is complex or unusually lengthy.

In this chapter we'll build several *select* objects using different types of data. *Select* objects often use the functions and special formatting discussed in Chapter 4 and Appendix C; but by comparison to *population* and *where* objects, *select* objects are simple. Enjoy their variety. Note too that the figures in this chapter start to assemble previously constructed objects into completed SQL programs. When this happens, writing ad hoc queries becomes much easier; you're just manipulating objects, not translating into SQL.

Character Data

Sort Name

Reports that list people's names often get sorted alphabetically by last name, first name, and then middle name. It's often convenient to create a single column by concatenating last, first, and middle names and then ordering the report by this constructed data column. This also saves space on the report. Three columns for last, first, and middle names may require 20, 15, and 15 spaces respectively, while a single sort name column may require only 30 characters.

Previous chapters introduced and used a sort name formed by concatenating last, first, and middle names. Figure 9–1 shows a sort name object and a report based on the object.

Initialed Name

For some reports it may be sufficient to display a person's last name and the initials of the first and middle names. Here's the task: construct a data column by concatenating the last name with the first character of the first name and the first character of the middle name, making sure that the initials appear as capital letters and that a space appears before the last name.

The chapter on *population* objects discussed the mapping of a verbal or written query request into SQL defining the report population. Constructing *select* objects requires much the same mapping, but is generally easier because words get mapped into SQL operators, functions, and formats. The key elements of the present assignment include the words "first character," "initials appear as capitals," and "concatenating." These map directly into the substring function *substr*, the initial capital function *initcap* or the uppercase function *upper*, and the concatenation operator.

Figure 9–2 on page 192 shows a report using a constructed data column of initialed names. It also shows the object and the help file corresponding to this object. The object might look somewhat formidable at first, but let's break it into elements. These elements fit together in a very logical fashion. For example, initcap(name_first) ensures that the first letter in name_first is uppercase. When this is placed within the *substr* function as substr(initcap(name_first),1,1), the value returned is just the first (capitalized) letter of name_first. A similar procedure capitalizes and returns the first character of the middle name. These are then concatenated to the last name. Simple.

REPORT

```
SQL> select
  2       recruit_id,
  3       n1.name_last||', '||n1.name_first||' '||n1.name_middle "sort_name"   [1]
  4  from
  5       name n1,
  6       recruit
  7  where
  8  [2] recruit_term = '199509'
  9            and recruit_level = 'UG'
 10      and n1.name_id = recruit_id
 11            and n1.name_seriesno =
 12  [3]       (select max(n2.name_seriesno)
 13            from name n2
 14            where n2.name_id = n1.name_id)
 15  order by 2
 16  /
ENTER to continue ...
    id sort_name
------ ------------------------
  2574 Abraham, Alicia
  2215 Abraham, Shannon V.
  1910 Acosta, Monica Eduarda
  3163 Adams, Amy
  3534 Adams, Angela
  ...
```

Objects used:
1. selsname.obj
2. poprecr.obj
3. whrname.obj

HELP

```
object:        selsname.obj
date created:  13-nov-1994
author:        glewis
revisions:

Purpose:       Creates a name as name_last, name_first, and name_middle.
               This name is useful in listings sorted by name.

Usage:         1. Use with the where object whrname.obj.
               2. Unless "sort_name" is the last data column in the select
               clause, place a comma at the end of the object.

Hints:         none
```

OBJECT

```
     n1.name_last||', '||n1.name_first||' '||n1.name_middle "sort_name"
```

Figure 9–1. *Select* object and report for a sort name.

REPORT

```
SQL> column first format a12
SQL> column middle format a12
SQL> column last format a15
SQL> select
  2     applicant_id,
  3     n1.name_first "first",
  4     n1.name_middle "middle",
  5     n1.name_last "last",
  6     substr(initcap(n1.name_first),1,1)||
  7           substr(initcap(n1.name_middle),1,1)
  8           ||' '||n1.name_last     "initials_name"      [1]
  9  from
 10     name n1,
 11     applicant
 12  where
 13     applicant_term = '199509'
 14 [2]       and applicant_level = 'UG'
 15           and applicant_college = 'AS'
 16     and n1.name_id = applicant_id
 17 [3]       and n1.name_seriesno =
 18           (select max(n2.name_seriesno)
 19           from name n2
 20           where n2.name_id = n1.name_id)
 21  /
ENTER to continue ...
    id first        middle       last            initials_name
------ ------------ ------------ --------------- ---------------
    44 Angela                    McCarthy        A McCarthy
    77 Tammy                     Chen            T Chen
    97 Stephen      V.           Chen            SV Chen
   114 Danielle                  Price           D Price
   133 Wai                       Kuang           W Kuang
   135 Omar         Andre        Campbell        OA Campbell
   145 Ryan                      Blake           R Blake
   151 Ryan         P.           Hill            RP Hill
   ...
```

Objects used:
1. selinname.obj
2. popapp.obj
3. whrname.obj

HELP

```
object:        selinname.obj
date created:  13-nov-1994
author:        glewis
revisions:

Purpose:       Creates a name using the initials of the
               first and middle names and concatenating
               these to name_last.
Usage:         1. Use with the where object whrname.obj.
               2. Unless "initials_name" is the last data
               column in the select clause, place a comma
               at the end of the object.

Hints:         none
```

OBJECT

```
    substr(initcap(n1.name_first),1,1)||
          substr(initcap(n1.name_middle),1,1)
          ||' '||n1.name_last "initials_name"
```

Figure 9–2. *Select* object and report for an initialed name.

This object could be extended in several ways. Suppose you wanted periods after the first and middle initials. This becomes a bit trickier because null values are possible for either first or middle names. It's unattractive to display a name as "R.. Price" or ".A. Pfeiffer," so you must find some way to concatenate a period (.) only when the first or middle name is not null. Give it some thought or come back to the question after the next section.

City, State, Zip, and Nation

Addresses commonly appear in roster reports when people or organizations form the report population. It's possible to display individual data columns for city, state, zip code, and nation, but often it's more convenient and saves report space to display a single concatenated column.

You could concatenate the data columns as:

```
address_city||', '||address_state||' '||address_zip||
' '||address_nation
```

This gets the job done for normal situations where a complete address exists. But what happens if you use one of the class 2u *where* objects that returns a row even if the address is null? In this situation the concatenated string shown above displays only a comma (the one between the city and state). Another problem occurs when address_city is unknown. In this case the constructed string begins with a comma. For a quick and dirty report neither situation creates a problem, but if you're trying to present a polished report you'll want to guard against the possible presence of missing data.

What's needed is an "if ... then ... else" structure. If the address is null, don't print anything; if the city is missing, just print state, zip, and nation; otherwise print the concatenated string shown above. Luckily the *decode* function provides this structure.

Recall from Chapter 4 and Appendix C that *decode* compares two values and returns a third value. It's general form is decode(value, comparison1, result1, comparison2, result2, ..., alternative). It works by comparing "value" to "comparison1" and returning "result1" if they match. If they don't match it then compares "value" with "comparison2" and returns "result2" if a match occurs. This process continues until all the comparison values are evaluated. If no matches occur, the decode function returns the "alternative" value if one is provided. As an "if ... then ... else" structure the *decode* function translates to "if 'value' = 'comparison' then 'result' else 'alternative.' "

The *decode* function finds considerable use in *select* objects. There is only one drawback - decodes can quickly become complex. When decodes get nested within each other, the syntax becomes confusing. Maintaining complex decodes, particularly if they were constructed by someone else, can present problems. The complexity can be minimized somewhat if you create structure in the *decode*, where the structure helps decipher what's occurring.

But back to the question at hand. You want a city, state, zip, and nation object that is robust enough to handle missing address data. Let's first work out the solution in pseudo-SQL. Let "cszn" represent the concatenated string of city, state, zip, and nation; also let "szn" represent the concatenated string of state, zip, and nation. We can state the problem as follows: if cszn is null, then return a null; else if city is null, return szn; else return cszn. In pseudo-SQL the corresponding *decode* is decode(cszn, null, null, decode(city, null, szn, cszn)). This says that if cszn is null, then return a null. Otherwise do the alternative, which evaluates city. If city is null, return szn. Otherwise do the alternative, which returns the full cszn string.

Figure 9–3 shows a report using a constructed data column concatenating city, state, zip, and nation. It also shows the object and corresponding help file. Note that the object uses aliases that coordinate with the aliases used in class 2u *where* objects. This facilitates assembly of objects into completed SQL.

The *decode* in Figure 9–3 looks messy, but examine it closely element by element and notice how the structure of the *decode* corresponds to the pseudo-SQL just discussed. When you use *decode*, I urge you to incorporate structure so that when you read the SQL at a later time you'll understand it better. Of course, if you save the *decode* as an object, you'll quickly become accustomed to manipulating the object. When this happens, the complexity in an object becomes transparent; you only deal with the object and not its contents.

Numeric Data

Objects constructed from numeric data columns use arithmetic operators and functions. They can be simple or complex, involve one or many data columns, and require straightforward calculations or convoluted algorithms. Numeric *select* objects are limited only by the needs of the query writer. Here we'll look at two such objects that provide only a flavor of what's possible.

Rank in Class

In a college admissions office, rank in the high school graduating class provides one measure of academic performance. An applicant's high school

The nested decodes control what happens if missing data exists (e.g., ensuring that a leading comma doesn't get printed if the address_city is missing).

Objects used:
1. selsname.obj
2. selcszn.obj
3. popapp.obj
4. whrname.obj
5. whraddr.obj

REPORT

```
SQL> select applicant_id "id"
        n1.name_last||', '||n1.name_first||' '||n1.name_middle "sort_name",      [1]
        d1.address_city "city",
        d1.address_state "st",
        d1.address_zip "zip",
        d1.address_nation "natn",
        decode(d1.address_city||d1.address_state||d1.address_zip||d1.address_nation,   [2]
              null, null,
              decode(d1.address_city,
                     null, d1.address_state||' '||d1.address_zip||' '||
                            d1.address_nation,
                     d1.address_city||', '||d1.address_state||' '||
                            d1.address_zip||' '||d1.address_nation)) "cszn"
from address d1, name n1, applicant
where    applicant_term = '199509'
[3]           and applicant_level = 'UG'
              and applicant_college = 'AS'
        and n1.name_id = applicant_id
              and n1.name_seriesno =
              (select max(n2.name_seriesno)
[4]            from name n2
              where n2.name_id = n1.name_id)
        and d1.address_id(+) = applicant_id
              and d1.address_type(+) = 'PR'
              and nvl(d1.address_seriesno, 1) =
              (select max(nvl(d2.address_seriesno, 1))
              from
[5]                   address d2,
                     person
              where
                     person_id = applicant_id
                     and d2.address_id(+) = person_id
                         and d2.address_type(+) = 'PR');
ENTER to continue ...
   id sort_name              city            st zip   natn cszn
----- -------------------- --------------- -- ----- ---- ----------
   44 McCarthy, Angela     Brooklyn        NY 10467      Brooklyn, NY 10467
   77 Chen, Tammy          Salem           NH 03079      Salem, NH 03079
   97 Chen, Stephen V.                     MA            MA
  114 Price, Danielle      Stamford        CT 06902      Stamford, CT 06902
  133 Kuang, Wai           Princeton       NJ 08540      Princeton, NJ 08540
```

HELP

```
object:        selcszn.obj
date created:  13-nov-1994
author:        glewis
revisions:

Purpose:       Creates a single display column by concatenating
               address_city,address_state, address_zip, and
               address_nation.

Usage:         1. Use with one of the class 2u or 2m where
               objects that access the ADDRESS table:
               whraddr.obj, whradhi.obj,or whraddrm.obj.
               2. Unless "cszn" is the last data column in the
               select clause, place a comma at the end of the object.

Hints:         none
```

OBJECT

```
decode(d1.address_city||d1.address_state||d1.address_zip||
d1.address_nation, null, null,
     decode(d1.address_city,
          null, d1.address_state||' '||d1.address_zip||' '||
                d1.address_nation,
          d1.address_city||', '||d1.address_state||' '||
                d1.address_zip||' '||d1.address_nation)) "cszn"
```

Figure 9–3. *Select* object and report for a city, state, zip, and nation.

transcripts generally provide high school rank as a raw value. That is, the rank might be 153 out of a class of 976. To make comparisons of high school rank easier, the raw values normally get converted into percentages. An applicant ranking 153 in a class of 976 would be in the sixteenth percentile.

Here's the task. The ACADEMIC table contains raw rank as academic_rankclass and class size as academic_sizeclass. Construct a display column of percent rank in class with numbers ranging between 0 percent and 100 percent rounded to the nearest integer (no decimals). Since division by zero produces an error, make the object robust enough to handle situations where academic_sizeclass might (inappropriately) be zero.

Figure 9–4 shows one solution. Let's take it apart element by element. The solution first uses the *sign* function to check academic_sizeclass. If the value is zero, the *sign* returns a -1 since (academic_sizeclass - 0.1) is negative. A value of -1 does not occur in the *decode* so no action is taken. If academic_sizeclass is a valid integer, *sign* returns a +1 and the calculation occurs. Rank is divided by class size and this ratio multiplied by 100 to convert it to a scale ranging from 0 to 100. The calculation is then rounded to zero decimal places (i.e., to a whole number). Figure 9–4 also shows the object and associated help file.

Note in Figure 9–4 that it's unnecessary to deal specifically with missing data. The ratio of rank to class size is not computed if either academic_rankclass or academic_sizeclass is null. Other solutions also exist for checking if academic_sizeclass is zero. Try to devise an object based on the *decode* function.

Combined SAT Scores

Many college admissions offices scrutinize an applicant's standardized test scores, believing that tests like the SAT measure general aptitude for college-level work. The SAT test consists of two parts, a math score and a verbal score. These test scores often get added together to create a combined SAT score that provides a single aptitude measure.

Here's the task. The TEST table contains test scores in the data column test_score. Use a class 2u *where* object to return the highest SAT math score and the highest SAT verbal score. Then construct a combined SAT score as the sum of the math and verbal scores.

The object in this case is trivial; in pseudo-SQL it's just (SAT math + SAT verbal). The only trick is that you must access the TEST table once to return the high SAT math score and then access it again to return the high SAT verbal score. Figure 9–5 shows one solution using the *where* object whrtest.obj twice in the same report. Table aliases that appear in the object

REPORT

```
SQL> select
        applicant_id,
        n1.name_last||', '||n1.name_first||' '||n1.name_middle "sort_name",
        academic_instcode,
        academic_rankclass,
        academic_sizeclass,
        decode(sign(academic_sizeclass - 0.1), 1,
              round((academic_rankclass/academic_sizeclass)*100, 0)) "pctrank"
    from
        academic,
        name n1,
        applicant
    where
        applicant_term = '199509'
              and applicant_level = 'UG'
              and applicant_college = 'AS'
        and n1.name_id = applicant_id
              and n1.name_seriesno =
              (select max(n2.name_seriesno)
              from name n2
              where n2.name_id = n1.name_id)
     and academic_id = applicant_id
    /
ENTER to continue ...
                                   inst   rank   size    pct
    id sort_name                   code   class  class
------ ------------------------- ------ ------ ------
   379 Martin, Emily               3434
   387 Williams, Stephanie D.      335[illegible]
   408 Campbell, Cindy C.
   455 Norris, Karen               [illegible]   33      0
   690 Baker, Bri[illegible]       0304
   693 Ivan[illegible]             0709    304   1170     26
   70[illegible]            [illegible]a A.     3433
       [illegible]ebecca           2219
       [illegible]illiams, Stephen R.  0085
  [illegible]238 Nelson, Adam L.   3004     99    582     17
   ...
```

1

2

3

4

If academic_sizeclass is zero, the sign(academic_sizeclass - 0.1) = -1 and no percent rank gets computed. This prevents an error when trying to divide by zero.

Objects used:
1. sel[illegible]
[illegible].obj
[illegible]. popapp.obj
4. whrname.obj

HELP

```
object:         selprank.obj
date created:   13-nov-1994
author:         glewis
revisions:

Purpose:        Computes a person's rank in high school based on class
                size and class rank.

Usage:          1. Use with a class 2u or class 2m object that accesses
                the ACADEMIC table.
                2. Unless "pctrank" is the last data column in the select
                clause, place a comma at the end of the object.

Hints:          none
```

OBJECT

```
decode(sign(academic_sizeclass - 0.1), 1,
      round((academic_rankclass/academic_sizeclass)*100, 0)) "pctrank"
```

Figure 9–4. *Select* object and report for a computed percentile rank in high school class.

must be changed the second time the object gets used, but other than this the report requires only simple assembly of existing objects. Figure 9–5 also shows a combined SAT object and help file.

Dates

Reformulation of dates provides another source of *select* objects ranging from the simple to the esoteric. On the simple end are objects that change the standard DD-MON-YY format into a preferred format. At the other extreme are objects that require complicated date arithmetic. This section examines three objects that use fairly simple arithmetic calculations with dates.

Age

A person's age can be computed based on knowledge of his or her birthdate. You need only calculate the number of years between today's date and the birthdate. Common convention says that you're one age until your next birthdate; that is, you're 24 years old until your 25th birthdate.

Figure 9–6 on page 200 shows a report that calculates the ages of applicants based on their birthdate and the date the report was run (i.e., the sysdate). The computation uses the *months_between* function to determine the months that separate a person's birthdate and the sysdate. This value is divided by 12 to convert months into years. Note that the *floor* function is also used; *floor*(n) returns the largest integer less than or equal to n. This equates nicely with the convention of rounding ages down no matter how close a person's next birthday might be. Figure 9–6 also shows this age computation as an object.

Reminder Date 1

Receipt of an admissions application sets off a chain reaction of events whose sense of urgency depends on the amount of time available for receiving all supporting documentation so that the application can be read, evaluated, and an admissions decision made. Under these circumstances it's helpful to include deadline dates in reports; that is, dates that show when various events should occur.

Here's the task. Suppose that each Monday the admissions office runs a roster of applicants and wants to show a due date for receipt of high school transcripts, recommendations, and other supporting documentation. They set the due date as the Monday that follows one month after the date the application was received. Your job is to construct the due date.

REPORT

```
SQL> select
  2        applicant_id,
  3        t1.test_score "satm",
  4        t3.test_score "satv",
  5        (t1.test_score + t3.test_score) "satc"
  6  from
  7        test t3,
  8        test t1,
  9        applicant
 10  where
 11        applicant_term = '199509'
 12              and applicant_level = 'UG'
 13              and applicant_college = 'AS'
 14        and t1.test_id(+) = applicant_id
 15              and t1.test_type(+) = 'SATM'
 16              and to_char(nvl(t1.test_score,800
 17                    to_char(nvl(t1.test_date,'
 18                    (select max(to_char(nvl(t2
 19                          to_char(nvl(t2.test
 20                    from
 21                          test t2,
 22                          person
 23                    where person_id = applicant_id
 24                          and t2.test_id(+) = person_id
 25                          and t2.test_type(+) = 'SATM')
 26        and t3.test_id(+) = applicant_id
 27              and t3.test_type(+) = 'SATV'
 28              and to_char(nvl(t3.test_score,800))||
 29                    to_char(nvl(t3.test_date,'01-JAN-50'),'YYYYMMDD') =
 30                    (select max(to_char(nvl(t4.test_score,800))||
 31                          to_char(nvl(t4.test_date,'01-JAN-50'),'YYYYMMDD'))
 32                    from
 33                          test t4,
 34                          person
 35                    where person_id = applicant_id
 36                          and t4.test_id(+) = person_id
 37                          and t4.test_type(+) = 'SATV')
 38  /
ENTER to continue ...
    id        satm        satv   satc
------  ----------  ----------  -----
    44         560         470   1030
    77         560         440   1000
    97         720         480   1200
   114         580         570   1150
```

1 2 3 4

HELP

```
object:         selsatc.obj
date created:   14-nov-1994
author:         glewis
revisions:

Purpose:        Calculates a combined SAT score as the sum of SAT math and
                SAT verbal scores.

Usage:          1. Use with the where object whrtest.obj to access the TEST
                table for SAT math. Include "test t1" in the from clause.
                2. Use the where object whrtest.obj again to access the TEST
                table for SAT verbal, but change all t1 aliases to t3 and
                all t2 aliases to t4.  Include "test t3" in the from clause.
                3. Unless "satc" is the last data column in the
                select clause, place a comma at the end of the object.

Hints:          none
```

OBJECT

```
     (t1.test_score + t3.test_score) "satc"
```

The class 2u object whrtest.obj was used twice, once to access TEST for the SAT math scores and a second time to retrieve the SAT verbal scores.

Objects used:
1. selsatc.obj
2. popapp.obj
3. whrtest.obj (SATM)
4. whrtest.obj (SATV)

Figure 9–5. *Select* object and report for a combined SAT score.

REPORT

```
SQL> column today heading 'report|date'
SQL> select
  2        applicant_id,
  3        n1.name_last||', '||n1.name_first||' '||n1.name_middle "sort_name",   [1]
  4        sysdate "today",
  5        person_birthdate,
  6        floor(months_between(sysdate, person_birthdate)/12) "age"              [2]
  7   from
  8        person,
  9        name n1,
 10        applicant
 11   where
 12  [3]   applicant_term = '199509'
 13           and applicant_level = 'UG'
 14           and applicant_college = 'AS'
 15        and n1.name_id = applicant_id
 16  [4]      and n1.name_seriesno =
 17           (select max(n2.name_seriesno)
 18           from name n2
 19           where n2.name_id = n1.name_id)
 20        and person_id = applicant_id
 21   order by 2
 22   /
ENTER to continue ...

                                      report    birth
    id  sort_name                     date      date       age
------  ----------------------------  --------- ---------  ----
  2574  Abraham, Alicia               15-NOV-94
  3163  Adams, Amy                    15-NOV-94 04-FEB-75    19
  6260  Allen, Adam                   15-NOV-94
  4846  Allen, Kristen                15-NOV-94 21-DEC-75    18
  3655  Amaral, Stephen               15-NOV-94
  3005  Anderson, Christine V         15-NOV-94 30-APR-76    18
  3390  Anderson, Cindy               15-NOV-94 24-JUL-74    20

   ...
```

Objects used:

1. selname.obj
2. selage.obj
3. popapp.obj
4. whrname.obj

HELP

```
object:          selage.obj
date created:    13-nov-1994
author:          glewis
revisions:

Purpose:     Computes a person's age based on sysdate (the report date)
             and the person's birthdate.

Usage:       1. Use with the where object whrpersn.obj.
             2. Unless "age" is the last data column in the select
             clause, place a comma at the end of the object.

Hints:       none
```

OBJECT

```
floor(months_between(sysdate, person_birthdate)/12) "age"
```

Figure 9–6. *Select* object and report for a computed age.

This turns out to be a fairly simple task using available date functions (see Table C-3 in Appendix C). The application date is found in the APPLICANT table as application_appldate. One month after that date is found by using the *add_months* function as add_months (applicant_appldate, 1). The Monday that follows this date is found using the *next_day* function. The general form of *next_day* is next_day(date1, day) = date2. It shows the date for the first day that follows "date1."

Figure 9–7 on the following page shows a report using the constructed due date. It also shows the due date object and associated help file.

Reminder Date 2

Let's make the due date slightly more complicated. Suppose it's now set as exactly 7 weeks following receipt of the application.

Seven weeks is 49 days. You could solve the task if there was some way to add 49 days to a date and return the new date. This involves a bit of a trick using Julien dates. A Julien date is the number of days since 01-January 4712 BC; so the Julien date for today is one less than the Julien date for tomorrow. This provides a mechanism for doing date arithmetic. You just add a specified number of days to a Julien date and then convert it into a traditional date format.

Here's how it works. First we'll convert the applicant_appldate into a Julien date using the *to_char* function as to_char(applicant_appldate, 'J'). The J format creates the Julien date (see Table C-6 in Appendix C). Then we convert this Julien date to a number using the *to_number* function as to_number(to_char(applicant_appldate, 'J')). Then add the 49 days to the number and convert it back to a traditional date as to_date(to_number(to_char(applicant_appldate, 'J')) + 49, 'J'). The second J format informs the *to_date* function that the date appears as a Julien date. The date returned appears in traditional DD-MON-YY format. Ah, the wily ways we must sometimes devise.

Figure 9–8 on page 203 shows a report using this due date. It also shows the due date as an object available for later use.

Recoded Data

At times it's useful to recode data columns for display in reports. This generally occurs in three situations:

REPORT

```
SQL> column date1 heading 'appldate|+1month'
SQL> select
  2          applicant_id,
  3          applicant_appldate,
  4          add_months(applicant_appldate, 1) "date1",
  5          next_day(add_months(applicant_appldate, 1), 'MONDAY') "reminder1"   [1]
  6  from
  7          applicant
  8  where
  9  [2]     applicant_term = '199509'
 10                  and applicant_level = 'UG'
 11                  and applicant_college = 'AS'
 12  /
ENTER to continue ...
                             reminder
      appl       appldate    monday>
   id date       +1month     appl+1mon
------ --------- ---------   ---------
    44 09-JAN-95 09-FEB-95   13-FEB-95
    77 31-OCT-94 30-NOV-94   05-DEC-94
    97 09-FEB-95 09-MAR-95   13-MAR-95
   114 06-DEC-94 06-JAN-95   09-JAN-95
   133 21-OCT-94 21-NOV-94   28-NOV-94
   135 02-DEC-94 02-JAN-95   09-JAN-95
   145 06-OCT-93 06-NOV-93   08-NOV-93
   151 15-DEC-94 15-JAN-95   16-JAN-95
   161 30-MAR-93 30-APR-93   03-MAY-93
   163 08-NOV-94 08-DEC-94   12-DEC-94
...
```

Objects used:
1. selrmnd1.obj
2. popapp.obj

HELP

```
object:         selrmnd1.obj
date created:   14-nov-1994
author:         glewis
revisions:

Purpose:        Calculates a "reminder date" as the Monday that follows
                the date of application plus one month.

Usage:          1. Use with one of the population objects that access
                the APPLICANT table.
                2. Unless "reminder1" is the last data column in the
                select clause, place a comma at the end of the object.

Hints:          none
```

OBJECT

```
next_day(add_months(applicant_appldate, 1), 'MONDAY') "reminder1"
```

Figure 9–7. *Select* object and report for a reminder date (version 1).

REPORT

```
SQL> select
  2          applicant_id,
  3          applicant_appldate,
  4          to_date(to_number(to_char(applicant_appldate,'J'))+49,'J') "reminder2"   [1]
  5  from
  6          applicant
  7  where
  8          applicant_term = '199509'
  9  [2]           and applicant_level = 'UG'
 10                and applicant_college = 'AS'
 11  /
ENTER to continue ...
                   reminder
       appl        7wks>
    id date        appldate
------ ---------   ---------
    44 09-JAN-95   27-FEB-95
    77 31-OCT-94   19-DEC-94
    97 09-FEB-95   30-MAR-95
   114 06-DEC-94   24-JAN-95
   133 21-OCT-94   09-DEC-94
   135 02-DEC-94   20-JAN-95
   145 06-OCT-93   24-NOV-93
   ...
```

Objects used:
1. selrmnd2.obj
2. popapp.obj

HELP

```
object:          selrmnd2.obj
date created:    14-nov-1994
author:          glewis
revisions:

Purpose:         Calculates a "reminder date" as 7 weeks (49 days)
                 after the application date.

Usage:           1. Use with one of the population objects that access
                 the APPLICANT table.
                 2. Unless "reminder2" is the last data column in the
                 select clause, place a comma at the end of the object.

Hints:           none
```

OBJECT

```
to_date(to_number(to_char(applicant_appldate,'J'))+49,'J') "reminder2"
```

Figure 9–8. *Select* object and report for a reminder date (version 2).

- A coded data column provides too much detail when "lumpier" groupings would actually be better,
- An institutional definition is based on a coded data column and that definition should be standard across the organization, or
- The user prefers to see a data range (e.g., 1000 - 2000) rather than the actual data value.

In this section we'll build *select* objects to demonstrate each of these situations.

More Aggregate Groupings

Sometimes data columns provide too much detail. Reducing that detail would actually improve a user's ability to read and understand a report. Consider, for example, a roster of applicants at Komenda that shows their anticipated majors. Figure 9–9 shows the majors available at Komenda. There are twenty-seven major codes used. Sometimes reports may require this degree of detail; but for other purposes more aggregate groupings would suffice.

Here's the task. Group anticipated majors into the academic departments responsible for those majors. Include Business, Arts, Sciences, Social Sciences, Languages, Philosophy and Religion, and Physical Education. Also include categories for "other" and "unknown" majors.

Completing the task requires collapsing the twenty-seven major codes into the seven departments listed above and the two additional categories for "other" and "unknown." Again, the *decode* function provides a solution, allowing a mapping from each major to a single department. Figure 9–10 on page 206 shows this mapping. Note that the constructed data column, called "majorcat," looks nasty. It's straightforward but long, making it a perfect candidate for an object (rekeying the complete *decode* would quickly become tiresome).

Figure 9–10 also shows the object and associated help file for collapsing academic majors into aggregate groupings.

Institutional Definitions

The previous chapter discussed two class 1 population modifiers for "international" and "minority." Both represent concepts employed at Komenda College when conducting normal business activities. Visa codes defined international status, while ethnic codes were used to define minority status. *Select* objects constructed from these definitions improve a report's readabil-

```
REPORT

SQL> select * from cmajor order by 1;
ENTER to continue ...
code  major                          datestamp
----- ------------------------------ ---------
ACCT  Accountancy                    17-MAR-94
ART   Art                            17-MAR-94
BCOM  Business Communications        17-MAR-94
BIOL  Biology                        17-MAR-94
CHEM  Chemistry                      17-MAR-94
CIS   Computer Information Systems   17-MAR-94
ECON  Economics                      17-MAR-94
ENGL  English                        17-MAR-94
FIN   Finance                        17-MAR-94
GBU   General Business               17-MAR-94
GOV   Government                     17-MAR-94
HIST  History                        17-MAR-94
LANG  Modern Languages               17-MAR-94
MATH  Mathematics                    17-MAR-94
MGT   Management                     17-MAR-94
MKT   Marketing                      17-MAR-94
MUSC  Music                          17-MAR-94
OBU   Other Business                 17-MAR-94
OLA   Other Liberal Arts             17-MAR-94
OT    Other                          17-MAR-94
PEDC  Physical Education             17-MAR-94
PHIL  Philosophy                     17-MAR-94
PHYS  Physics                        17-MAR-94
PSYC  Psychology                     17-MAR-94
RELG  Religion                       17-MAR-94
SOC   Sociology                      17-MAR-94
UN    Unknown                        17-MAR-94

27 rows selected.
```

Figure 9–9. Major codes from the CMAJOR table.

ity whenever detailed visa or ethnic codes are not required. But more importantly, international or minority *select* objects capture institutional definitions that can then be used uniformly throughout the organization. There are times when differing local definitions of a single concept may be appropriate, but uniform definitions ensure accurate external reporting and internal comparative reporting across offices or departments.

Here's the task. Build a *select* object that identifies whether an individual is an international. Make the object return a "Y" to indicate international and an "N" otherwise. Recall from Chapter 8 that Komenda College classifies someone as an international if he or she is not a U.S. citizen or a permanent resident of the United States. Translated into data columns

REPORT

```
SQL> select
  2         applicant_id,
  3         applicant_major,
  4         decode(applicant_major, 'ACCT', 'Business', 'ART', 'Arts',
  5                'BCOM', 'Business', 'BIOL', 'Sciences', 'CHEM', 'Sciences',
  6                'CIS', 'Business', 'ECON', 'SocialSci', 'ENGL', 'Languages',
  7                'FIN', 'Business', 'GBU', 'Business', 'GOV', 'SocialSci',
  8                'HIST', 'SocialSci', 'LANG', 'Languages', 'MATH', 'Sciences',
  9                'MGT', 'Business', 'MKT', 'Business', 'MUSC', 'Arts',
 10                'OBU', 'Business', 'OLA', 'Other', 'OT', 'Other',
 11                'PEDC', 'PhysEduc', 'PHIL', 'PhilRelg', 'PHYS', 'Sciences',
 12                'PSYC', 'SocialSci', 'RELG', 'PhilRelg', 'SOC', 'SocialSci',
 13                'UN', 'Unknown') "majorcat"
 14   from
 15         applicant
 16   where
 17         applicant_term = '199509'
 18                and applicant_level = 'UG'
 19                and applicant_college = 'AS'
 20   /
ENTER to continue ...
    appl  major
 id major dept
------ ----- ----------
    44 UN    Unknown
    77 UN    Unknown
    97 ART   Arts
   145 PSYC  SocialSci
   161 GOV   SocialSci
   163 BIOL  Sciences
   181 MATH  Sciences
   207 HIST  SocialSci
   227 MATH  Sciences
   233 SOC   SocialSci
   253 UN    Unknown
   255 CHEM  Sciences
   324 ENGL  Languages
   351 PHYS  Sciences
   460
   770 PHIL  PhilRelg
   ...
```

Objects used:
1. selmajr.obj
2. popapp.obj

HELP

```
object:         selmajr.obj
date created:   16-nov-1994
author:         glewis
revisions:

Purpose:        Collapses anticipated majors into academic departments.

Usage:          1. Use with a population object that accesses the APPLICANT
                table.
                2. Unless "majorcat" is the last data column in the
                select clause, place a comma at the end of the object.

Hints:          none
```

OBJECT

```
decode(applicant_major, 'ACCT', 'Business', 'ART', 'Arts',
       'BCOM', 'Business', 'BIOL', 'Sciences', 'CHEM', 'Sciences',
       'CIS', 'Business', 'ECON', 'SocialSci', 'ENGL', 'Languages',
       'FIN', 'Business', 'GBU', 'Business', 'GOV', 'SocialSci',
       'HIST', 'SocialSci', 'LANG', 'Languages', 'MATH', 'Sciences',
       'MGT', 'Business', 'MKT', 'Business', 'MUSC', 'Arts',
       'OBU', 'Business', 'OLA', 'Other', 'OT', 'Other',
       'PEDC', 'PhysEduc', 'PHIL', 'PhilRelg', 'PHYS', 'Sciences',
       'PSYC', 'SocialSci', 'RELG', 'PhilRelg', 'SOC', 'SocialSci',
       'UN', 'Unknown') "majorcat"
```

Figure 9–10. *Select* object and report for a recode of majors..

this means that a visa code must exist and it must not be "PR" (i.e., permanent resident).

The *decode* function easily captures this definition in SQL. Just use *decode* to check visa_type. If visa_type is null, the person is presumed a U.S. citizen and receives an N for international status. Similarly if visa_type is PR, the international status gets set to N. For all other visa_codes, the international status is Y. Figure 9–11 on the following page shows a report based on these definitions. It also shows the international *select* object.

Creating Data Ranges

Admissions offices get bombarded annually with questionnaires and surveys from various external organizations requesting information about admissions practices and results. Much of this information ends up compiled into the college guidebooks that help students evaluate and compare colleges and universities so they can decide where to submit admissions applications.

One of the favorite questions on admissions surveys concerns standardized test scores of applicants, accepted applicants, and new enrolling students. College guidebooks like to provide this information so that potential applicants can compare their own scores against the scores of other students who applied to the college in previous years. Information like this is always summary in nature. External reports never provide individual detail unless it's solicited by a government agency for audit or research purposes.

Questionnaires often request standardized test score information reported in data ranges. That is, they want to know how many applicants had SAT math scores between 200 and 299, between 300 and 399, and so on. The database, of course, stores only the raw scores.

Your task, then, is to convert raw test scores into data ranges. Suppose the ranges for reporting SAT scores are those just mentioned, 200 to 299 and so on up to 700 to 800. We must find some way to recode raw scores into data ranges.

This type of report request actually pushes SQL to the edge of its capabilities. Statistical packages handle data recodes with ease. But these programs were designed for data analysis; SQL is a reporting tool and was never intended to provide rich analytical functionality like maps or graphs or trend line summaries. But a gray area does exist where reporting tools and analysis tools overlap. Data recodes of continuous data like test scores fall into that gray area.

The solution to data recodes in SQL*PLUS rests on a trick I gratefully acknowledge I first found discussed by George Koch (see the References sec-

REPORT

```
SQL> select
  2          applicant_id,
  3          n1.name_last||', '||n1.name_first||' '||n1.name_middle "sort_name",   [1]
  4          v1.visa_type,
  5          decode(v1.visa_type, null, 'N', 'PR', 'N', 'Y') "intl"   [2]
  6  from
  7          visa v1,
  8          name n1,
  9          applicant
 10  where
 11          applicant_term = '199509'
 12   [3]        and applicant_level = 'UG'
 13                 and applicant_college = 'AS'
 14          and n1.name_id = applicant_id
 15                 and n1.name_seriesno =
 16   [4]           (select max(n2.name_seriesno)
 17                 from name n2
 18                 where n2.name_id = n1.name_id)
 19          and v1.visa_id(+) = applicant_id
 20  /
ENTER to continue ...
                                   visa
    id sort_name                   type intl
------ ------------------------    ---- ----
    44 McCarthy, Angela                 N
    77 Chen, Tammy                      N
    97 Chen, Stephen V.                 N
   114 Price, Danielle                  N
   133 Kuang, Wai                  PR   N
   266 Diaz, Edward                     N
   269 Peterson, Brian D.               N
   279 Stephens, Allison           F1   Y
   351 Sanchez, Stephanie               N
   352 Brown, Michelle                  N
   379 Martin, Emily                    N
   387 Williams, Stephanie D.           N
   408 Campbell, Cindy C.               N
   517 Ramy, Hazel                 F1   Y
   ...
```

Objects used:
1. selsname.obj
2. selintl.obj
3. popapp.obj
4. whrname.obj

HELP

```
object:         selintl.obj
date created:   13-nov-1994
author:         glewis
revisions:

Purpose:        Identifies a person as an "international" based on their
                visa status.

Usage:          1. Include the VISA table in the from clause
                with an alias v1.
                2. Unless "international" is the last data column in the select
                clause, place a comma at the end of the object.

Hints:          none
```

OBJECT

```
decode(v1.visa_type, null, 'N', 'PR', 'N', 'Y')  "intl"
```

Figure 9–11. *Select* object and report on international applicants.

tion). The trick uses the *sign* and *decode* functions. Consider the test score range from 500 to 599 and an individual score like 530 that falls in this range. Subtracting the upper limit of the range (599) from the individual value results in a negative number. The *sign* of a negative number is -1. Once we find a negative *sign* function, then we've located the test range a score belongs in. Consider 530 again. Is it in the 200 to 299 range? Operationally we can test this by subtracting 299 from 530. Is the sign of this number -1 (or 0 for an exact match)? No. So then test the range 300 to 399. Is 530 minus 399 negative? Again the answer is no. Continue until you find the -1 sign that occurs when subtracting 599 from 530. This procedure can be used with any test score to locate the range within which it falls.

Figure 9–12 on the following page shows two reports based on this solution. Note that the six test score ranges required nesting the decodes six levels deep. This works but it isn't pretty. That's why having constructed it once, you want to save it as an object for later reuse. Figure 9–12 also shows the object and associated help file.

Formatting *Select* Objects

Chapter 6 discussed how default column headings and formats could be set using an object embedded in a shell program (see Figure 6-4). This object standardizes the appearance of reports and also eliminates the need to repeatedly reset preferred headings or formats. Normally this object (called owncol.obj) gets built piecemeal. You find yourself using a data column a lot, so you add it to owncol.obj with the ***column*** command that sets the heading and format. After some time, you've built up a hefty object containing the data columns you commonly use in reports.

This same procedure should be followed with *select* objects. For each *select* object that you construct, add a ***column*** command to the owncol.obj object. Every time a SQL program gets run from the standard report shell, these commands get executed, creating your column headings and formats. Figure 9–13 on page 211 shows an extract of owncol.obj for the *select* objects constructed in this chapter.

Object Inventory

It's important to keep a current inventory of objects available for use. Table 9–1 adds the *select* objects just constructed to the *population* and *where* objects constructed in earlier chapters. Later chapters will add more

REPORT 1

```
SQL> select
  2       applicant_id,
  3       t1.test_score,
  4       decode(sign(t1.test_score-299),-1,'200-299',0,'200-299',
  5               decode(sign(t1.test_score-399),-1,'300-399',0,'300-399',
  6               decode(sign(t1.test_score-499),-1,'400-499',0,'400-499',
  7               decode(sign(t1.test_score-599),-1,'500-599',0,'500-599',
  8               decode(sign(t1.test_score-699),-1,'600-699',0,'600-699',
  9               decode(sign(t1.test_score-800),-1,'700-800',0,'700-800'))))))
 10               "testcat"
 11 from
 12       test t1,
 13       applicant
 14 where
 15       applicant_term = '199509'
 16               and applicant_level = 'UG'
 17               and applicant_college = 'AS'
 18       and t1.test_id(+) = applicant_id
 19               and t1.test_type(+) = 'SATM'
 20               and to_char(nvl(t1.test_score,800))||
 21                       to_char(nvl(t1.test_date,'01-JAN-
 22                       (select max(to_char(nvl(t2.test_s
 23                               to_char(nvl(t2.test_date,
 24                       from
 25                               test t2,
 26                               person
 27                       where person_id = applicant_id
 28                               and t2.test_id(+) = perso
 29                               and t2.test_type(+) = 'SA
 30 /
ENTER to continue ...
               test test
    id        score range
------ ---------- --------
    44        560 500-599
    77        560 500-599
    97        720 700-800
   161        690 600-699
   163        640 600-699
   181
   207        590 500-599
   ...
```

1

2

3

Objects used:
1. seltestr.obj
2. popapp.obj
3. whrtest.obj

REPORT 2

```
ENTER to continue ...
test
range         count
-------- ----------
200-299           2
300-399           5
400-499          55
500-599         234
600-699         262
700-800          39
Unknown         103
         ----------
sum             700
```

HELP

```
object:       seltestr.obj
datecreated:  14-nov-1994
author:       glewis
revisions:

Purpose:      Calculates a test range (e.g.,400-499) that an SAT score
              falls within.  Useful for frequency distributions by ranges.

Usage:        1.Use with the where object whrtest.obj that accesses the
              TEST table.
              2.Unless "testcat" is the last data column in the
              select clause, place a comma at the end of the object.

Hints:        none
```

OBJECT

```
decode(sign(t1.test_score-299),-1,'200-299',0,'200-299',
       decode(sign(t1.test_score-399),-1,'300-399',0,'300-399',
       decode(sign(t1.test_score-499),-1,'400-499',0,'400-499',
       decode(sign(t1.test_score-599),-1,'500-599',0,'500-599',
       decode(sign(t1.test_score-699),-1,'600-699',0,'600-699',
       decode(sign(t1.test_score-800),-1,'700-800',0,'700-800'))))))
       "testcat"
```

Figure 9–12. *Select* object and report on recoded SAT math scores.

OWNCOL.SQL

```
/* constructed */
column sort_name format a25
column age format 999
column pctrank heading 'pct|rank' format 99999
column cszn format a30
column intl format a4
column initials_name format a25
column reminder1 heading 'reminder|monday>|appl+1mon'
column reminder2 heading 'reminder|7wks>|appldate'
column testcat heading 'test|range' format a8
column satc format 99999
column majorcat heading 'major|dept' format a10
```

Figure 9–13. Additions to owncol.sql to set headings and formats for *select* objects.

objects to the inventory, which then finds use in Chapter 13 when constructing reports and in Chapter 14 when automating objects.

Table 9–1. Inventory of SQL objects.

Class	Name	Purpose
POPULATION	popacapp	Applicants accepted for admissions for a specified term, level, and college
	popapp	Applicants for admissions for a specified term, level, college
	popenrl	Accepted applicants for a specified term, level, and college who are expected to enroll
	poprecr	Recruits for a specified term and level
WHERE 1	whrintl	Defines the term "international" and modifies a population so only internationals are included
	whrmnrty	Defines the term "minority" and modifies a population so only individuals of color are included
WHERE 2u	whraddr	Provides access to the ADDRESS table for the most recent address of a specified type
	whradhi	Provides access to the ADDRESS table in a hierarchical fashion. Returns an address of a specified type (e.g., local). If this type of address is not available, it returns an address of a second specified type (e.g., permanent)
	whrname	Provides access to the NAME table for the most recent name
WHERE 2u	whrpersn	Provides access to the PERSON table
	whrphon	Provides access to the PHONE table for the most recent phone of a specified type and associated with an address of a specified type
	whrtest	Provides access to the TEST table for the highest test score of a specified type

(Continued)

Table 9–1. Inventory of SQL objects.

Class	Name	Purpose
WHERE 2m	whraddrm	Provides access to the ADDRESS table for all addresses of a specified type
	whrdcmnt	Provides access to all documents in the DOCUMENT table for a population of applicants
SELECT	selage	Computes a person's age based on sysdate (the report date) and the person's birthdate
	selcszn	Creates a single display column by concatenating address_city, address_state, address_zip, and address_nation
	seliname	Creates a name using the initials of the first and middle names and concatenating these to name_last
	selintl	Identifies a person an "international" based on their visa status
	selmajr	Collapses anticipated majors into academic departments
	selprank	Computes a person's percent rank in high school based on class size and class rank
	selrmnd1	Calculates a "reminder date" as the Monday that follows the date of application plus one month
	selrmnd2	Calculates a "reminder date" as 7 weeks (49 days) after the application date
	selsatc	Calculates a combined SAT score as the sum of SAT math and SAT verbal scores
	selsname	Creates a name by concatenating name_last, name_first, and name_middle
	seltestr	Calcualtes a test range (e.g., 400–499) that an SAT score falls within. Useful for frequency distributions by score ranges

Chapter 10

Building *Report* Objects

Ad hoc queries come in an infinite variety. Report populations, requested data columns, constructed expressions, sorting order, summary computations, and the physical appearance can all differ from one report to another. But under all this variation lie distinctly different report structures that distinguish major types of reports.

Some of the major report types can't be prepared using SQL. Others can only be prepared with difficulty. In these situations other tools provide greater flexibility than SQL. Since it's important to recognize when these situations occur, the chapter begins with a discussion of what reports you should not try with SQL. It then identifies several common reports where SQL is an appropriate query tool and concludes by building objects so that you can prepare these reports easily.

Report objects serve as templates for ad hoc queries. They provide the backbone around which other objects get assembled. You begin knowing how the user wants the report to appear. You then select a *report* object that produces this type of report. Then insert the *population*, *where*, and *select* objects to complete the *report* object. When combined with a *shell* object, the package is complete and ready to be run.

What Not to Try

Ad hoc reports are by nature simple in design. In part this occurs because the questions being asked tend to be quite specific, but in part the simplicity occurs because SQL and SQL*PLUS cannot handle, and were not designed to handle, complex reports.

Suppose the director of admissions requests a single report showing a count of applicants, accepted applicants, and new enrolling students by their gender. She'd like a table that computed accept rates and yield rates as shown in Table 10–1. This report cannot be done in SQL with one pass at the data.

To understand why, think back to the chapter on *population* objects. Each ad hoc query consists of a single population. Table 10–1 includes three populations: applicants, accepted applicants, and new enrolled students. Using SQL you can retrieve counts by gender, but it would require separate queries for each of the three populations. You'd then be faced with the task of computing transition rates (i.e., accepts/applicants and enrolled/accepts). Many options exist. You could compute the transition rates manually and type the final table. You could rekey the numbers from the three SQL queries into a spreadsheet program and create formulas to perform the rate calculations. You could even automate the process somewhat by using macros to import the three SQL reports, retrieve the relevant data, insert the data into the appropriate table cells, perform the calculations, and print the report. Or you could use a procedural programming language that provides complete control over data access, manipulation, and display.

Table 10–1. Sample report with multiple populations.

		Accepted		Enrolled	
Sex	Applicants	No.	Acc/App	No.	Enr/Acc
Female	378	238	63%	83	35%
Male	322	212	66%	69	33%
Total	700	450	64%	152	34%

When should you choose SQL and SQL*PLUS as the query tool for a given report? It's an interesting question. I use a very simple criteria when deciding if SQL is appropriate. If I can't get the data needed for a report with one pass at the data tables using SQL, I choose another tool unless the request is very simple (as is Table 10–1). This means I generally don't use SQL for reports with multiple populations. But the criteria also excludes other commonly requested report types. Suppose you're asked to prepare a report like the one shown in Table 10–2. This report shows counts of applicants by their anticipated academic major. It also shows the counts of specific majors as a percentage of the total applicant count. In SQL this report cannot be done with one data pass. It requires an initial pass to determine the total number of applicants. This number must be inserted into a temporary table and used during a second pass of the data to compute the percentage distributions.

Table 10–2. Sample report with percentage distributions.

Major	No.	Pct.
Art	15	2%
Biology	65	9%
Chemistry	31	4%
Economics	56	8%
English	30	4%
Government	40	6%
History	36	5%
Languages	31	4%
Mathematics	18	3%
Music	26	4%
Phys Educ	17	2%
Philosophy	4	1%
Physics	12	2%
Psychology	33	5%
Religion	5	1%
Sociology	31	4%
Unknown	250	36%
Total	700	100%

I think reports like percentage distributions overextend SQL and are better handled by procedural programming languages or by SQL used as a front end to spreadsheet, graphical, or statistical packages. You can prepare all the reports in this chapter with a single data pass. This still includes a wide variety of reports.

Report Roadmap

Figure 10–1 provides a roadmap through several major report types. The figure is structured around a series of questions in a decision tree. Answering the questions about a specific report request can help identify what *report* object to use.

Here's how the roadmap works. Start at the top of the figure. Does the requested report include group summaries like sums, counts, or averages? If yes, proceed along one path; if no, proceed along the other. Continue through the roadmap by asking and answering the questions until you reach an endpoint. That endpoint identifies a major report type and the name of the *report* object you can use to prepare reports of this type.

Roadmap Questions

The roadmap contains several questions. Each needs a little elaboration.

- Group functions? Does the report include any group summaries like sums, counts or averages?
- Counts? Does the report include counts?
- Averages? Does the report include averages?
- Mixed functions? Does the report include two or more group summaries?
- Detail? Does the report include any data other than that summarized for groups? That is, does it include any data column reported for individual table rows?
- Blocked? Does the report require that some data columns be "blocked" instead of appearing as columns across the top of the report? Blocked data consists of data columns placed underneath each other as in an address. Blocked reports commonly get used whenever many data columns appear in the report. When this happens the physical line size of the page is exceeded and line or column wrapping makes the report unattractive.
- Repeating detail? Does the detail report include duplicate information that could be suppressed to improve the legibility of the report? Duplicate information commonly occurs when joining to a table where individual items in the population may appear more than once (e.g., when joining to the DOCUMENT table to show all documents submitted by an applicant).

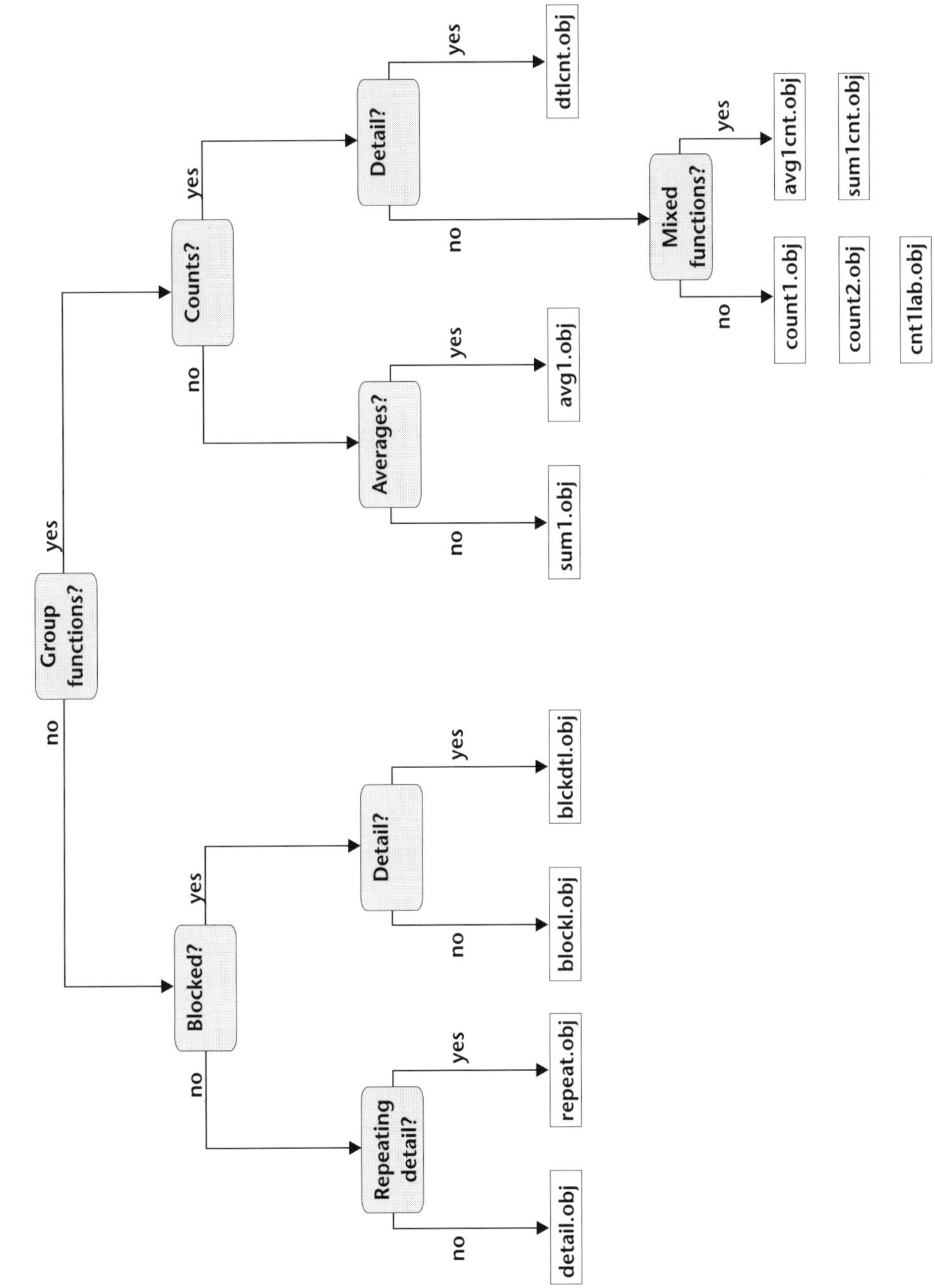

Figure 10–1. Roadmap of *report* objects built in this chapter.

```
REPORT

major      count
----- ----------
ART           15
BIOL          65
CHEM          31
ECON          56
ENGL          30
GOV           40
HIST          36
LANG          31
MATH          18
MUSC          26
PEDC          17
PHIL           4
PHYS          12
PSYC          33
RELG           5
SOC           31
UN           211
              39
      ----------
sum          700

18 rows selected.
```

The report shows counts of applicants by their anticipated academic major.

Figure 10–2. Example of a 1-way frequency distribution.

Figure 10–2 shows a report of counts. Suppose you wanted to prepare a report that looked roughly like Figure 10–2. What *report* object would you use? With modest experience using *report* objects, the answer is immediately clear. But until then the roadmap in Figure 10–1 helps. Let's work through this example. Does the report include group summaries? Yes. Does the report include counts? Again the answer is yes. Does the report include any detail on individual population items? No. This path ends in *report* objects that produce 1-way frequency distributions (count1.obj), 2-way cross-tabulations (count2.obj), and specially labeled 1-way frequency distributions (cnt1lab.obj). As we'll see shortly, Figure 10–2 is an example of a 1-way frequency distribution created with the count1.obj object.

Report Sketches

This chapter discusses three major types of ad hoc reports, each with several subcategories for more specific reports. Detail, summary, and hybrid reports form the three principal report classes. Detail reports contain information on individual items in the report population. Summary reports aggregate the detailed information and summarize it. Hybrid reports provide both detail and summary. Visually, the three report classes look distinctly different.

Detail Reports

Detail reports contain information on individual items in the report population. How much information the report contains and the type of information determine specific report subclasses.

Detail Only

For day-to-day operational use the simple roster or listing is a mainstay. In appearance this report looks like a spreadsheet table of rows and columns. Rows contain population items; each population item appears in only one row. Columns contain data table columns or expressions. Individual cells where rows and columns intersect show a specific data value for a population item. Figure 10–3 on the following page shows an example of a detail-only report, listing the I.D. number, name, sex, student type, intention to apply for financial aid, degree, and major for a population of applicants.

Repeating Detail

In appearance, repeating detail reports look similar to detail reports except that each population item may appear on more than one report row. This occurs whenever the query uses a table where population items appear more than once. For example, applicants can each have several standardized test scores. Suppose an applicant has four test scores. Listing the I.D., name, and test score will result in four report rows—one for each test score. The I.D. and name will appear repetitively on each of the four rows. This duplicated information is best suppressed. Figure 10–4 on page 221 shows a repeating detail report where duplicate information appears; Figure 10–5 on page 222 shows the same report using a cleaner style that suppresses duplicate information.

Blocked

Printed reports have physical limitations based upon the page size and the font used for printing. Standard "green-bar" paper in a line printer commonly provides 132 characters for display. Laser printing in landscape mode with a compressed pitch of 16.7 characters/inch provides about 160 display

```
REPORT

                                   student      aid      appl     appl
    id sort_name                   sex type     intent   degree   major
------ -------------------------   --- -------  -------  -------  -----
  2574 Abraham, Alicia                 F        Y        BA       GOV
  3163 Adams, Amy                  F   F        N        UN       UN
  2687 Adams, Samuel               M   T        N        BA       CHEM
  8584 Adams, Thomas P.            M   F        Y        UN       ECON
  1897 Affsa, Rita A.              F   F        Y        BA       LANG
  6287 Agnew,, Angela              F   F        Y        BA       HIST
  6260 Allen, Adam                 M   F        Y        BA       SOC
  3004 Allen, Alicia                   F        Y        BA       HIST
  2698 Allen, Cahren                   F        Y        UN       ART
  3650 Allen, Christine            F   F        N        UN       BIOL
  8672 Allen, Justin               M   F        Y        UN       UN
  5898 Allen, Karen                F   F        Y        BA       UN
  4846 Allen, Kristen              F   F        Y        BA       UN
  4970 Allen, Michael R.           M   F        Y        BA       LANG
  8128 Allen, Shawn W.             M   T        N        BA       MUSC
  4958 Allen, Shawnee                  F        Y        UN       UN
  5041 Amaral, Kris                M   F        Y        BA       BIOL
  3655 Amaral, Stephen             M   F        Y        BA       UN
  3005 Anderson, Christine V.      F   F        Y        BA       BIOL
  3390 Anderson, Cindy                 F        N        BA       UN
   ...
```

In a detail-only report, population items appear in rows and data columns appear in report columns. This is the classic roster or listing report.

Figure 10–3. Example of a detail-only report.

characters depending on margins. Sometimes so much information gets requested about population items that the physical line size dimensions are exceeded.

When this happens you have two options. First, you can reset column formats so the columns take up less space. As long as the "wrap" system variable is enabled (the default), no information will be truncated. But this can result in messy looking reports with data columns wrapping to another line.

The second option abandons the row-and-column format and prints detail data columns one under another in a block. Figure 10–6 on page 223 shows a blocked detail report with labels attached to each row for ease of use.

```
REPORT

                                         appl   appl  doc
   id sort_name                   sex degree major code document
------ ------------------------- --- ------ ----- ---- ------------------------------ ---------
  2574 Abraham, Alicia                BA     GOV   PRT1 Part 1 of application          24-OCT-94
  2574 Abraham, Alicia                BA     GOV   RANK Official high school rank      09-JAN-95
  2574 Abraham, Alicia                BA     GOV   XOFF Unofficial test scores         12-JAN-95
  2574 Abraham, Alicia                BA     GOV   FEE  Application fee                11-MAR-95
  3163 Adams, Amy                 F   UN     UN    TEST SAT, ACT, Achievement scores   03-NOV-94
  3163 Adams, Amy                 F   UN     UN    PRT1 Part 1 of application          29-DEC-94
  3163 Adams, Amy                 F   UN     UN    PRT2 Part 2 of application          25-FEB-95
  3163 Adams, Amy                 F   UN     UN    RANK Official high school rank      12-MAY-95
  2687 Adams, Samuel              M   BA     CHEM  FEE  Application fee                07-JAN-95
  2687 Adams, Samuel              M   BA     CHEM  PRT1 Part 1 of application          09-JAN-95
  2687 Adams, Samuel              M   BA     CHEM  TRAN High sch or college transcript 30-JAN-95
  2687 Adams, Samuel              M   BA     CHEM  XOFF Unofficial test scores
  8584 Adams, Thomas P.           M   UN     ECON  XOFF Unofficial test scores         08-OCT-94
  8584 Adams, Thomas P.           M   UN     ECON  PRT1 Part 1 of application          05-NOV-94
  8584 Adams, Thomas P.           M   UN     ECON  TEST SAT, ACT, Achievement scores   12-NOV-94
  8584 Adams, Thomas P.           M   UN     ECON  FEE  Application fee                18-FEB-95
  1897 Affsa, Rita A.             F   BA     LANG  TEST SAT, ACT, Achievement scores   20-NOV-94
  1897 Affsa, Rita A.             F   BA     LANG  TRAN High sch or college transcript 06-FEB-95
  1897 Affsa, Rita A.             F   BA     LANG  XOFF Unofficial test scores         18-FEB-95
  1897 Affsa, Rita A.             F   BA     LANG  PRT1 Part 1 of application          27-APR-95
   ...
```

In structure, a repeating detail report looks identical to a detail-only roster. However, a portion of the report contains duplicate information. For example, this report shows repeating data for applicant 2687.

Figure 10–4. Example of a repeating detail report with duplicate information.

REPORT

```
                                              appl   appl  doc
    id sort_name                         sex degree major code document
------ ------------------------- --- ------ ----- ---- ------------------------------ ---------
  2574 Abraham, Alicia                   BA     GOV   PRT1 Part 1 of application          24-OCT-94
                                                      RANK Official high school rank      09-JAN-95
                                                      XOFF Unofficial test scores         12-JAN-95
                                                      FEE  Application fee                11-MAR-95
  3163 Adams, Amy                    F   UN     UN    TEST SAT, ACT, Achievement scores   03-NOV-94
                                                      PRT1 Part 1 of application          29-DEC-94
                                                      PRT2 Part 2 of application          25-FEB-95
                                                      RANK Official high school rank      12-MAY-95
  2687 Adams, Samuel                 M   BA     CHEM  FEE  Application fee                07-JAN-95
                                                      PRT1 Part 1 of application          09-JAN-95
                                                      TRAN High sch or college transcript 30-JAN-95
                                                      XOFF Unofficial test scores
  8584 Adams, Thomas P.              M   UN     ECON  XOFF Unofficial test scores         08-OCT-94
                                                      PRT1 Part 1 of application          05-NOV-94
                                                      TEST SAT, ACT, Achievement scores   12-NOV-94
                                                      FEE  Application fee                18-FEB-95
  1897 Affsa, Rita A.                F   BA     LANG  TEST SAT, ACT, Achievement scores   20-NOV-94
                                                      TRAN High sch or college transcript 06-FEB-95
                                                      XOFF Unofficial test scores         18-FEB-95
                                                      PRT1 Part 1 of application          27-APR-95
   ...
```

This report is identical to the report in Figure 10–4 except that the duplicate information has been suppressed, making the report easier to read.

Figure 10–5. Example of a repeating detail report with duplicate information suppressed.

```
REPORT

id:             2574
name:           Abraham, Alicia
sex:
student_type:   F
aid_intent:     Y
degree:         BA
major:          GOV

id:             31663
name:           Adams, Amy
sex:            F
student_type:   F
aid_intent:     N
degree:         UN
major:          UN

id:             2687
name:           Adams, Samuel
sex:            M
student_type:   T
aid_intent:     NA
degree:         BA
major:          CHEM
 ...
```

In a block detail report, data columns appear as report rows rather than report columns. Each row (i.e., data column) has a label to identify it.

Figure 10–6. Example of a block detail report with labeled rows.

Detail and Block

A detail report structure and a block structure can be combined in the same report. This commonly occurs when printing addresses. You might want to display an I.D. number, name, and other population information on a single line but then block the address data. Figure 10–7 on the following page shows an example of a detail and block report.

Summary Reports

Summary reports aggregate detail data and summarize it using counts, averages, sums, or other group functions. These reports frequently get sent up the organizational command line where policy rather than day-to-day operations is the issue of interest.

Frequency Distribution (1-way)

Many ad hoc queries require counts by subgroups in the population. For example, to allocate an appropriate number of dormitory rooms for men or women, the Komenda College housing office will require a gender

```
REPORT

    id sort_name                 sex PR address
------ ------------------------- --- ------------------------------------
  2574 Abraham, Alicia               264 Park Street
                                     Fort Smith, AR 72903

  3163 Adams, Amy                F   39 Hickory Road Apt. #279
                                     Wayne, NJ 07479

  2687 Adams, Samuel             M   9950 Edgewater St Apt. #28C
                                     San Juan, PR 00911

  8584 Adams, Thomas P.          M   3361 Hickoy Tiempos Lane West
                                     Leysin, CH-1854 SUI

  1897 Affsa, Rita A.            F   23389 Meadown Drive
                                     Newark, NJ 07104
  6287 Agnew, Angela             F   1136 Victoria Hollow Drive
                                     Chesterfield, MO 63005

  ...
```

A detail and block report includes some data columns in a blocked format and other data columns that appear as report columns. In this report the address is blocked; information on I.D. number, name, and sex is not.

Figure 10–7. Example of a detail and block report.

breakdown of applicants expected to enroll. They need a count of the population by sex, showing the number of men and the number of women.

Reports of this type are called frequency distributions. They break the total population into counts for mutually exclusive subgroups, essentially showing how the population is distributed among these subgroups. Figure 10–8 shows an example of a frequency distribution. Visually, it's a two column report: the first column contains the categorical data column (e.g., sex) and the second column contains the corresponding counts.

Cross-tabulation (2-way Frequency Distribution)

Sometimes a 1-way breakdown of population counts doesn't provide enough detail. Suppose the dean of the College of Arts & Sciences wants a report to help with academic planning. He requests a report of applicants, showing counts by gender and by degree. He's particularly interested in the students who expect to get a joint BA and MBA degree. You could give the dean two reports—one showing the degree distribution of men and a second showing the degree distribution of women. However, the same information can be presented more conveniently in a single report showing counts by gender and by degree.

Reports of this type are called 2-way frequency distributions or cross-tabulations. Figure 10–9 shows a cross-tabulation of applicants by gender and anticipated academic degree. Note that the report appears as three

```
REPORT

sex       count
---  ----------
F           316
M           260
            124
     ----------
sum         700
```

A 1-way frequency distribution counts the report population by the values in one categorical data column. Here a population has been counted by sex.

Figure 10–8. Example of a 1-way frequency distribution.

```
REPORT

     appl
sex  degree       count
---  ------  ----------
F    BA             219
     BAMBA           20
     UN              77
***          ----------
sum                 316

M    BA             183
     BAMBA           14
     UN              63
***          ----------
sum                 260

     BA              87
     BAMBA            5
     UN              32
***          ----------
sum                 124

             ----------
sum                 700
```

A 2-way frequency distribution counts a report population by the values in two categorical data columns. This type of report is also called a cross-tabulation.

Figure 10–9. Example of a 2-way frequency distribution (a cross-tabulation).

columns: one column showing the gender categories, a second column showing the degree categories, and a third column showing counts. This report format is identical to a cross-tabulation report with gender in rows, degrees in columns, and counts in the cells.

Frequency distributions can be extended to include any number of categorical data columns, producing 3-way, 4-way, or n-way reports. As the number of categorical data columns increases, however, the ease of interpretation decreases. Trying to make sense out of a 4-way frequency distribution (i.e., a table in four dimensional space) displayed on a two dimensional printed page can prove a challenge.

N-way Sum or Average Reports

In a manner completely analogous to the n-way count reports just discussed, you can construct n-way reports of averages or sums. For simplicity let's stick to 1-way and 2-way reports. A 1-way report of sums looks exactly like a 1-way report of counts. The first column again displays the categorical data column, but the second column now contains sums instead of counts. Similarly, a 2-way report of sums is equivalent to a table of rows and columns with the cell values containing sums. Reports of averages from 1-way to n-way are constructed similarly.

Figure 10–10 shows an example of a 1-way average report, showing the average SAT math scores of applicants by gender.

N-way Mixed Reports

Reporting sums and averages without also reporting corresponding counts only invites misinterpretation. Suppose Komenda received two applications from students in Minnesota and 100 applications from students in New York. If the average SAT math score of the two Minnesota applicants is 50

REPORT

```
      avg
sex   satm
---   -----
F       591
M       591
na      583
```

A 1-way report of averages shows the average of a numeric data column for each value in a categorical column.

Figure 10–10. Example of a 1-way report of averages.

points less than the average score of the 100 New York applicants, that describes the population at one point in time. But based upon a sample of two applicants, you'd be unlikely to conclude that seeking applicants from Minnesota lowers the quality of the applicant pool. To guard against misinterpretations like this, counts should commonly appear in reports displaying averages and sums.

Mixed summary reports generally contain counts and one or more other summary calculations. Figure 10–11 shows a report combining counts and averages.

Hybrid Reports

Detail reports only contain information on specific population items. Summary reports only group the detail and summarize it. Hybrid reports offer both detail and summary in the same report. Since they offer double value, hybrid reports provide an attractive option to users.

Detail and Count

Suppose the director of admissions requests a report showing the I.D., name, gender, and major of applicants. She'd like the report sorted by major and a subtotal at the end of each major that displays the number of applicants in that major. This request combines a detail report with a summary count report. Figure 10–12 on the following page shows an example of a report mixing detail and counts.

Other common hybrid reports combine detail with averages, sums, averages and counts, sums and counts, or other combinations of sums, averages, and counts.

```
REPORT

      avg
sex   satm        count
---  -----   ----------
F      591          316
M      591          260
       583          124
             ----------
sum                 700
```

This report shows average SAT Math scores by sex. It also includes a count of how many test scores were included in the averages.

Figure 10–11. Example of a 1-way report of counts and averages.

```
REPORT

        id sort_name                sex major
---------- ------------------------ --- ------
      2698 Allen, Cahren                ART
      1798 Baker, Evelyn            F
      7899 Burke, Karl W.           M
        97 Chen, Stephen V.         M
      5761 Collins, Shawnee
      7080 DeMarco, Danielle
      7312 Doyle, John              M
      6234 Green, Allison           F
       532 Lee, Christopher         M
       379 Martin, Emily            F
      5159 Moore, Thomas K.         M
      6582 Patel, William           M
      8265 Pierce, Amy
      6031 Stephens, Christine      F
      3253 Thompson, Karen
----------                              ******
        15                              count

      3650 Allen, Christine         F   BIOL
      5041 Amaral, Kris             M
      3005 Anderson, Christine V    F
       ...
      8944 White, Michael           M
      6680 Williams, Jason          M
      6418 Wong, Sharon             F
      7579 Wood, Lori               F
      2655 Ysona, Grant
----------                              ******
        65                              count
...
----------
       700
700 rows selected
```

This report shows detail about population items, but also includes a count summarizing subgroups of the population.

Figure 10–12. Example of a hybrid report showing detail and summary.

***Report* Objects**

Each of the report classes and subclasses just described has a unique SQL and SQL*PLUS structure. Capturing this structure in an object makes it easy to prepare reports of a specific type. You merely select the appropriate *report* object and then complete it with *population*, *where*, and *select* objects.

This section discusses how to build and use *report* objects. The objects are not meant to be exhaustive, only illustrative of what is possible. Some business offices predominantly use reports of one or two subclasses. For example, a financial office might extensively use mixed summary reports showing total and subtotal sums, averages, and counts. You'd expect to see *report* objects vary between different business offices, as one office emphasized and developed objects of one subclass while a second office emphasized and developed objects in another subclass.

Detail Report *Objects*

Detail reports include detail-only reports in simple column and row format, repeating detail reports where repetitive information gets suppressed, blocked detail reports to handle large amounts of information, and combined detail and block reports. None of the *report* objects that produce these reports is complex.

Detail Only

Least complex is the object that produces a detail-only report. Figure 10–13 shows this object and the associated help file that describes how to use the object.

HELP

```
object:        detail.obj
date created:  20-nov-1994
author:        glewis
revisions:

Purpose:       A report object producing a simpe roster (i.e., listing)
               of data columns.

Usage:         1. <<columns>>: Replace with the list of data columns
               appearing in the select clause.
               2. <<population>>: Replace with a population object.
               3. <<where>>: Replace with one or more class 1 or class 2u
               where objects.  Remove if none is required.
               4. <<columns_subset>>: Replace with desired sorting order
               (e.g., 3 asc sorts the listing in ascending order
               using the third data column in the select clause).

Hints:         None
```

OBJECT

```
select
       <<columns>>
<<population>>
<<where>>
order by
       <<columns_subset>>
/
```

Figure 10–13. *Report* object and help file for a detail-only report.

Suppose the director of admissions requests a report of Arts & Sciences applicants showing their I.D. number, name, sex, student type, degree, major, and whether they expect to apply for financial assistance. She'd like the report sorted in alphabetical order by sort name.

Figure 10–14 shows the sequence of steps using the detail-only object to produce this report. In step 1, the *population* object popapp.obj gets inserted into the *report* object. This defines the report population. The admissions director requested data columns appearing in the APPLICANT, PERSON, and NAME tables. The *population* object only provides access to the APPLICANT table, so you'll need to add *where* objects accessing PERSON and NAME. Step 2 shows the two *where* objects whrpersn.obj and whrname.obj inserted into the *report* object. The only *select* object that you can use is selsname.obj that creates a sort name. Step 3 shows this object inserted into the detail *report* object. It also shows the manual addition of the other data columns requested by the admissions director and a choice of the sorting order.

Executing this completed object produces the report shown in Figure 10–15 on page 232.

Repeating Detail

Repeating detail reports occur whenever a class 2m *where* object appears in the query. The singularity of the report population gets lost because each population item may appear more than once in the joined table. You could use the detail-only *report* object (detail.obj) to produce a report under these circumstances, but it would look awkward because of repetitive information.

The secret to a repeating detail object lies in distinguishing the two types of data columns present in these reports. These are:

- Data columns showing duplicate information, generated from tables where the join criteria enforces singularity; and
- Data columns that do *not* show duplicate information, generated from the class 2m join that relaxes population singularity.

If you place the data columns with duplicate data first in the *select* clause, then there's a convenient way to eliminate the duplication by using the ***break*** command. Figure 10–16 on page 233 shows the repeating detail *report* object and its associated help file. Note that using the object entails several steps. Each data column showing duplicate data must receive an

OBJECT

```
select
      <<columns>>
<<population>>
<<where>>
order by
      <<columns_subset>>
/
```

STEP 1: Add *population* object popapp.obj

```
select
        <<column>>
from
        applicant
where
        applicant_term = '199509'
                and applicant_level = 'UG'
                and applicant_college = 'AS'
<<where>>
order by
        <<columns_subset>>
/
```

Step 2: Add *where* objects whrpersn.obj and whrname.obj

```
select
        <<column>>
from
        name n1,
        person
where
        applicant_term = '199509'
                and applicant_level = 'UG'
                and applicant_college = 'AS'
        and person_id = applicant_id
        and n1.name = applicant_id
                and n1.name_seriesno =
                (select max(n2.name_seriesno)
                from name n2
                where n2.name_id = n1.name_id)
order by
        <<columns_subset>>
/
```

STEP 3: Add *select* object selname.obj, other data columns and *order by*

```
select
     applicant_id,
     n1.name_last||', '||n1.name_first||' '||name_middle
                  "sort_name",
     person_gender,
     applicant_student_type,
     applicant_aid_intent,
     applicant_degreee,
     applicant_major
from
     name n1,
     person,
     applicant
where
     applicant_term ='199509'
                  and applicant_level = 'UG'
                  and applicant_college = 'AS'
     and person_id = applicant_id
     and n1.name = applicant_id
                  and n1.name_seriesno =
                  (select max(n2.name_seriesno)
                  from name n2
                  where n2.name_id = n1.name_id)
order by
     2, 6
/
```

Figure 10–14. An example of a query using the detail-only *report* object.

SQL

```
select
        applicant_id,
        n1.name_last||', '||n1.name_first||' '||name_middle "sort_name",
        person_gender,
        applicant_student_type,
        applicant_aid_intent,
        applicant_degreee,
        applicant_major
from
        name n1,
        person,
        applicant
where
        applicant_term ='199509'
                and applicant_level = 'UG'
                and applicant_college = 'AS'
        and person_id = applicant_id
        and n1.name = applicant_id
                and n1.name_seriesno =
                (select max(n2.name_seriesno)
                from name n2
                where n2.name_id = n1.name_id)
order by
        2, 6
/
```

REPORT

```
                                                    student aid     appl    appl
    id sort_name                               sex type    intent  degree  major
------ --------------------------------------- --- ------- ------- ------- -----
  2574 Abraham, Alicia                             F       Y       BA      GOV
  3163 Adams, Amy                              F   F       N       UN      UN
  2687 Adams, Samuel                           M   T       N       BA      CHEM
  8584 Adams, Thomas P.                        M   F       Y       UN      ECON
  1897 Affsa, Rita A.                          F   F       Y       BA      LANG
  6287 Agnew,, Angela                          F   F       Y       BA      HIST
  6260 Allen, Adam                             M   F       Y       BA      SOC
  3004 Allen, Alicia                               F       Y       BA      HIST
  2698 Allen, Cahren                               F       Y       UN      ART
  3650 Allen, Christine                        F   F       N       UN      BIOL
  8672 Allen, Justin                           M   F       Y       UN      UN
  5898 Allen, Karen                            F   F       Y       BA      UN
  4846 Allen, Kristen                          F   F       Y       BA      UN
  4970 Allen, Michael R.                       M   F       Y       BA      LANG
  8128 Allen, Shawn W.                         M   T       N       BA      MUSC
  4958 Allen, Shawnee                              F       Y       UN      UN
  5041 Amaral, Kris                            M   F       Y       BA      BIOL
   ...
```

Figure 10–15. A detail-only report from the query in Figure 10–14.

HELP

```
object:        repeat.obj
date created:  21-nov-1994
author         glewis
revisions:

Purpose:       Produce a detail report where repeating data
               gets suppressed (e.g., if an applicant has ten
               MAIL items the report shows all ten mailings
               but the applicant's name only once).

Usage:         1. Data columns in the select clause appear in
               two groups: i) columns where data repeats and
               should be shown only once; and ii) data columns
               causing the repeating data. Data columns in the
               first group should appear before data columns in
               the second group.
               2. column c#n '<<heading#n>>' format <format#n>:
               Each repeating column that appears in the select
               clause has a corresponding "column" command with
               a heading and format.
               3. <<col#1>> to <<col#n>>: Replace with repeating
               data column names that appear in the select clause
               (i.e., group 1i above).
               4. <<col#1R>> to <<col#mR>>: Replace with the names
               of the data columns that cause the repetition (i.e.,
               group 1ii above).
               5. <<population>>: Replace with a population object.
               6. <<where>>: Replace with one or more where
               objects, one of which is a class 2m where object.
               7. <<columns_subset>>: replace with desired sorting
               order (e.g., 3 asc sorts the listing in ascending
               order using the third data column in the select
               clause).

Hints:         None
```

OBJECT

```
column c#1 heading '<<heading#1>>' format <<format#1>>
...
column c#n heading '<<heading#n>>' format <<format#n>>
break on c#1 ... on c#n skip 1
select
       <<col#1>> "c#1",
       ...
       <<col#n>> "c#n"
       <<col#1R>>,
       ...
       <<col#mR>>
<<population>>
<<where>>
order by
       <<column_subset>>
/
```

Figure 10–16. Repeating detail *report* object and help file.

alias and a corresponding ***column*** command that sets the desired heading and format. The ***break*** command then suppresses duplicate data so it only appears once in the report. Figure 10–17 on the following page shows a completed repeating detail object and the resulting report.

SQL

```
SQL> column c1 heading 'id'
SQL> column c2 heading 'sort_name' format a25
SQL> column c3 heading 'sex' format a3
SQL> column c4 heading 'degree' format a6
SQL> column c5 heading 'major' format a5
SQL> break on c1 on c2 on c3 on c4 on c5 skip 1
SQL> select
        applicant_id "c1"
        n1.name_last||', '||n1.name_first||' '||n1.name_middle "c2",     [2]
        person_gender "c3",
        applicant_degree "c4",
        applicant_major "c5",
        document_code,
        cdocument_translation,
        document_receivedate
  from cdocument, document, name n1, person, applicant
  where
   [3]  applicant_term = '199509'
            and applicant_level = 'UG'
            and applicant_college = 'AS'
        and person_id = applicant_id                                    <-- [4]
   [5]  and n1.name_id = applicant_id
            and n1.name_seriesno =
            (select max(n2.name_seriesno)
            from name n2
            where n2.name_id = n1.name_id)
   [6]  and document_id(+) = applicant_id
            and document_applicant_term(+) = applicant_term
            and document_applicant_seriesno(+) = applicant_seriesno
        and cdocument_code(+) = document_code
  order by 2, 8;
```

Objects used:
1. repeat.obj
2. selsname.obj
3. popapp.obj
4. whrpersn.obj
5. whrname.obj
6. whrdcmnt.obj

REPORT

```
                                                doc                                  receive
     id sort_name                 sex degree major code document                     date
------- ------------------------- --- ------ ----- ---- ---------------------------- ---------
   2574 Abraham, Alicia               BA     GOV   PRT1 Part 1 of application        24-OCT-94
                                                   RANK Official high school rank    09-JAN-95
                                                   XOFF Unofficial test scores       12-JAN-95
                                                   FEE  Application fee              11-MAR-95

   3163 Adams, Amy                F   UN     UN    TEST SAT, ACT, Achievement scores 03-NOV-94
                                                   PRT1 Part 1 of application        29-DEC-94
                                                   PRT2 Part 2 of application        25-FEB-95
                                                   RANK Official high school rank    12-MAY-95
   ...
```

Figure 10–17. Repeating detail SQL and report.

Blocked

Because the data columns in blocked reports appear in rows instead of report columns, the header information is lost. If the content in the data columns is clear, there may be no need to print identifying labels. This is particularly true if the person requesting the report is very familiar with the data and can recognize the data columns by inspection. It's safer, however, to use a block labeled *report* object and include identifying labels.

Figure 10–18 shows the *report* object that produces a labeled block report and its associated help file. Figure 10–19 on the following page shows

HELP

```
object:        block.obj
date created:  20-nov-1994
author:        glewis
revisions:

Purpose:       A report object producing a simple roster (i.e., listing)
               of data columns in a blocked format.  Instead of appearing
               in columns across the report, data columns appear in rows
               down the report.  Labels are attached to the blocked columns.

Usage:         1. column c#n fold_after 1:  Each data column appearing in
               the select clause must have a corresponding "column" command.
               If there are 7 data columns in the select clause, there
               should be 7 column commands: column c#1 fold_after 1; column
               c#2 fold_after 1; etc.
               2. <<label#1>> to <<label#n>>: Replace with the labels that
               describe each of the data columns appearing in the select
               clause.
               3. <<col#1>> to <<col#n>>: Replace with the data column names
               appearing in the select clause.
               4. <<population>>: replace with a population object.
               5. <<where>>: Replace with one or more class 1 or class 2u
               where objects.  Remove if none is required.
               6. <<column_subset>>: Replace with desired sorting order
               (e.g., 3 asc sorts the listing in ascending order
               using the third data column in the select clause).

Hints:         None
```

OBJECT

```
set heading off
column c#1 fold_after 1
...
column c#n fold_after 1
select
       '<<label#1>>',
       <<col#1>> "c#1",
       ...
       '<<label#n>>',
       <<col#n>> "c#n"
<<population>>
<<where>>
order by
       <<columns_subset>>
/
```

Figure 10–18. Blocked *report* object.

SQL

```
SQL> set heading off
SQL> column c1 fold_after 1
SQL> column c2 fold_after 1
SQL> column c3 fold_after 1
SQL> column c4 fold_after 1
SQL> column c5 fold_after 1
SQL> column c6 fold_after 1
SQL> column c7 fold_after 1
SQL> select
  2         'id:          ',
  3         applicant_id "c1",
  4         'name:                       ',
  5         n1.name_last||', '||n1.name_first||' '||n1.name_middle "c2",
  6         'sex:                        ',
  7         person_gender "c3",
  8         'student_type: ',
  9         applicant_student_type "c4",
 10         'aid_intent:   ',
 11         applicant_aid_intent "c5",
 12         'degree:                     ',
 13         applicant_degree "c6",
 14         'major:                      ',
 15         applicant_major "c7"
 16   from
 17         name n1,
 18         person,
 19         applicant
 20   where
 21         applicant_term = '199509'
 22                and applicant_level = 'UG'
 23                and applicant_college = 'AS'
 24         and person_id = applicant_id
 25         and n1.name_id = applicant_id
 26                and n1.name_seriesno =
 27                (select max(n2.name_seriesno)
 28                from name n2
 29                where n2.name_id = n1.name_id)
 30   order by
 31         4
 32   /
```

Note the use of "fold_after 1" in the ***column*** commands to insert carriage returns, and the labeling applied to each column.

Objects used:
1. blockl.obj
2. popapp.obj
3. whrpersn.obj
4. whrname.obj

REPORT

```
id:            2574
name:          Abraham, Alicia
sex:
student_type:  F
aid_intent:    Y
degree:        BA
major:         GOV

id:            3163
name:          Adams, Amy
sex:           F
student_type:  F
aid_intent:    N
degree:        UN
major:         UN

id:            2687
name:          Adams, Samuel
sex:           M
student_type:  T
aid_intent:    N
degree:        BA
major:         CHEM

 ...
```

Figure 10–19. Block report and SQL.

an SQL query using the object; it also shows the final report. The secret to producing a blocked report lies in giving each data column an alias and then using the ***column*** command with the "fold_after 1" option. This inserts a carriage return after the data value is printed, ensuring that the next data value appears on a new line.

Block and Detail

Block and detail *report* objects also distinguish between two types of data columns appearing in the *select* clause. Appearing first are the unblocked columns; appearing last are the blocked columns. Give an alias to each of the blocked data columns in the *select* clause. Then use a ***column*** command with the "fold_after 1" option to insert carriage returns. A spacer is used to align the blocked data values underneath each other. This consists of a character string of spaces, with the number of spaces determining the alignment of the next blocked data value. When objects are used manually, the number of spaces must be determined by the query writer; when objects are automated (see Chapter 14), the spacer can be generated based on the data columns selected in the query.

Figure 10–20 on the following page shows the *report* object that produces a block and detail report. The figure also shows the help file that describes how to use the object. Figure 10–21 on page 239 shows an SQL query and report that uses the object.

Summary Report *Objects*

Summary reports include frequency distributions and cross-tabulations showing counts by one, two, or many categorical data columns; exactly analogous reports with counts replaced by averages or sums; and reports where counts, averages, sums or other summaries appear in any combination. All summary *report* objects utilize a *group by* clause in the SQL ***select*** command. They also use coordinated ***break*** and ***compute*** commands.

N-way Count Reports

Komenda College faces deteriorating interest in its business programs. This decline has been particularly noticeable among women. Suppose the president of Komenda asks the director of admissions to prepare a report showing the gender distribution of applicants for admission at the two colleges (Business and Arts & Sciences). The president would like to see if efforts to attract women into the Business College have had any effect. The director of admissions then turns to you for reports on applicants for next fall. She

HELP

```
object:        blckdtl.obj
date created:  21-nov-1994
author:        glewis
revisions:

Purpose:       Produces a combined detail and blocked detail report.

Usage:         1. Data columns in the select clause appear in two groups:
               i) columns that are not blocked (col#1 to col#n), and
               ii) data columns that are blocked (colb#1 to colb#m).
               Data columns in the first group should appear before data
               columns in the second group.
               2. <<block_format>>: Replace with a format for the block
               (e.g., a40).
               3. <<blanks>>: Replace with the number of spaces that will
               align colb#2 under colb#1.
               4. <<population>>: Replace with a population object.
               5. <<where>>: Replace with one or more where objects, one
               of which is a class 2m where object.
               6. <<columns_subset>>: Replace with desired sorting order
               (e.g., 3 asc sorts the listing in ascending order
               using the third data column in the select clause).

Hints:         Column headings are controlled using the shell object
               shltt3.obj.
```

OBJECT

```
set heading off
column b#1 format <<block_format>> fold_after 1
column b#2 fold_after 1
...
column b#m fold_after 1
select
      <<col#1>>,
      ...
      <<col#n>>,
      <<colb#1>>,
      '<<blanks>>',
      <<colb#2>>,
      '<<blanks>>',
      ...
      <<colb#m>>
<<population>>
<<where>>
order by
      <<column_subset>>
/
```

Figure 10–20. Block and *detail* report object and help file.

already has final reports from last fall that will form the base year for comparisons needed to demonstrate progress in attracting more women into business programs.

Frequency distributions and cross-tabulations provide answers to questions that ask how a population (of applicants) is distributed by one or more categorical data columns (sex and college in this case). Figure 10–22 on page 240 shows the *report* object that produces a 1-way

SQL

```
SQL> column b1 format a35 fold_after 1
SQL> column b2 format a30 fold_after 1
SQL> select
         applicant_id,
         n1.name_last||', '||n1.name_first||' '||n1.name_middle "sort_name",
         person_gender,
         d1.address_street1 "b1",
         '                                        ',
         decode(d1.address_city||d1.address_state||d1.address_zip||d1.address_nation,
                 null, null,
                 decode(d1.address_city,
                         null, d1.address_state||' '||d1.address_zip||' '||
                                 d1.address_nation,
                         d1.address_city||', '||d1.address_state||' '||
                                 d1.address_zip||' '||d1.address_nation)) "b2"
 from address d1, name n1, person, applicant
 where applicant_term = '199509'
           and applicant_level = 'UG'
           and applicant_college = 'AS'
  and person_id = applicant_id
  and n1.name_id = applicant_id
           and n1.name_seriesno =
           (select max(n2.name_seriesno)
           from name n2
           where n2.name_id = n1.name_id)
  and d1.address_id(+) = applicant_id
           and d1.address_type(+) = 'PR'
           and nvl(d1.address_seriesno, 1) =
           (select max(nvl(d2.address_seriesno, 1))
           from
                   address d2,
                   person
           where
                   person_id = applicant_id
                   and d2.address_id(+) = person_id
                           and d2.address_type(+) = 'PR')
 order by 2;
```

Objects used:
1. blckdtl.obj
2. selsname.obj
3. selcszn.obj
4. popapp.obj
5. whrpersn.obj
6. whrname.obj
7. whraddr.obj

REPORT

```
    id sort_name                 sex PR address
------ ------------------------- --- ------------------------------
  2574 Abraham, Alicia               264 Park Street
                                     Fort Smith, AR 72903

  3163 Adams, Amy                F   39 Hickory Road Apt. #279
                                     Wayne, NJ 07470

  2687 Adams, Samuel             M   9950 Edgewater St Apt. #28C
                                     San Juan, PR 00911

  8584 Adams, Thomas P.          M   3361 Hickory Tiempos Lane West
                                     Leysin,  CH-1854 SUI

  1897 Affsa, Rita A.            F   23389 Meadown Drive
                                     Newark, NJ 07104

  6287 Agnew, Angela             F   1136 Victoria Hollow Drive
                                     Chesterfield, MO 63005

   ...
```

Figure 10–21. Block and detail report and SQL.

REPORT

```
SQL> break on report
SQL> compute sum of count on report
SQL> select
  2         person_gender,
  3         count(*) "count"
  4  from
  5         person,
  6         applicant
  7  where
  8         applicant_term = '199509'
  9                and applicant_level = 'UG'
 10                and applicant_college = 'AS'
 11         and person_id = applicant_id
 12  group by
 13         person_gender
 14  /
ENTER to continue ...
sex      count
--- ----------
F          316
M          260
           124
    ----------
sum        700
```

Objects used:
1. count1.obj (report)
2. popapp.obj

HELP

```
object:       count1.obj
date created: 09-may-1994
author:       glewis
revisions:

Purpose:      Produces a report counting the report population by
              categories in one coded data column (i.e., a 1-way
              frequency distribution).

Usage:        1. <<col1>>: Replace with the name of the data column upon
              which the frequency counts will be done
              (eg,applicant_degree).
              2. <<population>>: Replace with a population object.
              3. <<where>>: Replace with one or more class 1 or class 2u
              where objects.  Remove if none is required.

Hints:        None
```

OBJECT

```
break on report
compute sum of count on report
select
      <<col1>>,
      count(*) "count"
<<population>>
<<where>>
group by
      <<col1>>
/
```

Figure 10–22. 1-way frequency distribution object, help file, and sample report.

frequency distribution. Note that the ***break*** and ***compute*** commands work together to include a grand total in the report. The figure also shows the help file, the SQL query for a frequency distribution of applicants in Arts & Sciences by gender, and the report itself.

Figure 10–23 on the following page shows a 2-way report of applicants by gender and by college. The figure also shows the object that produces this type of report. Note that this structure provides subtotals as well as grand totals.

The basic 1-way and 2-way objects shown in Figure 10–22 and Figure 10–23 frequently get modified to include code descriptors. This probably isn't necessary in the two reports just shown. Users won't have difficulty determining that a gender code of F means Female; nor will they misinterpret the college codes. Not all codes are this clear or well known, however. In such circumstances it's best to include code translations in the report. Figure 10–24 on page 243 shows a modified 1-way frequency report that includes code translations. Note that the *report* object producing this modified 1-way count differs very little from the basic 1-way object; only an additional *select* and *group by* column are needed.

N-way Sum or Average Reports

To produce 1-way, 2-way or n-way reports of averages or sums requires very few changes to the corresponding frequency *report* objects just discussed. Instead of a "count(*)," the object contains a "avg(avg_column)" or "sum(sum_column)." Figure 10–25 on page 244 shows the *report* object producing a 1-way breakdown of average SAT math scores by gender. Figure 10–26 on page 245 shows the *report* object producing a 1-way breakdown of collected application fees (i.e., sums) by gender.

N-way Mixed Reports

It is also easy to extend n-way *report* objects by including two or more summary computations; for example, by including counts in the basic reports showing sums or averages. Figure 10–27 on page 246 shows a 1-way breakdown of average SAT math scores by gender. It also shows how many test scores are included in the averages. Reports of sums and counts are entirely analogous. Figure 10–28 on page 247 shows the object needed to produce a 1-way sum and count report.

REPORT

```
SQL> column sex format a3
SQL> break on report on sex skip 1
SQL> compute sum of count on report sex
SQL> select
  2         person_gender "sex",
  3         applicant_degree,
  4         count(*) "count"
  5  from   person, applicant
  6  where
  7         applicant_term = '199509'
  8                 and applicant_level = 'UG'
  9                 and applicant_college = 'AS
 10         and person_id = applicant_id
 12  group by
 13         person_gender,
 14         applicant_degree
 15  /
ENTER to continue ...
    appl
sex degree        count
--- ------ ----------
F   BA              219
    BAMBA            20
    UN               77
***        ----------
sum                 316

M   BA              183
    BAMBA            14
    UN               63
***        ----------
sum                 260

    BA               87
    BAMBA             5
    UN               32
***        ----------
sum                 124

           ----------
sum                 700
```

Objects used:
1. count2.obj (report)
2. popapp.obj

HELP

```
object:         count2.obj
date created:   20-nov-1994
author:         glewis
revisions:

Purpose:        Produces a report counting the report population by
                categories of two coded data columns (i.e., a 2-way cross-
                tabulation).

Usage:          1. <<alias1>>: Replace with an alias for the first data
                column.
                2. <<fmt1>>: Replace with a format for the first data
                column (e.g., a8).
                3. <<col1>>: Replace with the name of the first data column
                appearing in the select clause.
                4. <<col2>>: Replace with the name of the second data column
                appearing in the select clause.
                5. <<population>>: Replace with a population object.
                6. <<where>>: Replace with one or more class 1 or class 2u
                where objects. Remove if none is required.

Hints:          None
```

OBJECT

```
column <<alias1>> format <<fmt1>>
break on report on <<alias1>> skip 1
compute sum of count on report <<alias1>>
select
       <<col1>> "<<alias1>>",
       <<col2>>,
       count(*) "count"
<<population>>
<<where>>
group by
       <<col1>>,
       <<col2>>
/
```

Figure 10–23. 2-way frequency distribution (cross-tabulation) object, help file, and sample report.

Objects used:
1. cnt1lab.obj (report)
2. popapp.obj

REPORT

```
SQL> break on report
SQL> compute sum of count on report
SQL> select
  2         person_ethnic,
  3         cethn_translation,
  4         count(*) "count"
  5  from
  6         cethn,
  7         person,
  8         applicant
  9  where
 10         applicant_term = '199509'
 11                 and applicant_level = 'UG'
 12                 and applicant_college = 'AS
 13         and person_id = applicant_id
 14         and cethn_code(+) = person_ethnic
 15  group by
 16         person_ethnic,
 17         cethn_translation
 18  /
ENTER to continue ...
ethnic ethnic status                          count
------ ------------------------------------ ----------
A      Asian-American                              15
B      Black                                        8
C      Caucasian                                  114
H      Hispanic                                    14
I      American Indian                              1
N      Non-resident                                35
X      Unknown                                    378
                                                  135
                                            ----------
sum                                               700

8 rows selected.
```

HELP

```
object:         cnt1lab.obj
date created:   20-nov-1994
author:         glewis
revisions:

Purpose:        Produces a report counting the report population by
                categories in a single coded data column.  Includes a
                column that provides the code translation.

Usage:          1. <<col1>>: Replace with the name of the data column upon
                which the frequency counts will be done (eg,
                (applicant_degree).
                2. <<col2>>: Replace with the name of the data column
                containing the code translations for <<col1>> (e.g., cdegree
                contains codes and their translation for applicant_degree).
                3. <<population>>: Replace with a population object.
                4. <<where>>: Replace with one or more class 1 or class 2u
                where objects.  One of these must access the code translation
                table containing <<col2>>.

Hints:          None
```

OBJECT

```
break on report
compute sum of count on report
select
      <<col1>>,
      <<col2>>,
      count(*) "count"
<<population>>
<<where>>
group by
      <<col1>>,
      <<col2>>
/
```

Figure 10–24. Labeled 1-way frequency distribution object, help file, and sample report.

REPORT

```
SQL> column avg heading 'avg|satm' format 9999
SQL> select
  2          person_gender,
  3          avg(t1.test_score) "avg"
  4  from
  5          test t1,
  6          person,
  7          applicant
  8  where
  9          applicant_term = '199509'
 10                  and applicant_level = 'UG'
 11                  and applicant_college = 'AS'
 12          and person_id = applicant_id
 13          and t1.test_id(+) = applicant_id
 14                  and t1.test_type(+) = 'SATM'
 15                  and to_char(nvl(t1.test_score,800))||
 16                          to_char(nvl(t1.test_date,'01-JAN-50')
 17                          (select max(to_char(nvl(t2.test_score
 18                                  to_char(nvl(t2.test_date,'01-
 19                          from
 20                                  test t2,
 21                                  person pn1
 22                          where pn1.person_id = applicant_id
 23                                  and t2.test_id(+) = pn1.perso
 24                                  and t2.test_type(+) = 'SATM')
 25  group by
 26          person_gender
 27  /
ENTER to continue ...
      avg
sex  satm
--- -----
F     591
M     591
      583
```

[2] (lines 9–11) [3] (line 12) [4] (lines 13–24)

Objects used:
1. avg1.obj (report)
2. popapp.obj
3. whrpersn.obj
4. whrtest.obj

HELP

```
object:         avg1.obj
date created:   20-nov-1994
author:         glewis
revisions:

Purpose:        A report OBJECT showing the average of a data column
                broken down by the categories of a coded data column (e.g.,
                showing average test scores by gender).

Usage:          1. <<heading>>: Replace with column header for data column
                being averaged.
                2. <<format>>: Replace with format (e.g., 9,999) for data
                column being averaged.
                2. <<col1>>: Replace with the name of the categorical
                (i.e., coded) data column.
                3. <<avg_col>>: Replace with the name of the numeric data
                column upon which averages will be computed.
                4. <<population>>: Replace with a population object.
                5. <<where>>: Replace with one or more class 1 or class 2u
                where objects.  Remove if none is required.

Hints:          Report does not show a grand-total average.
```

OBJECT

```
column avg heading '<<heading>>' format <<format>>
select
        <<col1>>,
        avg(<<avg_col>>) "avg"
<<population>>
<<where>>
group by
        <<col1>>
/
```

Figure 10–25. 1-way average object, help file, and sample report.

REPORT

```
SQL> column total heading 'est|fees' format $999,990
SQL> select
  2        person_gender,
  3        sum(decode(applicant_aid_intent, 'Y', 50, 'N', 200, 100)) "total"
  4  from
  5        person,
  6        applicant
  7  where
  8        applicant_term = '199509'
  9               and applicant_level = 'UG'
 10               and applicant_college = 'AS'
 11        and person_id = applicant_id
 12  group by
 13        person_gender
 14  /
ENTER to continue ...
            est
sex        fees
--- ---------
F     $27,050
M     $22,900
      $11,150
```

Objects used:
1. sum1.obj (report)
2. popapp.obj
3. whrpersn.obj

HELP

```
object:        sum1.obj
date created:  21-nov-1994
author:        glewis
revisions:

Purpose:       A report object showing the sum of a data column
               broken down by the categories of a coded data column (e.g.,
               showing total fees by gender).

Usage:         1. <<heading>>: Replace with column header for data column
               being averaged.
               2. <<format>>: Replace with format (e.g., 9,999) for data
               column being averaged.
               2. <<col1>>: Replace with the name of the categorical (i.e.,
               coded) data column.
               3. <<sum_col>>: Replace with the name of the numeric data
               column upon which sums will be computed.
               4. <<population>>: Replace with a population object.
               5. <<where>>: Replace with one or more class 1 or class 2u
               where objects.  Remove if none is required.

Hints:
```

OBJECT

```
column total heading '<<heading>>' format <<format>>
select
      <<col1>>,
      sum(<<sum_col>>) "total"
<<population>>
<<where>>
group by
      <<col1>>
/
```

Figure 10–26. 1-way sum object, help file, and sample report.

REPORT

```
SQL> column avg heading 'avg|satm' format 9999
SQL> break on report
SQL> compute sum of count on report
SQL> select
          person_gender,
          avg(t1.test_score) "avg",
          count(*) "count"
     from
          test t1,
          person,
          applicant
     where
          applicant_term = '199509'
                and applicant_level = 'UG'
                and applicant_college = 'AS'
          and person_id = applicant_id
          and t1.test_id(+) = applicant_id
                and t1.test_type(+) = 'SATM'
                and to_char(nvl(t1.test_score,800))|
                        to_char(nvl(t1.test_date,'0
                        (select max(to_char(nvl(t2.
                                to_char(nvl(t2.test
                        from
                                test t2,
                                person pn1
                        where pn1.person_id = applic
                                and t2.test_id(+) =
                                and t2.test_type(+)
     group by
          person_gender
     /
ENTER to continue ...
      avg
sex  satm      count
---  ----- ----------
F     591        316
M     591        260
      583        124
           ----------
sum              700
```

Objects used:
1. avg1cnt.obj (report)
2. popapp.obj
3. whrpersn.obj
4. whrtest.obj

HELP

```
object:        avg1cnt.obj
date created:  20-nov-1994
author:        glewis
revisions:

Purpose:       A report object showing the average of a data column
               broken down by the categories of a coded data column (e.g.,
               showing average test scores by gender).  The report includes
               counts of items averaged.

Usage:         1. <<heading>>: Replace with column header for data column
               being averaged.
               2. <<format>>: Replace with format (e.g., 9,999) for data
               column being averaged.
               2. <<col1>>: Replace with the name of the categorical (i.e.,
               coded) data column.
               3. <<avg_col>>: Replace with the name of the numeric data
               column upon which averages will be computed.
               4. <<population>>: Replace with a population object.
               5. <<where>>: Replace with one or more class 1 or class 2u
               where objects.  Remove if none is required.

Hints:         Report does not show a grand-total average.
```

OBJECT

```
column avg heading '<<heading>>' format <<format>>
break on report
compute sum of count on report
select
        <<col1>>,
        avg(<<avg_col>>) "avg",
        count(*) "count"
<<population>>
<<where>>
group by
        <<col1>>
/
```

Figure 10–27. 1-way average and count object, help file, and sample report.

Objects used:
1. sum1.obj
2. popapp.obj
3. whrpersn.obj

REPORT

```
SQL> column total heading 'est|fees' format $999,990
SQL> break on report
SQL> compute sum of count total on report
SQL> select
  2         person_gender,
  3         sum(decode(applicant_aid_intent, 'Y', 50, 'N', 200, 100)) "total",
  4         count(*) "count"
  5  from
  6         person,
  7         applicant
  8  where
  9         applicant_term = '199509'
 10                 and applicant_level = 'UG'
 11                 and applicant_college = 'AS'
 12         and person_id = applicant_id
 13  group by
 14         person_gender
 15  /
ENTER to continue ...
          est
sex      fees       count
--- --------- ----------
F     $27,050        316
M     $22,900        260
      $11,150        124
    --------- ----------
sum   $61,100        700
```

HELP

```
object:        sumlcnt.obj
date created:  21-nov-1994
author:        glewis
revisions:

Purpose:       A report object showing the sum of a data column
               broken down by the categories of a coded data column (e.g.,
               showing total fees by gender).  The report includes counts
               of items summed.

Usage:         1. <<heading>>: Replace with column header for data column
               being averaged.
               2. <<format>>: Replace with format (e.g., 9,999) for data
               column being averaged.
               2. <<col1>>: Replace with the name of the categorical (i.e.,
               coded) data column.
               3. <<sum_col>>: Replace with the name of the numeric data
               column upon which sums will be computed.
               4. <<population>>: Replace with a population object.
               5. <<where>>: Replace with one or more class 1 or class 2u
               where objects.  Remove if none is required.

Hints:
```

OBJECT

```
column total heading '<<heading>>' format <<format>>
break on report
compute sum of count total on report
select
       <<col1>>,
       sum(<<sum_col>>) "total",
       count(*) "count"
<<population>>
<<where>>
group by
       <<col1>>
/
```

Figure 10–28. 1-way sum and count object, help file, and sample report.

Hybrid Report *Objects*

Hybrid reports combine detail and summary into one report. The common summaries include counts, averages, sums, and combinations of these. It's possible, then, to have detail and count reports; detail and sum reports; detail and average reports; detail, sum, and count reports; and so on. This section discusses only a detail and count *report* object. Extending this object to other subclasses should be obvious based on objects discussed in previous sections.

Detail and Count

A detail and count report is just a detail report sorted by one (or more) data columns with counts of population items appearing in each sort category. For example, a report of applicants sorted by major would include a count of applicants within each major; a report of applicants sorted by ethnic status would include a count within each ethnic code.

Figure 10–29 shows the object that produces a detail and count report. It also shows the associated help file describing how to use the object. Figure 10–30 on page 250 shows an SQL query and report based on the object.

Object Inventory

Report objects serve as a foundation for constructing SQL queries. All other object classes except *shell* objects get assembled within the structure provided by *report* objects. However, you need not be limited to reports illustrated in this chapter. For example, you could construct a detail *report* object producing mailing labels. You could also design a *report* object producing a delimited flat file without headers and suitable for importing into spreadsheet or statistical packages. You could also modify any of the objects in this chapter, making them more suitable for your own work.

This chapter built twelve *report* objects. Table 10–3 on page 251 adds these objects to our running inventory that provides the basis for the ad hoc reporting done in Chapter 13.

HELP

```
object:        dtlcnt.obj
date created:  21-nov-1994
author:        glewis
revisions:

Purpose:       Produces a combined detail and count report.

Usage:         1. There are two special data columns that appear in the
               select clause: i) A data column that will be counted (e.g.,
               an id number) that appears as the first column in the select,
               and ii) A data column that the report is sorted on and
               broken on so that sub-totals can be computed.
               2. <<count_col>>: Replace with an alias for the data column
               that will be counted.
               3. <<headingc>>: Replace with a heading for the counted data
               column.
               4. <<formatc>>: Replace with a format for the counted data
               column.
               5. <<break_col>>: Replace with an alias for the data column
               that will be sorted and broken on.
               6. <<headingb>>: Replace with a heading for the break column.
               7. <<formatb>>: Replace with a format for the break column.
               5. <<population>>: Replace with a population object.
               6. <<where>>: Replace with one or more where objects, one
               of which is a class 2m where object.
               7. <<#n>>: Replace with the number identifying the position
               of the break column <<break_col>> in the select clause.

Hints:               None
```

OBJECT

```
column <<count_col>> heading <<headingc>> format <<formatc>>
column <<break_col>> heading '<<headingb>>' format <<formatb>>
break on report on <<break_col>> skip 1
compute count of <<count_col>> on report <<break_col>>
select
      <<col#1>> "<<count_col>>",
      ...
      <<col#n>> "<<break_col>>",
      ...
      <<col#t>>
<<population>>
<<where>>
order by
      <<#n>>
/
```

Figure 10–29. Detail and count object and help file.

SQL

```
SQL> column id heading 'id'
SQL> column major heading 'major' format a6
SQL> break on report on major skip 1
SQL> compute count of id on report major
SQL> select
        applicant_id "id",
        n1.name_last||', '||n1.name_first||' '||n1.name_middle "sort_name",
        person_gender,
        applicant_major "major"
  from
        name n1,
        person,
        applicant
  where
        applicant_term = '199509'
              and applicant_level = 'UG'
              and applicant_college = 'AS'
        and person_id = applicant_id
        and n1.name_id = applicant_id
              and n1.name_seriesno =
              (select max(n2.name_seriesno)
              from name n2
              where n2.name_id = n1.name_id)
  order by
        4, 2
  /
```

Objects used:
1. dtlcnt.obj
2. selsname.obj
3. popapp.obj
4. whrpersn.obj
5. whrname.obj

REPORT

```
ENTER to continue ...
        id sort_name                  sex major
---------- -------------------------- --- ------
      2698 Allen, Cahren                  ART
      1798 Baker, Evelyn              F
      7899 Burke, Karl W.             M
        97 Chen, Stephen V.           M
      5761 Collins, Shawnee
      7080 DeMarco, Danielle
      7312 Doyle, John                M
      6234 Green, Allison             F
       532 Lee, Christopher           M
       379 Martin, Emily              F
      5159 Moore, Thomas K.           M
      6582 Patel, William             M
      8265 Pierce, Amy
      6031 Stephens, Christine        F
      3253 Thompson, Karen
----------                                ******
        15                                count

      3650 Allen, Christine           F   BIOL
      5041 Amaral, Kris               M
      3005 Anderson, Christine V      F
...
      2655 Ysona, Grant
----------                                ******
        65                                count

...

----------
       700
```

Figure 10–30. SQL and report for a detail and count report.

Table 10–3. Inventory of SQL objects.

Class	Name	Purpose
POPULATION	popacapp	Applicants accepted for admissions for a specified term, level, and college
	popapp	Applicants for admissions for a specified term, level, college
	popenrl	Accepted applicants for a specified term, level, and college who are expected to enroll
	poprecr	Recruits for a specified term and level
WHERE 1	whrintl	Defines the term "international" and modifies a population so only internationals are included
	whrmnrty	Defines the term "minority" and modifies a population so only individuals of color are included
WHERE 2u	whraddr	Provides access to the ADDRESS table for the most recent address of a specified type
	whradhi	Provides access to the ADDRESS table in a hierarchical fashion. Returns an address of a specified type (e.g., local). If this type of address is not available, it returns an address of a second specified type (e.g., permanent)
	whrname	Provides access to the NAME table for the most recent name
	whrpersn	Provides access to the PERSON table
	whrphon	Provides access to the PHONE table for the most recent phone of a specified type and associated with an address of a specified type
	whrtest	Provides access to the TEST table for the highest test score of a specified type
WHERE 2m	whraddrm	Provides access to the ADDRESS table for all addresses of a specified type
	whrdcmnt	Provides access to all documents in the DOCUMENT table for a population of applicants
SELECT	selage	Computes a person's age based on sysdate (the report date) and the person's birthdate
	selcszn	Creates a single display column by concatenating address_city, address_state, address_zip, and address_nation
	seliname	Creates a name using the initials of the first and middle names and concatenating these to name_last
	selintl	Identifies a person as an "international" based on their visa status
	selmajr	Collapses anticipated majors into academic departments
	selprank	Computes a person's percent rank in high school based on class size and class rank
	selrmnd1	Calculates a "reminder date" as the Monday that follows the date of application plus one month
	selrmnd2	Calculates a "reminder date" as 7 weeks (49 days) after the application date

(Continued)

Table 10–3. Inventory of SQL objects.

Class	Name	Purpose
SELECT	selsatc	Calculates a combined SAT score as the sum of SAT math and SAT verbal scores
	selsname	Creates a name by concatenating name_last, name_first, and name_middle
	seltestr	Calculates a test range (e.g., 400-499) that an SAT score falls within. Useful for frequency distributions by score ranges
REPORT	avg1	Produces a report showing the average of a data column broken down by the categories of a coded data column (e.g., showing average test scores by gender)
	avg1cnt	Produces a report showing the average of a data column broken down by the categories of a coded data column. Includes counts of items averaged
	blckdtl	Produces a combined detail and blocked detail report
	blockl	Produces a simple roster (i.e., listing) of data columns in a blocked format. Instead of appearing in columns across the report, data columns appear in rows down the report. Labels are attached to the blocked columns
	cnt1lab	Produces a report counting the report population by categories in a coded data column. Includes the code translations
	count1	Produces a report counting the report population by categories in a coded data column (i.e., a 1-way frequency distribution)
	count2	Produces a report counting the report population by categories in two coded data columns (i.e., a 2-way cross-tabulation)
	detail	Produces a simple roster or listing of data columns for the report population
	dtlcnt	Produces a combined detail and count report
	repeat	Produces a detail report where repeating data gets suppressed (e.g., if an applicant has ten MAIL items the report shows all ten mailings but the applicant's name only once)
	sum1	Produces a report showing the sum of a data column broken down by the categories of a coded data column (e.g., showing total fees by gender)
	sum1cnt	Produces a report showing the sum of a data column broken down by the categories of a coded data column. Includes counts of the items summed

Chapter 11

Building *Shell* Objects

By controlling many physical characteristics of the final report, *shell* objects perform a special function when preparing ad hoc reports. They control the final destination (printer, file, or screen), line sizes and page sizes, column headings, report titles, and stamping with date, time, and other documentation. *Shell* objects also control runtime interactions with the user. Queries can be generalized with embedded prompts that accept user responses. These responses get incorporated into the SQL and SQL*PLUS programs for one run of the report; the next run might use another set of responses yet requires no change in the program.

Earlier chapters, particularly Chapter 6 on the SQL*PLUS primer, discussed *shell* objects in some detail. Most of this chapter builds examples of *shell* objects that perform functions not previously discussed. This includes objects that prompt users and accept responses, capture those responses for inclusion in report titles, detect (and sometimes correct) errors in the responses, permit users to exit the program whenever errors are detected, and control column headings for specialized reports like the detail and block report.

SQL

```
select
      applicant_id,
      n1.name_last||', '||n1.name_first||' '||n1.name_middle "sort_name",
      academic_instcode,
      cinst_name,
      cinst_state
from
      cinst,
      academic e1,
      name n1,
      applicant
where
      applicant_term = '199509'
             and applicant_level = 'UG'
             and applicant_college = 'AS'
      and n1.name_id = applicant_id
             and n1.name_seriesno =
             (select max(n2.name_seriesno)
             from name n2
             where n2.name_id = n1.name_id)
      and e1.academic_id(+) = applicant_id
             and nvl(e1.academic_degree,'HS') = 'HS'
             and to_char(nvl(e1.academic_datestamp,'01-JAN-50'),'YYYYMMDD
                    (select max(to_char(nvl(e2.academic_datestamp,'01-JAN
                    from

      and cinst
order by 2
/
```

SHELL

```
set termout off
start &&object_dir.\clears
start &&object_dir.\hpprintr
start &&object_dir.\date
start &&object_dir.\time
start &&object_dir.\owncol
start &&object_dir.\escape

ttitle left xEscape skip 1-
      'Last high school attended by undergrad applicants to Arts
and Sciences: Fall 1995' -
        right 'Report name: fig11-1.lis' skip 1 -
      left 'Date: ' xDate '     Time: ' xTime -
      right 'SQL name:    fig11-1.sql' skip 1 -
      right 'Page: ' format 999 sql.pno skip 2;

spool fig11-1.lis
      start xfig11-1
      start &&object_dir.\reset
spool off

start &&object_dir.\clears
start &&object_dir.\screen
```

REPORT

```
Last high school attended by undergrad applicants to Arts and Sciences: Fall 1995        Report name: fig11-1.lis
Date: 04-DEC-1994     Time: 07:59                                                        SQL name:    fig11-1.sql
                                                                                               Page:     1

                                  inst
    id sort_name                  code   school_name                    state
------ ------------------------- ------ ------------------------------ -----
  2574 Abraham, Alicia            0401   Soutside High School           AR
  3163 Adams, Amy                 3104   Wallkill Valley Regional HS    NJ
  2687 Adams, Samuel              5459   Episcopal Cathedral School     PR
  8584 Adams, Thomas P.           7968   College Du Leman
  1897 Affsa, Rita A.             3108   Barringer High School          NJ
  6287 Agnew, Angela              2609   Lafayette High School          MO
  6260 Allen, Adam                0708   Trumbull High School           CT
  3004 Allen, Alicia              3314   Commack High School North      NY
  2698 Allen, Cahren              0709   Wethersfield High School       CT
  3650 Allen, Christine
  8672 Allen, Justin              2635   Waynesville Senior High School MO
   ...
```

Figure 11–1. Sample report produced from a completed shell program and a main SQL program.

Summary of *Shell* Objects

Chapter 6 (e.g., see Figure 6–10) used *shell* objects to discuss SQL*PLUS commands. These objects each perform a specific job, summarized here:

- **Screen.sql** controls characteristics of reports sent to the monitor. This includes whether the report pauses at the end of each page or scrolls continuously from start to end. The object also sets the page dimensions (how many characters fit across a line and how many lines fit on the screen), and determines if SQL commands get echoed to the screen as they are executed.
- **Clears.sql** performs clean-up functions. It clears away all previously set ***column*** definitions, ***compute*** statements, and ***break*** commands, providing a blank slate for the construction of a new query and report.
- **Printer.sql** defines the physical dimensions of reports destined for a printer. It controls line size and page size. It turns off the pausing used when reading reports from a monitor; prevents the appearance of SQL code in the final report (this sometimes concerns users); and enables the feedback option that prints how many rows were selected for the report.
- **Date.sql** and **time.sql** capture the date and time when the query was executed. These values then get used in the report title to provide documentation about the report. If the information in a report is time sensitive, a report without a run date quickly loses all utility.
- **Escape.sql** generates the escape sequences that control many printers. As the object appears in Chapter 6, it sets a Hewlett-Packard LaserJet printer for landscape compressed mode.
- **Reset.sql** sends the printer an escape sequence that resets the printer to its normal mode.
- **Shell.obj** is the meta-shell object that provides a home for all other *shell* objects. It also starts the SQL command file that actually accesses the database and retrieves data for the report.

Figure 11–1 shows a completed shell program containing each of the objects mentioned above. It also shows the main SQL program and the

```
OBJECT

/*
        sql:     <shell_name>
        date:    <date>
        author:  <author>
        purpose: <purpose_text>
*/
set termout off
start &&object_dir.\clears
start &&object_dir.\hpprintr
start &&object_dir.\date
start &&object_dir.\time
start &&object_dir.\owncol
start &&object_dir.\escape

<prompts>
<title>

spool <report_name>
        start <subprogram>
        start &&object_dir.\reset
spool off

start &&object_dir.\clears
start &&object_dir.\screen
```

```
HELP

Object:        shell.obj
date created:  09-may-1994
author:        glewis
revisions:

Purpose:       Provides a shell for each ad hoc report from which the
               SQL program is started. Controls printer and screen
               characteristics, report titles, column headers, and other
               features of the finished report.

Usage:         1. <shell_name>: Replace with name for SQL (e.g.,
                       example1.sql).
               2. <date>: Replace with date report was created.
               3. <author>: Replace with author of report.
               4. <purpose_text>: Replace with a brief statement of why the
                       report was created.
               5. <prompts>: Replace with any objects needed to prompt
                       users for responses (e.g., using shlprmpt.obj).
                       Remove if not needed.
               6. <title>: Replace with one of the title objects (e.g.,
                       shlttl1.obj). Remove if not needed.
               7. <report_name>: Replace with the name of the file that
                       will contain the output report.
               8. <main_program>: Replace with the name of the SQL program
                       that will actually retrieve the data for the report.

Hints: None
```

Figure 11–2. Principal *shell* object.

resulting report. Together the shell program and the main SQL program comprise a completed ad hoc query. Figure 11–2 shows the meta-shell object used to produce the shell program in Figure 11–1. Note that two items must be replaced. One refers to user interactions, the second to report titles.

User Interaction

All of the *population* and *where* objects built in earlier chapters contained items that needed replacement when the objects actually were used. Figure 11–3 shows, for example, the *population* object defining applicants for admissions. In order to use the object, you must replace <term>, <level>, and <college> with appropriate values.

Objects used in this fashion presume manual manipulation. That is, a programming editor must be used to substitute values for each of the items enclosed by brackets. This works fine, and is easy to do. It even performs a valuable service by forcing you to look at the SQL again. Sometimes definitions change or your understanding of how the database design interacts

HELP

```
object:        popapp.obj
date created:  13-oct-1994
author:        glewis
revisions:

Purpose:       Defines the population of applicants for a specified
               term, level, and college (Arts & Sciences, Business)

Usage:         1. <term>: replace with term (eg, 199409 for Fall 1994)
               2. <level>: replace with level (eg, UG for Undergrad)
               3. <college>: replace with college (eg, AS or BU)

Hints:         none
```

OBJECT

```
from
     applicant
where
     applicant_term = '<term>'
            and applicant_level = '<level>'
            and applicant_college = '<college>'
```

Figure 11–3. Applicant *population* object and help file discussed in Chapter 7.

with the data becomes more sophisticated. When this happens, it's useful to examine objects again just to ensure that the SQL code is current. Using an editor to assemble objects provides this opportunity.

But most end users do not want to use editors to assemble or manipulate objects. They require some degree of automation (Chapter 14 discusses this in detail). Users may also hesitate to tweak an existing SQL query so it runs with slightly different criteria. For example, a report summarizing February expenses works well until March. It would be nice if some method existed to generalize queries. This makes the query more useful; it also eliminates the need for users to perform minor programming changes.

HELP

```
object:       popxapp.obj
date created: 30-nov-1994
author:       glewis
revisions:

Purpose:      Defines the population of applicants for a specified
              term, level, and college (Arts & Sciences, Business).
              Accepts prompts for term, level, and college.

Usage:        1. Use with shell objects that prompt for applicant
              term, level, and college.

Hints:        none
```

OBJECT

```
from
        applicant
where
        applicant_term = '&&xTerm'
              and applicant_level = '&&xLevel'
              and applicant_college = '&&xCollege'
```

This applicant *population* object uses substitution variables for term, level, and college. Values for substitution variables get entered by users when they run the query.

Figure 11–4. Generalized *population* object that uses runtime responses from users.

Fortunately, objects can be generalized with substitution variables. Recall from Chapter 6 that a substitution variable is a user-defined variable identified by one or two ampersands (&) in front of the variable name. When programs containing substitution variables get executed, SQL replaces the variable with its actual value. Figure 11–4 shows the *population* object of admissions applicants now generalized with substitution variables for term, level, and college.

Generalizing objects incurs a cost, however. Users must attach specific values to the substitution variables at runtime. This means prompting users for what value they want to use, capturing the input for use when documenting the report, detecting any input errors, and determining a course of action when errors occur. All these require additional objects that must work in coordination with the *population* or *where* objects containing the substitution variables.

Figure 11–5 on the following page shows an object that prompts users for values of substitution variables. Figure 11–6 on page 261 shows the object actually used in an example. Let's see what it does. The example prompts for admissions level (i.e., undergraduate or graduate) and consists of five parts. Part 1 is a place-setter, preparing for the main work of the object. Part 5 is the reverse of Part 1, providing an exit from the object that cleans up any changes made in Part 1. Part 2 prompts the user for the admissions level and accepts the input into the substitution variable called &&level. Part 3 converts this response to uppercase because the codes for applicant_level are all uppercase. It also assigns this uppercase value to a new substitution variable called &&xLevel. Part 4 searches the code table CLEVEL that contains valid admissions level codes. If the code is located, the user is prompted to continue by pressing any key. If the code is not found in CLEVEL, then a warning is issued and a suggestion made that the user abort the program.

The object shown in Figure 11–6 is functional but not elegant. Minimizing, detecting, and handling errors occur in parts 3 and 4 of the object, but only through cumbersome code. SQL and SQL*PLUS get stretched to perform these operations, which are actually much easier to do with a procedural language. When more fully automating objects, procedural languages become essential.

```
HELP

object:         shlprmpt.obj
date created:   01-dec-1994
author:         glewis
revisions:

Purpose:        Prompts user for a coded data column (e.g., term, level,
                college, etc).  Verifies that response is valid.  Provides
                break opportunity if response is invalid.

Usage:          1. Use with any population or where object (e.g.,
                popxapp.obj) that accepts prompts.
                2. <variable_name>: Replace with a variable name for the
                coded data column (e.g., if prompting for applicant_term then
                you might choose 'term').
                3. <text>: Enter text string for prompt (e.g., 'Enter term: ').
                4. <define_var>: Enter another variable name for the coded
                data column, to use in a DEFINE command (e.g., 'xTerm').
                5. <code_table>: Enter name of code table containing valid
                values for the coded data column (e.g., the cterm table if
                checking applicant_term).
                6. <code_table.coded_data_column>: Replace with name of data
                column in <code_table> that contains the valid codes (e.g.,
                cterm_code in the table cterm).

Hints:              none
```

```
OBJECT

set termout off
ttitle off
set feedback off
set heading off

set verify off
set termout on
accept <variable_name> prompt '<text>'

set termout off
spool defines.sql
     select 'define <define_var> = ', '&&<variable_name>' from dual;
spool off
start defines

break on foundOK
column foundOK new_value xFlag
select count(*) foundOK from <code_table> where <code_table.coded_data_column> = '&&<define_var>';
set termout on
select decode(&&xFlag, 0, 'Invalid <variable_name>.  Press break key (e.g., ^C) to end.', null) from dual;
prompt Press any key to continue.
pause

set termout off
set feedback on
set heading on
ttitle on
```

Figure 11–5. *Shell* object used to prompt users at runtime for substitution variables.

OBJECT

```
set termout off
ttitle off
set feedback off
set heading off                                  [1]

set verify off
set termout on
accept level prompt 'Level:   '                  [2]

set termout off
spool defines.sql
      select 'define xLevel = ', upper('&&level') from dual;      [3]
spool off
start defines

break on foundOK
column foundOK new_value xFlag
select count(*) foundOK from clevel where clevel_code = '&&xLevel';      [4]
set termout on
select decode(&&xFlag,0,'Invalid level. Press break key (e.g., ^C) to end.', null) from dual;
prompt Press any key to continue.
pause

set termout off
set feedback on
set heading on
ttitle on                                        [5]
```

The prompting object contains five elements:

1. Gets ready to prompt.
2. Prompts.
3. Defines new variable based on user response.
4. Checks for errors in response.
5. Cleans up prior to exiting the object.

Figure 11–6. Completed *shell* object that prompts users for admission level.

Report Titles

Report titles are the second item that must be replaced to make the meta-shell object operational. Report titles often reflect preferences of individual query writers. I commonly use three different types.

Standard Title

A standard report title includes a line of text describing the report, the date the query ran, the time the query ran, a page number, the name of the output file containing the report, and the name of the shell program that produced the report. This standard title contains enough information to describe the report population for users; it also contains enough documentation to make later referral to the report or its underlying SQL easy.

Figure 11–7 shows the object and help file for a standard report title. To use it you need only insert a description of the report, the name of the output report file, and the name of the SQL program that produced the report. The title shown in Figure 11–1 provides an example of a standard report title.

Modified Standard Title

A modified standard title is used whenever the SQL includes user prompts. I like to capture user responses and display them in report titles. The modified standard report title contains all the elements in the standard report title, but it also includes any responses that the user made to run-time prompts.

HELP

```
object:        shlttl.obj
date created:  01-dec-1994
author:        glewis
revisions:

Purpose:       Inserts a standard top title into a report.

Usage:         1. <report_title_text>: Replace with the text you wish to
               appear at the top of each page of the report.
               2. <report_name>: Replace with the name of the file that
               will contain the output report.
               3. <shell_name>: Replace with the name of the SQL shell for
               the report.

Hints:         none
```

OBJECT

```
ttitle left xEscape skip 1-
       '<report_title_text>' -
       right 'Report name: <report_name>' skip 1 -
       left 'Date: ' xDate '     Time: ' xTime -
       right 'SQL name:    <shell_name>' skip 1 -
       right 'Page: ' format 999 sql.pno skip 2;
```

Figure 11–7. *Shell* object that produces a standard report title.

Figure 11–8 shows the object and help file that produce a modified standard title. You must insert the names of variables used to accept responses from users at runtime. Figure 11–9 on the following page shows a sample report that prompts the user for admissions term, level, and college. These three items appear in the title printed on each page of the report.

Column Heading Title

A special report title must be used whenever column headings are deliberately disabled. For example, the detail and block report discussed in Chapter 10 requires that column headings be set off. This prevents the structure of a block and detail report from creating an unattractive multiple-line

HELP

```
object:        shlttl2.obj
date created:  01-dec-1994
author:        glewis
revisions:

Purpose:       Inserts a top title into a report, including information on
               user responses to prompts.

Usage:         1. <report_title_text>: Replace with the text you wish to
               appear at the top of each page of the report.
               2. <variable_name>: Replace with variable name given to
               coded data column in shlprmpt.obj (e.g., 'Term').
               3. <define_var>: Replace with variable name given to coded
               data column and used in the DEFINE command in shlprmpt.obj
               (e.g., 'xTerm').
               4. <report_name>: Replace with the name of the file that
               will contain the output report.
               5. <shell_name>: Replace with the name of the SQL shell for
               the report.

Hints:         none
```

OBJECT

```
ttitle left xEscape skip 1-
       '<report_title_text>' -
       right 'Report name: <report_name>' skip 1 -
       left 'Date: ' xDate '      Time: ' xTime -
       right 'SQL name:    <shell_name>' skip 1 -
       left '<variable_name>: ' <define_var> -
       right 'Page: ' format 999 sql.pno skip 2;
```

Figure 11–8. *Shell* object that produces a standard title modified to capture user response to runtime prompts.

REPORT

```
Sample report using prompting objects                              Report name: elev-1.lis
Date: 01-DEC-1994     Time: 06:06                                  SQL name:     xelev-1.sql
Term: 199509     Level: UG     College: AS                                       Page:     1

ethnic      count
------ ----------
A              15
B               8
C             114
H              14
I               1
N              35
X             378
              135
       ----------
sum           700

8 rows selected.
```

SHELL

```
set termout off
start &&object_dir.\clears
start &&object_dir.\hpprintr
start &&object_dir.\date
start &&object_dir.\time
start &&object_dir.\owncol
start &&object_dir.\escape

start &&object_dir.\term
start &&object_dir.\level
start &&object_dir.\college

ttitle left xEscape skip 1-
       'Sample report using prompting objects' -
       right 'Report name: elev-1.lis' skip 1 -
       left 'Date: ' xDate '     Time: ' xTime -
       right 'SQL name:    xelev-1.sql' skip 1 -
       left 'Term: ' xTerm '     Level: ' xLevel '     College: ' xCollege -
       right 'Page: ' format 999 sql.pno skip 2;


spool elev-1.lis
       start xelev-1
       start &&object_dir.\reset
spool off

start &&object_dir.\clears
start &&object_dir.\screen
```

This line in the ***ttitle*** command produces the title highlighted in the report.

Figure 11–9. Completed shell and report using a modified standard report title.

column heading. But disabling column headings creates another problem: unless the data columns are obvious, it makes the user guess what data the columns contain. An alternative exists. You can create your own column headings and insert them into the report title. Column heading titles contain all elements in the standard report title, but they also contain text that identifies each column appearing in the report.

Figure 11–10 shows the object and help file that produce a column heading title. To use it you must insert a line of text containing the column headings for the report. Figure 11–11 on the following page shows a sample detail and block report using this type of title.

HELP

```
object:        shlttl3.obj
date created:  01-dec-1994
author:        glewis
revisions:

Purpose:       Inserts a top title into a detail and block report, where
               column headings are set off and must be controlled
               directly.

Usage:         1. <column_headings>: Replace with a line of text containing
                       the column headings (e.g., '     id sort_name ...').
               2. <line>: Replace with a line to use under the column
                       headings (e.g., '-------------------------').
               3. <report_title_text>: Replace with the text you wish to
                       appear at the top of each page of the report.
               4. <report_name>: Replace with the name of the file that
                       will contain the output report.
               5. <shell_name>: Replace with the name of the SQL shell for
                       the report.

Hints:         none
```

OBJECT

```
set heading off
define xCols = '<column_headings>'
define xLine = '<line>'
ttitle left xEscape skip 1-
       '<report_title_text>' -
       right 'Report name: <report_name>' skip 1 -
       left 'Date: ' xDate '     Time: ' xTime -
       right 'SQL name:    <shell_name>' skip 1 -
       right 'Page: ' format 999 sql.pno skip 2 -
       left xCols skip 1 -
       left xLine skip 1;
```

Figure 11–10. *Shell* object that produces a special title needed by the detail and block report.

REPORT

```
Example of detail and block report                    Report name: fig11-11.lis
Date: 04-DEC-1994     Time: 10:27                     SQL name:    fig11-11.sql
                                                                     Page:    1

   id sort_name                   sex PR address
---------------------------------------------------------------------------
 2574 Abraham, Alicia                   264 Park Street
                                        Fort Smith, AR 72903

 3163 Adams, Amy                  F     39 Hickory Road Apt. #279
                                        Wayne, NJ 07470

 2687 Adams, Samuel               M

 8584 Adams, Thomas P.            M

 1897 Affsa, Rita A.              F

 6287 Agnew, Angela               F

  ...
```

SHELL

```
set termout off
start &&object_dir.\clears
start &&object_dir.\hpprintr
start &&object_dir.\date
start &&object_dir.\time
start &&object_dir.\owncol
start &&object_dir.\escape

define xCols = '    id sort_name                    sex PR address'
define xLine = '-----------------------------------------------------------------'

ttitle left xEscape skip 1-
       'Example of detail and block report' -
       right 'Report name: fig11-11.lis' skip 1 -
       left 'Date: ' xDate '      Time: ' xTime -
       right 'SQL name:    fig11-11.sql' skip 1 -
       right 'Page: ' format 999 sql.pno skip 2 -
       left xCols skip 1 -
       left xLine skip 1;

spool fig11-11.lis
       start xfig11-11
       start &&object_dir.\reset
spool off

start &&object_dir.\clears
start &&object_dir.\screen
```

Defining xCols and xLine and including them in the ***ttitle*** command produces column headings in a detail and block report.

Figure 11–11. Completed shell and report using a special title needed by detail and block reports.

Inventory of Objects

Table 11–1 provides an inventory of objects built so far. It includes objects in each of the major object classes. In Chapter 13 we'll use these objects to construct ad hoc queries and reports; in the process we'll actually build several new objects. But first, it's important to understand how objects should be tested and debugged so that they perform well together.

Table 11–1. Inventory of SQL objects.

Class	Name	Purpose
POPULATION	popacapp	Applicants accepted for admissions for a specified term, level, and college
	popapp	Applicants for admissions for a specified term, level, college
	popenrl	Accepted applicants for a specified term, level, and college who are expected to enroll
	poprecr	Recruits for a specified term and level
	popxapp	Applicants for a specified term, level, and college. Accepts prompts for term, level, and college
WHERE 1	whrintl	Defines the term "international" and modifies a population so only internationals are included
	whrmnrty	Defines the term "minority" and modifies a population so only individuals of color are included
WHERE 2u	whraddr	Provides access to the ADDRESS table for the most recent address of a specified type
	whradhi	Provides access to the ADDRESS table in a hierarchical fashion. Returns an address of a specified type (e.g., local). If this type of address is not available, it returns an address of a second specified type (e.g., permanent)
	whrname	Provides access to the NAME table for the most recent name
	whrpersn	Provides access to the PERSON table
	whrphon	Provides access to the PHONE table for the most recent phone of a specified type and associated with an address of a specified type
	whrtest	Provides access to the TEST table for the highest test score of a specified type
WHERE 2m	whraddrm	Provides access to the ADDRESS table for all addresses of a specified type
	whrdcmnt	Provides access to all documents in the DOCUMENT table for a population of applicants
SELECT	selage	Computes a person's age based on sysdate (the report date) and the person's birthdate
	selcszn	Creates a single display column by concatenating address_city, address_state, address_zip, and address_nation

(Continued)

Table 11–1. Inventory of SQL objects.

Class	Name	Purpose
SELECT	seliname	Creates a name using the initials of the first and middle names and concatenating these to name_last
	selintl	Identifies a person as an "international" based on their visa status
	selmajr	Collapses anticipated majors into academic departments
	selprank	Computes a person's percent rank in high school based on class size and class rank
	selrmnd1	Calculates a "reminder date" as the Monday that follows the date of application plus one month
	selrmnd2	Calculates a "reminder date" as 7 weeks (49 days) after the application date
	selsatc	Calculates a combined SAT score as the sum of SAT math and SAT verbal scores
	selsname	Creates a name by concatenating name_last, name_first, and name_middle
	seltestr	Calculates a test range (e.g., 400–499) that an SAT score falls within. Useful for frequency distributions by score ranges
REPORT	avg1	Produces a report showing the average of a data column broken down by the categories of a coded data column (e.g., showing average test scores by gender)
	avg1cnt	Produces a report showing the average of a data column broken down by the categories of a coded data column. Includes counts of items averaged
	blckdtl	Produces a combined detail and blocked detail report
	blockl	Produces a simple roster (i.e., listing) of data columns in a blocked format. Instead of appearing in columns across the report, data columns appear in rows down the report. Labels are attached to the blocked columns
	cnt1lab	Produces a report counting the report population by categories in a coded data column. Includes the code translations
	count1	Produces a report counting the report population by categories in a coded data column (i.e., a 1-way frequency distribution)
	count2	Produces a report counting the report population by categories in two coded data columns (i.e., a 2-way cross-tabulation)
	detail	Produces a simple roster or listing of data columns for the report population
	dtlcnt	Produces a combined detail and count report
	repeat	Produces a detail report where repeating data gets suppressed (e.g., if an applicant has 10 MAIL items the report shows all 10 mailings but the applicant's name only once)
	sum1	Produces a report showing the sum of a data column broken down by the categories of a coded data column (e.g., showing total fees by gender)
	sum1cnt	Produces a report showing the sum of a data column broken down by the categories of a coded data column. Includes counts of the items summed

(Continued)

Table 11–1. Inventory of SQL objects.

Class	Name	Purpose
SHELL	shell.obj	Provides a shell for each ad hoc report. Starts the main SQL that retrieves data for the report. Houses other shell objects that control printer and screen characteristics, report titles,column headers, and other features of the finished report
	shlprmpt.obj	Prompts user for a report parameter to use at runtime. Verifies that the response is correct
	shlttl1.obj	Produces a standard top title for a report, including descriptive text, date stamp, time stamp, page number, and names of the files containing the SQL and the report output
	shlttl2.obj	Produces a modified standard report that also includes user responses to prompts
	shltt3.obj	Produces a standard title and column headings for a detail and block report

Chapter 12

Testing, Debugging, and Tuning SQL Objects

Objects have an interesting life-cycle. They originally get built for a requested report. You don't sit down one day and just decide to write five or six objects; rather, you get asked for a report that requires a new chunk of SQL code. If the new SQL seems useful for other queries, you then create an object and a help file. The object obviously gets tested so it works in the requested report. But this test represents just the first of many testings that all objects should receive.

An SQL query for a specific report gets done at one point in time under one set of circumstances. The fact that the SQL works at that time under those circumstances does not guarantee it will work at a later point in time or under other circumstances. It may work well within one constellation of objects, but does it work with all possible combination of objects? An object may work fine for one set of business rules, but what if those rules change? If the database administrator creates a new index to optimize certain types of queries, does an object perform well under these new conditions? If you upgrade from one version of the ORACLE RDBMS to another, what effect does that have on an object?

You should never stop testing the objects you build. This doesn't mean you must have a formal rigorous testing program. But with each query you write, you should subject the SQL to a minimal level of testing just to ensure that *under the conditions at the moment* the objects still work well. Objects evolve; as conditions change your objects must adapt.

This chapter is based on a request for a single report. The director of admissions at Komenda College wants a report on women applicants to the undergraduate college of Arts & Sciences for Fall 1995. She'd like to see a roster of applicants showing their I.D. number, name, the high school they're attending (or last attended), the state in which the high school is located, and the last admissions decision for the applicant.

Objects that we've already built provide much, but not all, of the required SQL. Figure 12–1 shows an initial query constructed by assembling some existing objects and writing some new but untested SQL. The existing objects define the population of applicants (popapp.obj), provide access to the PERSON table (whrpersn.obj), provide access to the NAME table (whrname.obj), and create a sort name expression (selsname.obj). The new SQL accesses the ACADEMIC table and the DECISION table. We'll first see if problems exist in the SQL (they do). The task then becomes one of finding the problems. Is it in the SQL or in the data? If it's in the SQL, what part of the code causes the problem? Once we've isolated the problem, how then do we fix it? This chapter addresses those questions.

Sometimes the population for a report is very large. Testing and debugging queries in this situation can try your patience while waiting for the test to complete. Processing a large number of table rows also puts an additional burden on system performance. Using a sample of the population can dramatically improve query completion times and relieve stress on you and on the computer system. The chapter also describes two procedures for sampling from a large population.

The chapter concludes by discussing query performance. As mentioned earlier, I use a "good enough" strategy with my queries. If they work in a reasonable time then I'm happy. I don't try to squeeze every last ounce of speed out of the query. But occasionally you'll find a query that takes more than a reasonable time even though the population size is small or moderate. When this happens, you need to analyze your SQL for performance problems. Where does the problem originate in the SQL and how can you fix it? Sometimes even a small change in the SQL can have tremendous impact on performance. My personal best is a query that a user aborted after two hours of running. Revising one line of SQL changed the entire strategy the ORACLE engine used to execute the query; it then completed in less than 30 seconds with a population of two!

SQL

```
select
        applicant_id,
        n1.name_last||', '||n1.name_first||' '||n1.name_middle "sort_name",     [1]
        academic_instcode,
        cinst_name,
        cinst_state,
        person_gender,
        decision_code,
        cdecision_translation
from
        cdecision,
        decision c1,
        cinst,
        academic e1,
        name n1,
        person,
        applicant
where
        applicant_term = '199509'                      [2]
                and applicant_level = 'UG'
                and applicant_college = 'AS'           [3]
        and person_id = applicant_id
                and person_gender = 'F'
        and n1.name_id = applicant_id
                and n1.name_seriesno =
                (select max(n2.name_seriesno)          [4]
                from name n2
                where n2.name_id = n1.name_id)
        and e1.academic_id(+) = applicant_id
                and nvl(e1.academic_seriesno,1) =
                (select max(nvl(e2.academic_seriesno,1))
                from
                        academic e2,
                        person
                where person_id = applicant_id
                        and e2.academic_id(+) = person_id)
        and cinst_code(+) = nvl(e1.academic_instcode,'unkn')
        and c1.decision_id = applicant_id
                and c1.decision_applicant_term = applicant_term
                and c1.decision_applicant_seriesno = applicant_seriesno
                and c1.decision_seriesno =
                        (select max(c2.decision_seriesno)
                        from decision c2
                        where c2.decision_id = c1.decision_id
                        and c2.decision_applicant_term = c1.decision_applicant_term
                        and c2.decision_applicant_seriesno = c1.decision_applicant_seriesno)
        and cdecision_code = c1.decision_code
/
```

Objects used:

1. selsname.obj
2. popapp.obj
3. whrpersn.obj
4. whrname.obj

Figure 12–1. Initial SQL query.

Maintaining Population Size

Each query has a population. Once the size of that population is determined, your SQL must prevent the two types of errors discussed in earlier chapters. Falling through a join causes population loss; multiplying through a join (or loss of singularity) causes population increase. Each SQL query must be tested for the presence of these two types of errors. Either type of error may exist individually or they may both exist simultaneously. You first test queries to see if problems exist. You then isolate those problems to portions of the SQL. Finding the table rows that create the errors often helps diagnose the problem. Then the issue becomes one of fixing the problem.

Identifying Problems

I know I've said this several other places, but it is important. The concept of a report population is absolutely central in an ad hoc query. You must be able to state in words what the population is; you must then translate those words into SQL. In the report requested by Komenda's director of admissions the population is "women applicants to the undergraduate college of Arts & Sciences for Fall 1995." Figure 12–2 shows the portion of the query that identifies this population.

Step 1: What Is the Population Size?

Start testing each query by determining the population size. Do this using a count(*) to count the number of rows the query returns. Use a count(distinct ...) to count the number of distinct items in the population. In Figure 12–2 the distinct count occurs on applicant_id because you want to know how many applicants exist in the population. Figure 12–2 shows that both counts are 318. There are 318 distinct applicants and 318 rows returned by the SQL defining the population.

The count(*) and count(distinct ...) must be identical at this point. If they are not, it means you have not identified the population correctly. Usually this just requires a change in your thinking about what constitutes the population. Suppose the director of admissions had requested a report on all admissions decisions for the women applicants to the undergraduate college of Arts & Sciences for Fall 1995. If you think of the population as applicants, the count(*) will differ from the count(distinct applicant_id) because

SQL

```
SQL> select
         count(*), count(distinct applicant_id)
     from
         person,
         applicant
     where
         applicant_term = '199509'
                 and applicant_level = 'UG'
                 and applicant_college = 'AS'
         and person_id = applicant_id
                 and person_gender = 'F'
     /
ENTER to continue ...
  COUNT(*) COUNT(DISTINCTAPPLICANT_ID)
---------- ---------------------------
       318                         318
```

The population includes 318 applicants with one row per applicant.

Figure 12–2. Counts of the report population.

each applicant can have more than one admissions decision. But if you think of the population as the admissions decisions of these women, the two counts will be identical; that is, the count(*) and a count(distinct applicant_id||decision_seriesno) will be the same.

Step 2: Does the SQL Change Population Size?

Next determine if the remainder of your SQL changes the size of the population. Do this using the count(*) and count(distinct ...) but now applied to the entire query. Figure 12–3 on the following page shows the results. We've got problems. The query should return 318 rows, one for each applicant. Instead it returns 344 rows on 315 applicants. Three applicants fell through the joins. Other applicants multiplied through the joins.

The report from this query will be wrong. But if you don't test the query, you won't know the SQL is wrong until you (or the end user) examine the report. It's better to catch the error early in the process. As we did here, do this by counting the population size and then comparing this number to a count of the report population based on the entire SQL.

SQL

```
SQL> select
        count(*), count(distinct applicant_id)
from
     cdecision,
     decision c1,
     cinst,
     academic e1,
     name n1,
     person,
     applicant
where
     applicant_term = '199509'
            and applicant_level = 'UG'
            and applicant_college = 'AS'
     and person_id = applicant_id
            and person_gender = 'F'
     and n1.name_id = applicant_id
            and n1.name_seriesno =
            (select max(n2.name_seriesno)
            from name n2
            where n2.name_id = n1.name_id)
     and e1.academic_id(+) = applicant_id
            and nvl(e1.academic_seriesno,1) =
            (select max(nvl(e2.academic_seriesno,1))
            from
                   academic e2,
                   person
            where person_id = applicant_id
                   and e2.academic_id(+) = person_id)
     and cinst_code(+) = nvl(e1.academic_instcode,'unkn')
     and c1.decision_id = applicant_id
            and c1.decision_applicant_term = applicant_term
            and c1.decision_applicant_seriesno = applicant_seriesno
            and c1.decision_seriesno =
                   (select max(c2.decision_seriesno)
                   from decision c2
                   where c2.decision_id = c1.decision_id
                   and c2.decision_applicant_term = c1.decision_applicant_term
                   and c2.decision_applicant_seriesno = c1.decision_applicant_seriesno)
     and cdecision_code = c1.decision_code
 /
ENTER to continue ...
  COUNT(*) COUNT(DISTINCTAPPLICANT_ID)
---------- ---------------------------
       344                         315
```

Some applicants fell through the SQL; others appear more than once.

Figure 12–3. Counts of the population included in the initial query.

Isolating Problems

Sometimes just knowing that a problem exists provides enough knowledge to diagnose and fix the problem. You can examine the SQL and immediately find the problem. But most often this is not true. The objects used in our query were all used successfully in other queries. They could be at fault, but the problem more likely occurs in the newly written SQL. The problem could also exist in the data; maybe our SQL is fine but the data is corrupted. We need to isolate the problem.

Step 3: Stepping Through Joins

We know the entire query produced counts of 344 for count(*) and 315 for the count(distinct applicant_id). For the purpose of easy referral, I'll denote this as counts of 344/315. The query should return counts of 318/318. The objective in testing and debugging the SQL is to reach these 318/318 counts.

Isolating the problem requires systematic disassembly of the constructed SQL query. Start at the bottom of the query and remove the last join. Also remove the table from the *from* clause (if you forget to do this you'll get a Cartesian product and your query will take forever). Then do the count(*) and count(distinct ...) on this revised SQL query. If the counts change, then the portion of the SQL you removed contains a problem. Proceed through the joins in this fashion, one join at a time, until the remaining SQL defines the population.

This process is called "stepping through the joins." It provides an easy way to pinpoint what part of the SQL is involved in the problem. Figure 12–4 on the following page steps through the last join in our query—the join to the code table called CDECISION. Note that the counts changed from 344/315 to 345/316. Apparently one applicant fell through this join. We now need to find out who it was and why the joined failed.

Step 4: Finding the Affected Table Rows

The strategy used to find rows affected by join failures depends on the type of error encountered. Falling through a join requires one strategy; loss of singularity requires another. In this case the problem occurs because an applicant fell through the join to CDECISION. The table rows affected by falling through a join can be identified using a *not exists* subquery. Figure 12–5 on page 279 shows that the applicant with I.D. number 7156 is the unlucky

SQL

```
SQL> select
        count(*), count(distinct applicant_id)
from
        decision c1,
        cinst,
        academic e1,
        name n1,
        person,
        applicant
where
        applicant_term = '199509'
                and applicant_level = 'UG'
                and applicant_college = 'AS'
        and person_id = applicant_id
                and person_gender = 'F'
        and n1.name_id = applicant_id
                and n1.name_seriesno =
                (select max(n2.name_seriesno)
                from name n2
                where n2.name_id = n1.name_id)
        and e1.academic_id(+) = applicant_id
                and nvl(e1.academic_seriesno,1) =
                (select max(nvl(e2.academic_seriesno,1))
                from
                        academic e2,
                        person
                where person_id = applicant_id
                        and e2.academic_id(+) = person_id)
        and cinst_code(+) = nvl(e1.academic_instcode,'unkn')
        and c1.decision_id = applicant_id
                and c1.decision_applicant_term = applicant_term
                and c1.decision_applicant_seriesno = applicant_seriesno
                and c1.decision_seriesno =
                        (select max(c2.decision_seriesno)
                        from decision c2
                        where c2.decision_id = c1.decision_id
                        and c2.decision_applicant_term = c1.decision_applicant_term
                        and c2.decision_applicant_seriesno =
c1.decision_applicant_seriesno)
/
ENTER to continue ...
  COUNT(*) COUNT(DISTINCTAPPLICANT_ID)
---------- ---------------------------
       345                         316
```

One applicant apparently fell through the CDECISION join (the count of distinct applicants increased by 1 to 316 when the CDECISION join was removed).

Figure 12–4. Stepping through the joins: removal of the CDECISION join.

SQL

```
SQL> select
  2        applicant_id
  3  from
  4        decision c1,
  5        person,
  6        applicant
  7  where
  8        applicant_term = '199509'
  9              and applicant_level = 'UG'
 10              and applicant_college = 'AS'
 11        and person_id = applicant_id
 12              and person_gender = 'F'
 13        and c1.decision_id = applicant_id
 14              and c1.decision_applicant_term = applicant_term
 15              and c1.decision_applicant_seriesno = applicant_seriesno
 16              and c1.decision_seriesno =
 17                   (select max(c2.decision_seriesno)
 18                    from decision c2
 19                    where c2.decision_id = c1.decision_id
 20                    and c2.decision_applicant_term = c1.decision_applicant_term
 21                    and c2.decision_applicant_seriesno = c1.decision_applicant_seriesno)
 22        and not exists
 23        (select * from cdecision
 24        where cdecision_code = c1.decision_code)
 25  /
ENTER to continue ...
APPLICANT_ID
------------
      7156
```

This subquery identifies applicant 7156 as having fallen through the CDECISION join.

Figure 12–5. Using a *not exists* subquery structure to identify population items falling through joins.

person who fell through the CDECISION join. Figure 12–6 shows the applicant's admissions decisions. Our query requests only the last decision, so that's the data we need to inspect. Note that the decision code for the last decision is DO. This is not a valid decision code. Because there's no DO in CDECISION, applicant 7156 gets eliminated from the query.

Step 5: Fixing the Problem

Applicant 7156 falls through the CDECISION join because of a data problem, not because of anything wrong with the SQL. You could rewrite the SQL to get around the data problem, but the better choice is to fix the data. You'd want to report the error to the admissions office and get the supervisor of data input to pull the admissions folder for the applicant, investigate the problem, and change the DO code. Most likely the DO is just an input error; probably it should be CO.

This problem actually might go deeper than just a data input error. It may also identify a design error in the database itself. ORACLE provides a mechanism to prevent the entry of invalid codes. Database designers can place constraints on data columns like decision_code, so that only valid codes in the CDECISION table get committed to the data table. Apparently this constraint was not placed on decision_code. You'd want to discuss the issue with the database administrator and determine if this was an oversight or done for a reason.

Step 6: Repeat Steps 3, 4, and 5

We solved one problem, but it left the counts at 345/316 and we need to get to 318/318. Isolate the next problem by stepping through more joins until the counts change again. Figure 12–7 on page 282 shows what happens when the join to the DECISION table is removed from the query. The counts increase to 347/318. Apparently two applicants fell through this join.

Using a *not exists* subquery structure, Figure 12–8 on page 283 identifies the two applicants and shows their admissions decisions. Apparently one applicant (1136) does not have any admissions decisions. The other (4665) has two decisions but they're for Fall 1994. This might be a data entry error but the decision dates make them appear legitimate. Apparently this person applied for admission in Fall 1994 and again in Fall 1995. So he or she has data in the DECISION table; it's just not the right term.

We're left with the two types of problems discussed in Chapter 8 when building *where* objects: (1) one situation where an applicant has no data in the DECISION table, and (2) a second situation where an applicant has data

DECISION data:

```
SQL> select decision_id, decision_applicant_seriesno, decision_applicant_term,
  2  decision_seriesno, decision_code
  3  from decision
  4  where decision_id = 7156;
ENTER to continue ...
        applicant appl      decision decsn
    id   seriesno term      seriesno code
------ ---------- ------ ---------- -----
  7156          1 199509          1 DR
  7156          1 199509          2 SR
  7156          1 199509          3 WL
  7156          1 199509          4 AC
  7156          1 199509          5 DO
```

Applicant 7156 falls through the CDECISION join because his or her last decision code is DO, and this is an invalid code.

CDECISION codes:

```
SQL> select * from cdecision order by 1;
ENTER to continue
decision                                       accept cancel enrl
code     decision                              ind    ind    ind    datestamp
-------- ------------------------------ ------ ------ ------ ---------
AC       Accept regular                        Y                    20-MAR-94
AD       Accept deferred                       Y      Y             20-MAR-94
AE       Accept early                          Y                    20-MAR-94
CI       Cancel, incomplete                           Y             20-MAR-94
CO       Cancel by office                             Y             20-MAR-94
CP       Canceled after paid                          Y             20-MAR-94
CS       Canceled before decision                     Y             20-MAR-94
CZ       Canceled after accept                        Y             20-MAR-94
DR       Deferred to regular                                        20-MAR-94
HL       Decision pending                                           20-MAR-94
PD       Paid enrollment deposit                             Y      20-MAR-94
RJ       Rejected                                     Y             20-MAR-94
SR       Second reading                                             20-MAR-94
WA       Wait-list accept                      Y                    20-MAR-94
WC       Wait-list cancel by appl                     Y             20-MAR-94
WL       Wait-listed                                                20-MAR-94
WR       Rejected from wait-list                      Y             20-MAR-94
```

Figure 12–6. Examining the data for an applicant who fell through the CDECISION join.

```
SQL

SQL> select
        count(*), count(distinct applicant_id)
 from
        cinst,
        academic e1,
        name n1,
        person,
        applicant
 where
        applicant_term = '199509'
                and applicant_level = 'UG'
                and applicant_college = 'AS'
        and person_id = applicant_id
                and person_gender = 'F'
        and n1.name_id = applicant_id
                and n1.name_seriesno =
                (select max(n2.name_seriesno)
                from name n2
                where n2.name_id = n1.name_id)
        and e1.academic_id(+) = applicant_id
                and nvl(e1.academic_seriesno,1) =
                (select max(nvl(e2.academic_seriesno,1))
                from
                        academic e2,
                        person
                where person_id = applicant_id
                        and e2.academic_id(+) = person_id)
        and cinst_code(+) = nvl(e1.academic_instcode,'unkn')
 /
ENTER to continue ...
  COUNT(*) COUNT(DISTINCTAPPLICANT_ID)
---------- ---------------------------
       347                         318
```

Two more applicants fell through the DECISION join.

Figure 12–7. Stepping through the DECISION join.

in the DECISION table but it's not the kind we want. Chapter 8 showed how to use outer joins to handle both types of problems. The solution appears in Figure 12–9 on page 284.

The counts in Figure 12–9 are now 347/318. We've found and fixed all the problems generated by falling through joins. But we're still left with loss of singularity—the fact that some applicants appear more than once in the report. To solve this problem, you must continue stepping through the joins.

Removing the join to the code table CINST produces no changes in the counts. They remain at 347/318. But removing the join to the ACADEMIC table does have an effect. Now the counts go to 318/318 (see Figure 12–10 on page 285). The loss of singularity occurs in the ACADEMIC join.

SQL

```
SQL> select
  2         applicant_id
  3  from
  4         person,
  5         applicant
  6  where
  7         applicant_term = '199509'
  8                and applicant_level = 'UG'
  9                and applicant_college = 'AS'
 10         and person_id = applicant_id
 11                and person_gender = 'F'
 12         and not exists
 13         (select * from decision c1
 14         where c1.decision_id = applicant_id
 15                and c1.decision_applicant_term = applicant_term
 16                and c1.decision_applicant_seriesno = applicant_seriesno
 17                and c1.decision_seriesno =
 18                       (select max(c2.decision_seriesno)
 19                       from decision c2
 20                       where c2.decision_id = c1.decision_id
 21                       and c2.decision_applicant_term = c1.decision_applicant_term
 22                       and c2.decision_applicant_seriesno =c1.decision_applicant_seriesno))
 23  /
ENTER to continue ...
    id
------
  1136
  4665
```

DECISION data

```
SQL> select decision_id, decision_applicant_seriesno, decision_applicant_term,
  2  decision_code, decision_seriesno, decision_datestamp
  3  from decision
  4  where decision_id in (1136, 4665)
  5  order by 1, 5
  6  /
ENTER to continue ...
        applicant appl   decsn   decision
    id   seriesno term   code    seriesno datestamp
------ ---------- ------ ----- ---------- ---------
  4665          1 199409 AC             1 11-NOV-93
  4665          1 199409 CO             2 21-MAR-94
```

Applicant 1136 has no admissions decisions; applicant 4665 only has decisions for Fall 1994.

Figure 12–8. Identifying applicants who fell through the DECISION join.

SQL

```
SQL> select
        count(*), count(distinct applicant_id)
  from
        decision c1,
        cinst,
        academic e1,
        name n1,
        person,
        applicant
  where
        applicant_term = '199509'
                and applicant_level = 'UG'
                and applicant_college = 'AS'
        and person_id = applicant_id
                and person_gender = 'F'
        and n1.name_id = applicant_id
                and n1.name_seriesno =
                (select max(n2.name_seriesno)
                from name n2
                where n2.name_id = n1.name_id)
        and e1.academic_id(+) = applicant_id
                and nvl(e1.academic_seriesno,1) =
                (select max(nvl(e2.academic_seriesno,1))
                from
                        academic e2,
                        person
                where person_id = applicant_id
                        and e2.academic_id(+) = person_id)
        and cinst_code(+) = nvl(e1.academic_instcode,'unkn')
        and c1.decision_id(+) = applicant_id
                and c1.decision_applicant_term(+) = applicant_term
                and c1.decision_applicant_seriesno(+) = applicant_seriesno
                and nvl(c1.decision_seriesno,1) =
                        (select max(nvl(c2.decision_seriesno,1))
                        from
                                decision c2,
                                person
                        where person_id = applicant_id
                        and c2.decision_id(+) = person_id
                                and c2.decision_applicant_term(+) = applicant_term
                                and c2.decision_applicant_seriesno(+) = applicant_seriesno)
  /
ENTER to continue ...
  COUNT(*) COUNT(DISTINCTAPPLICANT_ID)
---------- ---------------------------
       347                         318
```

The outer joins in the main query and the subquery prevent applicants 1136 and 4665 from falling through the DECISION join.

Figure 12–9. An outer join prevents applicants from falling through the DECISION join.

SQL

```
SQL> select
  2         count(*), count(distinct applicant_id)
  3  from
  4         name n1,
  5         person,
  6         applicant
  7  where
  8         applicant_term = '199509'
  9                 and applicant_level = 'UG'
 10                 and applicant_college = 'AS'
 11         and person_id = applicant_id
 12                 and person_gender = 'F'
 13         and n1.name_id = applicant_id
 14                 and n1.name_seriesno =
 15                 (select max(n2.name_seriesno)
 16                 from name n2
 17                 where n2.name_id = n1.name_id)
 18  /
ENTER to continue ...
  COUNT(*) COUNT(DISTINCTAPPLICANT_ID)
---------- ---------------------------
       318                         318
```

The loss of singularity occurs in the ACADEMIC join (i.e., the count(*) drops from 347 to 318 when the ACADEMIC join is removed).

Figure 12–10. Stepping through the CINST and ACADEMIC joins.

To find table rows affected by loss of singularity, a "*group by ... having* count(*) > 1" structure is used. Figure 12–11 on the following page identifies the applicants with multiple rows returned. The figure also shows some of the ACADEMIC data for these applicants. The applicants all attended more than one high school. So apparently the SQL that translated "the high school they're attending (or last attended)" contains faulty logic. The problem becomes immediately clear by comparing the data in Figure 12–11 with the join to the ACADEMIC table (e.g., see Figure 12–7). The subquery in the join retrieves a maximum academic_seriesno for each applicant. But look at the data for applicant 1885 in Figure 12–11. He or she attended two schools and they both have an academic_seriesno of 1. Returning the maximum academic_seriesno includes both these rows.

Apparently the query writer misinterpreted the meaning of academic_seriesno and believed it contained a sequential number that identified the order of school attendance. Using this logic, someone with two schools should have academic_seriesno of 1 and 2. But they don't. The data dictionary (Table A–3 in Appendix A) makes clear why;

SQL

```
SQL> select
             applicant_id,
             count(*)
     from
             academic e1,
             name n1,
             person,
             applicant
     where
             applicant_term = '199509'
                     and applicant_level = 'UG'
                     and applicant_college = 'AS'
             and person_id = applicant_id
                     and person_gender = 'F'
             and n1.name_id = applicant_id
                     and n1.name_seriesno =
                     (select max(n2.name_seriesno)
                     from name n2
                     where n2.name_id = n1.name_id)
             and e1.academic_id(+) = applicant_id
                     and nvl(e1.academic_seriesno,1) =
                     (select max(nvl(e2.academic_seriesno,1))
                     from
                             academic e2,
                             person
                     where person_id = applicant_id
                             and e2.academic_id(+) = person_id)
     group by applicant_id
     having count(*) > 1
     /
ENTER to continue ...
    id   COUNT(*)
------ ----------
   265          2
   799          2
  1447          2
  1489          2
  1570          2
  1885          2
  2137          2
  2292          2
 ...
```

ACADEMIC data

```
SQL> select academic_id, academic_seriesno, academic_instcode,
     academic_degree, academic_degreedate
     from academic
     where academic_id in (1885, 2137, 2292)
     order by 1, 2
     /
ENTER to continue ...
             inst inst          degree
    id   seriesno code   degree date
------ ---------- ------ ------ ---------
  1885          1 0305
  1885          1 1007
  2137          1 0609
  2137          1 0708   HS     17-JUN-93
  2292          1 0533
  2292          1 0606
```

Note that each person attended two prior schools. The max(academic_seriesno) returns both rows because academic_seriesno equals 1 for each.

This report lists all applicants with more than one ACADEMIC row returned by the join.

Figure 12–11. A *having* structure to identify loss of singularity.

academic_seriesno actually distinguishes if someone attended a single school more than once. This is unlikely at the undergraduate level where the prior schools are high schools. But at the graduate level, an applicant may have attended one school and received a bachelor's degree and then attended the same school at a later time and received a master's degree.

The problem here is faulty logic in the SQL. The solution requires another translation into SQL. Figure 12–12 shows a solution based on selecting the school where an applicant received a high school diploma or, if this does not exist, the last school input or updated in the ACADEMIC table for the applicant. The SQL solution in Figure 12–12 should look familiar. It's similar to the class 2u *where* objects built in Chapter 8.

SQL

```
SQL> select
         count(*), count(distinct applicant_id)
     from
         academic e1,
         name n1,
         person,
         applicant
     where
         applicant_term = '199509'
                 and applicant_level = 'UG'
                 and applicant_college = 'AS'
         and person_id = applicant_id
                 and person_gender = 'F'
         and n1.name_id = applicant_id
                 and n1.name_seriesno =
                 (select max(n2.name_seriesno)
                 from name n2
                 where n2.name_id = n1.name_id)
         and e1.academic_id(+) = applicant_id
                 and decode(e1.academic_degree,'HS','HS',null)||
                 to_char(nvl(e1.academic_datestamp,'01-JAN-50'),'YYYYMMDD') =
                 (select max(decode(e2.academic_degree,'HS','HS',null)||
                 to_char(nvl(e2.academic_datestamp,'01-JAN-50'),'YYYYMMDD'))
                 from
                         academic e2,
                         person
                 where person_id = applicant_id
                         and e2.academic_id(+) = person_id)
     /
ENTER to continue ...
  COUNT(*) COUNT(DISTINCTAPPLICANT_ID)
---------- --------------------------
       318                        318
```

This structure now preserves singularity through the ACADEMIC join.

Figure 12–12. Revision of the ACADEMIC join.

The counts now stand at 318/318. This definitely looks promising. But one final test remains.

Step 7: Test the Entire SQL Again

One last test remains before running the shell and main SQL program. In the process of testing and debugging the SQL we've stepped through one join after another, fixing each join if needed but also eliminating them from further testing. It is possible for a solution in one join to interact with a join

SQL

```
SQL> select
        count(*), count(distinct applicant_id)
from
        cdecision,decision c1,cinst,academic e1,name n1,person,applicant
where
        applicant_term = '199509'
                and applicant_level = 'UG'
                and applicant_college = 'AS'
        and person_id = applicant_id
                and person_gender = 'F'
        and n1.name_id = applicant_id
                and n1.name_seriesno =
                (select max(n2.name_seriesno)
                from name n2
                where n2.name_id = n1.name_id)
        and e1.academic_id(+) = applicant_id
                and decode(e1.academic_degree,'HS','HS',null)||
                to_char(nvl(e1.academic_datestamp,'01-JAN-50'),'YYYYMMDD') =
                (select max(decode(e2.academic_degree,'HS','HS',null)||
                to_char(nvl(e2.academic_datestamp,'01-JAN-50'),'YYYYMMDD'))
                from
                        academic e2,
                        person
                where person_id = applicant_id
                        and e2.academic_id(+) = person_id)
        and cinst_code(+) = nvl(e1.academic_instcode,'unkn')
        and c1.decision_id(+) = applicant_id
                and c1.decision_applicant_term(+) = applicant_term
                and c1.decision_applicant_seriesno(+) = applicant_seriesno
                and nvl(c1.decision_seriesno,1) =
                        (select max(nvl(c2.decision_seriesno,1))
                        from
                                decision c2,
                                person
                        where person_id = applicant_id
                        and c2.decision_id(+) = person_id
                                and c2.decision_applicant_term(+) = applicant_term
                                and c2.decision_applicant_seriesno(+) = applicant_seriesno)
        and cdecision_code(+) = c1.decision_code
/
ENTER to continue ...
  COUNT(*) COUNT(DISTINCTAPPLICANT_ID)
---------- ---------------------------
       318                         318
```

The SQL preserves population size through all the joins.

Figure 12–13. Testing the final SQL program.

already eliminated from further testing. As a final test you should check for these interactions by doing count(*) and count(distinct ...) on the entire SQL program again, essentially testing all joins in combination.

In our example the counts turn out to be 316/316 instead of the 318/318 expected! Fixing each join individually and then putting them back together resulted in two applicants falling through the joins. To find the problem you'd start stepping through the joins from the bottom, one join at a time. But in this case the problem is pretty obvious. When the outer joins were added to the DECISION table, it produced null rows for the two applicants (1136 and 4665) who had no admissions decisions for Fall 1995. However, we neglected to add an outer join to the CDECISION table. These same two applicants now fall through this join. Adding this outer join produces counts of 318/318 as shown in Figure 12–13. A portion of the final report appears in Figure 12–14 on the following page.

The SQL program we just built included several existing objects but also required two new sections of code—one joining the DECISION table and a second joining the ACADEMIC table. Both joins qualify as class 2u *where* objects that maintain population size. Both joins could prove useful in other queries that accessed either the DECISION or ACADEMIC tables. When this happens, it's best to create objects from the new sections of code, capturing the time and effort of development and testing so the next time you can just insert the object into a program. Figure 12–15 on page 291 shows the object joining DECISION, while the ACADEMIC object appears in Figure 12–16 on page 292.

Sampling Populations

It should be clear from the previous example that testing and debugging an SQL program can require considerable effort. Each step through a join requires another execution of the program. Each time you locate an error, additional SQL programs must be written and run to find the affected table rows. When the population size is small, this doesn't present a problem.

However, when the population is large, testing and debugging can produce a drain on the computer system as well as on the query writer. Under these circumstances it's useful to sample from the population. For the one error that appears in every 100,000 table rows, sampling won't prove helpful. But choosing a reasonably sized sample from a large population makes it possible to catch common errors and still get good response times from the query.

```
REPORT
                                      inst                                      inst      decsn
    id sort_name                      code    inst_name                         state sex code  decision
------ ------------------------- ------ ------------------------------ ----- --- ----- ------------------------------
  3163 Adams, Amy                 3104    Wallkill Valley Regional HS      NJ    F   CO    Cancel by office
  1897 Affsa, Rita A.             3108    Barringer High School            NJ    F   CO    Cancel by office
  6287 Agnew, Angela              2609    Lafayette High School            MO    F   RJ    Rejected
  3650 Allen, Christine                                                          F   RJ    Rejected
  5898 Allen, Karen               2221    Wakefield High School            MA    F   PD    Paid enrollment deposit
  4846 Allen, Kristen             0704    New Canaan High School           CT    F   RJ    Rejected
  3005 Anderson, Christine V                                                     F   CZ    Canceled after accept
  2407 Anderson, Jennifer         2410    Hawley High School               MN    F   CS    Canceled before decision
   ...
```

Figure 12–14. Final report.

HELP

```
object:        whrdecsn.obj
date created:  13-dec-1994
author:        glewis
revisions:

Purpose:       Provides access to the DECISION table for information on
               the last admissions decision.

Usage:         1. Need to include DECISION and CDECISION in the from clause.
               Give the DECISION table an alias of "c1".
               2. Assumes that the APPLICANT table also appears in the from
               clause.

Hints:
```

OBJECT

```
and c1.decision_id(+) = applicant_id
        and c1.decision_applicant_term(+) = applicant_term
        and c1.decision_applicant_seriesno(+) = applicant_seriesno
        and nvl(c1.decision_seriesno,1) =
                (select max(nvl(c2.decision_seriesno,1))
                from
                        decision c2,
                        person
                where person_id = applicant_id
                and c2.decision_id(+) = person_id
                        and c2.decision_applicant_term(+) = applicant_term
                        and c2.decision_applicant_seriesno(+) = applicant_seriesno)
and cdecision_code(+) = c1.decision_code
```

Figure 12–15. Class 2u *where* object returning last admissions decision.

Sampling can occur in two ways. One is quick but may yield a biased sample. The second requires more effort but also provides a more representative sample. The easy method utilizes a "pseudo-column" called ROWNUM. When an SQL query returns a row that meets all the *where* conditions, the row gets assigned a sequential number. This row assignment occurs before any *order by* processing. ROWNUM may be accessed in any query just like a real data column, but since it is not actually stored in a table no deletes, inserts, or updates of the column can occur.

ROWNUM provides a convenient way to limit the number of rows returned in a query. In this sense it provides a sample of the population for testing and debugging. To use ROWNUM, just include it in the *where* clause. For example, the statement "where ... and rownum <= 100" returns the first 100 rows that meet the *where* conditions.

This procedure provides a sample, but it may not be a very good one. It's certainly not a random sample. The sequential order of data rows often

```
HELP

object:        whracad.obj
date created:  13-dec-1994
author:        glewis
revisions:

Purpose:       Provides access to the ACADEMIC table for information on
               the last high school attended.

Usage:         1. Need to include ACADEMIC and CINST in the from
               clause. Give the ACADEMIC table an alias of "e1".
               2. Assumes that the APPLICANT table also appears in the
               from clause.

Hints:
```

```
OBJECT

    and e1.academic_id(+) = applicant_id
            and decode(e1.academic_degree,'HS','HS',null)||
            to_char(nvl(e1.academic_datestamp,'01-JAN-50'),'YYYYMMDD') =
            (select max(decode(e2.academic_degree,'HS','HS',null)||
            to_char(nvl(e2.academic_datestamp,'01-JAN-50'),'YYYYMMDD'))
            from
                    academic e2,
                    person
            where person_id = applicant_id
                    and e2.academic_id(+) = person_id)
    and cinst_code(+) = nvl(e1.academic_instcode,'unkn')
```

Figure 12–16. Class 2u *where* object returning last high school attended.

contains a rough chronological element. That is, rows returned near each other in sequence may have been created near each other in time (allowing, of course, for deletions and later insertions of new rows that alter the time sequence). By sampling the first N rows you sample a window of time. If the sample is small, you might return rows input by a single data entry clerk over a period of a week. If the population actually covers input occurring over a year, one week of data may not represent the year very well. Too many things can change.

You get a more useful sample by choosing every Nth record from a population. This reduces the impact that chronology can have on the sample. But choosing every Nth row demands a bit more work than choosing the first N rows. It requires that a new table be created to hold two data columns—one for the population primary key (e.g., applicant_id) and the second for ROWNUM. This new table then gets filled with the key and ROWNUM for each item in the population. The table contains the report population and can serve as the driving table in SQL being tested and debugged. Any number of algorithms can be used to sample from the newly created population table and the ROWNUM column it contains.

Figure 12–17 on the following page shows the 318 applicants in our example inserted into a new table called SAVELIST. The table includes the two data columns called savelist_id and savelist_rownum, one containing applicant_id and the other a ROWNUM value. Figure 12–17 also shows a portion of the SAVELIST table and a query that samples eight evenly spaced rows from the 318. With a population this small there is no need for a sample. But the query in Figure 12–17 illustrates how this sampling procedure can limit the rows used to test and debug SQL programs.

The sampling algorithm shown in Figure 12–17 can be generalized to select N rows from a population of size M. In this form it makes a good object for later reuse. Figure 12–18 on page 295 shows a population object based on this systematic sampling procedure.

Improving Performance

As a query writer you must first ensure the accuracy of a report. If the SQL logic is wrong, the report is worthless and oftentimes misleading. The query may run with blistering speed, but the report is still wrong. So ensure accuracy first. Once having done that, then worry about performance.

As mentioned earlier, I believe SQL queries should hit an acceptable window of performance rather than try to optimize performance. In an ideal situation you'd choose the single SQL query that produced the right results in the shortest amount of time. But there are trade-offs to be made. How long will it take to find the fastest performing query? Can you ever be sure when you've found it? How many system resources will be expended trying to find that query? And, perhaps most importantly, how should you balance your own time against CPU time? Can you afford a half day optimizing a query to save two minutes of elapsed execution time?

I have no special measure for acceptable performance. What's acceptable on one database may be inappropriate for another. Experience spent running many different queries provides a gut-level check on performance. I know, for example, that against certain tables my reports should complete in five minutes. I also know that against other tables a report might take 40 minutes, give or take some time for what's happening elsewhere on the system. This knowledge provides rough benchmarks against which query performance can be judged. I'll forget sometimes to join a table that appears in the *from* clause. But seldom will I let the resulting Cartesian product run to completion, simply because I know when a query takes too long.

Forgetting to join a table certainly degrades query performance. But it's an easy problem to detect because it also produces the wrong results. Far

SAVELIST

```
SQL> insert into savelist (savelist_id, savelist_rownum)
  2  select
  3          applicant_id,
  4          rownum
  5  from
  6          person,
  7          applicant
  8  where
  9          applicant_term = '199509'
 10                  and applicant_level = 'UG'
 11                  and applicant_college = 'AS'
 12          and person_id = applicant_id
 13                  and person_gender = 'F'
 14  /

318 rows created.

SQL> select * from savelist order by 2;
ENTER to continue ...
        id    rownum
---------- ----------
        44          1
       114          2
       133          3
       161          4
       207          5
       227          6
       253          7
       265          8
       279          9
       289         10
       309         11
       324         12
       351         13
       352         14
       379         15
       ...
```

SAMPLE

This selects a sample of 8.
The driving table is SAVELIST.

```
SQL> select
  2          applicant_id,
  3          savelist_rownum
  4  from
  5          cdecision,
  6          decision c1,
  7          cinst,
  8          academic e1,
  9          name n1,
 10          person,
 11          applicant,
 12          savelist s1
 13  where
 14          s1.savelist_rownum in
 15                  (select round(s2.savelist_rownum*(318/8))
 16                  from savelist s2
 17                  where s2.savelist_rownum <= 8)
 18          and applicant_id = savelist_id
 19                  and applicant_term = '199509'
 20                  and applicant_level = 'UG'
 21                  and applicant_college = 'AS'
 22          and person_id = applicant_id
 23                  and person_gender = 'F'
            [rest of SQL removed ...]

ENTER to continue ...
    id     rownum
------ ----------
  1059         40
  2665         80
  3719        119
  4979        159
  6200        199
  7116        239
  7906        278
  8994        318

8 rows selected.
```

Figure 12–17. Example of a savelist used to sample a population.

```
HELP

object:        popsampl.obj
date created:  06-Dec-1994
author:        glewis
revisions:

Purpose:       Selects Nsample rows from a population of size Npop, for use
               in testing and debugging objects when the population size is
               large.  Assumes population size is known.

Usage:         1. <query_tables>: Replace with list of table names used in
               the SQL query.
               2. <Npop>: Replace with the number of items in the population.
               3. <Nsample>: Replace with the number of items you want in
               the sample.
               4. <query_driving_table>: Replace with the name of the driving
               table in the SQL query.
               5. <remainder_of_query>: Replace with the rest of the SQL
               query.

Hints:         none
```

```
OBJECT

from
      <query_tables>,
      savelist s1
where
      s1.savelist_rownum in
              (select round(s2.savelist_rownum*(<Npop>/<Nsample>))
              from savelist s2
              where s2.savelist_rownum <= <Nsample>)
      and <query_driving_table>_id = savelist_id
      and <remainder_of_query>
```

Figure 12–18. *Population* object for selecting a sample.

more difficult are queries that produce the right results on a sample but fall outside the acceptable window of performance when run against the entire population. When this happens you need to revise the SQL to improve performance. You have at your disposal one tool that ORACLE provides and guidelines/folklore accumulated by many programmers running many queries over considerable time. Let's discuss each, starting with the tool.

EXPLAIN PLAN

Before an SQL (SQL*PLUS) program retrieves data rows, it passes through an ORACLE optimizer that determines a strategy for implementing the SQL that you've written. This implementation plan then directs the actual retrieval of data. By changing the SQL, sometimes in seemingly minor ways, you can influence the strategy the optimizer chooses and thus the amount of runtime. Improving performance then becomes a matter of revising the SQL so that the ORACLE optimizer chooses a better strategy for data retrieval.

With version 7 of ORACLE there are now two types of optimizers. One is the rules-based optimizer that provided the only option in earlier versions of ORACLE. This optimizer chooses an implementation strategy based on existing indexes and a set of predefined rules. The second optimizer is called a cost-based optimizer. To use it the database administrator must first perform analysis routines that gather information about the data tables; for example, how many rows they contain, how the rows are clustered in physical proximity to each other, and what indexes exist. This information gets stored and used to select an implementation strategy. Theoretically the cost-based optimizer provides more information about your specific database and brings more intelligence to bear on the implementation strategy. With ORACLE version 7 you can choose which optimizer to use. You can also include optimization hints within the SQL itself. These then influence the strategy chosen to retrieve data rows.

Regardless of whether you're running ORACLE version 6 or version 7, or whether you choose a cost-based or rules-based optimizer, ORACLE provides a tool that lets you analyze the data retrieval strategy selected by the optimizer. You can use the tool to identify bottlenecks in data retrieval. For example, does the strategy use available indexes? Does it do full table scans on large tables? Based on this information you can then tweak your SQL or provide alternative optimization hints. This process continues iteratively. Revise the SQL, analyze the execution plan selected by the optimizer, and test the performance. If necessary go through the process again and again until performance improves or you exhaust your ideas for improving performance.

The performance tool that analyzes an execution plan operates through a statement called EXPLAIN PLAN. Here's how it works. At the top of a query you wish to analyze, place the statement "explain plan into <table_name> for." In this case <table_name> is the name of a table that will contain the results of the analysis. ORACLE provides a script to create this table—which is often called plan_table. See your database administrator for the script. By running a simple SQL program you can output a report analyzing the execution plan.

I'll illustrate EXPLAIN PLAN using the query we constructed earlier in this chapter. But first a word of caution. The output from EXPLAIN PLAN depends on the ORACLE optimizer being used. What you're about

```
EXPLAIN PLAN

parent id     pos    query_plan
------ ------ ------ ------------------------------------------------------------------
       1      0        SORT GROUP BY
1      2      1          FILTER
2      19     3            SORT GROUP BY
19     20     1              INDEX RANGE SCAN NAME_KEY
2      21     4            SORT GROUP BY
21     22     1              NESTED LOOPS OUTER
22     23     1                INDEX UNIQUE SCAN PERSON_KEY
22     24     2                TABLE ACCESS BY ROWID ACADEMIC
24     25     1                  INDEX RANGE SCAN ACADEMIC_KEY
2      3      1            NESTED LOOPS OUTER
3      18     2              INDEX UNIQUE SCAN CINST_KEY
3      4      1              NESTED LOOPS OUTER
4      16     2                TABLE ACCESS BY ROWID ACADEMIC
16     17     1                  INDEX RANGE SCAN ACADEMIC_KEY
4      5      1                NESTED LOOPS
5      15     2                  INDEX RANGE SCAN NAME_KEY
5      6      1                  NESTED LOOPS OUTER
6      14     2                    INDEX UNIQUE SCAN CDECISION_KEY
6      7      1                    NESTED LOOPS OUTER
7      8      1                      NESTED LOOPS
8      9      1                        TABLE ACCESS FULL APPLICANT
8      10     2                        TABLE ACCESS BY ROWID PERSON
10     11     1                          INDEX UNIQUE SCAN PERSON_KEY
7      12     2                      TABLE ACCESS BY ROWID DECISION
12     13     1                        INDEX RANGE SCAN DECISION_KEY
2      26     5            SORT GROUP BY
26     27     1              NESTED LOOPS OUTER
27     28     1                INDEX UNIQUE SCAN PERSON_KEY
27     29     2                INDEX RANGE SCAN DECISION_KEY
```

Figure 12–19. EXPLAIN PLAN results for query in Figure 12–13.

to see are results from a rules-based ORACLE version 6 optimizer. Output from other versions using different optimizers may differ. Regardless, it's useful to go through the process so you get the general idea even if the specifics may differ in your situation.

Figure 12–19 shows the results of EXPLAIN PLAN on the final query we developed earlier (see Figure 12–13). If you've not previously seen the results of an EXPLAIN PLAN, they can appear somewhat obtuse. Let's begin the interpretation of Figure 12–19 by backtracking. I'd like to take you through a process that experienced query writers normally eliminate. But it's a very informative process.

Figure 12–20 on the following page shows our final query divided into ten blocks. Each block constitutes a new join or a new subquery. I want to

```
SQL

select
        count(*), count(distinct applicant_id)
from
        cdecision,decision c1,cinst,academic e1,name n1,person,applicant
where
1       applicant_term = '199509'
                and applicant_level = 'UG'
                and applicant_college = 'AS'
2       and person_id = applicant_id
                and person_gender = 'F'
3       and n1.name_id = applicant_id
                and n1.name_seriesno =
4               (select max(n2.name_seriesno)
                from name n2
                where n2.name_id = n1.name_id)
5       and e1.academic_id(+) = applicant_id
                and decode(e1.academic_degree,'HS','HS',null)||
                to_char(nvl(e1.academic_datestamp,'01-JAN-50'),'YYYYMMDD') =
                (select max(decode(e2.academic_degree,'HS','HS',null)||
                to_char(nvl(e2.academic_datestamp,'01-JAN-50'),'YYYYMMDD'))
                from
6                       academic e2,
                        person
                where person_id = applicant_id
                        and e2.academic_id(+) = person_id)
7       and cinst_code(+) = nvl(e1.academic_instcode,'unkn')
        and c1.decision_id(+) = applicant_id
8               and c1.decision_applicant_term(+) = applicant_term
                and c1.decision_applicant_seriesno(+) = applicant_seriesno
                and nvl(c1.decision_seriesno,1) =
                        (select max(nvl(c2.decision_seriesno,1))
                        from
                                decision c2,
9                               person
                        where person_id = applicant_id
                        and c2.decision_id(+) = person_id
                                and c2.decision_applicant_term(+) = applicant_term
                                and c2.decision_applicant_seriesno(+) = applicant_seriesno)
10      and cdecision_code(+) = c1.decision_code;
```

The query includes 10 sections:
1. APPLICANT join
2. PERSON join
3. NAME join
4. NAME subquery
5. ACADEMIC join
6. ACADEMIC subquery
7. CINST join
8. DECISION join
9. DECISION subquery
10. CDECISION join

Figure 12–20. Sections in the final SQL query from Figure 12–13.

rebuild the query step-by-step using these ten blocks and run an EXPLAIN PLAN at each of the ten steps. By doing this we can determine which parts of the full execution plan (in Figure 12–19) came from which block of SQL. We can then graphically reformat the execution plan and analyze it to interpret how the optimizer retrieves data.

The first step appears in Figure 12–21. This figure shows the execution plan when only the block accessing the APPLICANT table appears in the query. Note the execution plan contains only two lines. I'll provide definitions for the terms used in the execution plan shortly, but it appears (correctly) that the query requires a sequential row-by-row scan of the entire APPLICANT table.

Next we want to add block 2 joining the PERSON table into the query. We'd run another EXPLAIN PLAN and use the results to identify which lines in the full execution plan got created because of the PERSON join. We'd proceed in this fashion through all ten blocks of SQL in the full query.

Figure 12–22 on the following page shows the final results of mapping SQL blocks to the execution plan. It shows you exactly how the execution plan relates to the SQL. For example, the outer join to the CDECISION table (block 10) produced the two lines in the execution plan that read "nested loops outer ... index unique scan cdecision_key."

This information proves useful if we recast the execution plan in a hierarchical parent-child format. You can prepare this reformulation directly from the full execution plan using the three columns of numbers that appear in the plan (see Figure 12–22). Each step in the execution plan is given an I.D. number. This I.D. appears as column 2 in the execution plan. Each step except one also has a PARENT_ID that appears as column 1 in the execution plan. For example, step 2 in Figure 12–22 is the filter step. It's parent

EXPLAIN PLAN

```
parent id     pos    query_plan
------ ------ ------ --------------------------------------------------------
       1      0        SORT GROUP BY
1      2      1           TABLE ACCESS FULL APPLICANT
```

The query includes only section 1 (the APPLICANT join) of the 10 sections in the full query.

Figure 12–21. EXPLAIN PLAN results for section 1 of the query.

EXPLAIN PLAN

```
parent id     pos    query_plan
------ ------ ------ --------------------------------------------------------
       1      0        SORT GROUP BY
1      2      1          FILTER
2      19     3            SORT GROUP BY
19     20     1              INDEX RANGE SCAN NAME_KEY
2      21     4            SORT GROUP BY
21     22     1              NESTED LOOPS OUTER
22     23     1                INDEX UNIQUE SCAN PERSON_KEY
22     24     2                TABLE ACCESS BY ROWID ACADEMIC
24     25     1                  INDEX RANGE SCAN ACADEMIC_KEY
2      3      1            NESTED LOOPS OUTER
3      18     2              INDEX UNIQUE SCAN CINST_KEY
3      4      1              NESTED LOOPS OUTER
4      16     2                TABLE ACCESS BY ROWID ACADEMIC
16     17     1                  INDEX RANGE SCAN ACADEMIC_KEY
4      5      1                NESTED LOOPS
5      15     2                  INDEX RANGE SCAN NAME_KEY
5      6      1                  NESTED LOOPS OUTER
6      14     2                    INDEX UNIQUE SCAN CDECISION_KEY
6      7      1                    NESTED LOOPS OUTER
7      8      1                      NESTED LOOPS
8      9      1                        TABLE ACCESS FULL APPLICANT
8      10     2                        TABLE ACCESS BY ROWID PERSON
10     11     1                          INDEX UNIQUE SCAN PERSON_KEY
7      12     2                      TABLE ACCESS BY ROWID DECISION
12     13     1                        INDEX RANGE SCAN DECISION_KEY
2      26     5            SORT GROUP BY
26     27     1              NESTED LOOPS OUTER
27     28     1                INDEX UNIQUE SCAN PERSON_KEY
27     29     2                INDEX RANGE SCAN DECISION_KEY
```

The query includes 10 sections:

1. APPLICANT join
2. PERSON join
3. NAME join
4. NAME subquery
5. ACADEMIC join
6. ACADEMIC subquery
7. CINST join
8. DECISION join
9. DECISION subquery
10. CDECISION join

Figure 12–22. EXPLAIN PLAN results mapped to sections of the query.

is step 1 (sort group by). We'll find out shortly what these mean. Right now you just need to know that the results from performing a step get passed up the line to the parent. When step 2 performs its function, the results get passed to step 1.

If a parent has more than one child, the order of processing gets determined by the step's POSITION. The POSITION appears as column 3 in Figure 12–22. Note, for example, that steps 18 and 4 each have step 3 as a parent. The results of step 4 get processed by the parent first because it's POSITION is 1.

Figure 12–23 reformats the execution plan graphically in a parent-child relationship. When two or more children have the same parent, the POSITION order is represented left to right in the figure. For example, note that steps 4 and 18 both connect to the parent step 3. But step 4 appears to the left of step 18 in the figure. This indicates that the results of step 4 get passed up to the parent before the results from step 18.

Now here's the interesting part. What happens when we combine the graphical execution plan (Figure 12–23) with the mapping of SQL blocks and execution steps (Figure 12–22)? The answer appears in Figure 12–24 on the following page. This format let's us verbally describe the data retrieval strategy selected by the ORACLE optimizer.

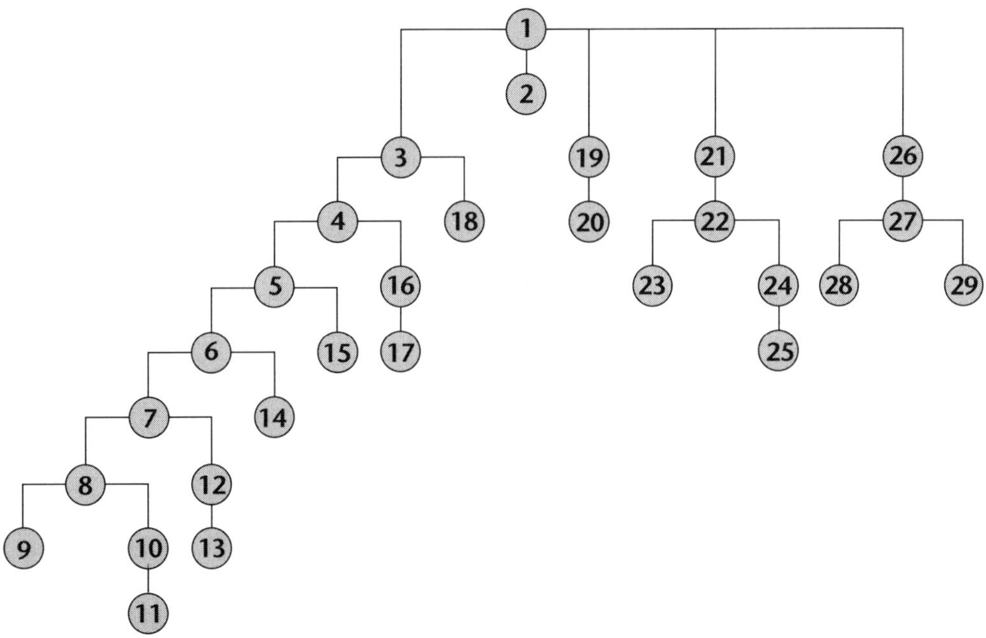

Figure 12–23. EXPLAIN PLAN results arranged in a parent-child format.

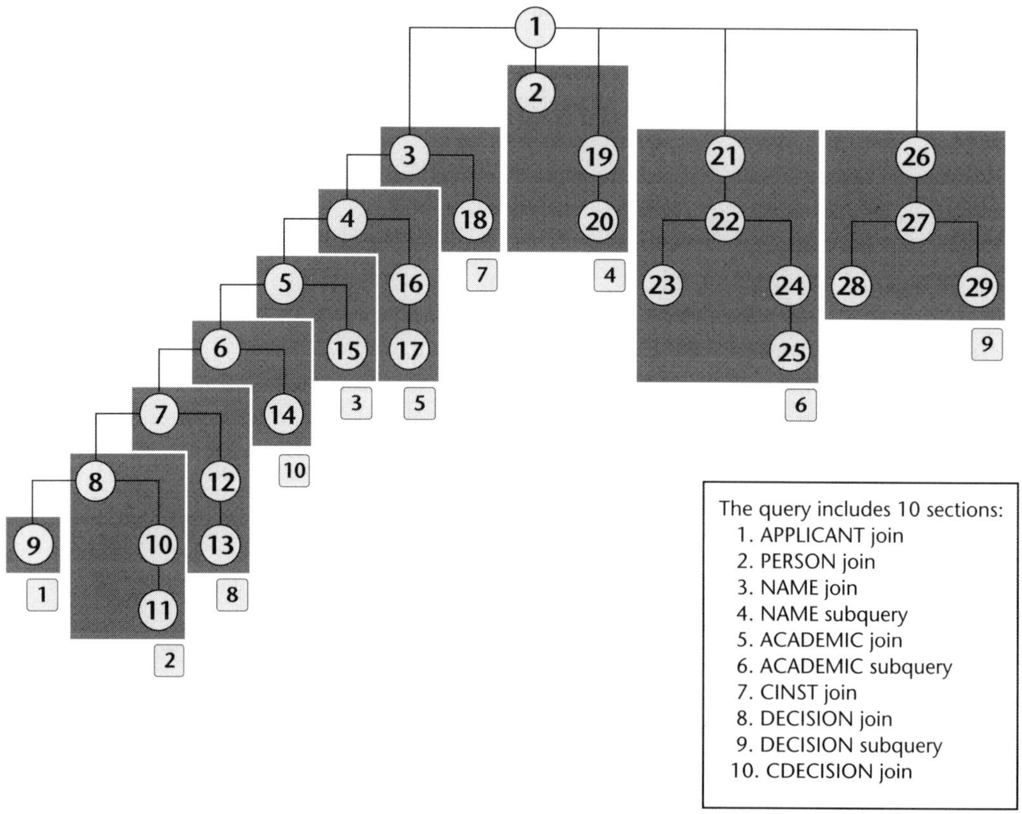

Figure 12–24. EXPLAIN PLAN results mapped to the query sections.

The process starts down in the lower left-hand corner of Figure 12–24 with the APPLICANT table. This table gets read row by row until a row is found that matches the *where* conditions (applicant_term = '199509' and applicant_level = 'UG' and applicant_college = 'AS'). When this row is found the next step joins to the PERSON table. This is followed by the join to the DECISION table. The full sequence of steps for this one applicant row is:

1. Retrieve a row from the APPLICANT table that meets the *where* conditions.
2. Join to the PERSON table.
3. Join to the DECISION table.
4. Join to the CDECISION table.
5. Join to the NAME table.

6. Join to the ACADEMIC table.
7. Join to the CINST table.
8. Perform the NAME subquery that returns the latest name information.
9. Perform the ACADEMIC subquery that returns the last high school attended.
10. Perform the DECISION subquery that returns the last admissions decision.

The process then begins again with a search for the next APPLICANT row that qualifies. These procedures occur over and over until the entire APPLICANT file has been processed.

So now you know the basic execution strategy. But to influence that strategy you must understand more about the terminology used in the execution plan. Table 12–1 on the following page lists the various operations used in execution plans. Some occur with options and the table also lists these. For example, when the execution plan in Figure 12–22 says "index unique scan cdecision_key" it means that this step directly looks up a cdecision_code using the unique index cdecision_key. When the execution plan says "nested loops outer" for the CINST join it means this join is an outer join.

With the information in Table 12–1 we can add a bit more substance to the execution strategy described above. The strategy starts with a full table scan of the APPLICANT table, searching each row in the table until a row matching the *where* conditions is found. When this first match is found, the following steps occur:

1. Retrieve the row from the APPLICANT table.
2. Join to the PERSON table. The applicant_id is known from step 1, the join criteria in the query equates applicant_id and person_id, and person_id is the unique index in PERSON (see Table A–2 in Appendix A). This means that a lookup of person_id in the index returns the precise ROWID locating the PERSON data. Access and retrieval of the PERSON data is direct. Only rows with person_gender = F get retained for further operations.
3. Perform an outer join to the DECISION table. As shown in Table A–2 the unique index decision_key uses decision_id, decision_applicant_term, decision_applicant_seriesno, and decision_seriesno. The first three items in the index are known

Table 12–1. EXPLAIN PLAN operations.

Operation	Option	Action
AND-EQUAL		Intersections of ROWIDs using index searches
CONNECT BY		Executes the CONNECT BY clause in ***select*** commands
CONCATENATION		A retrieval using a UNION ALL operation of tables
COUNTING		Counts the number of rows returned from a table
FILTER		Restricts rows returned from a table
FIRST ROW		Retrieves only the first row of a query
FOR UPDATE		Places locks on selected rows for update
INDEX	UNIQUE SCAN	Uses index to look up a unique value
	RANGE SCAN	Uses index to look up non-unique values (more than one row)
INTERSECTION		Retrieves rows common to two tables
MERGE JOIN		Joins two tables by sorting and then merging
	OUTER	Performs an outer join
MINUS		Retrieves rows in one table that don't appear in a second table
NESTED LOOPS		Joins performed on two child operations. Each time the first child operation returns a row, the second child operation occurs
	OUTER	Performs an outer join
PROJECTION		Retrieves a subset of columns from a table
REMOTE		Retrieves rows from a remote database
SEQUENCE		Utilizes a sequence generator
SORT	UNIQUE	Sorts to produce unique values
	GROUP BY	Sorts for the *group by* clause
	JOIN	Sorts for merge joins
	ORDER BY	Sorts for ordering the query results
TABLE ACCESS	BY ROWID	Access a table using a ROWID retrieved from an index
	FULL	Access a table by scanning the full table
	CLUSTER	Access a table using a cluster key
UNION		Retrieves rows in either of two tables. Eliminates duplicates
VIEW		Retrieves from a data view (a virtual table)

from the join criteria. The table rows cannot be accessed directly because the full index is not known; but the index does provide approximate row locations. It says essentially that DECISION data for the applicant is between ROWID x and ROWID y. A scan of the DECISION table from ROWID x to ROWID y locates the correct data for retrieval.

4. Perform an outer join to the CDECISION table. The correct CDECISION row is accessed directly because all the data needed by the unique index cdecision_key is known.

5. Join to the NAME table. The unique index in NAME is name_id and name_seriesno (see Table A–2). Only the name_id is known, so NAME data for the applicant must be located using a range scan based on information provided by the index name_key.
6. Perform an outer join to the ACADEMIC table. The unique index for the ACADEMIC table is academic_key. This uses academic_id, academic_instcode, and academic_seriesno. Only academic_id is known going into this join, so ACADEMIC data for the applicant must be located using a range scan based on information provided by the index. A filter is applied to retain only those rows with nvl(academic_degree, 'HS') = HS.
7. Perform an outer join to the CINST table. The correct CINST row is accessed directly because all the information needed by the unique index cinst_key is known.
8. Perform the NAME subquery to return the latest name information. Only name_id is known going into the subquery. The range of rows in NAME is scanned using information provided by the index name_key. These are then sorted on the basis of name_seriesno and only the row with max(name_seriesno) is retained for further operations.
9. Perform the ACADEMIC subquery to return the last high school attended. This subquery uses the PERSON table to correlate with the main query. The known I.D. number permits direct access to the PERSON row through the index person_key. An outer join between PERSON and ACADEMIC then occurs. This uses a range scan of ACADEMIC based on information provided by the index academic_key. The results are sorted by academic_datestamp and only the row with the maximum date is retained for further operations.
10. Perform the DECISION subquery to return the last admissions decision. This subquery also uses the PERSON table to correlate with the main query. The correct PERSON row is accessed directly because the person_id is known. An outer join between PERSON and DECISION then occurs. This uses a range scan of DECISION based on information provided by the decision_key index. The results get sorted by decision_seriesno and only the row with max(decision_seriesno) gets retained.

The process then begins again with the next APPLICANT row that meets the *where* conditions. This continues iteratively until all rows in the APPLICANT table have been processed.

You can use the information provided by EXPLAIN PLAN to affect response time. Already you might see some opportunities. Can we get rid of any full table scans? Can we influence when the filters occur so that later operations have fewer rows to process? Do the operations make best use of the available indexes? We'll consider these questions shortly, but first a brief review of the accumulated wisdom of SQL tuners is needed.

Tuning Folklore

In their documentation and in the release notes that accompany version upgrades, Oracle provides a ranking of query paths from fastest to slowest. Improving performance then becomes a task of choosing the faster query paths over the slower query paths whenever alternative paths are available.

Table 12–2 shows Oracle's ranking of query paths for version 7. In broad terms this ranking implies the following general rules for improving performance:

- Indexes provide better performance than full table scans.
- Unique indexes provide better performance than non-unique indexes.
- Entire concatenated indexes provide better performance than the leading edge of concatenated indexes.
- Operations like *order by*, *max*, *min*, *is null*, and *like* '%C%' provide the worst performance.

In actual practice, however, the rankings shown in Table 12–2 merely provide guidelines for tuning a query. For example, full table scans appear near the bottom of the rankings in Table 12–2. But the performance of some queries can actually be improved by consciously disabling an index so that you force a full table scan.

Particularly with the rules-based optimizers, tuning an SQL query remains more an art form than an engineering feat. You test query performance, analyze the query with EXPLAIN PLAN, modify the SQL to alter the execution plan, and test query performance again. Tuning continues in this fashion until you run out of ideas or performance improves to a satisfactory point.

Table 12–2. Oracle's ranking of query paths by order of speed.

Rank	Path
1	ROWID = constant
2	unique indexed column = constant
3	entire unique concatenated index = constant
4	entire cluster key = corresponding cluster key in another table in same cluster
5	entire cluster key = constant
6	entire non-unique concatenated index = constant
7	non-unique index = constant
8	entire concatenated index = lower bound
9	most leading concatenated index specified
10	unique index column BETWEEN low value AND high value or unique indexed column LIKE 'C%' (bounded range)
11	non-unique indexed column BETWEEN low value and high value, or non-unique indexed column LIKE 'C%'
12	unique indexed column or constant (unbounded range)
13	non-unique indexed column or constant (unbounded range)
14	sort/merge (joins only)
15	MAX or MIN of single indexed column
16	ORDER BY entire index
17	full table scans
18	unindexed column = constant, or column IS NULL, or column LIKE '%C%' (full table scan)

Notes:

1. The lower the rank, the faster the query path.
2. These rankings are subject to change with changes in optimizers.

Over time query tuners have developed some rules of thumb that guide them through the tuning process. The rankings in Table 12–2 provide the backdrop; the guidelines shown in Table 12–3 on the following page provide more specific tuning strategies.

Tuning a query requires concentration on two parts of the SQL: the *from* clause and the *where* clause. Each affects performance individually or through interactions with the other. In the *from* clause the order of the tables affects performance; in the *where* clause the conditions and join statements affect performance based on how they use indexes.

Initially it might seem surprising that the order of tables listed in the *from* clause could affect performance. But consider a simple situation with two tables, one table containing 1 row and the other table containing 1000 rows. Assume each table is indexed on the same key. Two execution strategies exist. You could do a full table scan of 1000 rows and then perform the

Table 12–3. Guidelines for tuning SQL queries.

from clause	
1	In a query with two tables, use the table returning the fewest rows as the driving table. The driving table is listed last in the *from* clause.
2	In queries with more than two tables, use the intersection table as the driving table. The intersection table is the one on which many other tables are dependent.
3	Use table aliases if there's any chance of ambiguity (e.g., in subqueries).
4	Don't include views in the query.
where clause, indexes	
5	If the query returns fewer than x% of the rows in a table, use an index. Otherwise use a full table scan. The value of x varies but is usually set at 10%, 20%, or 30%. This is known as the 90/10, 80/20, or 70/30 rule.
6	Use a function (for character data types) or an arithmetic operation (for number data types) to deliberately disable an index. Avoid using functions or performing calculations on indexed data columns unless trying to disable the index.
7	If used on indexed data columns, the following disable the index: !=, <>, NOT IN, IS NULL, IS NOT NULL. Seek alternatives unless deliberately trying to disable an index.
8	Avoid mismatching data types in an expression using indexed data columns. This also disables an index.
9	When using OR, the clause returning the fewest rows should appear first.
10	Avoid using joins that require a DISTINCT on the *select* clause.

Sources:

1. Corrigan, Peter and Mark Gurry. *ORACLE Performance Tuning.* Sebastopol, CA: O'Reilly & Associates, Inc., 1993.
2. Nordeen, Kenneth E. "A Practical Guide to SQL Application Tuning." International Computer Consultants (photocopy).

join for 1 row. Or you could do a full table scan of 1 row and then perform the join for one of the 1000 rows. Obviously the second strategy requires fewer operations and produces better response times.

The table used as a starting point in a query is known as the *driving table.* The driving table should appear last in the query list. In simple queries with two tables, the driving table should be the one with the fewest rows returned. In queries joining more than two tables, the driving table should be the intersection table. Your *population* object identifies the intersection table: it's the one at the heart of the query; the one that describes the population; the one on which other tables are dependent. As you'll see shortly, choosing the correct driving table can dramatically affect performance.

The *where* clause affects performance through its use of indexes. You must consciously choose to enable or disable the available indexes, meaning that the tuning objective becomes one of managing the use of indexes. As mentioned above, a full table scan can yield faster results under some conditions than the use of an index. The situations when this occurs will vary, but tuners generally employ an 80/20 or similar rule. That is, if fewer than 20 percent of the rows in a table will be returned from a query, then an index provides the fastest access. If the number of returned rows exceeds 20 percent, then a full table scan provides faster access. But be cautious; these are guidelines only. The dividing line for your query may occur at a different point.

Queries often suffer when indexes are unintentionally disabled. Applying a function to an indexed column or performing an arithmetic operation on an indexed column disables the index. Using NOT conditions such as != or <> or NOT IN also disables an indexed data column. The trick becomes one of finding alternative structures. For example, using NOT EXISTS is preferable to using NOT IN.

Tables 12–2 and 12–3 provide tuning help. But truthfully you're on your own when you tune a query. You need to experiment with alternative SQL structures, to test the effect of disabling an index to force a full table scan, and to determine which of two competing indexes provides the better performance. All this takes time, which is why I recommend you abandon an optimizing tuning policy. When a query takes too long, then tune it until performance is acceptable. Otherwise spend your time writing other queries.

Tuning an SQL Query

The SQL query in Figure 12–13 accurately produced the report requested by Komenda's director of admissions. But can we improve the query so it produces an accurate report in a faster time? Let's find out.

Tuning a query requires a number of steps. These include:

- Determine how fast the initial query performs so that this can be used as a benchmark to judge changes in the query.
- Identify bottlenecks in the query that require the most execution time.
- Analyze the bottlenecks and devise alternative methods of accomplishing the same task.

- Determine how fast the new query runs and compare it to the benchmark. If it's significantly faster, then keep the change; if not, then discard it.
- Continue in this fashion iteratively until you run out of ideas. Assume this is the best query.

Table 12–4 shows timing statistics gathered by using the *set* command to "set timing on."

Table 12–4. Query performance before tuning query.

		No. Rows		Cumulative		Step	
Section	**Description**	**Processed**	**Returned**	**Seconds**	**Pct**	**Seconds**	**Pct**
1	Full table scan of APPLICANT	1045	700	1.76	8.5%	1.59	7.7%
2	Join to PERSON	700	318	2.96	14.3%	1.20	5.8%
8	Join to DECISION	318	616	4.39	21.1%	1.43	6.9%
10	Join to CDECISION	616	616	4.83	23.3%	0.44	2.1%
3	Join to NAME	616	996	9.17	44.2%	4.34	20.9%
5	Join to ACADEMIC	996	1082	13.46	64.8%	4.29	20.7%
7	Join to CINST	1082	1082	14.94	71.9%	1.48	7.1%
4	NAME subquery	1082	671	15.60	75.1%	0.66	3.2%
6	ACADEMIC subquery	671	616	19.17	92.3%	3.57	17.2%
9	DECISION subquery	616	318	20.77	100.0%	1.60	7.7%

Note:

1. Section numbers refer to the numbering scheme shown in Figure 12–20.

The table breaks the query into the ten sections discussed earlier. Note that the entire query took 20.77 seconds to complete. This number is actually an average value obtained by running the query ten times. On a single-user database using a processor running no other applications, the variation in performance times is fairly small. The standard deviation in the ten runs in Table 12–4 is only 0.189 seconds. This provides a good benchmark against which variations in the query may be judged. If this was a statistical test, we'd assume that any performance times within plus or minus two standard deviations of the mean were not statistically different from the mean. Any times that fell outside of this range apparently occurred because the revised SQL legitimately affected performance.

Examine Table 12–4 closely. The first two columns identify the ten major sections in the query. The next two columns show how many rows each section of the query processed and how many rows it returned for processing in later operations. For example, section 1 in the query did a full scan of the APPLICANT table. The operation processed 1045 rows and retained 700 for processing. The next two columns in Table 12–4 show timing statistics for each of the ten query sections. The times are added cumulatively and a percentage distribution provided. These are determined by removing sections of the query and gathering timing statistics for the revised query. For example, a query including only sections 1, 2, 8, and 10 completes in 4.83 seconds. This represents 23.3 percent of the average completion time of 20.77 seconds. The last two columns show the time that each section of the query requires individually. For example, section 10 requires 0.44 seconds (i.e., 4.83 seconds minus 4.39 seconds). This represents 2.1 percent of the average completion time of 20.77 seconds.

Table 12–4 immediately identifies the bottlenecks in the query. Note that three sections consume almost 60 percent of the average completion time. These offending sections are 3 (the NAME join), 5 (the ACADEMIC join) and 6 (the ACADEMIC subquery), and they provide opportunities to improve performance.

Before trying to improve performance, note one other thing in Table 12–4. Look at the pattern of rows processed. The query starts with a full table scan of 1045 rows and returns 700. The report population actually consists of the 318 rows resulting from the PERSON join that occurs in section 2 of the query. From this point the number of rows increases to a maximum of 1082 as joins into tables with repeating rows occur. Then the subqueries kick in and the row counts begin to decline again until the last step returns 318. Limiting the increase in rows could also improve performance. For example, if you could structure the query so that fewer than 1082 rows got processed at maximum, then the query should run faster.

Table 12–5 on the following page shows results from a fishing expedition of tuning efforts. We know that the biggest improvements are likely to occur in the NAME and ACADEMIC joins. But Table 12–5 includes a number of other strategies just to illustrate some points.

Table 12–5. Effects on performance for selected changes in the SQL query.

Strategy	Description	Time (sec)	Changes from Baseline
A	Baseline: full query in Figure 12–20	20.77	None (baseline)
B	Smallest table last in *from* clause	20.76	None
C	Make NAME the driving table	40.70	Full table scan on NAME
D	Move APPLICANT condition and PERSON join to bottom	21.04	Different order for subqueries
E	Random location of the 10 query sections	20.54	Different order for subqueries
F	Correlate NAME subquery differently	18.73	Uses unique index on NAME
G	Alternative structure for ACADEMIC join and subquery	19.99	Uses more of the ACADEMIC index but creates greater complexity in the subquery
I	Strategies G and F combined	18.18	Combined effect of strategies G and F

Note:

1. Ten trials of strategy A produced a standard deviation of 0.189 seconds and a mean of 20.768 seconds. The range within 2 standard deviations of the mean extends from 20.58 seconds to 20.96 seconds.

Let's start with a strategy that doesn't appear in Table 12–5. The query performs a full table scan of APPLICANT. Normally full table scans should set off alarms. But in this case the query returns almost 70 percent of the rows in the APPLICANT table (700 out of the 1045). It's unlikely that creating an index would improve performance. If you did choose to experiment with an index, the index should include applicant_term, applicant_level, and applicant_college. The index would be non-unique.

Strategy B in Table 12–5 represents a common error. Query writers sometimes select a driving table by placing the smallest table last in the *from* clause. If you follow this advice strictly, the smallest table is often a code table. In our query the smallest table is actually the code table CDECISION that includes approximately two dozen decision codes. Table 12–5 shows that code tables don't operate as driving tables. In fact, placing CDECISION last in the *from* clause produced no change in the execution plan and no significant change in performance (20.76 seconds).

Strategy C, however, had a dramatic impact on performance. Choosing the NAME table as the driving table in the query forced a full scan of the NAME table. Performance nearly doubled to 40.70 seconds. The correct choice for the driving table in this query is APPLICANT. It's the intersection table, the one that defines the population.

Sometimes you hear the advice that the most restrictive *where* conditions should appear last in the *where* clause. This advice is offered because parsing of the query occurs from bottom to the top. If the most restrictive conditions appear at the end of the SQL, then they get parsed first. That doesn't mean they appear first in the execution plan, however, and that's what counts. Table 12–5 shows two strategies that alter the location of the ten sections in the query. Strategy D moves the *population* object (i.e., the APPLICANT and PERSON join) to the bottom of the SQL query. This does produce a different execution plan (not shown). The order of processing the subqueries changes. However, performance actually got a little worse (21.04 seconds). Strategy E takes the reorganization effort to an extreme. In this query each section was randomly assigned a location. For example, the NAME join might appear first in the SQL, but the NAME subquery might be in location 7. This structure also produced an execution plan that processed the subqueries differently from the baseline execution plan. But there was no change in performance (20.54 seconds).

Strategy F addresses one of the bottlenecks in the query. It makes a subtle change in the correlating condition between the NAME subquery and the main query. This change is shown in Figure 12–25 on the following page. Instead of correlating the NAME subquery with the main query through a join of n2.name_id = n1.name_id, it joins n2.name_id = applicant_id. In other words, the correlating criteria uses the driving table. The change makes better use of the index NAME_KEY, causing a unique scan of the index instead of a range scan. Performance time improves significantly to 18.73 seconds.

Strategy G struggles with the other bottlenecks, which occur in the ACADEMIC join and subquery. At least two approaches should be considered when revising this portion of the SQL. First, note that the subquery uses the PERSON table to correlate with the APPLICANT table in the main query. This structure prevents applicants without ACADEMIC data from falling through the subquery. Recall from Chapter 8 that an alternative structure using OR provides the same results without requiring the PERSON join. We should try this alternative structure.

Second, we should look for ways to better use the index on the ACADEMIC table. The unique index consists of academic_id, academic_instcode, and academic_seriesno (see Table A–2 in Appendix A). Our query only utilizes the leading edge of this index because only academic_id is known. We should try to revise the SQL so that the next portion of the index, academic_instcode, also gets used.

Figure 12–25 on the next page shows revisions in the ACADEMIC join to better use the index and to use an alternative structure. The effect is a

SQL

```
select
       count(*), count(distinct applicant_id)
from cdecision, decision c1, cinst, academic e1, name n1, person, applicant
where
       applicant_term = '199509'
               and applicant_level = 'UG'
               and applicant_college = 'AS'
       and person_id = applicant_id
               and person_gender = 'F'
       and n1.name_id = applicant_id
               and n1.name_seriesno =
               (select max(n2.name_seriesno)
               from name n2
               where n2.name_id = applicant_id)
       and e1.academic_id(+) = applicant_id
               and
               (
               (e1.academic_instcode is null)
               OR
               (e1.academic_instcode =
               (select e2.academic_instcode
               from academic e2
               where e2.academic_id = applicant_id
               and decode(e2.academic_degree,'HS','HS',null)||
               to_char(e2.academic_datestamp,'YYYYMMDD') =
                        (select max(decode(e3.academic_degree,'HS','HS',null)||
                        to_char(e3.academic_datestamp,'YYYYMMDD'))
                        from academic e3
                        where e3.academic_id = applicant_id)))
               )
       and cinst_code(+) = nvl(e1.academic_instcode,'unkn')
       and c1.decision_id(+) = applicant_id
               and c1.decision_applicant_term(+) = applicant_term
               and c1.decision_applicant_seriesno(+) = applicant_seriesno
               and nvl(c1.decision_seriesno,1) =
                        (select max(nvl(c2.decision_seriesno,1))
                        from
                                decision c2,
                                person
                        where person_id = applicant_id
                        and c2.decision_id(+) = person_id
                                and c2.decision_applicant_term(+) = applicant_term
                                and c2.decision_applicant_seriesno(+) = applicant_seriesno)
       and cdecision_code(+) = c1.decision_code;
```

The two changes each make better use of existing indexes.

Figure 12–25. The tuned SQL program.

modest improvement in performance. Table 12–5 shows that performance improves from 20.77 seconds to 19.99 seconds.

When strategies F and G are combined, performance improves even more. The combined effect of these changes produces a query that completes in 18.18 seconds. This represents a 12.5 percent improvement over the original query. Table 12–6 shows performance in each of the major sections of the query. Figure 12–26 on the following page shows the execution strategy for this query. Note that revising the NAME join rearranged the order of processing so that the NAME join occurred third. This reduces the number of rows that get processed in later steps. In the original query the maximum number of rows processed was 1082 (see Table 12–4), but in the tuned query the maximum is only 671. Reducing the rows carried from step to step in the query helps improve response time.

Table 12–6. Query performance after tuning query.

		No. Rows		Cumulative		Step	
Section	Description	Processed	Returned	Seconds	Pct	Seconds	Pct
1	Full table scan of APPLICANT	1045	700	1.32	7.3%	1.26	6.9%
2	Join to PERSON	700	318	3.19	17.5%	1.87	10.3%
3,4	Join to NAME	318	318	6.75	37.1%	3.56	19.6%
8	Join to DECISION	318	616	7.91	43.5%	1.16	6.4%
10	Join to CDECISION	616	616	9.66	53.1%	1.75	9.6%
5	Join to ACADEMIC	616	671	12.75	70.1%	3.09	17.0%
7	Join to CINST	671	671	13.73	75.5%	0.98	5.4%
6	ACADEMIC subquery	671	616	16.92	93.1%	3.19	17.5%
9	DECISION subquery	616	318	18.18	100.0%	1.26	6.9%

Note:

1. Section numbers refer to the numbering scheme shown in Figure 12–20.

Was the tuning worth the effort? In this case, no. Queries that complete in 21 seconds fall well within my "good enough" range. But remember the query only processed about 1000 rows. If the query had run against a million rows, then the time spent tuning the query may have been useful. By making some assumptions about scaling of performance times, the tuned

```
EXPLAIN PLAN

parent id     pos    query_plan
------ ------ ------ ------------------------------------------------------------
       1      0        SORT GROUP BY
1      2      1          FILTER
2      18     3            FILTER
18     19     1              TABLE ACCESS BY ROWID ACADEMIC
19     20     1                INDEX RANGE SCAN ACADEMIC_KEY
18     21     2              SORT GROUP BY
21     22     1                TABLE ACCESS BY ROWID ACADEMIC
22     23     1                  INDEX RANGE SCAN ACADEMIC_KEY
2      3      1            NESTED LOOPS OUTER
3      17     2              INDEX UNIQUE SCAN CINST_KEY
3      4      1              NESTED LOOPS OUTER
4      16     2                INDEX RANGE SCAN ACADEMIC_KEY
4      5      1                NESTED LOOPS OUTER
5      15     2                  INDEX UNIQUE SCAN CDECISION_KEY
5      6      1                  NESTED LOOPS OUTER
6      13     2                    TABLE ACCESS BY ROWID DECISION
13     14     1                      INDEX RANGE SCAN DECISION_KEY
6      7      1                    NESTED LOOPS
7      8      1                      NESTED LOOPS
8      9      1                        TABLE ACCESS FULL APPLICANT
8      10     2                        TABLE ACCESS BY ROWID PERSON
10     11     1                          INDEX UNIQUE SCAN PERSON_KEY
7      12     2                      INDEX UNIQUE SCAN NAME_KEY
2      24     4            SORT GROUP BY
24     25     1              NESTED LOOPS OUTER
25     26     1                INDEX UNIQUE SCAN PERSON_KEY
25     27     2                INDEX RANGE SCAN DECISION_KEY
```

The tuned SQL makes better use of the indexes NAME_KEY and ACADEMIC_KEY. However it also makes the ACADEMIC subquery more complex.

Figure 12–26. EXPLAIN PLAN results after tuning query.

query could reduce total runtime by 40 minutes if one million rows got processed. That's good; unless, of course, it took you three hours to achieve a one-time improvement of 40 minutes.

There is another benefit from tuning SQL; it can often improve the quality of objects. For example, based on the tuning exercise in this chapter, you'd want to revise the objects whrname.obj and whracad.obj that access the NAME and ACADEMIC tables. With use, continuous testing, and occasional tuning, objects improve with age. Table 12–7 updates the inventory list with the new objects developed in this chapter.

Table 12–7. Inventory of SQL objects.

Class	Name	Purpose
POPULATION	popacapp	Applicants accepted for admissions for a specified term, level, and college
	popapp	Applicants for admissions for a specified term, level, college
	popenrl	Accepted applicants for a specified term, level, and college who are expected to enroll
	poprecr	Recruits for a specified term and level
	popsampl	Selects Nsample rows from a population of size Npop, for use in testing and debugging objects when the population size is large. Assumes the population size is known
	popxapp	Applicants for a specified term, level, and college. Accepts prompts for term, level and college
WHERE 1	whrintl	Defines the term "international" and modifies a population so only internationals are included
	whrmnrty	Defines the term "minority" and modifies a population so only individuals of color are included
WHERE 2u	whracad	Provides access to the ACADEMIC table for information on the last high school attended
	whraddr	Provides access to the ADDRESS table for the most recent address of a specified type
	whradhi	Provides access to the ADDRESS table in a hierarchical fashion. Returns an address of a specified type (e.g., local). If this type of address is not available, it returns an address of a second specified type (e.g., permanent)
	whrdecsn	Provides access to the DECISION table for information on the last admissions decision
	whrname	Provides access to the NAME table for the most recent name
	whrpersn	Provides access to the PERSON table
	whrphon	Provides access to the PHONE table for the most recent phone of a specified type and associated with an address of a specified type
	whrtest	Provides access to the TEST table for the highest test score of a specified type
WHERE 2m	whraddrm	Provides access to the ADDRESS table for all addresses of a specified type
	whrdcmnt	Provides access to all documents in the DOCUMENT table for a population of applicants
SELECT	selage	Computes a person's age based on sysdate (the report date) and the person's birthdate
	selcszn	Creates a single display column by concatenating address_city, address_state, address_zip, and address_nation
	seliname	Creates a name using the initials of the first and middle names and concatenating these to name_last

(Continued)

Table 12–7. Inventory of SQL objects.

Class	Name	Purpose
SELECT	selintl	Identifies a person as an "international" based on their visa status
	selmajr	Collapses anticipated majors into academic departments
	selprank	Computes a person's percent rank in high school based on class size and class rank
	selrmnd1	Calculates a "reminder date" as the Monday that follows the date of application plus one month
	selrmnd2	Calculates a "reminder date" as 7 weeks (49 days) after the application date
	selsatc	Calculates a combined SAT score as the sum of SAT math and SAT verbal scores
	selsname	Creates a name by concatenating name_last, name_first, and name_middle
	seltestr	Calculates a test range (e.g., 400-499) that an SAT score falls within. Useful for frequency distributions by score ranges
REPORT	avg1	Produces a report showing the average of a data column broken down by the categories of a coded data column (e.g., showing average test scores by gender)
	avg1cnt	Produces a report showing the average of a data column broken down by the categories of a coded data column. Includes counts of items averaged
	blckdtl	Produces a combined detail and blocked detail report
	blockl	Produces a simple roster (i.e., listing) of data columns in a blocked format. Instead of appearing in columns across the report, data columns appear in rows down the report. Labels are attached to the blocked columns
	cnt1lab	Produces a report counting the report population by categories in a coded data column. Includes the code translations
	count1	Produces a report counting the report population by categories in a coded data column (i.e., a 1-way frequency distribution)
	count2	Produces a report counting the report population by categories in two coded data columns (i.e., a 2-way cross-tabulation)
	detail	Produces a list of data columns for the report population
	dtlcnt	Produces a combined detail and count report
	repeat	Produces a detail report where repeating data gets suppressed (e.g., if an applicant has 10 MAIL items the report shows all 10 mailings but the applicant's name only once)
	sum1	Produces a report showing the sum of a data column broken down by the categories of a coded data column (e.g., showing total fees by gender)
	sum1cnt	Produces a report showing the sum of a data column broken down by the categories of a coded data column. Includes counts of the items summed

(Continued)

Table 12–7. Inventory of SQL objects.

Class	Name	Purpose
SHELL	shell.obj	Provides a shell for each ad hoc report. Starts the main SQL that retrieves data for the report. Houses other shell objects that control printer and screen characteristics, report titles, column headers, and other features of the finished report
	shlprmpt.obj	Prompts user for a report parameter to use at run time. Verifies that the response is correct
	shlttl1.obj	Produces a standard top title for a report, including descriptive text, date stamp, time stamp, page number, and names of the files containing the SQL and the report output
	shlttl2.obj	Produces a modified standard report that also includes user responses to prompts
	shltt3.obj	Produces a standard title and column headings for a detail and block report

Part III
Using SQL Objects

Chapter 13

Reporting with SQL Objects

Previous chapters provided the elements necessary for reporting with SQL objects. This chapter actually uses those elements to prepare a series of ad hoc reports focused on a single policy issue at Komenda College. I hope to demonstrate the use of SQL objects in a reporting situation that closely approximates reality.

Summary of Reporting with SQL Objects

Each query constructed with SQL objects proceeds through a logical series of steps. These steps appeared throughout the previous chapters. At this point, however, it's useful to pull the steps together and summarize them in one place. Not all of the steps require action in each query, but they do all require attention. The steps are as follows:

- Each query begins with a request. Often that request is made verbally but sometimes it appears in writing.
- The request must be clarified. Often requests are incomplete or poorly thought out. Ask questions of the person making the request until you understand exactly what he or she wants. Sometimes this process is iterative. You arrive at an understanding of what's required, but then translating the request raises more questions which must be answered. Don't skimp on this step; nothing else matters if you don't get it right.

- Decide on the appropriate tool for the report. SQL*PLUS is only one possibility. Complicated research questions requiring considerable analysis should not be done with SQL. Even seemingly simple reports with multiple populations should not generally be done with SQL. I use a fairly stringent criteria when deciding on the appropriateness of SQL for a reporting question. If I can do the report with one pass at the data, I'll use SQL. Otherwise I'll use a procedural programming language or a statistical/reporting tool. In these situations SQL still serves a useful function because it can be embedded in many procedural languages or it can be used to create extract data sets for analysis. This step often involves negotiation with the person making the report request. He or she may ask for a report that is difficult with SQL, but may be satisfied with a similar report that SQL can handle easily.
- Assuming that SQL qualifies as the tool of choice, the request must be translated from words into a ***select*** statement. It's here that the real utility of SQL objects becomes evident. Objects already incorporate standard business concepts. So you seldom need to translate directly from words into SQL; you merely translate from words into SQL objects.
- Start the translation by identifying the report population. Use the *population* object that most closely approximates the verbal request. You might not have a *population* object for "female applicants for admission" but you do have one for "applicants for admission." Start with what you've already got and then add modifying *where* objects to qualify the population. You must be absolutely clear about the population, otherwise later testing won't be meaningful.
- Now focus on what type of data the user requested in the report. What pieces of information about the population does he or she want to see? Any data columns that appear in tables used in the main query (as opposed to subqueries) of the *population* object are already available for reporting. Identify those data columns that need additional joins. Then map the joins to the closest *where* objects. Pay particular attention here to the issue of singularity. For each item in the population, should the join return a single value or several values? It's this step and the previous one that require the most attention. For example, consider the request to show permanent addresses of female applicants for admission. If you

take the report population to be "female applicants for admission" then you must use a *where* object that prevents anyone in the population from falling through the report. However, if you take the report population to be "female applicants for admission who have permanent addresses" then the *where* object becomes part of the population definition and you need not worry about population loss. In this case the presence of a permanent address acts as just another qualifier like "female." Make sure you know whether a *where* object acts to qualify the population—and therefore becomes part of the population definition—or if it acts to retrieve information about the population. There's an enormous difference.

- The previous two steps, of selecting and modifying *population* and *where* objects, may leave you with complete *from* and *where* clauses for the SQL ***select*** statement. If so, you can begin testing. If not, you'll need to add additional SQL to the query. For example, you may not have a *where* object that accesses the table containing a data column required in the report. Dig out the database schematics, check the index listings, examine the data dictionary, and talk with other query writers who may already have solved this join problem. Write the necessary SQL. After testing it may serve as the basis for a new object.
- At this point you have completed the *from* and *where* clauses for the SQL ***select***. It's now time to test the query. Start by stepping through the joins. Do a count(*) and count(distinct ...) on just that portion of the SQL that contains the population. Do another count(*) and count(distinct ...) on the entire SQL. Set the timing on when you do this last test. Use the two sets of results to determine if population items fall through the SQL or generate unwanted multiples. For example, a count(*) and count(distinct applicant_id) of 150 for an applicant population would trigger concern if the entire SQL counts were both 148 (apparently two people fell through the joins). If you uncover problems, you'll need to step through the joins one by one, identify the population items affected, and then rewrite the SQL. Don't ignore this testing and debugging step. Even robust objects need continual testing. Conditions change and objects need revision. This testing also serves as a quality control on data input, because you may find the problem is not in your SQL but in the data itself.

- Use the timing statistics from your testing in the previous step to determine whether the SQL needs tuning. If performance falls outside of your acceptable range, or if you know the query will run against a large number of rows, diagnose performance bottlenecks. Run an EXPLAIN PLAN against the query. Graphically plot the EXPLAIN PLAN results. Break the query into units of joins and subqueries. Then get timing statistics on each unit by stepping through the units one by one. That is, time the entire query and then eliminate one query unit and time the new query. Proceed in this manner until only one unit remains in the query. Use these results to identify which parts of the SQL take the most time. Concentrate your revision efforts on these parts of the SQL. Try to make better use of indexes and keep in mind the performance guidelines discussed in Chapter 12.
- Identify the type of report requested. Does the user want a roster? If so, should it be blocked? Does the report include repeating data that should be suppressed for easier reading? Were any group summaries requested? Choose the *report* object that most closely approaches the type of report requested by the user.
- Assemble the tested SQL and the *report* object. Then complete the *report* object, using any *select* objects that are needed. At this point you have a finished SQL ***select*** statement.
- Create a shell program to start the SQL completed in the previous step. Use the basic *shell* object and modify it with additional *shell* objects that prompt users for runtime input or add special titles to the report. At this point you have a finished shell program.
- Start the completed shell program from the SQL prompt. You may get an error here, but it's likely to be a minor one because of the testing done previously. For example, I'll sometimes forget to put a comma after a data column or expression that appears in the *select* clause. Make the necessary corrections and run the shell program again until you get a completed report.
- Print the report and examine it. If you made any blunders when assembling the objects, they may be apparent. Identify anything in the report that needs discussion with the user.
- When satisfied with the report, deliver it to the person requesting it. If necessary, discuss the report with him or her.

- At this point you might be done. But often the user returns with another request—"yes, this is helpful but what I really wanted was ..." or "this is very interesting, but I'd like to check ..." or some other variation. If this happens consider the query a success. You got the user thinking about something and actually using the report.

A Sequence of Queries

As described earlier in Chapter 3, Komenda College has suffered recent enrollment loss in its undergraduate business college. In a tuition-dependent institution like Komenda, enrollment decline translates directly into financial loss. Consequently the Dean of Enrollment Management has faced increasing pressure to reverse or at least stem the enrollment decrease among business students. Senior administrators and trustees all know that national demographic trends and declining interest among high school seniors in business contribute heavily to Komenda's problem. So the Dean is not directly blamed for the decline; nonetheless, she feels pressure. Monitoring business recruits, applicants, and new student enrollment has assumed even greater importance.

Despite considerable effort with new recruiting and marketing programs directed at potential business students, Komenda's Fall 1995 enrollment in the Business College appears to be declining. The Dean wants to understand why. She asks your help. The request begins this way: "The yield among business accepts seems lower than among accepts in arts and sciences. Can you get me a report to see if this is true?" The remainder of this chapter explores this policy issue. As the Dean asks questions, you write queries using SQL objects, and you both interpret the results.

Query 1

An analyst familiar with enrollment research would understand the Dean's request without need for clarification. But let's assume that you, the query writer, want to make sure you understand what she wants. The words "business accepts" seem clear enough. It's just undergraduate applicants for Fall 1995 who were accepted for admission to the Business College. The words "accepts in arts and sciences" are also clear. The only term that needs clarification is "yield." The Dean explains that a yield rate is the percentage of applicants accepted for admission who actually enroll. If 100 students get accepted and 30 of them enroll, then the yield rate is 30 percent.

In her request to you, it's clear the Dean believes the yield rate for Fall 1995 differs by the college of application—that a higher percentage of those accepted into the Arts & Sciences College actually enroll compared to those accepted into the Business College. At this point the verbal request is clear.

You can now begin to map the request into SQL objects. This mapping process will help determine if SQL is actually an appropriate query tool. In this case it is, although one minor glitch appears. Start by identifying the report population. The Dean's request is based on two populations! The yield rate is the ratio of newly enrolled students to accepted applicants. You'll need one report where the population is accepted applicants. You'll need a second report for newly enrolled students. Using the two reports, you can compute yield rates. While not ideal, this seems simple enough.

Table 13–1 shows the table you'll need to complete before computing yield rates. The two report populations—for accepts and new enrollees—appear as columns in the table. The rows refer to the two colleges (i.e., Business and Arts & Sciences). The cell values contain counts.

Table 13–1. Format for computing yield rates by undergraduate college.

College	Accepts	Enrolled	Yield %
Arts & Science			
Business			
Totals			

Note:
1. Yield % = (Enrolled/Accepts)*100

Table 13–1 makes mapping the verbal request into SQL objects easy. The column on accepted applicants maps directly to the object popacapp.obj. The column on new enrolled students maps directly to the object popenrl.obj. Each object specifies a term (Fall 1995), a level (undergraduate), and a college. The Dean's request uses no other population qualifiers, so you could use the two objects as they exist. You would then run four reports: one to count business accepts, one to count arts and sciences accepts, one to count business enrollees, and one to count arts and sciences enrollees.

It's easier, however, to modify the objects slightly and get all the information in just two reports. Each column in Table 13–1 is just a frequency distribution. For example, the column of accepted applicants shows the distribution by college. The *report* object count1.obj produces 1-way frequency distributions like the counts in each column of Table 13–1.

Here's the approach. Insert the popacapp.obj object into the count1.obj *report* object. Modify the popacapp.obj object to include both AS and BU colleges instead of a single college (see Figure 13–1). If necessary use the help files to complete the requested information in the objects. When this is done you have the SQL program. Test the SQL using count(*) and count(distinct applicant_id). These results appear in Figure 13–1. Note that some applicants were accepted to both colleges. Then use the objects called shell.obj and shlttl1.obj to prepare a shell program with a standard report title. The completed shell, SQL, and report appear in Figure 13–2 on the following page.

You would follow the exact steps for a report on new enrolled students. With the two reports, you can compute yield rates. These are shown in Table 13–2 on page 331. The Dean's statement was correct. Yield rates do differ by college: 34 percent of accepted applicants in Arts & Sciences enroll but only 26 percent of those in the Business College do so.

```
SQL> select
        count(*), count(distinct applicant_id)
     from
        applicant
     where
        applicant_term = '199509'
                and applicant_level = 'UG'
        and exists
        (select 'x'
        from
                cdecision,
                decision
        where
                decision_id = applicant_id
                        and decision_applicant_term = applicant_term
                        and decision_applicant_seriesno = applicant_seriesno
                and cdecision_code = decision_code
                        and cdecision_accept_ind = 'Y')
     /
ENTER to continue ...
  COUNT(*) COUNT(DISTINCTAPPLICANT_ID)
---------- ---------------------------
       606                         578
```

The *population* object popacapp.obj was modified by removing the criteria that specified a college (i.e., AS or BU).

Some applicants were accepted by both the Business College and the Arts & Sciences College.

Figure 13–1. Test on the population of accepted undergraduate applicants for Fall 1995.

Objects used:
1. count1.obj
2. popacapp.obj modified

SHELL

```
/*
       sql:      fig13-2
       date:     03-jan-1995
       author:   glewis
       purpose:  Figure 13-2 for Chapter 13
*/
set termout off
start &&object_dir.\clears
start &&object_dir.\hpprintr
start &&object_dir.\date
start &&object_dir.\time
start &&object_dir.\owncol
start &&object_dir.\escape

ttitle left xEscape skip 1-
       'Counts of accepted applicants by col
       right 'Report name: fig13-2.lis' skip
       left 'Date: ' xDate '      Time: ' xTi
       right 'SQL name:    fig13-2.sql' skip
       right 'Page: ' format 999 sql.pno ski


spool fig13-2.lis
       start xfig13-2
       start &&object_dir.\reset
spool off

start &&object_
start &&object_
```

SQL

```
break on report
compute sum of count on report
select
      applicant_college,
      count(*) "count"
from
      applicant
where
      applicant_term = '199509'
              and applicant_level = 'UG'
      and exists
      (select 'x'
      from cdecision, decision
      where
              decision_id = applicant_id
                     and decision_applicant_term = applicant_term
                     and decision_applicant_seriesno = applicant_seriesno
              and cdecision_code = decision_code
                     and cdecision_accept_ind = 'Y')
group by
      applicant_college
```

REPORT

```
Counts of accepted applicants by college: Fall 1995          Report name: fig13-2.lis
Date: 03-JAN-1995     Time: 04:41                              SQL name:    fig13-2.sql
                                                                Page:     1


coll      count
---- ----------
AS          450
BU          156
     ----------
sum         606

2 rows selected.
```

Figure 13–2. Completed shell program, SQL program, and report for query 1.

Table 13–2. Yield rates by undergraduate college: Fall 1995.

College	Accepts	Enrolled	Yield %
Arts & Science	450	152	34%
Business	156	41	26%
Totals	606	193	32%
Total unique	578	193	33%

Note:
1. Yield % = (Enrolled/Accepts)*100

Query 2

You succeeded in substantiating the Dean's claim that yield rates differ by college. But she's unlikely to let the matter rest. She'll want to know why the rates differ. Is it something Komenda is doing? Are arts and sciences accepts treated differently than business students? Do they receive more individualized attention from admissions counselors, or better financial aid packages, or preferential assignments into dormitory spaces? This might be disturbing and embarrassing news, but at least the Dean could take some solace if the problem was responsive to internal policy control. Alternatively, the yield rates might differ for reasons largely unrelated to Komenda. It could be some characteristic of the students or some external factor that caused the difference in yield rates. Perhaps the high school academic achievement of business accepts is superior to those in arts and sciences and the business accepts also get accepted at a greater number of other colleges. They'd then have more options. Or perhaps Komenda is simply getting beaten by a competitor business college for those students that each accepts for admissions.

All of these thoughts occur to the Dean as she digests your report. But first she decides to ask for more background information. She likes the tabular format you presented and asks that this analysis be expanded to include all conversion rates: "This is great, but it would be really helpful if I had the same kind of report starting at the recruit stage and tracking them through the admissions process."

So you and the Dean chat. You need to understand what she really wants, not what she said she wanted or what you think she wanted. After some discussion you arrive at an understanding. She'd like to see a single table of recruits, applicants, the application rate (i.e., applicants/recruits), accepts, the accept rate (i.e., accepts/applicants), enrollees, and the yield rate (i.e., enrollees/accepts). She'd like this broken down by the two colleges.

You begin by mapping the request to SQL objects and evaluating the appropriateness of SQL as a query tool. This time the final report requires four populations; one each for recruits, applicants, accepts, and new enrollees. This means at least four SQL reports, but since two are already done you decide to proceed using SQL.

Applicants map directly to the *population* object popapp.obj. But you hit a snag with the recruit population. A recruit *population* object does exist (poprecr.obj), but it doesn't include anything about the college of the recruit. In fact, by examining the data dictionary for the RECRUIT table you find that no data column identifies the college. Recruits are simply recruits to a level (undergraduate or graduate) and not to a specific college. It's time for more clarification. You need to ask the Dean, the director of admissions, the director of marketing, or the supervisor of records how a business recruit differs from an arts and sciences recruit.

You find out that Komenda makes the distinction based on the interests that a recruit identifies when responding to mailings. Once a student enters Komenda's database as a recruit, he or she begins to receive regular mailings in efforts to sustain an interest in the college. Some mailings contain response forms that allow a student to request information that interests him or her specifically. For example, some may request more information about the men's baseball team or about availability of financial assistance. Based on these responses, future mailings to recruits are individualized. Whenever a recruit checks off an interest in the business programs, he or she becomes a business recruit. Similarly, by expressing interest in arts and sciences programs, the recruit becomes an arts and sciences recruit. Students might express interest in both programs. In this case they're a recruit to both the Business and the Arts & Sciences colleges. You find that business recruits receive a special mailing coded "BUS" for business; arts and sciences recruits receive a mailing coded "LA" for liberal arts.

With this information, you can plot a strategy for the report. Again you'll use the count1.obj *report* object. For the applicant report you can use popapp.obj. For the recruit report you can start with the *population* object poprecr.obj, but you'll need to modify it based on the definitions for business and arts and sciences recruits. The mailings received by recruits distinguish them as business or arts and sciences recruits. Our inventory of objects shows no objects that access the MAIL table.

Lucky you. You get to translate a verbal request into SQL, thereby building a new object and adding a new vocabulary item to your object inventory. The next time someone asks for a report on business recruits, you'll have the object already available.

You examine the data dictionary for the MAIL table (see Table A–8 in Appendix A). It's a very simple table. The only data columns in the table identify who received the mailing, the type of mailing sent, and the date it was sent. The table does have an index, but it's a non-unique index consisting of mail_id, mail_code, and mail_date (see Table A–2 in Appendix A). Use SQL to look at some of the data just to get a feeling for it. Then list the various MAIL codes so you know what codes exist. Sometimes people providing definitions get the codes wrong or they omit a code that should be included. For example, maybe there are two business mailings coded "BUS" and "BUS1." If so, does receipt of either mailing identify a business recruit? You'd need to find out. Figure 13–3 lists legitimate mail codes at Komenda. Note that the relevant codes are indeed BUS and LA.

The question then becomes one of modifying the *population* object. You have several choices. You could include the MAIL table in the main query in poprecr.obj by adding a join between the MAIL table and the RECRUIT table. Figure 13–4 on the following page shows this solution. Apparently this wasn't a good idea. Your testing shows that the count(*) differs from count(distinct recruit_id). This means that some recruits actually receive multiple business mailings. Every time you used the new object the reports would generate multiple rows simply because a recruit had multiple business mailings!

Recall from the chapter on *population* objects that the comparison operators *exists* and *not exists* serve very useful functions when defining populations. They allow you to test for the presence or absence of some characteristic of a population item. In this case you can test to see if a BUS

```
SQL> select cmail_code, cmail_translation from cmail order by 1;
ENTER to continue ...
mail
code   mail
------ -----------------------------
ADVSR  Notification of advisor
AWARD  Financial aid award
BUS    Business
FOLLOW Aid follow information
HOUS   Housing
INTL   International
INTRST Outside interest
INTV   Interview
LA     Liberal arts
PRE    Pre-print of application
REFUND Enrollment refund

11 rows selected.
```

Figure 13–3. Mail codes from the code table CMAIL.

```
SQL> select count(*), count(distinct recruit_id)
     from
          mail,
          recruit
     where
          recruit_term = '199509'
                  and recruit_level = 'UG'
          and mail_id = recruit_id
                  and mail_code = 'BUS'
     /
ENTER to continue ...
 COUNT(*) COUNT(DISTINCTRECRUIT_ID)
---------- -------------------------
      3412                      2695
```

Some recruits receive more than one business mailing, perhaps different versions.

Figure 13–4. Undergraduate recruits for Fall 1995 who received a BUS (business) mailing.

mailing exists for a recruit. If so, that person is a business recruit. Both the *exists* and *not exists* structures preserve singularity, so you need not worry about generating unwanted multiples. However, they do use a subquery and therefore may not be appropriate in all circumstances. Suppose someone requested a report on female applicants. You could use an *exists* to access the PERSON table to see if person_gender = F. This works fine unless the user wanted to include sex as one of the report columns. Buried in a subquery, the join to PERSON makes person_gender unavailable for display.

Figure 13–5 shows the population of business recruits using *exists* to determine if Komenda sent a recruit a business mailing. Note the SQL preserves singularity in the population. Figure 13–6 shows the generalization of this population into a *population* object and its associated help file.

After running the recruit and applicant reports, you can complete the table requested by the Dean. Table 13–3 on page 336 provides those results. Two things of interest appear in this table. First, the Arts & Sciences College apparently does a better job at converting recruits into applicants than does the Business College. The two conversion rates are 12 percent and 8 percent, respectively. Second, the Business College accepts applicants at a higher rate than the Arts & Sciences College, perhaps operating under pressure to raise enrollments in the Business College. Both findings may deserve the Dean's attention. But neither one gets at her core concern over yield rates.

```
SQL> select
 2        count(*), count(distinct recruit_id)
 3   from
 4        recruit
 5   where
 6        recruit_term ='199509'
 7                and recruit_level = 'UG'
 8        and exists
 9        (select 'x'
10        from mail
11        where mail_id = recruit_id
12        and mail_code = 'BUS')
13  /
ENTER to continue ...
  COUNT(*) COUNT(DISTINCTRECRUIT_ID)
---------- -------------------------
      2695                      2695
```

> This SQL preserves singularity in the population by using *exists.*

Figure 13–5. A second definition of the Fall 1995 undergraduates with a BUS (business) mailing.

OBJECT

```
from
      recruit
where
      recruit_term='<term>'
              and recruit_level = '<level>'
      and exists
      (select 'x'
      from mail
      where mail_id = recruit_id
      and mail_code = '<mail_code>')
```

HELP

```
object:          poprecml.obj
date created:    03-jan-1995
author:          glewis
revisions:

Purpose:         Defines the population of recruits for a specified
                 term and level who also received a mailing of a
                 specified type.

Usage:           <term>: replace with term (eg, 199509 for Fall 1995)
                 <level>: replace with level (eg, UG for Undergrad)
                 <mail_code>: replace with code for type of mailing
                         (e.g., 'BUS' for Business mailing)

Hints:           none
```

Figure 13–6. *Population* object and help file for recruits who receive a specific mailing.

Table 13–3. Conversion rates for recruits, applicants, and enrollees: Fall 1995.

College	Recruits	Applicants		Accepts		Enrolled	
		No.	Appl %	No.	Accept %	No.	Yield %
Arts & Science	5896	700	12%	450	64%	152	34%
Business	2695	228	8%	156	68%	41	26%
Totals	8591	928	11%	606	65%	193	32%
Total unique	6996	859	12%	578	67%	193	33%

Notes:

1. Application rate = Appl % = (Applicants/Recruits)*100
2. Accept rate = Accept % = (Accepts/Applicants)*100
3. Yield rate = Yield % = (Enrolled/Accepts)*100

Query 3

After she's thought about the results in Table 13–3, the Dean calls you on the phone and says: "I'd like to test two ideas. One, are we doing something wrong? Or, two, do the students in the Arts & Sciences College differ from those in Business College? Let's start with the first question. Could you get me a report that lists all accepted business applicants who did not enroll? I'd like to see their name, sex, major, and a list of all the mailings we sent to them. That'll give me some idea if we didn't stay in touch with them or if something looks strange in our contacts with them."

You begin by running through a mental checklist of query items. What's the population? It's clearly defined as "accepted business applicants who did not enroll." There's no existing object for that population but either popacapp.obj or popenrl.obj could be modified easily enough. The Dean wants names in the report; that will come from the whrname.obj object. She also wants a report column showing gender; you can access that with the whrpersn.obj object. Academic major appears in the APPLICANT table and is already available because APPLICANT is used in the *population* object. As yet, no *where* object exists to join the MAIL table but that should be trivial after completing the previous query. Singularity will be lost in the MAIL join because each accepted applicant could have multiple mailings; the report population will actually be "mailings sent to accepts who did not enroll," rather than "accepts who did not enroll." The Dean wants a roster report. To suppress the appearance of repeating name, sex, and major information for each mailing, you'll need to use the *report* object called repeat.obj. This is clearly a simple SQL report against a single population.

Begin constructing the query by assembling the SQL objects. Figure 13–7 on the following page shows the SQL for the report population. It required only a minor modification to the *population* object popenrl.obj, turning an *exists* into a *not exists*. This excludes any accepted applicant expected to enroll. Then add the two *where* objects whrname.obj and whrpersn.obj to this population definition. Finish by writing the MAIL join. Figure 13–8 on page 339 shows the assembled objects and a standard test of joins. The tests provide no cause for concern. The population consists of 115 people. This number can be verified against Table 13–3; here the count of accepted business applicants is 156 and the count of new enrolled business students is 41. The population of 156-41 = 115 appears correct. Figure 13–8 also shows that the counts for the entire SQL are 1024/115. You expected generation of multiples through the MAIL join. This test also confirms that nobody fell through any of the joins. Timing statistics fall within an acceptable range.

At this point you embed the SQL into the *report* object (i.e., repeat.obj), add the *select* clause columns, complete the requested items in repeat.obj, and write a shell program using the objects shell.obj and shlttl1.obj. Figure 13–9 on page 340 shows the shell, SQL, and completed report. From start to finish this report should take less than 20 minutes to do.

Query 4

"Thanks for the report," says the Dean. "I gave it to the director of admissions to review. She didn't find anything that looked unusual. Now let's go to the other item we discussed last time. I'd like to see if business accepts differ from arts and sciences accepts. If they were better qualified academically, they probably got accepted by more universities and have a broader range of enrollment options. That would explain why our yield is lower among business accepts. Could you get me a report that compares the average SAT scores of business and arts and sciences accepts? Use the combined SAT scores, ok?"

You sigh, but the Dean is on a hunt and won't be satisfied until she finds out why the yield rates differ. And, at their best, ad hoc queries probe data, provoke thought, and probe again in a complex Brownian movement through a policy problem. Take satisfaction from participating in the quest; someday databases will be so easy to query that the Dean won't need an interpreter.

```
SQL> select count(*), count(distinct applicant_id)
 from
        applicant
 where
        applicant_term = '199509'
                and applicant_level = 'UG'
                and applicant_college = 'BU'
        and exists
        (select 'x'
        from
                cdecision cd0,
                decision d0
        where
                d0.decision_id = applicant_id
                        and d0.decision_applicant_term = applicant_term
                        and d0.decision_applicant_seriesno = applicant_seriesno
                and cd0.cdecision_code = d0.decision_code
                        and cd0.cdecision_accept_ind = 'Y')
        and not exists
        (select 'x'
        from
                cdecision cd1,
                decision d1
        where
                d1.decision_id = applicant_id
                        and d1.decision_applicant_term = applicant_term
                        and d1.decision_applicant_seriesno = applicant_seriesno
                and cd1.cdecision_code = d1.decision_code
                        and cd1.cdecision_enrl_ind = 'Y'
                and not exists
                (select 'x'
                from
                        cdecision cd2,
                        decision d2
                where
                        d2.decision_id = applicant_id
                                and d2.decision_applicant_term = applicant_term
                                and d2.decision_applicant_seriesno = applicant_seriesno
                        and cd2.cdecision_code = d2.decision_code
                                and cd2.cdecision_cancel_ind = 'Y'))
 /
ENTER to continue ...
  COUNT(*) COUNT(DISTINCTAPPLICANT_ID)
---------- ---------------------------
       115                         115
```

Compare this structure with the population object popenrl.obj for new enrollees (see Figure 7–14). The two are very similar yet define non-intersecting subgroups of accepted applicants.

Figure 13–7. Accepted applicants to the Business College who did not enroll.

```
SQL> select count(*), count(distinct applicant_id)
from
      name n1,
      person,
      cmail,
      mail,
      applicant
where
[population from Figure 13-7]
      and mail_id = applicant_id
      and cmail_code = mail_code
      and person_id = applicant_id
      and n1.name_id = applicant_id
              and n1.name_seriesno =
              (select max(n2.name_seriesno)
              from name n2
              where n2.name_id = applicant_id)
/
ENTER to continue ...
  COUNT(*) COUNT(DISTINCTAPPLICANT_ID)
---------- --------------------------
      1024                        115
real: 33620
```

The SQL from Figure 13–7 appears here but was removed for clarity.

Nobody in the population falls through the joins (i.e., the distinct count is still 115). The query completes in about 34 seconds.

Figure 13–8. Testing the full SQL for query 3.

After your momentary lapse into self-pity, you begin mapping the request to objects. The report population is simple; it's just "accepted applicants." This translates directly to the object popacapp.obj. The Dean wants SAT averages by college; that would mean an avg1cnt.obj report. She wants a combined SAT score computed by adding an accept's SAT math and SAT verbal scores. You do have a *where* object called whrtest.obj that returns the highest test score of a specified type. This could be used once to get SAT math scores and used again to get SAT verbal scores. Then it should be a simple matter to add the two scores together.

As always, begin assembling objects with the *population* object (popacapp.obj). Add the *where* object whrtest.obj so it returns SAT math. Then add whrtest.obj again, but this time for the SAT verbal score. To use the same object twice in a single query, you'll need to alter the table aliases the second time that whrtest.obj is used. Figure 13–10 on page 341 shows the results of this object assembly and the join tests.

SHELL

```
/*
        sql:     fig13-9.sql
        date:    21-dec-1994
        author:  glewis
        purpose: Figure 13-9 for Chapter 13
*/
set termout off
start &&object_dir.\clears
start &&object_dir.\hpprintr
start &&object_dir.\date
start &&object_dir.\time
start &&object_dir.\owncol
start &&object_dir.\escape

ttitle left xEscape skip 1-
        'Mailings sent to BU accepted applicants who have
        right 'Report name: fig13-9.lis' skip 1 -
        left 'Date: ' xDate '     Time: ' xTime -
        right 'SQL name:    fig13-9.sql' skip 1 -
        right 'Page: ' format 999 sql.pno skip 2;

spool fig13-9.lis
        start xfig13-9
        start &&object_dir.\reset
spool off

start &&object_dir.\clears
start &&object_dir.\screen
```

Objects used:
1. shell.obj
2. shlttl1.obj

SQL

```
column c#1 heading 'id' format 9999
column c#2 heading 'sort_name' format a30
column c#3 heading 'sex' format a3
column c#4 heading 'major' format a6
break on c#1 on c#2 on c#3 on c#4 skip 1
select
        applicant_id "c#1",
        n1.name_last||', '||n1.name_first||' '||n1.name_middle "c#2",
        person_gender "c#3",
        applicant_major "c#4",
        mail_code,
        cmail_translation,
        mail_date
from name n1, person, cmail, mail, applicant
where
        [population from Figure 13-7]
        and mail_id = applicant_id
        and cmail_code = mail_code
        and person_id = applicant_id
        and n1.name_id = applicant_id
                and n1.name_seriesno =
                (select max(n2.name_seriesno)
                from name n2
                where n2.name_id = applicant_id)
order by 2, 7
/
```

Objects used:
1. repeat.obj

REPORT

```
Mailings sent to BU accepted applicants who have no enrollment deposit: Fall 1995        Report name: fig13-9.lis
Date: 01-JAN-1995     Time: 09:54                                                         SQL name:    fig13-9.sql
                                                                                                       Page:     1

                                                   mail                                 mail
   id sort_name                        sex major  code   mail                           date
----- ------------------------------ --- ------ ------ ------------------------------ ---------
 1798 Baker, Evelyn                    F   FIN    INTRST Outside interest               17-JUL-94
                                                  BUS    Business                       26-JUL-94
                                                  INTRST Outside interest               25-OCT-94
                                                  FOLLOW Aid follow information         03-JUL-95

 6706 DeMarco, Amy                     F   BCOM   HOUS   Housing                        20-OCT-94
                                                  AWARD  Financial aid award            16-APR-95

   ...
```

Figure 13–9. Completed shell program, SQL program, and report for query 3.

```
SQL> select count(*), count(distinct applicant_id)
     from
             test t3,
             test t1,
             applicant
     where
             applicant_term = '199509'
                     and applicant_level = 'UG'
             and exists
             (select 'x'
             from
                     cdecision,
                     decision
             where
                     decision_id = applicant_id
                             and decision_applicant_term = applicant_term
                             and decision_applicant_seriesno = applicant_seriesno
                     and cdecision_code = decision_code
                             and cdecision_accept_ind = 'Y')
             and t1.test_id = applicant_id
                     and t1.test_type = 'SATM'
                     and to_char(t1.test_score)||
                             to_char(t1.test_date,'YYYYMMDD') =
                             (select max(to_char(t2.test_score)||
                                     to_char(t2.test_date,'YYYYMMDD'))
                             from test t2
                             where t2.test_id = applicant_id
                                     and t2.test_type = 'SATM')
             and t3.test_id = applicant_id
                     and t3.test_type = 'SATV'
                     and to_char(t3.test_score)||
                             to_char(t3.test_date,'YYYYMMDD') =
                             (select max(to_char(t4.test_score)||
                                     to_char(t4.test_date,'YYYYMMDD'))
                             from test t4
                             where t4.test_id = applicant_id
                                     and t4.test_type = 'SATV')
     /
ENTER to continue ...
  COUNT(*) COUNT(DISTINCTAPPLICANT_ID)
---------- ---------------------------
       516                         494

real: 40210
```

Objects used:
1. whrtest for SATM
2. whrtest for SATV (new aliases)

Timing statistics appear reasonable. As expected the counts differ because some applicants apply to both the Business and Arts & Sciences colleges.

Figure 13–10. Testing of SQL for query 4.

```
SQL> select count(*), count(distinct applicant_id)
     from
           applicant
     where
           applicant_term = '199509'
                   and applicant_level = 'UG'
           and exists
           (select 'x'
           from
                   cdecision,
                   decision
           where
                   decision_id = applicant_id
                           and decision_applicant_term = applicant_term
                           and decision_applicant_seriesno = applicant_seriesno
                   and cdecision_code = decision_code
                           and cdecision_accept_ind = 'Y')
           and exists
           (select 'x'
           from test t1
           where t1.test_id = applicant_id
                   and t1.test_type in ('SATM','SATV'))
     /
ENTER to continue ...
  COUNT(*) COUNT(DISTINCTAPPLICANT_ID)
---------- ---------------------------
       516                         494

 real: 7470
```

This subquery only returns rows where an SATM or SATV test type exists.

Figure 13–11. Undergraduate accepts for Fall 1995 who have SAT scores.

The test results on the SQL prove interesting. The timing statistics appear reasonable at 40 seconds. However the counts are 516 for count(*) and 494 for count(distinct applicant_id). The lack of singularity is not surprising. You already know that some applicants get accepted at both the Business College and the Arts & Sciences College. However, the numbers you expected to see were 606 and 578, respectively. These number appear in Table 13–3 under the accept column. You confirm these numbers by running a quick query counting the population of accepts; they're correct. Apparently some accepts fall through the TEST joins.

Two possibilities exist. First, the whrtest.obj object may be leaky. It might be poorly constructed and some legitimate accepts do fall through the join. Second, some accepts may not have SAT test scores. The SQL in whrtest.obj retrieves the high test score scores of a certain type. If no test scores of that type exist, then no row gets returned. This does not present a problem, because you should not include accepts without scores in a computed average. But it would mean you should revise your population definition. Instead of the report population consisting of "accepted applicants" it would now become "accepted applicants with SAT test scores." There's a difference and you need to recognize that difference.

You decide to run a quick test to see how many accepted applicants actually have SAT scores. Figure 13–11 shows the results. Happily the counts in this report are 516 and 494 again. You conclude that the whrtest.obj object does not leak and that you now have a report based on the population of accepted applicants with SAT scores.

Embed the SQL objects in the avg1cnt.obj *report* object, fill out the requested information, and construct a shell program from the shell.obj and shltt1.obj objects. Figure 13–12 on the following page shows the completed shell, SQL and report. You note ruefully that the Dean's supposition about the "quality" of accepted applicants is incorrect. In fact, the average SAT score of business accepts is actually lower (1059) than those of accepts in arts and sciences (1082). The two types of accepts may differ, but apparently not in ways that explain the differences in yield rates.

Query 5

You know the Dean will come back to you with another report request. This time you decide to take the initiative. There was something in the SAT report that triggered a thought. Instead of two types of accepts—those in the Business College and those in the Arts & Sciences College—there are actually three types of accepts. These are:

1. Applicants accepted only by the Business College
2. Applicants accepted only by the Arts & Sciences College
3. Applicants accepted by both the Business College and the Arts & Sciences College

You reason that maybe the difference in yield rates occurs because applicants accepted to both colleges preferentially enroll at the Arts & Sciences College over the Business College. Who are those applicants applying to both colleges? Why would they submit two applications to

SHELL

```
/*
    sql:          fig13-12.sql
    date:         21-dec-1994
    author:       glewis
    purpose:      Figure 13-12 for Chapter 13
*/
set termout off
start &&object_dir.\clears
start &&object_dir.\hpprintr
start &&object_dir.\date
start &&object_dir.\time
start &&object_dir.\owncol
start &&object_dir.\escape

ttitle left xEscape skip 1-
    'Average SAT scores of accepted applicants by und
    right 'Report name: fig13-12.lis' skip 1 -
    left 'Date: ' xDate '       Time: ' xTime -
    right 'SQL name:    fig13-12.sql' skip 1 -
    right 'Page: ' format 999 sql.pno skip 2;

spool fig13-12.lis
    start xfg13-12
    start &&object_dir.\reset
spool off

start &&object_dir.\clears
start &&object_dir.\screen
```

Objects used:
1. shell.obj
2. shlttl1.obj

SQL

```
column avg heading 'SAT|combined' format 9999
break on report
compute sum of count on report
select
       applicant_college,
       avg(t1.test_score + t3.test_score) "avg",
       count(*) "count"
from
       test t3,
       test t1,
       applicant
where
       applicant_term = '199509'
                and applicant_level = 'UG'
       and exists
       (select 'x'
       from
                cdecision,
                decision
       where
                decision_id = applicant_id
                        and decision_applicant_term = applicant_term
                        and decision_applicant_seriesno = applicant_seriesno
                and cdecision_code = decision_code
                        and cdecision_accept_ind = 'Y')
       [TEST joins from Figure 13-10]
```

Objects used:
1. count1.obj

REPORT

```
Average SAT scores of accepted applicants by undergrad college: Fall 1995          Report name: fig13-12.lis
Date: 03-JAN-1995     Time: 05:34                                                  SQL name:    fig13-12.sql
                                                                                          Page:    1

          SAT
coll combined      count
---- -------- ----------
AS       1082        379
BU       1059        137
                ----------
sum                  516

2 rows selected.
```

Figure 13–12. Completed shell program, SQL program, and report for query 4.

Komenda? Do they want to maximize the chance that they'll be admitted? If so, maybe they really prefer one college over the other but apply to both as a safety net, realizing that opportunities exist for later transfer between Business and Arts & Sciences.

You start by identifying the population of students who applied to both the Business and the Arts & Science colleges. No *population* object exists for this group of applicants, but it should be easy to modify the popapp.obj object. Figure 13–13 shows your modification. Similarly, no *population* object exists for the group of applicants accepted by both colleges, but again it should be easy to modify the popacapp.obj object (this is left as an exercise). You also want to know where the joint accepts actually decided to enroll. This requires a third report. Figure 13–14 on the following page shows the shell program and a pseudo-SQL program that defines the population and retrieves the data for this third report (completion of the SQL is left as an exercise). Note the query uses the *report* object called dtlcnt.obj that combines detail data with counts. The output report appears in Figure 13–15 on page 347. Figure 13–16 on page 348 shows a diagram of the findings from the various reports you ran.

The findings look dramatic. Of the 69 applicants who applied to both colleges, 28 were accepted by both. Of these 28 joint accepts, 18 enrolled in Arts & Sciences and only 5 enrolled in the Business College! When you tabulate the results, they're startling. Table 13–4 on page 348 shows that the yield at the Business College is only 19 percent among accepted applicants

```
SQL> select
        count(*), count(distinct p1.applicant_id)
     from
        applicant p1
     where
        p1.applicant_term = '199509'
               and p1.applicant_level = 'UG'
               and p1.applicant_college = 'AS'
        and exists
        (select 'x'
        from applicant p2
        where p2.applicant_id = p1.applicant_id
        and p2.applicant_term = '199509'
        and p2.applicant_level = 'UG'
        and p2.applicant_college = 'BU')
     /
ENTER to continue ...
  COUNT(*) COUNT(DISTINCTP1.APPLICANT_ID)
---------- ------------------------------
        69                             69
```

This subquery only returns rows if the person also applied to the Business College.

Figure 13–13. Modification of the popapp object to include applicants who applied to both the Business and Arts & Sciences colleges.

SHELL

```
/*
       sql:        fig13-14.sql
       date:       02-jan-1995
       author:     glewis
       purpose:    Figure 13-14
*/
set termout off
start &&object_dir.\clears
start &&object_dir.\hpprintr
start &&object_dir.\date
start &&object_dir.\time
start &&object_dir.\owncol
start &&object_dir.\escape

ttitle left xEscape skip 1-
       'Applicants accepted by both the Business and Arts and Sciences Colleges: Fall 1995' -
       right 'Report name: fig13-14.lis' skip 1 -
       left 'Date: ' xDate '      Time: ' xTime -
       right 'SQL name:    fig13-14.sql' skip 1 -
       right 'Page: ' format 999 sql.pno skip 2;

spool fig13-14.lis
       start xfg13-14
       start &&object_dir.\reset
spool off

start &&object_dir.\clears
start &&object_dir.\screen
```

Objects used:
1. shell.obj
2. shlttl1.obj

SQL

```
column college heading 'enrolled|college' format a8
break on report on college skip 1
compute count of id on report college
select
      p1.applicant_id "id",
      n1.name_last||', '||n1.name_first||' '||n1.name_middle "sort_name",
      p3.applicant_college "college"
from
      name n1,
      applicant p3,
      applicant p1
where
      [population of applicants accepted by BU and AS colleges: alias p1]
      [who enrolled: modification of popenrl.obj using alias p3]
      and n1.name_id = p1.applicant_id
                  and n1.name_seriesno =
                  (select max(n2.name_seriesno)
                  from name n2
                  where n2.name_id = p1.applicant_id)
order by 3, 2
/
```

Objects used:
1. dtlcnt.obj
2. selsname.obj
3. whrname.obj

The SQL for the report population is left as an exercise.

Figure 13–14. Completed shell program and SQL program for query 5.

REPORT

```
Applicants accepted by both the Business and Arts and Sciences Colleges: Fall 1995
Date: 03-JAN-1995     Time: 05:40

                                                enrolled
        id sort_name                            college
---------- ------------------------------------ --------
      7279 Chen, Cahren                         AS
       494 Cruz, Heather
      7124 DeMarco, Jennifer
      5586 Hall, John
      1814 Lam, Eric
      2055 Patel, Jacqueline
      8265 Pierce, Amy
      5408 Pierce, Stephanie
      2683 Rodriguez, John
      6684 Shaw, Brenda M.
      8500 Taylor, Stephanie
       161 Tobin, Michelle M.
      8370 Tran, Christine M.
      6183 Upchurch, Ryan D.
      5330 Walsh, Elizabeth L.
      5889 Welch, Cahren
      1077 Williams, Mary E.
      8716 Yang, Cynthia
----------                                      ********
        18                                      count

      7133 Berger, Kimberly                     BU
      6706 DeMarco, Amy
      8884 Garcia, Shawn L.
      7295 Hall, Victor
      5547 Lee, Carlos
----------                                      ********
         5                                      count

----------
        23

23 rows selected.
```

Note that 18 joint accepts enrolled in Arts & Sciences while only 5 enrolled in the Business College.

Figure 13–15. Final report for query 5.

who also applied to the Arts & Sciences College. The corresponding yield rate in Arts & Sciences is three times larger (57 percent). When you exclude applicants who applied to both colleges, the gap in the yield rate nearly disappears (32 percent in Arts & Sciences versus 30 percent in Business, as shown in Table 13–5 on page 349). This gives the Dean a place to start. You put the two tables into interoffice mail and fire off an e-mail to the Dean about the results.

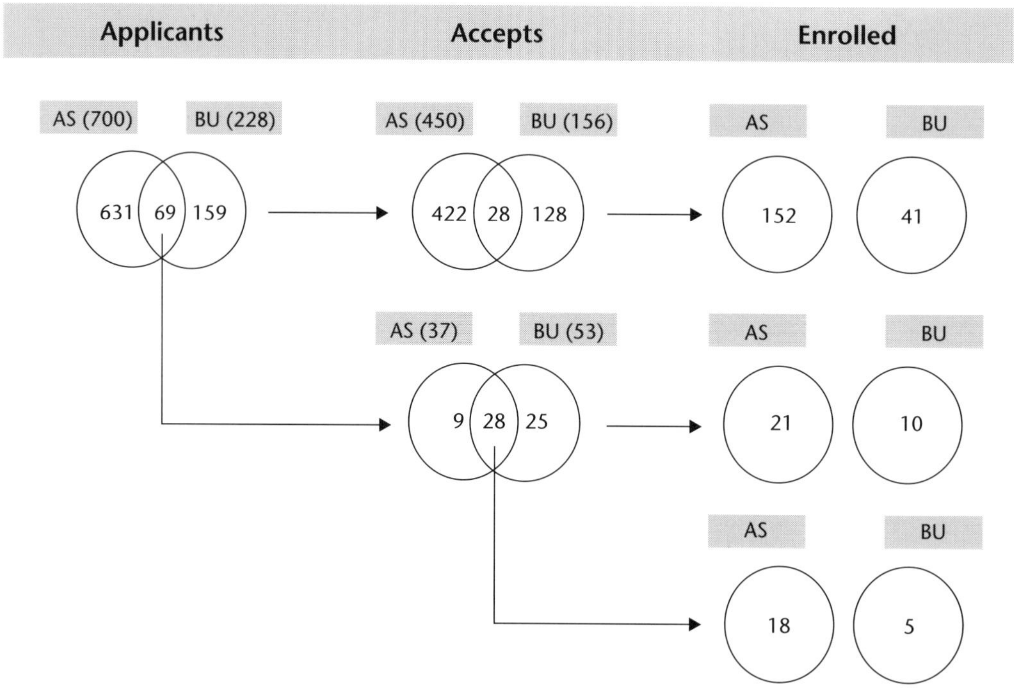

Figure 13–16. Diagram of findings for query 5.

Table 13–4. Accept and yield rates for applicants who applied to both the Business and Arts & Sciences colleges: Fall 1995.

		Accepts		Enrolled	
College	**Applicants**	**No.**	**Accept %**	**No.**	**Yield %**
Arts & Science	69	37	54%	21	57%
Business	69	53	77%	10	19%
Total unique	69	62	90%	31	50%

Notes:

1. Accept rate = Accept % = (Accepts/Applicants)*100
2. Yield rate = Yield % = (Enrolled/Accepts)*100

Table 13–5. Accept and yield rates excluding applicants who applied to both the Business and Arts & Sciences colleges: Fall 1995.

		Accepts		Enrolled	
College	Applicants	No.	Accept %	No.	Yield %
Arts & Science	631	413	65%	131	32%
Business	159	103	65%	31	30%
Total unique	790	516	65%	162	31%

Notes:

1. Accept rate = Accept % = (Accepts/Applicants)*100
2. Yield rate = Yield % = (Enrolled/Accepts)*100

A few days later the Dean calls. "Thanks for that last analysis. It really helps. We'll have to look at our policy of permitting applications to both colleges, or maybe the policy of allowing both colleges to accept the same applicant. But first I want to know everything possible about those 69 applicants who applied to the Business College and the Arts & Sciences College. Can you get me a roster with everything we have on them? I'd also like a separate listing of name, address, and phone number so we can do a phone survey. Maybe that way we'll find out what's going on. Thanks. I really do appreciate your help."

Before she finishes the conversation, you're already mapping the request into SQL objects. Let's see, the Dean wants "everything we have" on applicants accepted at both colleges. You already have SQL that defines the population. She wants a roster, but it's going to be huge. That means you'll have to block the report. That means a blockl.obj *report* object. And then you'll use the object ... and so on.

Final Object Inventory

The Dean took you on an analytical roller-coaster. After things settle down, you should identify what portions of the analysis can be converted to objects and reused later. Were any new populations identified that might

OBJECT

```
from
        applicant
where
```

1

```
        applicant_term = '<term>'
                and applicant_level = '<level>'
                and applicant_college = '<college>'
```

2

```
        and exists
        (select 'x'
        from
                cdecision cd0,
                decision d0
        where
                d0.decision_id = applicant_id
                        and d0.decision_applicant_term = applicant_term
                        and d0.decision_applicant_seriesno = applicant_seriesno
                and cd0.cdecision_code = d0.decision_code
                        and cd0.cdecision_accept_ind = 'Y')
```

3

```
        and not exists
        (select 'x'
        from
                cdecision cd1,
                decision d1
        where
                d1.decision_id = applicant_id
                        and d1.decision_applicant_term = applicant_term
                        and d1.decision_applicant_seriesno = applicant_seriesno
                and cd1.cdecision_code = d1.decision_code
                        and cd1.cdecision_enrl_ind = 'Y'
                and not exists
                (select 'x'
                from
                        cdecision cd2,
                        decision d2
                where
                        d2.decision_id = applicant_id
                                and d2.decision_applicant_term = applicant_term
                                and d2.decision_applicant_seriesno = applicant_seriesno
                        and cd2.cdecision_code = d2.decision_code
                                and cd2.cdecision_cancel_ind = 'Y'))
```

HELP

```
object:           popacxen.obj
date created:     03-jan-1995
author:           glewis
revisions:

Purpose:          Defines the population of applicants accepted for admissions
                  for a specified term, level and college who did not enroll.

Usage:            <term>: replace with term (eg, 199509 for Fall 1995)
                  <level>: replace with level (eg, UG for Undergrad)
                  <college>: replace with college code (eg, BU for Business)

Hints:            none
```

The SQL defines a population of:

1. Applicants for a specified term, level and college.
2. Who were accepted.
3. And who do not have an active enrollment deposit.

Figure 13–17. *Population* object and help file for accepted applicants who do not enroll.

warrant an object? Were any new report formats required? Were any new expressions used that could become *select* objects? Were any new population modifiers created that might become a *where* class 1 object? Were any joins made to new tables for the purpose of retrieving data columns?

Not every query should be carved up into new objects. Some are so idiosyncratic that the objects would never be used again. But the series of reports above did include several object candidates. For example, the following might make good objects:

- The population of accepted applicants who did not enroll (see Figure 13–17)
- The population of applicants who applied to both the Business College and the Arts & Sciences College (see Figure 13–18)
- The two joins to the TEST table to return SAT math and SAT verbal scores so that a combined score could be computed (see Figure 13–19 on the following page)

OBJECT

```
from
      applicant p1
where
      p1.applicant_term = '<term>'
              and p1.applicant_level = '<level>'
              and p1.applicant_college = '<college1>'
      and exists
      (select 'x'
      from applicant p2
      where p2.applicant_id = p1.applicant_id
      and p2.applicant_term = p1.applicant_term
      and p2.applicant_level = p1.applicant_level
      and p2.applicant_college = '<college2>')
```

HELP

```
object:        popjtapp.obj
date created: 03-jan-1995
author:        glewis
revisions:

Purpose:       Defines the population of applicants for a specified
               term, level, and college who also applied to a second
               college for that term and level.

Usage:         <term>: replace with term (eg, 199509 for Fall 1995)
               <level>: replace with level (eg, UG for Undergrad)
               <college1>: replace with college code (eg, AS or BU)
               <college2>: replace with college code

Hints:         none
```

Figure 13–18. *Population* object and help file for applicants common to two Komenda colleges.

```
OBJECT

    and t1.test_id = <driving_table>_id
            and t1.test_type = 'SATM'
            and to_char(t1.test_score)||
                    to_char(t1.test_date,'YYYYMMDD') =
                    (select max(to_char(t2.test_score)||
                            to_char(t2.test_date,'YYYYMMDD'))
                    from test t2
                    where t2.test_id = applicant_id
                            and t2.test_type = 'SATM')
    and t3.test_id = <driving_table>_id
            and t3.test_type = 'SATV'
            and to_char(t3.test_score)||
                    to_char(t3.test_date,'YYYYMMDD') =
                    (select max(to_char(t4.test_score)||
                            to_char(t4.test_date,'YYYYMMDD'))
                    from test t4
                    where t4.test_id = applicant_id
                            and t4.test_type = 'SATV')
```

```
HELP

object:        whrsatc.obj
date created:  03-jan-1995
author:        glewis
revisions:

Purpose:       For each person with SAT scores, this object returns the
               high SAT Math score and the high SAT Verbal score.

Usage:         Need to include the TEST table twice in the main query,
               once with an alias of "t1" and once with an
               alias of "t3".
               <driving_table>: replace with name of table driving the
               query (e.g., APPLICANT)

Hints:         Note this object qualifies a population.  It only returns
               rows if a population item has SAT scores.
```

Figure 13–19. *Where* object returning SAT math and SAT verbal scores.

Table 13–6 shows the final inventory of objects created in this book. For a query writer it represents a dictionary. As with any dictionary, an object inventory is a living document that changes. New words appear in a language; new objects appear in an inventory. Old words get used in new ways; old objects get modified as circumstances change. Old words sometimes disappear; old objects wither from lack of use. Words are the building blocks for constructing sentences; objects are the building blocks for constructing queries. You just need to map report requests into the object inventory and then assemble objects into queries.

Table 13–6. Inventory of SQL objects.

Class	Name	Purpose
POPULATION	popacapp	Applicants accepted for admissions for a specified term, level, and college
	popapp	Applicants for admissions for a specified term, level, college
	popenrl	Accepted applicants for a specified term, level, and college who are expected to enroll
	popjtapp	Applicants for a specified term, level, and college who also applied to a second college for that term and level
	poprecr	Recruits for a specified term and level
	popsampl	Selects Nsample rows from a population of size Npop, for use in testing and debugging objects when the population size is large. Assumes the population size is known
	popxapp	Applicants for a specified term, level, and college. Accepts prompts for term, level, and college.
WHERE 1	whrintl	Defines the term "international" and modifies a population so only internationals are included
	whrmnrty	Defines the term "minority" and modifies a population so only individuals of color are included
	whrsatc	Returns high SAT math and high SAT verbal test scores for individuals who have SAT scores
WHERE 2u	whracad	Provides access to the ACADEMIC table for information on the last high school attended
	whraddr	Provides access to the ADDRESS table for the most recent address of a specified type
	whradhi	Provides access to the ADDRESS table in a hierarchical fashion. Returns an address of a specified type (e.g., local). If this type of address is not available, it returns an address of a second specified type (e.g., permanent)
	whrdecsn	Provides access to the DECISION table for information on the last admissions decision
	whrname	Provides access to the NAME table for the most recent name
	whrpersn	Provides access to the PERSON table
	whrphon	Provides access to the PHONE table for the most recent phone of a specified type and associated with an address of a specified type
	whrtest	Provides access to the TEST table for the highest test score of a specified type
WHERE 2m	whraddrm	Provides access to the ADDRESS table for all addresses of a specified type
	whrdcmnt	Provides access to all documents in the DOCUMENT table for a population of applicants

(Continued)

Table 13–6. Inventory of SQL objects.

Class	Name	Purpose
SELECT	selage	Computes a person's age based on sysdate (the report date) and the person's birthdate
	selcszn	Creates a single display column by concatenating address_city, address_state, address_zip, and address_nation
	seliname	Creates a name using the initials of the first and middle names and concatenating these to name_last
	selintl	Identifies a person as "international" based on their visa status
	selmajr	Collapses anticipated majors into academic departments
	selprank	Computes a person's percent rank in high school based on class size and class rank
	selrmnd1	Calculates a "reminder date" as the Monday that follows the date of application plus one month
	selrmnd2	Calculates a "reminder date" as 7 weeks (49 days) after the application date
	selsatc	Calculates a combined SAT score as the sum of SAT math and SAT verbal scores
	selsname	Creates a name by concatenating name_last, name_first, and name_middle
	seltestr	Calculates a test range (e.g., 400-499) that an SAT score falls within. Useful for frequency distributions by score ranges
REPORT	avg1	Produces a report showing the average of a data column broken down by the categories of a coded data column (e.g., showing average test scores by gender)
	avg1cnt	Produces a report showing the average of a data column broken down by the categories of a coded data column. Includes counts of items averaged
	blckdtl	Produces a combined detail and blocked detail report
	blockl	Produces a simple roster (i.e., listing) of data columns in a blocked format. Instead of appearing in columns across the report, data columns appear in rows down the report. Labels are attached to the blocked columns
	cnt1lab	Produces a report counting the report population by categories in a coded data column. Includes the code translations
	count1	Produces a report counting the report population by categories in a coded data column (i.e., a 1-way frequency distribution)
	count2	Produces a report counting the report population by categories in two coded data columns (i.e., a 2-way cross-tabulation)
	detail	Produces a list of data columns for the report population
	dtlcnt	Produces a combined detail and count report
	repeat	Produces a detail report where repeating data gets suppressed (e.g., if an applicant has 10 MAIL items the report shows all 10 mailings but the applicant's name only once)
	sum1	Produces a report showing the sum of a data column broken down by the categories of a coded data column (e.g., showing total fees by gender)
	sum1cnt	Produces a report showing the sum of a data column broken down by the categories of a coded data column. Includes counts of the items summed

(Continued)

Table 13–6. Inventory of SQL objects.

Class	Name	Purpose
SHELL	shell.obj	Provides a shell for each ad hoc report. Starts the main SQL that retrieves data for the report. Houses other shell objects that control printer and screen characteristics, report titles, column headers, and other features of the finished report
	shlprmpt.obj	Prompts user for a report parameter to use at run time. Verifies that the response is correct
	shlttl1.obj	Produces a standard top title for a report, including descriptive text, date stamp, time stamp, page number, and names of the files containing the SQL and the report output
	shlttl2.obj	Produces a modified standard report that also includes user responses to prompts
	shltt3.obj	Produces a standard title and column headings for a detail and block report

Chapter 14

Automation of SQL Objects

Just like words in a dictionary, objects require organization to be fully useful. At first the number of objects is small and manageable with minimal effort. But with time the number of objects and the number of object users both increase. As more objects get built, the distinction between some objects blurs. Just like synonyms, one object might be used in one set of circumstances but a related object will be used in other circumstances. Keeping track of objects, ensuring users select the correct objects, and making objects work well together can all become problematic.

Solving the problems depends on recognizing two distinctions. First, end users possess widely different technical skills and computer literacy. At one extreme are "power users," the business analysts who could just as easily work in an information systems (IS) office. At the other extreme are people who only know that a database exists and that it contains data they need. In previous chapters objects required manual manipulation; assembling objects into programs, running error and performance tests, and revising SQL all assumed a knowledgeable individual performing the operations. This severely limits the number of end users who can benefit from SQL objects. So think of users in two broad categories:

1. those who feel comfortable manually manipulating objects, and
2. those totally focused on the end report who don't want to know anything about the mechanics that produce the report.

The second helpful distinction concerns the degree of difficulty in queries. As the previous chapters make abundantly clear, the complexity of queries varies considerably. Some queries are simple, while others require a struggle. I've found it useful to group queries into four categories:

1. those that only require assembly of existing objects,
2. those that require minor modifications to existing objects,
3. those where the testing uncovers errors that require analysis and object revision, and
4. those that require building and testing entirely new objects.

Users in each of the two skill categories can face any of the four levels of query difficulty. This creates 2*4 = 8 possible scenarios. Automating objects means something different in each scenario. Yet in each scenario IS staff should serve as a safety net; whenever the query difficulty exceeds the query writer's skill level, IS staff should be available for consultation and on-the-job training.

This chapter describes several ways to organize and manage objects so they serve a broad array of end users operating in a variety of query situations.

Organizing Objects for Use

When the number of objects remains small and the skill level of users high, objects require minimal organization. Each object exists in a separate file and has an associated documentation file that describes how to use it. Objects and their documentation get stored in a single location accessible by users. Access rights to the shared directory is read-only so that users may not alter and overwrite existing objects nor create new objects for general use. An object inventory resides on the shared subdirectory to assist the query writer in selecting appropriate objects. Assembly of objects into completed queries occurs in a local user subdirectory and is entirely manual. The user needs only an editor and the knowledge of SQL and SQL*PLUS presented in this book.

This level of object organization provides great flexibility but very little guidance. A user is limited only by what he or she knows and how skillfully he or she can apply that knowledge. This means only the highly skilled will use objects organized in this fashion.

Organizing Objects into Tables

Before objects can transition into wider use, their organization and management should become a database function. For example, an OBJECT table replaces the object inventory that previously listed available objects. Each object gets assigned a unique object_id identification number. Each object also gets assigned to one and only one object class (e.g., *population*, *shell*, etc.). A code table for object classes and their descriptions is necessary, and an object entry form is needed to input new objects and to update information on existing objects. Figure 14–1 shows an SQL utility program that users can run whenever they want a current listing of available objects. Figure 14–2 on the following page shows a portion of this report for the objects built throughout this book. It lists the file name where objects are stored, identifies the object class, and provides both a short and longer

SHELL

```
set termout off
start &&object_dir.\clears
start &&object_dir.\hpprintr
start &&object_dir.\date
start &&object_dir.\time
start &&object_dir.\owncol
start &&object_dir.\escape

ttitle left xEscape skip 1-
      'SQL objects available for use' -
      right 'Report name: objects.lis' skip 1 -
      left 'Date: ' xDate '      Time: ' xTime -
      right 'SQL name:    objects.sql' skip 1 -
      right 'Page: ' format 999 sql.pno skip 2;

spool objects.lis
      start xobjects
      start &&object_dir.\reset
spool off

start &&object_dir.\clears
start &&object_dir.\screen
```

SQL

```
column class format a5
column id format 9999
column desc format a40 word_wrapped
column help format a60 word_wrapped
set recsep off
break on class skip 2
select
      object_class "class",
      object_id "id",
      object_file "file",
      object_desc "desc",
      object_help "help"
from
      object
order by 1, 3
/
```

Figure 14–1. Shell and SQL program for a report on available objects.

REPORT

```
SQL objects available for use                                                Report name: objects.lis
Date: 06-JAN-1995     Time: 06:02                                            SQL name:    objects.sql
                                                                                         Page:     1

class    id file          desc                                     help
----- ----- ------------ ---------------------------------------- ------------------------------------------------------------
POP       1 popacapp.obj APPLICANT: accepts                        Applicants accepted for admission for a specified term,
                                                                   level, and college.
          8 popacxen.obj APPLICANT: accepts who do not enroll      Applicants accepted for admission for a specified term,
                                                                   level, and college who do not enroll.
         15 popapp.obj   APPLICANT: applicants for admission       Applicants for admission for a specified term, level, and
                                                                   college.
  ...

RPT      19 blockl.obj   Block report                              Produces a simple roster in a blocked format.  Instead of
                                                                   appearing in columns across the report, data columns appear
                                                                   in rows down the report.
         13 countl.obj   Frequency distribution                    Produces a report counting the report population by
                                                                   categories in a coded data column.
          6 detail.obj   Detail report                             Produces a list of data columns for the report population.
  ...

SEL       5 selage.obj   PERSON: age                               Computes an age based on sysdate and a birthdate.
         12 selcszn.obj  ADDRESS: city, state, zip and nation      Creates a single display column by concatenating
                                                                   address_city, address_state, address_zip, and address_nation.
         18 seliname.obj NAME: using initials                      Creates a name using the initials of the first and middle
                                                                   names and concatenating these to name_last.

  ...
SHL       7 shell.obj    Standard shell                            Provides a shell for each ad hoc report, starting the main
                                                                   SQL and housing other object that control report
                                                                   characteristics.
  ...
```

Items removed for clarity.

Figure 14–2. Report of available objects.

description of the object. The object file name also identifies the associated documentation file (e.g., the popacapp.obj object has a documentation file of popacapp.hlp). Alternatively, object documentation can be stored in a HELP table using object_id as part of the primary key.

At first this new level of object organization has little effect on the number of object users; it simply provides a little additional support. But it does represent a significant step for two reasons. First, managing objects through database tables and forms occurs only when the institution recognizes their utility and importance. As such it's a milestone, the initial entry of SQL objects into the fabric of the organization. Second, managing objects through tables provides a foundation for broadening their use among a larger number of users.

Automating Object Assembly

Highly skilled query writers working on complex queries may desire the flexibility that minimally organized objects provide. For most end users, however, this flexibility is a deterrent to object use. They need a more structured approach to SQL objects.

Completing routine reports with SQL objects quickly becomes boring if done manually. After you do enough of them, there's something very mechanical about preparing these queries. The most interesting part of the process actually occurs first when you must map the user request into SQL objects. This sometimes provides a little challenge. But after this step, things get pretty repetitive. You assemble objects in an editor, answer any embedded questions, prepare a shell program, test the joins for logic errors and performance problems, and then run the query. Almost all of this work can be effectively automated.

This section describes one method of automating objects for routine reports. The structure of this method provides a counterpoint to the flexible but largely unstructured organization of objects described in the previous section. The skill level of users matters little for these routine reports.

Functionality in a Menu Selection System

Most of the repetitive work with objects can be eliminated by using a simple menu-driven selection system. Users select objects from a series of menu screens. These objects then get assembled by a computer program into a shell program and an SQL program. The user merely runs the shell to produce the report.

In general terms a menu-driven object selection system should provide a number of features, including:

- Separate menus for each object class. Users should be able to select objects, unselect objects, and move easily between menus.
- A mechanism for making only valid objects available for selection. As a user makes object selections, some options should become unavailable. For example, selecting a *population* object should make all other *population* objects unavailable for selection until the original *population* object is unselected. This mechanism should ensure the validity of objects by making available for selection only those objects that work together.
- An additional menu for selection of data columns for the report. Once the user selects the *population* and *where* objects, the data tables appearing in the main query are known. The user should be able to select and unselect any data columns in these tables.
- The ability to qualify populations. The user should be able to place simple conditions on the report population. For a report on female applicants accepted for admission, the user would select a *population* object of "applicants accepted for admission" from the population screen. Then in a conditions screen the user would qualify the population with the *where* clause "and person_gender = 'F'."
- The ability to format data columns. A user should be able to override a default column header or format.
- Ready access to on-line help. Documentation on each object should be available as part of the system. For example, a user might place the cursor on an object name and then press a "Help" key to retrieve the help file associated with the object.
- A program that parses the selected objects. Many objects contain embedded messages that must be replaced with user responses at runtime. After a user has selected the objects for a report, the objects should be parsed for embedded messages. Any messages requiring user interaction should initiate a prompting question to the user, wait for a response, and verify that response if possible (e.g., entry of codes can be verified against code tables).

- A program that assembles the objects. Selected objects and user responses to embedded messages should be assembled into a shell program and an SQL program.
- A mechanism for testing the report population and the final SQL. The user should be warned whenever population items fall through the joins, whenever multiple rows appear unexpectedly, or whenever the query performance deteriorates below acceptable levels. For the user this warning serves notice that the report is no longer routine.

Example of a Menu Selection System

A menu system for selecting and assembling SQL objects could be implemented in many different ways. This section prototypes a simple SQL object system that uses Oracle's SQL*FORMS to provide the user interface. Object parsing and assembly happen behind the scenes using a procedural programming language (SQR).

Figure 14–3 on the following page shows a schematic of the object system. A user begins by selecting a report type (e.g., roster, frequency distribution, etc.), then selects the report population and proceeds to a menu of *where* objects. The user makes one, several, or no selections from the *where* menu. The system then asks if he or she would like to qualify the population. If so, a screen appears and the user enters a *where* clause that modifies the *population* object. Error detection occurs at this point and the user can reenter the qualifying criteria if necessary. The user then moves to a screen where data columns can be selected. He or she can also choose *select* objects from an expressions screen. Other data columns can be accessed by selecting a table name and then selecting one or more data column names within the table. In each menu, object selection occurs by using cursor keys to highlight an object and pressing a Select key to select or unselect the highlighted choice. At any point, the user may cycle back to earlier menus and make alternative choices. If these choices invalidate existing choices, a warning is issued. Once the user makes all selections he or she commits the query and control passes to the procedural language. This program parses the selected objects, prompts the user for responses to embedded messages, and then assembles the completed shell and SQL programs.

Figure 14–4 through Figure 14–11 on pages 365 through 368 illustrate this system used to prepare a simple roster report on female applicants

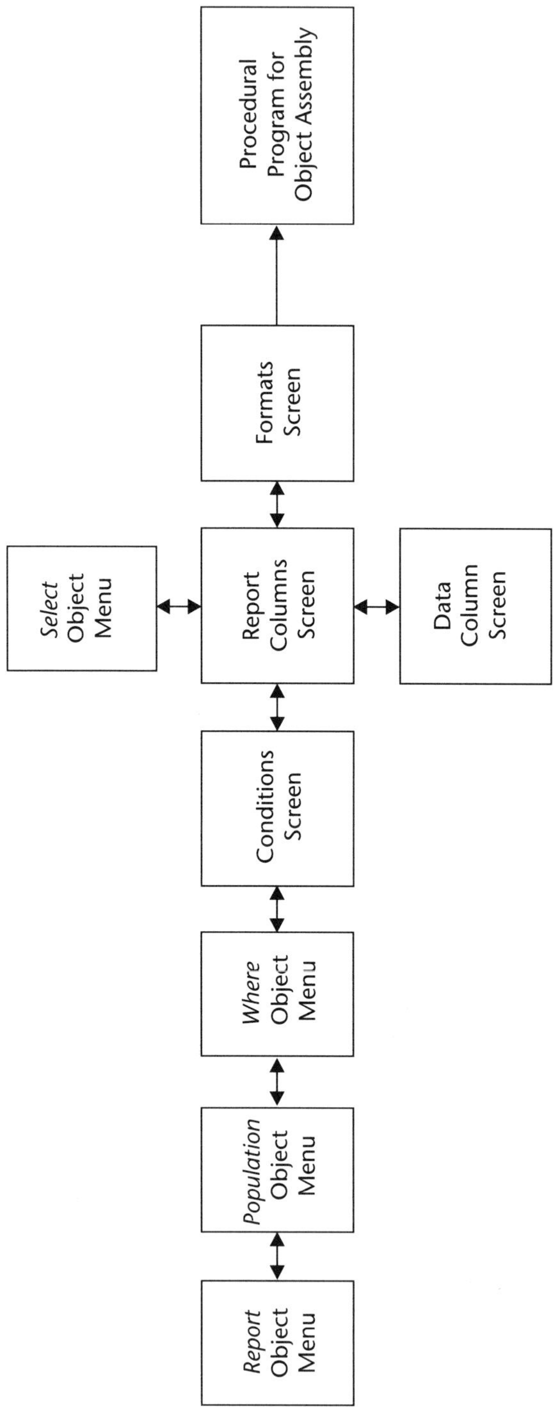

Figure 14–3. Schematic of one menu-driven object system.

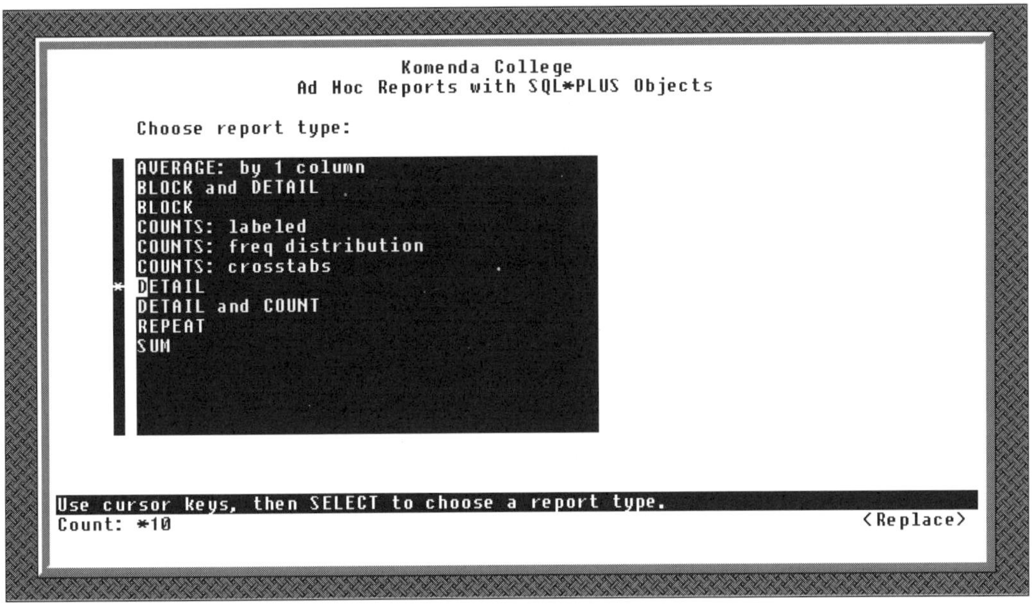

Figure 14–4. Menu of *report* objects.

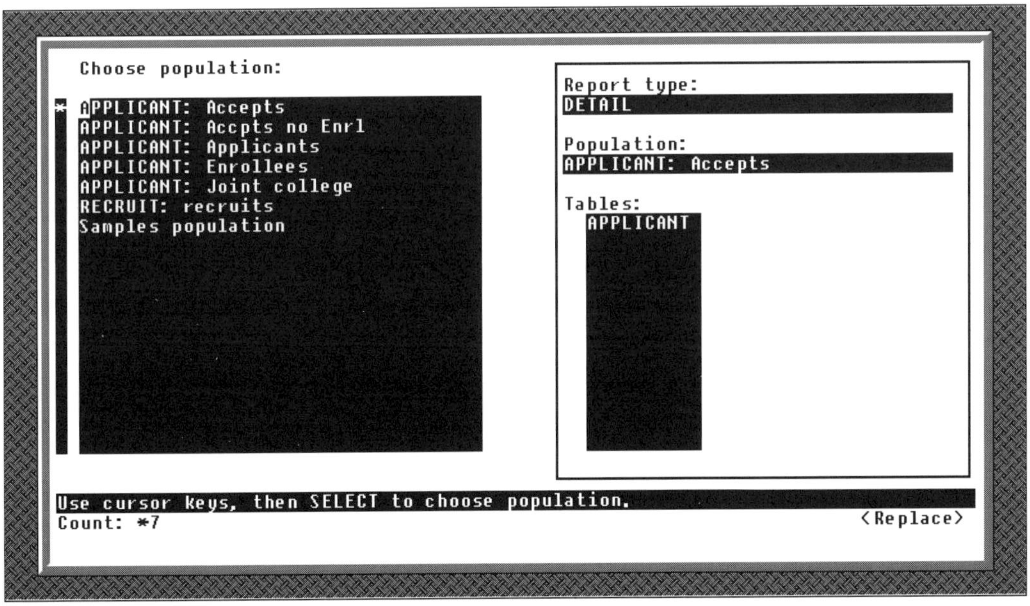

Figure 14–5. Menu of *population* objects.

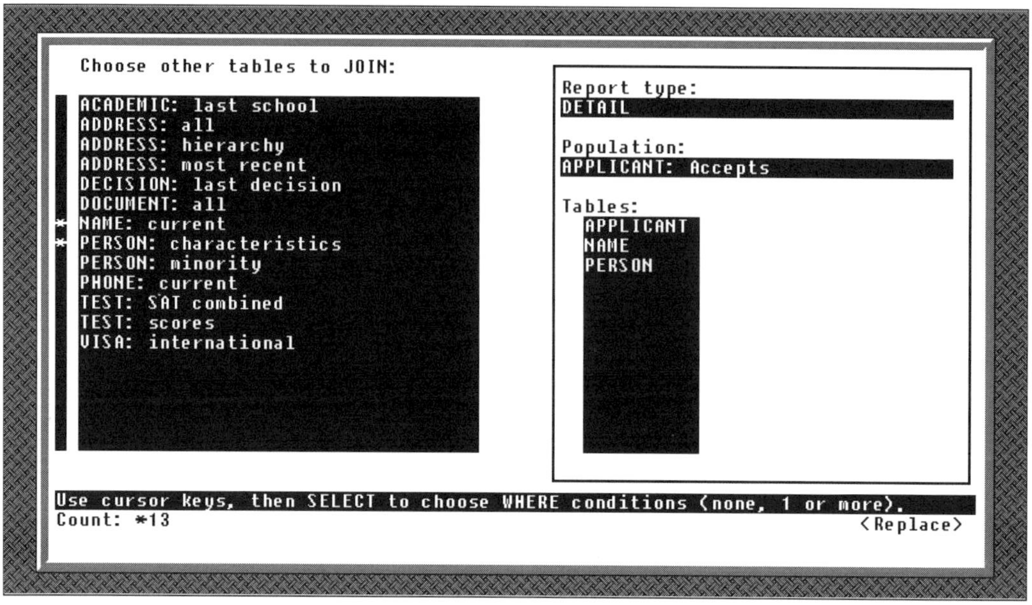

Figure 14–6. Menu of *where* objects.

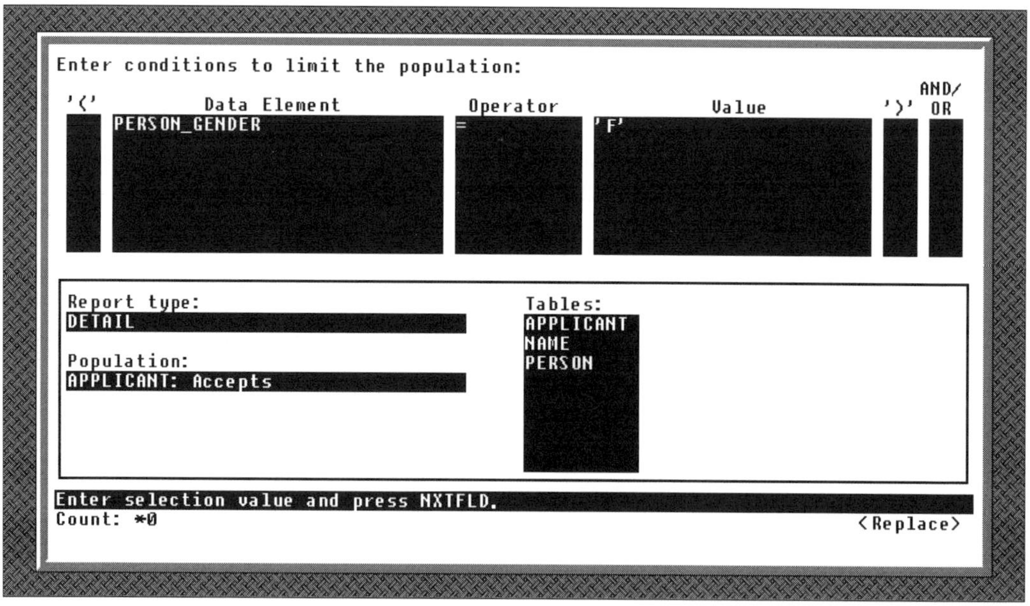

Figure 14–7. Screen for modifying population definitions.

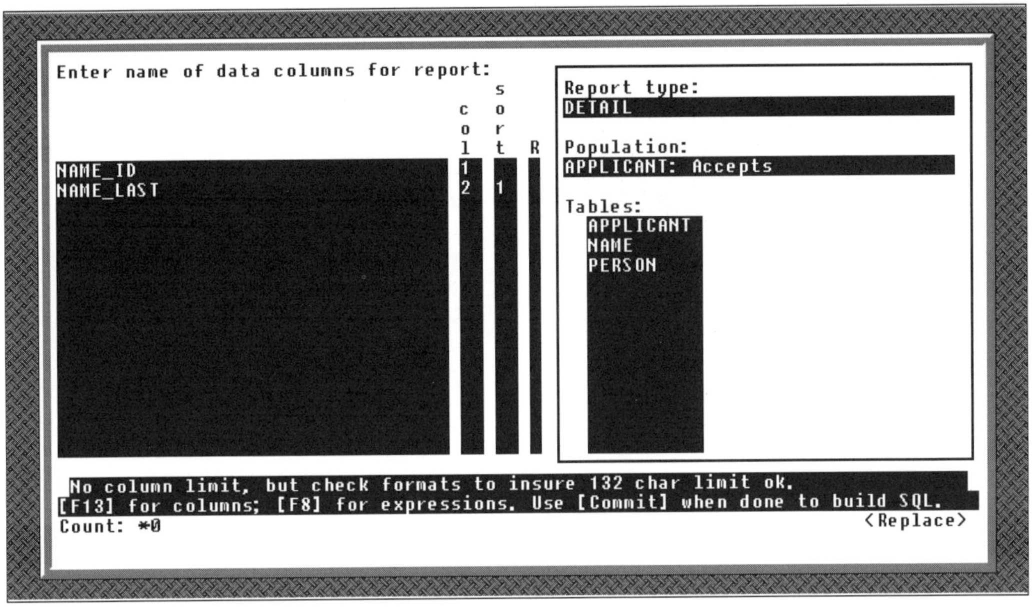

Figure 14–8. Screen for selecting data columns.

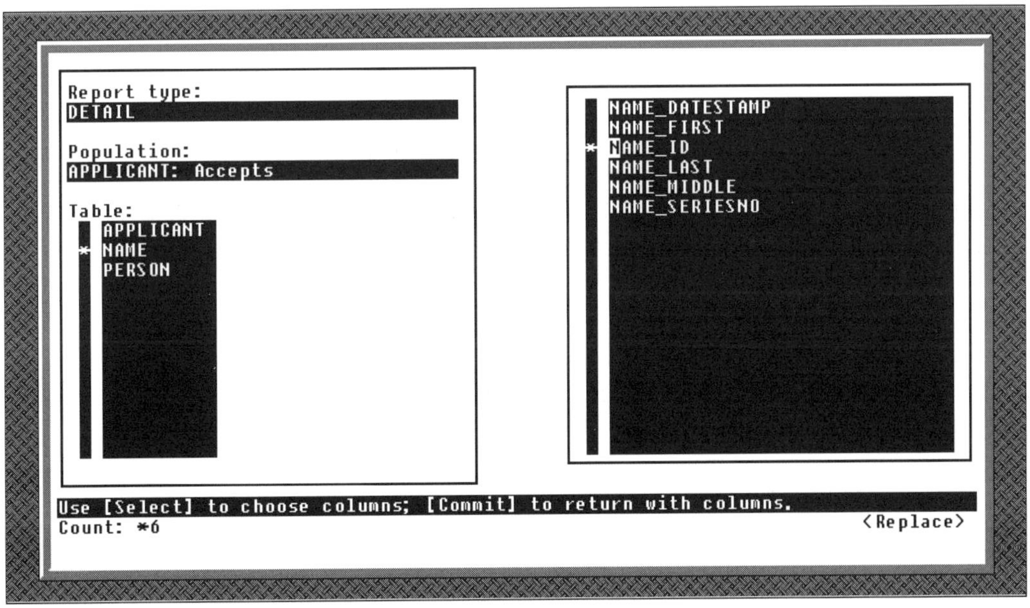

Figure 14–9. Menu of data columns.

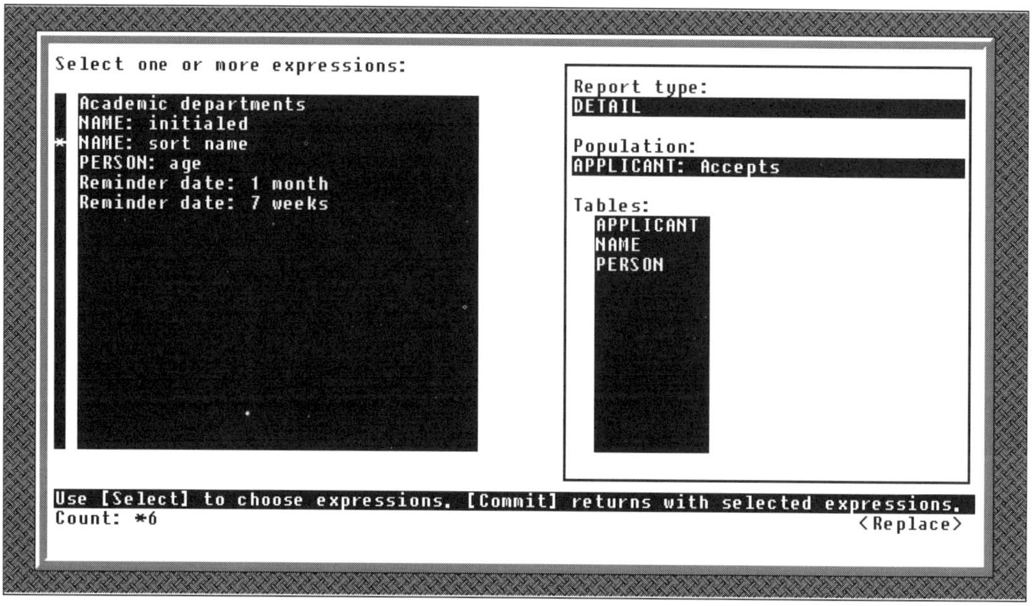

Figure 14–10. Menu of *select* objects.

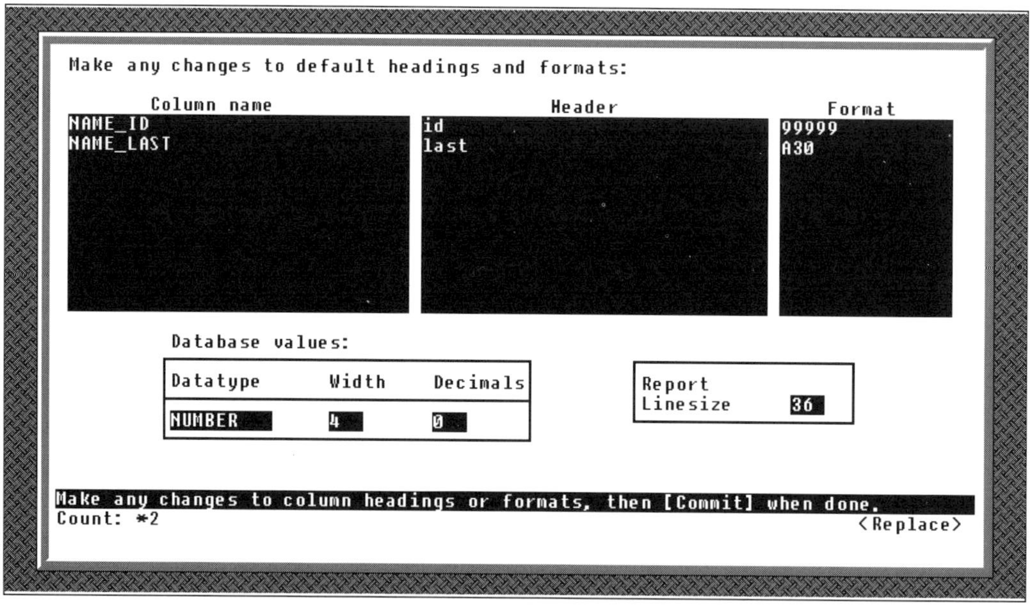

Figure 14–11. Screen for changing default column formats.

accepted for admission. From the *report* object menu (Figure 14–4), the user highlights and selects the detail report. He or she then passes to the *population* object menu (Figure 14–5) where the population of accepted applicants is highlighted and selected. The enclosed box on this menu and subsequent menus provides a running summary of objects selected and tables made available for reporting. From the *where* object menu (Figure 14–6), the user selects objects providing access to the NAME and PERSON tables. The conditions screen (Figure 14–7) provides the opportunity to limit the population to women by specifying that person_gender = F. From the data columns screen (Figure 14–8), the user can access two other screens to choose columns for the report. Data columns appearing in tables can be accessed from one of the two screens (Figure 14–9) by highlighting the table and selecting one or more columns from that table. Exiting this screen with selected data columns includes these columns in the report. Similarly, *select* objects can be chosen from an expressions screen (Figure 14–10). Exiting this screen with selected expressions includes the expressions in the report. From the central data column screen (see Figure 14–8 again), the column order and sort order may be specified. The user then passes to a screen (Figure 14–11) where default column headings and formats are displayed. The two boxes inserted in this screen provide the user with information useful when making changes to the default settings. In this case the user is informed that the data columns selected for the report only use 36 characters across the report page. This information is most pertinent when a large number of data columns appear in the report and exceeding the line size available for printing becomes an issue. By using the cursor keys to highlight a data column name, the user can also see the datatype and default column width. This default may be changed. At this point, the user commits the selections to database tables and control passes to the procedural language which parses and assembles the objects into completed SQL programs. At any time during the menu selection process, the user can cycle back to earlier menus to modify previous choices.

Constructing the query requires only a few keystrokes and less than a minute of time. By all accounts the query appears simple. But examine the shell and SQL programs in Figure 14–12 on the following page and the actual report in Figure 14–13 on page 371. The user has just constructed two programs complete with multiple joins, correlated subqueries, report titles and column headings, and printer control. Yet all of this is completely transparent to the user. The query is simultaneously simple and complex; simple for the user to conceive and execute but complex in its SQL and SQL*PLUS.

SHELL

```
/*
        sql:        fg14-13.sql
        date:       30-jan-1995
        author:     glewis
        purpose:    Figure 14-13
*/
set termout off
start &&object_dir.\clears
start &&object_dir.\hpprintr
start &&object_dir.\date
start &&object_dir.\time
start &&object_dir.\owncol
start &&object_dir.\escape

ttitle left xEscape skip 1-
        'Women applicants accepted to AS college: Fall 1995'
        right 'Report name: fg14-13.lis' skip 1 -
        left 'Date: ' xDate '     Time: ' xTime -
        right 'SQL name:    fg14-13.sql' skip 1 -
        right 'Page: ' format 999 sql.pno skip 2;

spool fg14-13.lis
        start xfg14-13
        start &&object_dir.\reset
spool off

start &&object_dir.\clears
start &&object_dir.\screen
```

SQL

```
select
      n1.name_id,
      n1.name_last
from
      person,
      name n1,
      applicant
where
      applicant_term = '199509'
              and applicant_level = 'UG'
              and applicant_college = 'AS'
      and exists
      (select 'x'
      from
              cdecision,
              decision
      where
              decision_id = applicant_id
                        and decision_applicant_term = applicant_term
                        and decision_applicant_seriesno = applicant_seriesno
              and cdecision_code = decision_code
                        and cdecision_accept_ind = 'Y')
      and n1.name_id = applicant_id
              and n1.name_seriesno =
              (select max(n2.name_seriesno)
              from name n2
              where n2.name_id = applicant_id)
      and person_id = applicant_id
              and person_gender = 'F'
order by
      2
/
```

Figure 14–12. SQL and shell programs built in Figure 14–4 through Figure 14–11.

```
REPORT

Women applicants accepted to AS college: Fall 1995          Report name: fg14-13.lis
Date: 30-JAN-1995      Time: 05:11                          SQL name:     fg14-13.sql
                                                                          Page:     1

    id last
------ ------------------------------
  1897 Affsa
  5898 Allen
  3005 Anderson
  5923 Arnold
  1634 Asay
   882 Baker
   956 Baker
   ...
```

Figure 14–13. Report from query shown in Figure 14–12.

Issues in Object Automation

Once you begin to automate objects, you generate a number of issues that require resolution. None of the issues are new. They all exist even when objects get used by highly skilled query writers using editors to assemble objects and craft queries. But skilled query writers resolve the issues on their own, query by query. In a menu-driven object system the issues must be addressed as the system is designed and developed.

The issues that arise when automating SQL objects include the following:

- Validation. How do you ensure that users can only select objects that work together? Clearly it should be impossible to choose the *select* object selsname.obj without first having chosen an object like whrname.obj that accesses the NAME table. Equally disastrous results occur if users can select a population of applicants and then a *where* object accessing their college grades—which, of course, they don't yet have. As users select objects from a menu system, the universe of available objects constantly changes. Somehow the system must know what objects make sense given whatever choices the user has already made.
- Recursive validation. A menu-driven object system is not a linear experience. Users frequently change their minds about a previous selection. Perhaps they make a mistake or maybe they just decide to do the report differently. For whatever reason, users should be able to alter their object selections. Doing so, however, requires revalidation of the selected objects. For example, suppose a user

selects a roster report, proceeds through the various selection screens, and identifies five data columns to appear in the report. But before committing the selection and generating the SQL, the user decides to change the report type to a frequency distribution. This change invalidates many of the previous objects. The system must recognize these situations and take some course of action. For example, a warning might be issued with a prompting question requesting confirmation from the user that the invalid objects should be dropped from the query.

- User groups. As the number of objects and users grow, the objects available to users should be segmented. Users in the admissions office should not have access to objects used by the registrar. A menu-driven system must accommodate different user groups, meaning that some mechanism must identify what objects are available for each user community.
- Query retrieval. Some queries get run repeatedly with minor variations. A menu-driven object system should store enough information about a query so that a user may retrieve it, make modifications to it, and then reexecute the query. This requires storing the name of the shell and SQL program files. But it also means storing information about what objects the user selected, because retrieval of a completed query should reselect the appropriate objects from the various menus. The user can then make changes and run the modified query.
- Default overrides. Many reports run well with the default assumptions implicit in objects. But sometimes those defaults must be overridden. For example, a user may wish to conserve space on the report by modifying column formats. A menu-driven object system should provide this opportunity. Besides column headings and formats, other defaults include the destination printer and the physical location of the SQL programs and output reports.
- Error trapping. Messages embedded in objects require runtime responses from users of menu-driven object systems. These responses should be validated if at all possible. If, for example, a user is prompted to enter a college code (e.g., AS or BU) then the response can be checked against the CCOLLEGE table to ensure the code is valid. Error trapping of coded responses is easy and should be done routinely. But even uncoded responses can be checked; for example, a number should not have any characters

in it, an SAT score may only range between 200 and 800, and so on. For objects assembled from a menu-driven system with runtime user responses, I'd also recommend that the user responses appear somewhere on the final report. Not all errors can be detected before running the SQL for a query. Documenting the runtime responses on the report provides a final opportunity for the user to detect any possible errors.

- Alias management. Many objects utilize table aliases. In order for objects to properly work together, the aliases must be coordinated when objects get assembled. What happens, for example, when you want to use the same object twice in a report? Such a request can certainly be legitimate. Recall the situation with SAT scores when whrtest.obj was used once to retrieve SAT math scores and used again in the same query to retrieve SAT verbal scores. Throughout this book, objects contain specific aliases—for example, d1 for the DECISION table. For automatic assembly, however, designation of aliases can occur in the procedural program that parses the objects and assembles them. This requires revising the objects somewhat. Specific aliases should be removed and replaced by some symbol that the parsing program recognizes. The program logic then assigns specific table aliases to all the objects used in a query.
- Embedded messages. When you automate object assembly, the messages that get embedded in the objects become richer and more complex. An individual constructing a query with an editor assumes all responsibility for assembling objects correctly. But when the assembly is controlled by a procedural program, it helps if the objects themselves contain general assembly instructions that can be read by the program. In this way the objects assist the procedural program when it creates the SQL query.
- *Report* objects. *Report* objects, in particular, require the most additional management when used in a menu-driven system. Each specific *report* object makes assumptions that must be resolved in the menu system. For example, a frequency distribution report assumes that only one data column will be selected and that it will be a categorical (as opposed to a continuous) data column. A menu system must then limit a user to one data column whenever he or she selects a frequency distribution report; it must also check that the data column selected is CHAR or VARCHAR2 and not

NUMBER. Similarly, the repeating detail report requires that a user distinguish between two types of data columns—those that repeat and those that do not. A menu system must accommodate this requirement. Other types of reports require still other forms of special attention, such as insertion of special report columns like "count(*)" or formatting statements like "fold_after 1."

Object Management System

The issues just discussed quickly create the need for an object management system; that is, some way to resolve the issues so that queries can be created in a menu-driven system. The user interface—the series of screens used to select objects and construct queries—merely becomes the pinnacle that sits on top of a supporting foundation.

Many different methods exist for implementing an object management system that can support automated assembly of objects. For example, the menu object system discussed previously used Oracle's SQL*FORMS to construct the user interface. Behind the scenes exist several data tables that support this system. These tables include:

- OBJECTS: a table identifying each object by id, class, physical file name, associated documentation, and short and long descriptions of the object.
- QUESTIONS: a table containing the questions used to prompt users for responses, including validation instructions used by the procedural program that assembles objects.
- TABLES_USED: a table identifying each table made available for reporting by each object, ensuring that users cannot select data columns unavailable for reporting.
- COLUMNS: a temporary table containing user-supplied overrides of default column headers and formats and also containing user-specified sorting requirements.
- DEFAULTS: a table containing default column headings and formats.
- VALIDATION: a table cross-validating objects to ensure they work with each other.
- USER_GROUPS and USER_OBJECTS: tables that create communities of users and then identify which objects each group may access.

- CONDITIONS: a temporary table containing the modifying criteria a user applies to the population definition.
- REPORTS: a table of special requirements needed by each *report* object.

As the user works through a query on the menu-driven system, the SQL*FORMS interface uses these tables. For example, a specific user belongs to one user group. The system identifies the user, looks up his or her user group, determines the objects the user can access, and then displays these objects for selection. As the user selects objects, the system accesses the VALIDATION table to ensure that he or she cannot select objects that don't work together. When the user selects data columns to appear in the report, the system accesses the TABLES_USED table to ensure that he or she cannot select unavailable data columns. The column selections get stored temporarily in the COLUMNS table. Any overrides of default column settings also appear here. If the user chooses to modify the population with a *where* clause, it gets stored temporarily in the CONDITIONS table. When he or she commits the query, control passes to the procedural program. This program parses each of the objects the user selected. It accesses the QUESTIONS table whenever an object requires a response from the user. Instructions for validating user responses also appear in the QUESTIONS table. The procedural program then assembles the objects. It accesses the COLUMNS and CONDITIONS tables, processes these rows, and adds them to the query. The program also reads the REPORTS table to determine any special assembly instructions for the report type chosen by the user.

Evolution in SQL Objects

Previous sections described two scenarios for object use. One presumed a highly skilled user operating with considerable flexibility but little support. The second made no presumption about user skill but required that objects be used in a structured and closed menu-driven system. Between these two extremes lies considerable room for development of a more comprehensive system for object use.

Many reports fall into this middle ground. For one reason or another, the reports are no longer routine. Population items may have fallen through a join, the performance may be poor, the report population may require minor modification to the SQL, or the *report* object may need revision to include a new feature. All of these circumstances create problems in a structured menu-driven object system. Yet none requires the skill of an object developer who uses data dictionaries, database schematics, indexes, and detailed knowledge of SQL to build new objects.

You could argue that a menu-driven system would evolve with time so that more and more reports became routine. That is, as the system matured the objects would become more robust and the occurrence of problems less frequent. Indeed I think this would happen. But I also think that even a mature menu-driven object system will leave gaps in the reports that users can accomplish on their own.

Not having done this, I offer the following suggestion as speculation. Constructing queries with SQL objects would seem an ideal application for an expert system. Imagine a computer program that took the place of the query writer in Chapter 13. A query starts with a request from someone. Between that start and the completed report many steps require judgment. Each of these steps would benefit from a knowledge base that helped guide user selection, manipulation, and assembly of objects. If the query writer is an expert system, then the person requesting the report could be the system user. Users need the power and the freedom to ask question after question of a database. Eliminating the middle person, the interpreter, simply must happen before users can truly pursue an ad hoc question.

Many steps in the query process would benefit from an expert system. These include the following:

- Query clarification. The most important step occurs first in a query. This involves clarifying what the user actually wants the report to do. Often a query is initially ill-formed and gets recast through discussion. Forcing a user to identify the report population, the type of report, and the data columns to appear in the report serves to clarify the request. But an opportunity should exist for the user to define any new terms as well. Through a query clarification module, an expert system could map the evolving query to the object database. This mapping process would generate interactions between the user and the expert system as the system attempted to clarify the request and simultaneously helped the user to clarify his or her thinking.
- Query tool selection. SQL is not an appropriate query tool for every ad hoc question. In the process of clarifying a user's request, an expert object system would gather sufficient information to determine if SQL objects represented a viable solution. The system might also suggest reformulation of a request.

- Population issues. The key to a successful report rests on accurately identifying the report population. Once the population is determined, no item in the population should fall through the SQL. This means distinguishing population qualifiers—female, international, freshman—from items about the population that should be displayed—addresses and phone numbers. It means knowing the difference between a population of "applicants and their home addresses" and a population of "applicants with home addresses." Defining populations also forces clarification of singularity. When is it acceptable to generate multiple report rows for each population item? Knowledge about falling and multiplying through joins could be built into an expert object system to help clarify population definitions.
- Query testing. Each query requires testing. Without it you cannot determine if population items fall through joins or multiply through joins. You also cannot determine if performance is acceptable. Yet users frequently skip the testing step entirely and rely on examination of the final report as their quality control step. Testing is an area where an expert object system could make major improvements in ad hoc reporting. Each query should be tested at least twice: once to count the population and once to gets counts for the entire SQL program. Comparing these two counts identifies problems.
- Problem resolution. If testing a query shows that a problem exists, a knowledgeable user operating manually then identifies the cause of the problem. This requires stepping through the joins one by one, getting counts at each step and comparing them to counts obtained from the previous step. Once the problem is localized to a segment of SQL code, the query writer uses the techniques described in Chapter 12 to locate the data rows causing the problem. Falling through a join requires one technique; multiplying through a join requires another. An expert object system could easily duplicate this process, stepping through joins whenever testing identified a problem. It could also write and run the SQL to find the offending data rows.
- Performance analysis. Sometimes queries run too slow. Or the query may be run against an enormous database. Either situation requires SQL tuning. Yet even programmers generally skip this step. An expert object system could make a major impact on ad

hoc reporting by improving the ease with which performance testing and tuning occurred. Such a system could run an EXPLAIN PLAN and then display those results graphically. It could identify logical sections of the SQL (i.e., joins and subqueries) and label these on the graph. An expert system could also gather the performance statistics needed to pinpoint the bottleneck. As demonstrated in Chapter 12, this requires stepping through the logical sections of a query and gathering timing statistics at each step. These results can then be displayed in a table. With the graphical interpretation of the optimizer plan and a table of timing statistics, a query writer knows what part of the SQL needs tuning. Tuning might eventually be part of an expert system, but initially that job should be left to the IS staff responsible for object development.

It's strange: we must simplify the process of ad hoc reporting, but do so without reducing its complexity. Ignoring the complexity only produces poor reports.

SQL Objects and Object-Oriented Systems

I began creating and using SQL objects in an entirely natural way; it just seemed logical to reuse chunks of code I'd already spent time developing. There's nothing special about this; programmers have always done it. Maybe they called it a subroutine or a procedure, but they've always saved and reused programming code that performed some useful function with applicability outside the program in which it was developed.

But the more I use SQL objects, the more I see parallels to formal object-oriented systems. Such a system has four characteristics. First, an object consists of a set of attributes that describes its state and a set of operations that defines its behavior. SQL objects meet these criteria. They have a data component consisting of the SQL code. They also have a procedural component; certainly a *report* object behaves differently from a *population* object. Second, an object-oriented system uses messages to communicate with objects. Again SQL objects meet these criteria; messages embedded in SQL objects communicate with the user and with the procedural program used to assemble the objects. Third, in an object-oriented system objects are grouped into classes. This is certainly true of SQL objects. The major classes are *report*, *population*, *where*, *select*, and *shell*. And fourth, in an object-oriented system, object attributes and operations are inherited through a class hierarchy. This may seem less true of SQL objects than some of the other characteristics. But the *where* class contains an element of inheritance. This class actually consists of two major subclasses: the population modifiers (the *where* 1 objects) and table accessers (the *where* 2 objects). The *where* 2 objects are further split into those that preserve population singularity (the *where* 2u objects) and those that do not (the *where* 2m objects). This hierarchical class structure seems consistent with inheritance of more general attributes and procedures from objects farther up in the hierarchy.

I'm not sure where this parallel between SQL objects and object-oriented systems would lead if developed more fully. But it is intriguing to think that as it applies to ad hoc reporting, the SQL language may be an object-oriented system.

Part IV
Appendixes

Appendix A

Data Dictionaries for Simulated Database

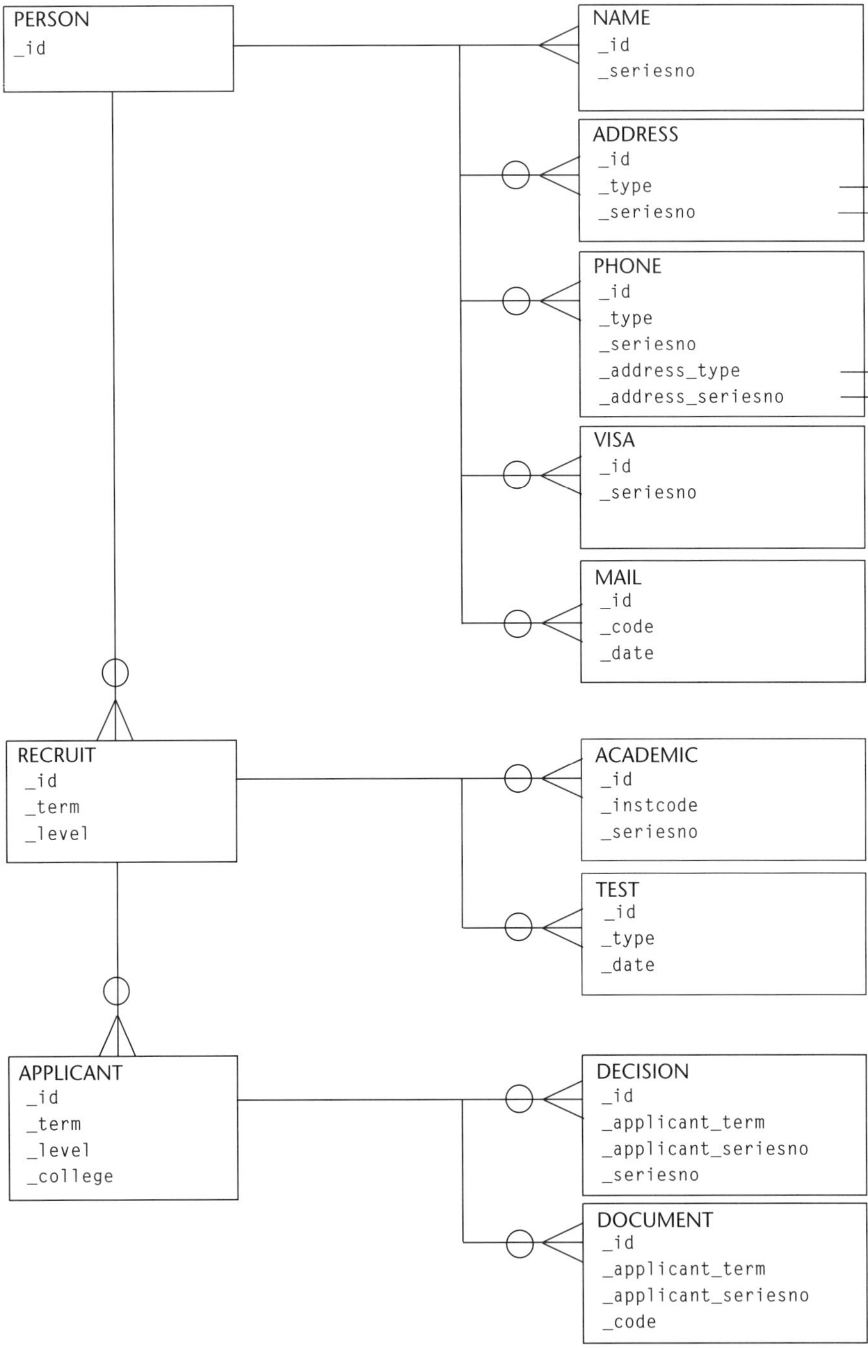

Figure A–1. Database schematic of simulated recruiting and admissions data.

Table A–1. Database tables owned by KOMENDA.

```
Tables for owner: KOMENDA                                                   Page:    1
Date: 09-OCT-1994     Time: 10:05                            Report name: komenda.lis
                                                             SQL name:     tables.sql
```

Name	Type	Owner	Comments
ACADEMIC	TABLE	KOMENDA	High School and Previous College Academic Records
ADDRESS	TABLE	KOMENDA	Address Information
APPLICANT	TABLE	KOMENDA	Applicant Information
CADDRESS	TABLE	KOMENDA	Address Type Code Translation Table
CAPPLICANT	TABLE	KOMENDA	Application Type Code Translation Table
CCOLLEGE	TABLE	KOMENDA	College Code Translation Table
CDECISION	TABLE	KOMENDA	Admissions Decision Code Translation Table
CDEGREE	TABLE	KOMENDA	Degree Code Translation Table
CDOCUMENT	TABLE	KOMENDA	Document Code Translation Table
CDORM	TABLE	KOMENDA	Residence Code Translation Table
CETHN	TABLE	KOMENDA	Ethnic Code Translation Table
CGENDER	TABLE	KOMENDA	Gender Code Translation Table
CINST	TABLE	KOMENDA	Institutions Code Translation Table
CLEVEL	TABLE	KOMENDA	Level Code Translation Table
CMAIL	TABLE	KOMENDA	Document Code Translation Table
CMAJOR	TABLE	KOMENDA	Major Code Translation Table
CNATION	TABLE	KOMENDA	Nation Code Translation Table
CPHONE	TABLE	KOMENDA	Phone Type Code Translation Table
CSTATE	TABLE	KOMENDA	State Code Translation Table
CSTYPE	TABLE	KOMENDA	Student Type Code Translation Table
CTERM	TABLE	KOMENDA	Term Code Translation Table
CTEST	TABLE	KOMENDA	Test Code Translation Table
CVISA	TABLE	KOMENDA	Visa Code Translation Table
DECISION	TABLE	KOMENDA	Admissions Decision Information
DOCUMENT	TABLE	KOMENDA	Admissions documents received
MAIL	TABLE	KOMENDA	Recruit and Applicant Correspondence
NAME	TABLE	KOMENDA	Table of Name Information
PERSON	TABLE	KOMENDA	Person Specific Information
PHONE	TABLE	KOMENDA	Telephone Information
RECRUIT	TABLE	KOMENDA	Prospects for Admission
TEST	TABLE	KOMENDA	Test Score Information
VISA	TABLE	KOMENDA	Visa Information for Internationals

Table A-2. Indexes on tables owned by KOMENDA

```
Indexes on tables owned by: KOMENDA                                              Page:     1
Date: 07-JAN-1995     Time: 06:51                                        Report name: indexes.lis
                                                                         SQL name:    indexes.sql
```

Table	Index	Uniqueness	Column	Position
ACADEMIC	ACADEMIC_KEY	UNIQUE	ACADEMIC_ID	1
			ACADEMIC_INSTCODE	2
			ACADEMIC_SERIESNO	3
ADDRESS	ADDRESS_KEY	UNIQUE	ADDRESS_ID	1
			ADDRESS_TYPE	2
			ADDRESS_SERIESNO	3
APPLICANT	APPLICANT_KEY1	UNIQUE	APPLICANT_ID	1
			APPLICANT_TERM	2
			APPLICANT_SERIESNO	3
	APPLICANT_KEY2	UNIQUE	APPLICANT_ID	1
			APPLICANT_TERM	2
			APPLICANT_LEVEL	3
			APPLICANT_COLLEGE	4
CDECISION	CDECISION_KEY	UNIQUE	CDECISION_CODE	1
CINST	CINST_KEY	UNIQUE	CINST_CODE	1
DECISION	DECISION_KEY	UNIQUE	DECISION_ID	1
			DECISION_APPLICANT_TERM	2
			DECISION_APPLICANT_SERIESNO	3
			DECISION_SERIESNO	4
DOCUMENT	DOCUMENT_KEY	UNIQUE	DOCUMENT_ID	1
			DOCUMENT_APPLICANT_TERM	2
			DOCUMENT_APPLICANT_SERIESNO	3
			DOCUMENT_CODE	4
MAIL	MAIL_KEY	NONUNIQUE	MAIL_ID	1
			MAIL_CODE	2
			MAIL_DATE	3
NAME	NAME_KEY	UNIQUE	NAME_ID	1
			NAME_SERIESNO	2

Table A-2. Indexes on tables owned by KOMENDA.

```
Indexes on tables owned by: KOMENDA                                                Page:    2
Date: 07-JAN-1995     Time: 06:51                                      Report name: indexes.lis
                                                                       SQL name:    indexes.sql
```

Table	Index	Uniqueness	Column	Position
NAME	NAME_LAST	NONUNIQUE	NAME_LAST	1
PERSON	PERSON_KEY	UNIQUE	PERSON_ID	1
PHONE	PHONE_KEY	UNIQUE	PHONE_ID	1
			PHONE_TYPE	2
			PHONE_SERIESNO	3
RECRUIT	RECRUIT_KEY	UNIQUE	RECRUIT_ID	1
			RECRUIT_TERM	2
			RECRUIT_LEVEL	3
SAVELIST	SAVELIST_KEY	UNIQUE	SAVELIST_ID	1
TEST	TEST_KEY	UNIQUE	TEST_ID	1
			TEST_TYPE	2
			TEST_DATE	3
VISA	VISA_KEY	UNIQUE	VISA_ID	1
			VISA_SERIESNO	2

Table A-3. Data dictionary for ACADEMIC table.

```
Date: 06-SEP-1994     Time: 05:25                    TABLE: ACADEMIC                              Page:    1
Report name: academic.dic                            Owner: KOMENDA                           SQL name: dic.sql
                                       High_School_and_Previous_College_Academic_Records
```

Column name	Type	Width	Scale	Nulls	Column comments
ACADEMIC_ID	NUMBER	4		NOT NULL	ID number of person
ACADEMIC_SERIESNO	NUMBER	2		NOT NULL	Sequential number if person attended a previous institution more than once
ACADEMIC_INSTCODE	CHAR	6		NOT NULL	Code of previous institution attended
ACADEMIC_DEGREE	CHAR	6		NULL	Degree obtained
ACADEMIC_DEGREEDATE	DATE	7		NULL	Date degree was obtained
ACADEMIC_SIZECLASS	NUMBER	5		NULL	Size of graduating class
ACADEMIC_RANKCLASS	NUMBER	5		NULL	Rank of person in graduating class
ACADEMIC_GPA	NUMBER	3	2	NULL	Grade point average at previous institution
ACADEMIC_DATESTAMP	DATE	7		NULL	Date when last update occurred

Table A-4. Data dictionary for ADDRESS table.

```
Date: 06-SEP-1994     Time: 05:26                    TABLE: ADDRESS                               Page:    1
Report name: address.dic                             Owner: KOMENDA                           SQL name: dic.sql
                                                   Address_Information
```

Column name	Type	Width	Scale	Nulls	Column comments
ADDRESS_ID	NUMBER	4		NOT NULL	ID number of person
ADDRESS_SERIESNO	NUMBER	2		NOT NULL	Sequential number if person has more than 1 address of a given type
ADDRESS_TYPE	CHAR	2		NOT NULL	Type of address
ADDRESS_BEGINDATE	DATE	7		NULL	First date address is current
ADDRESS_ENDDATE	DATE	7		NULL	Last date address is current
ADDRESS_DATESTAMP	DATE	7		NULL	Last date record was updated
ADDRESS_CITY	CHAR	20		NULL	City of address
ADDRESS_STATE	CHAR	2		NULL	State of address
ADDRESS_ZIP	CHAR	10		NULL	Zip code of address
ADDRESS_NATION	CHAR	5		NULL	Nation of address
ADDRESS_STREET1	CHAR	35		NULL	First line of street address
ADDRESS_STREET2	CHAR	35		NULL	Second line of street address

Table A-5. Data dictionary for APPLICANT table.

```
Date: 07-JAN-1995      Time: 07:00                    TABLE: APPLICANT                      Page:    1
Report name: applicant.dic                            Owner: KOMENDA                  SQL name: dic.sql
                                                   Applicant_Information
```

Column name	Type	Width	Scale	Nulls	Column comments
APPLICANT_ID	NUMBER	4		NOT NULL	ID number of applicant
APPLICANT_TERM	CHAR	6		NOT NULL	Anticipated term of enrollment
APPLICANT_LEVEL	CHAR	2		NOT NULL	Level (Undergrad, Grad) of applicant
APPLICANT_SERIESNO	NUMBER	2		NOT NULL	Sequential number if more than one application in single term
APPLICANT_RECRUIT_TERM	CHAR	6		NOT NULL	Anticipated enrollment term from recruit record
APPLICANT_COLLEGE	CHAR	2		NULL	College (Arts and Sciences, Business)
APPLICANT_DORM_INTENT	CHAR	1		NULL	Anticipated residence status (commuter or dorm)
APPLICANT_AID_INTENT	CHAR	1		NULL	Anticipated need for financial aid
APPLICANT_TYPE	CHAR	2		NULL	Type of application
APPLICANT_STUDENT_TYPE	CHAR	1		NULL	Type of student (freshman, transfer)
APPLICANT_DATESTAMP	DATE	7		NULL	Last date record was updated
APPLICANT_DEGREE	CHAR	6		NULL	Anticipated degree
APPLICANT_MAJOR	CHAR	4		NULL	Anticipated major
APPLICANT_APPLDATE	DATE	7		NULL	Date application received
APPLICANT_HOUSINGDATE	DATE	7		NULL	Date housing deposit received

Table A-6. Data dictionary for DECISION table.

```
Date: 07-JAN-1995      Time: 07:00                    TABLE: DECISION                       Page:    1
Report name: decision.dic                             Owner: KOMENDA                  SQL name: dic.sql
                                              Admissions_Decision_Information
```

Column name	Type	Width	Scale	Nulls	Column comments
DECISION_ID	NUMBER	4		NOT NULL	ID number of applicant
DECISION_APPLICANT_SERIESNO	NUMBER	2		NOT NULL	Sequential number of application in APPLICANT table for given term
DECISION_APPLICANT_TERM	CHAR	6		NOT NULL	Term of anticipated enrollment from APPLICANT table
DECISION_SERIESNO	NUMBER	2		NOT NULL	Sequential number if more than 1 decisions for this applicaiton
DECISION_CODE	CHAR	2		NOT NULL	Application decision code
DECISION_DATE	DATE	7		NOT NULL	Date of application decision
DECISION_DATESTAMP	DATE	7		NULL	Last date record was updated

Table A-7. Data dictionary for DOCUMENT table.

```
Date: 06-SEP-1994      Time: 05:45                        TABLE: DOCUMENT                         Page:    1
Report name: document.dic                                 Owner: KOMENDA                     SQL name: dic.sql
                                                     Admissions_documents_received
```

Column name	Type	Width	Scale	Nulls	Column comments
DOCUMENT_ID	NUMBER	4		NOT NULL	ID number of person
DOCUMENT_APPLICANT_SERIESNO	NUMBER	2		NOT NULL	applicant_series number from applicant table
DOCUMENT_APPLICANT_TERM	CHAR	6		NOT NULL	applicant_term from applicant table
DOCUMENT_CODE	CHAR	4		NOT NULL	Code for type of document
DOCUMENT_REQUIRED	CHAR	1		NULL	Document required (Y) for application to be complete
DOCUMENT_RECEIVEDATE	DATE	7		NULL	Date document was received
DOCUMENT_DATESTAMP	DATE	7		NULL	Last date of update

Table A-8. Data dictionary for MAIL table.

```
Date: 06-SEP-1994      Time: 05:32                         TABLE: MAIL                            Page:    1
Report name: mail.dic                                     Owner: KOMENDA                     SQL name: dic.sql
                                                 Recruit_and_Applicant_Correspondence
```

Column name	Type	Width	Scale	Nulls	Column comments
MAIL_ID	NUMBER	4		NOT NULL	ID number of person
MAIL_CODE	CHAR	6		NOT NULL	Type of correspondence
MAIL_DATE	DATE	7		NULL	Date correspondence sent
MAIL_DATESTAMP	DATE	7		NULL	Date when last update occurred

Table A-9. Data dictionary for NAME table.

```
Date: 06-SEP-1994      Time: 05:32                         TABLE: NAME                            Page:    1
Report name: name.dic                                     Owner: KOMENDA                     SQL name: dic.sql
                                                       Table_of_Name_Information
```

Column name	Type	Width	Scale	Nulls	Column comments
NAME_ID	NUMBER	4		NOT NULL	ID number of person
NAME_SERIESNO	NUMBER	2		NOT NULL	Sequential number for person if name changes exist
NAME_LAST	CHAR	30		NULL	Last name of person
NAME_DATESTAMP	DATE	7		NULL	Last date record was updated
NAME_FIRST	CHAR	15		NULL	First name of person
NAME_MIDDLE	CHAR	15		NULL	Middle name of person

Table A-10. Data dictionary for PERSON table.

```
Date: 06-SEP-1994      Time: 05:32                    TABLE: PERSON                        Page:    1
Report name: person.dic                               Owner: KOMENDA                   SQL name: dic.sql
                                                Person_Specific_Information
```

Column name	Type	Width	Scale	Nulls	Column comments
PERSON_ID	NUMBER	4		NOT NULL	ID number for person
PERSON_BIRTHDATE	DATE	7		NULL	Date of birth for person
PERSON_ETHNIC	CHAR	1		NULL	Ethnic status of person
PERSON_GENDER	CHAR	1		NULL	Gender of person
PERSON_DATESTAMP	DATE	7		NULL	Date record was last updated

Table A-11. Data dictionary for PHONE table.

```
Date: 06-SEP-1994      Time: 05:33                    TABLE: PHONE                         Page:    1
Report name: phone.dic                                Owner: KOMENDA                   SQL name: dic.sql
                                                  Telephone_Information
```

Column name	Type	Width	Scale	Nulls	Column comments
PHONE_ID	NUMBER	4		NOT NULL	ID number of person
PHONE_SERIESNO	NUMBER	2		NOT NULL	Sequential number if more than one phone of a specific type
PHONE_TYPE	CHAR	2		NOT NULL	Type of phone (car, residence, etc)
PHONE_STATUS	CHAR	1		NULL	Active (null) or inactive (I) status
PHONE_AREA	CHAR	3		NULL	Area code of phone number
PHONE_NUMBER	CHAR	7		NULL	Phone number
PHONE_ADDRESS_TYPE	CHAR	2		NULL	Address type associated with phone
PHONE_ADDRESS_SERIESNO	NUMBER	2		NULL	Sequential number in ADDRESS table for record associated with this phone.
PHONE_DATESTAMP	DATE	7		NULL	Last date record was updated

Table A-12. Data dictionary for RECRUIT table.

```
Date: 06-SEP-1994     Time: 05:33                            TABLE: RECRUIT                          Page:    1
Report name: recruit.dic                                     Owner: KOMENDA                      SQL name: dic.sql
                                                         Prospects_for_Admission

Column name                     Type     Width  Scale Nulls     Column comments
======================================================================================================================
RECRUIT_ID                      NUMBER       4        NOT NULL  ID number for recruit
RECRUIT_TERM                    CHAR         6        NOT NULL  Term that recruit would enroll if admitted
RECRUIT_LEVEL                   CHAR         2        NULL      Level (undergrad or graduate) for recruit
RECRUIT_DATESTAMP               DATE         7        NULL      Date record was last changed
RECRUIT_DEGREE                  CHAR         4        NULL      Anticipated degree for recruit
RECRUIT_STUDENT_TYPE            CHAR         1        NULL      Type of recruit (eg, freshman, transfer)
RECRUIT_RECRUITERID             NUMBER       4        NULL      ID number of Admissions staff member responsible for recruit
RECRUIT_MAJOR                   CHAR         4        NULL      Anticipated major of recruit
RECRUIT_DATEIN                  DATE         7        NULL      Date recruit record was created
```

Table A-13. Data dictionary for TEST table.

```
Date: 06-SEP-1994     Time: 05:33                            TABLE: TEST                             Page:    1
Report name: test.dic                                        Owner: KOMENDA                      SQL name: dic.sql
                                                         Test_Score_Information

Column name                     Type     Width  Scale Nulls     Column comments
======================================================================================================================
TEST_ID                         NUMBER       4        NOT NULL  ID number of person
TEST_TYPE                       CHAR         6        NOT NULL  Type of test
TEST_DATE                       DATE         7        NOT NULL  Date test taken
TEST_DATESTAMP                  DATE         7        NOT NULL  Last date record was updated
TEST_SCORE                      NUMBER       5      2 NOT NULL  Score on test
```

Table A-14. Data dictionary for VISA table.

```
Date: 06-SEP-1994     Time: 05:33                            TABLE: VISA                             Page:    1
Report name: visa.dic                                        Owner: KOMENDA                      SQL name: dic.sql
                                                    Visa_Information_for_Internationals

Column name                     Type     Width  Scale Nulls     Column comments
======================================================================================================================
VISA_ID                         NUMBER       4        NOT NULL  ID number of person
VISA_TYPE                       CHAR         2        NOT NULL  Type of visa (coded)
VISA_SERIESNO                   NUMBER       2        NOT NULL  Sequential number if more than one visa of a single type
VISA_CITIZEN                    CHAR         5        NULL      Country of citizenship for person
VISA_DATESTAMP                  DATE         7        NULL      Last date record was updated
```

Table A-15. Data dictionary for CADDRESS code table.

```
Date: 06-SEP-1994      Time: 05:27                              TABLE: CADDRESS                              Page:    1
Report name: caddress.dic                                       Owner: KOMENDA                          SQL name: dic.sql
                                                   Address_Type_Code_Translation_Table
```

Column name	Type	Width	Scale	Nulls	Column comments
CADDRESS_CODE	CHAR	2		NOT NULL	Address type code
CADDRESS_TRANSLATION	CHAR	30		NOT NULL	Description of code
CADDRESS_DATESTAMP	DATE	7		NOT NULL	Date of last update

Table A-16. Data dictionary for CAPPLICANT code table.

```
Date: 06-SEP-1994      Time: 05:27                              TABLE: CAPPLICANT                            Page:    1
Report name: capplicant.dic                                     Owner: KOMENDA                          SQL name: dic.sql
                                                 Application_Type_Code_Translation_Table
```

Column name	Type	Width	Scale	Nulls	Column comments
CAPPLICANT_CODE	CHAR	2		NOT NULL	Code for type of application
CAPPLICANT_TRANSLATION	CHAR	30		NOT NULL	Description of code
CAPPLICANT_DATESTAMP	DATE	7		NOT NULL	Date of last update

Table A-17. Data dictionary for CCOLLEGE code table.

```
Date: 06-SEP-1994      Time: 05:28                              TABLE: CCOLLEGE                              Page:    1
Report name: ccollege.dic                                       Owner: KOMENDA                          SQL name: dic.sql
                                                    College_Code_Translation_Table
```

Column name	Type	Width	Scale	Nulls	Column comments
CCOLLEGE_CODE	CHAR	2		NOT NULL	College code
CCOLLEGE_TRANSLATION	CHAR	30		NOT NULL	Description of code
CCOLLEGE_DATESTAMP	DATE	7		NOT NULL	Date of last update

Table A-18. Data dictionary for CDECISION code table.

```
Date: 06-SEP-1994     Time: 05:28                       TABLE: CDECISION                          Page:    1
Report name: cdecision.dic                               Owner: KOMENDA                     SQL name: dic.sql
                                             Admissions_Decision_Code_Translation_Table
```

Column name	Type	Width	Scale	Nulls	Column comments
CDECISION_CODE	CHAR	2		NOT NULL	Decision code
CDECISION_TRANSLATION	CHAR	30		NOT NULL	Description of code
CDECISION_ACCEPT_IND	CHAR	1		NULL	Indicator (Y) of accept decision
CDECISION_CANCEL_IND	CHAR	1		NULL	Indicator (Y) of canceled (inactive) decision
CDECISION_ENRL_IND	CHAR	1		NULL	Indicator (Y) that applicant expects to enroll
CDECISION_DATESTAMP	DATE	7		NOT NULL	Date of last update

Table A-19. Data dictionary for CDEGREE code table.

```
Date: 06-SEP-1994     Time: 05:28                       TABLE: CDEGREE                            Page:    1
Report name: cdegree.dic                                 Owner: KOMENDA                     SQL name: dic.sql
                                                  Degree_Code_Translation_Table
```

Column name	Type	Width	Scale	Nulls	Column comments
CDEGREE_CODE	CHAR	6		NOT NULL	degree code
CDEGREE_TRANSLATION	CHAR	30		NOT NULL	Description of code
CDEGREE_DATESTAMP	DATE	7		NOT NULL	Date of last update

Table A-20. Data dictionary for CDOCUMENT code table.

```
Date: 06-SEP-1994     Time: 05:28                       TABLE: CDOCUMENT                          Page:    1
Report name: cdocument.dic                               Owner: KOMENDA                     SQL name: dic.sql
                                                  Document_Code_Translation_Table
```

Column name	Type	Width	Scale	Nulls	Column comments
CDOCUMENT_CODE	CHAR	4		NOT NULL	Document code
CDOCUMENT_TRANSLATION	CHAR	30		NOT NULL	Description of code
CDOCUMENT_DATESTAMP	DATE	7		NOT NULL	Date of last update

Table A-21. Data dictionary for CDORM code table.

```
Date: 06-SEP-1994     Time: 05:28                    TABLE: CDORM                        Page:    1
Report name: cdorm.dic                               Owner: KOMENDA                  SQL name: dic.sql
                                          Residence_Code_Translation_Table
```

Column name	Type	Width	Scale	Nulls	Column comments
CDORM_CODE	CHAR	2		NOT NULL	Residence code
CDORM_TRANSLATION	CHAR	30		NOT NULL	Description of code
CDORM_DATESTAMP	DATE	7		NOT NULL	Date of last update

Table A-22. Data dictionary for CETHN code table.

```
Date: 06-SEP-1994     Time: 05:29                    TABLE: CETHN                        Page:    1
Report name: cethn.dic                               Owner: KOMENDA                  SQL name: dic.sql
                                            Ethnic_Code_Translation_Table
```

Column name	Type	Width	Scale	Nulls	Column comments
CETHN_CODE	CHAR	2		NOT NULL	Ethnic code
CETHN_TRANSLATION	CHAR	30		NOT NULL	Description of code
CETHN_DATESTAMP	DATE	7		NOT NULL	Date of last update

Table A-23. Data dictionary for CGENDER code table.

```
Date: 06-SEP-1994     Time: 05:29                    TABLE: CGENDER                      Page:    1
Report name: cgender.dic                             Owner: KOMENDA                  SQL name: dic.sql
                                            Gender_Code_Translation_Table
```

Column name	Type	Width	Scale	Nulls	Column comments
CGENDER_CODE	CHAR	1		NOT NULL	Gender code
CGENDER_TRANSLATION	CHAR	30		NOT NULL	Description of code
CGENDER_DATESTAMP	DATE	7		NOT NULL	Date of last update

Table A-24. Data dictionary for CINST code table.

```
Date: 06-SEP-1994      Time: 05:29                   TABLE: CINST                         Page:    1
Report name: cinst.dic                              Owner: KOMENDA                    SQL name: dic.sql
                                            Institutions_Code_Translation_Table
```

Column name	Type	Width	Scale	Nulls	Column comments
CINST_CODE	CHAR	4		NOT NULL	Institution code
CINST_NAME	CHAR	30		NOT NULL	Institution name
CINST_STREET	CHAR	30		NULL	Street address of institution
CINST_CITY	CHAR	20		NULL	City of institution
CINST_STATE	CHAR	2		NULL	State of institution
CINST_ZIP	CHAR	5		NULL	Zip code of institution
CINST_NATION	CHAR	3		NULL	Nation of institution
CINST_DATESTAMP	DATE	7		NOT NULL	Date of last update

Table A-25. Data dictionary for CLEVEL code table.

```
Date: 06-SEP-1994      Time: 05:29                   TABLE: CLEVEL                        Page:    1
Report name: clevel.dic                             Owner: KOMENDA                    SQL name: dic.sql
                                              Level_Code_Translation_Table
```

Column name	Type	Width	Scale	Nulls	Column comments
CLEVEL_CODE	CHAR	2		NOT NULL	Level code
CLEVEL_TRANSLATION	CHAR	30		NOT NULL	Description of code
CLEVEL_DATESTAMP	DATE	7		NOT NULL	Date of last update

Table A-26. Data dictionary for CMAIL code table.

```
Date: 06-SEP-1994      Time: 05:30                   TABLE: CMAIL                         Page:    1
Report name: cmail.dic                              Owner: KOMENDA                    SQL name: dic.sql
                                             Document_Code_Translation_Table.
```

Column name	Type	Width	Scale	Nulls	Column comments
CMAIL_CODE	CHAR	6		NOT NULL	Document code
CMAIL_TRANSLATION	CHAR	30		NOT NULL	Description of code
CMAIL_DATESTAMP	DATE	7		NOT NULL	Date of last update

Table A-27. Data dictionary for CMAJOR code table.

```
Date: 06-SEP-1994      Time: 05:30                          TABLE: CMAJOR                          Page:    1
Report name: cmajor.dic                                     Owner: KOMENDA                      SQL name: dic.sql
                                                     Major_Code_Translation_Table
```

Column name	Type	Width	Scale	Nulls	Column comments
CMAJOR_CODE	CHAR	6		NOT NULL	Major code
CMAJOR_TRANSLATION	CHAR	30		NOT NULL	Description of code
CMAJOR_DATESTAMP	DATE	7		NOT NULL	Date of last update

Table A-28. Data dictionary for CNATION code table.

```
Date: 06-SEP-1994      Time: 05:30                          TABLE: CNATION                         Page:    1
Report name: cnation.dic                                    Owner: KOMENDA                      SQL name: dic.sql
                                                     Nation_Code_Translation_Table
```

Column name	Type	Width	Scale	Nulls	Column comments
CNATION_CODE	CHAR	3		NOT NULL	Nation code
CNATION_TRANSLATION	CHAR	30		NOT NULL	Description of code
CNATION_DATESTAMP	DATE	7		NOT NULL	Date of last update

Table A-29. Data dictionary for CPHONE code table.

```
Date: 06-SEP-1994      Time: 05:30                          TABLE: CPHONE                          Page:    1
Report name: cphone.dic                                     Owner: KOMENDA                      SQL name: dic.sql
                                                  Phone_Type_Code_Translation_Table
```

Column name	Type	Width	Scale	Nulls	Column comments
CPHONE_CODE	CHAR	2		NOT NULL	Phone type code
CPHONE_TRANSLATION	CHAR	30		NOT NULL	Description of code
CPHONE_DATESTAMP	DATE	7		NOT NULL	Date of last update

Table A-30. Data dictionary for CSTATE code table.

```
Date: 06-SEP-1994     Time: 05:30                       TABLE: CSTATE                   Page:    1
Report name: cstate.dic                                 Owner: KOMENDA            SQL name: dic.sql
                                                 State_Code_Translation_Table
```

Column name	Type	Width	Scale	Nulls	Column comments
CSTATE_CODE	CHAR	2		NOT NULL	State type code
CSTATE_TRANSLATION	CHAR	30		NOT NULL	Description of code
CSTATE_DATESTAMP	DATE	7		NOT NULL	Date of last update

Table A-31. Data dictionary for CSTYPE code table.

```
Date: 06-SEP-1994     Time: 05:31                       TABLE: CSTYPE                   Page:    1
Report name: cstype.dic                                 Owner: KOMENDA            SQL name: dic.sql
                                             Student_Type_Code_Translation_Table
```

Column name	Type	Width	Scale	Nulls	Column comments
CSTYPE_CODE	CHAR	2		NOT NULL	Student type code
CSTYPE_TRANSLATION	CHAR	30		NOT NULL	Description of code
CSTYPE_DATESTAMP	DATE	7		NOT NULL	Date of last update

Table A-32. Data dictionary for CTERM code table.

```
Date: 06-SEP-1994     Time: 05:31                       TABLE: CTERM                    Page:    1
Report name: cterm.dic                                  Owner: KOMENDA            SQL name: dic.sql
                                                  Term_Code_Translation_Table
```

Column name	Type	Width	Scale	Nulls	Column comments
CTERM_CODE	CHAR	6		NOT NULL	Term code
CTERM_TRANSLATION	CHAR	30		NOT NULL	Description of code
CTERM_DATESTAMP	DATE	7		NOT NULL	Date of last update

Table A-33. Data dictionary for CTEST code table.

```
Date: 06-SEP-1994     Time: 05:31                  TABLE: CTEST                   Page:     1
Report name: ctest.dic                             Owner: KOMENDA             SQL name: dic.sql
                                          Test_Code_Translation_Table
```

Column name	Type	Width	Scale	Nulls	Column comments
CTEST_CODE	CHAR	5		NOT NULL	Test code
CTEST_TRANSLATION	CHAR	30		NOT NULL	Description of code
CTEST_DATESTAMP	DATE	7		NOT NULL	Date of last update

Table A-34. Data dictionary for CVISA code table.

```
Date: 06-SEP-1994     Time: 05:31                  TABLE: CVISA                   Page:     1
Report name: cvisa.dic                             Owner: KOMENDA             SQL name: dic.sql
                                          Visa_Code_Translation_Table.
```

Column name	Type	Width	Scale	Nulls	Column comments
CVISA_CODE	CHAR	2		NOT NULL	Visa type code
CVISA_TRANSLATION	CHAR	30		NOT NULL	Description of code
CVISA_DATESTAMP	DATE	7		NOT NULL	Date of last update

Appendix B

Database Simulation

Three concepts formed the basis for the database simulation used in this book: probability distributions, random number generators, and conditional relationships.

- Probability distributions: Possible values for a single data column have an associated probability of occurring. For example, three data values are possible for gender: M(ale), F(emale) or Not Reported. In the simulation performed here the probability of each value occurring was 39 percent, 45 percent and 16 percent, respectively. Changing the probability distributions changes the simulated data. Since all real databases contain messy data, the probability distributions used in this simulation contain small percentages of values that are illogical (e.g., could be attributed to data input error). Tables B–1 through B–12 list all the data columns where data was simulated using probability distributions. The tables also list how many possible values were used in the simulation of each data column.
- Random number generators: Specific data values got simulated using random number generators. Consider again the example of simulating gender. A random number between 0 and 1 was generated from a uniform distribution. That number then gets translated into a data value using the probability distribution of gender. If the number is between 0 and .39, a value of M is assigned; if it's between .39 and .84, a value of F is assigned; if it's between .84 and 1.0, then the gender is not reported and left null.

- Conditional relationships: Several data columns are conditional upon the values generated in other data columns. For example, a person's first name is conditional upon gender. The effect of this conditional relationship is that three separate probability distributions for values of first names must be used: one for males, one for females, and one for persons whose gender is not reported.

Conditional relationships can quickly become complex. For example, when simulating a sequence of events there is the logic of time—one event logically earlier than another should occur on an earlier date; an applicant for college admissions cannot logically pay an enrollment deposit before being accepted for admissions. The simulation, then, should build conditional probabilities into dates. But it does not; it didn't seem worth the extra effort. In deciding which conditional relationships to include I used a rough guideline. If the relationship reflected the conduct of a recruiting and admissions office, I built that relationship into the simulation. There's a simulated conditional relationship between student type (freshman/transfer) and school attended (high school/college), for example, because freshmen haven't previously attended a college. Tables B–1 through B–12 show all the conditional relationships built into the simulation.

I programmed the simulations with Microsoft QuickBasic for DOS, using a separate program for each data table. Conditional relationships that cut across data tables meant that the simulation had to proceed in a definite order (e.g., it wasn't possible to simulate names until the PERSON data was simulated so that a person's gender was known). An ASCII data file resulted from each simulation program. This data was loaded into ORACLE tables using the SQL*LOADER utility.

The simulation programs also included a variable for the size of the simulation. I first generated data values based on a recruit population of 1000 and loaded this data into ORACLE tables. Based on testing with this small database, I revised several of the simulation programs. I then reran the programs for a recruit population of 9000 and loaded that data as the final simulated database.

Table B–1. Data columns simulated in ACADEMIC table.

Column	No. values	Conditional upon	Note
academic_id		decision_code	1
academic_seriesno			
academic_instcode	1142	recruit_student_type	2
		address_nation	3
		address_zip	3
academic_degree		recruit_student_type	4
academic_degreedate	28		5
academic_sizeclass			6
academic_rankclass			6
academic_gpa	24	recruit_student_type	2
academic_datestamp			

Notes:

1. All applicants accepted for admissions have academic records; other recruits were randomly selected to have academic records.
2. Transfer students previously attended colleges, while freshmen attended high schools. Only transfer students have a grade point average (GPA) from a prior college attended.
3. The nation and zip code of a recruit's permanent residence were used to select an institution attended.
4. If they received a prior degree, transfer students got an Associate in Science (AS) degree while freshmen received a high school (HS) diploma.
5. Probabilities for year and month were used; days were randomly generated.
6. Percentile rank in class was simulated from a probability distribution; the class size was randomly determined, and rank in class computed from percentile rank and class size.

Table B–2. Data columns simulated in ADDRESS table.

Column	No. values	Conditional upon	Note
address_id			
address_seriesno			
address_type	3		
address_begindate	30		1
address_enddate	21		1
address_datestamp			
address_city	991		2
address_state	991		2
address_zip	991		2
address_nation	991		2
address_street1			3
address_street2			3

Notes:

1. Probabilities for year and month were used; days were randomly generated.
2. City, state, zip, and nation were simulated as a unit from a single probability distribution that contained 991 possible values.
3. Street addresses were simulated in several stages: 1) the type of street address (e.g., a basic three element address like 140 Pinto St.) was selected; 2) if the address type contained a number, that was randomly generated; 3) if the address type contained an apartment number, that was randomly generated; 4) if the address type contained a direction modifier (e.g., Northeast) that was randomly selected using a probability distribution with 8 values; 5) if the address type contained one street name, that was randomly selected from a probability distribution with 217 values; 6) if the address type contained two street names, the second name was randomly selected from a probability distribution with 157 values; and 7) the type of street (e.g., Road, Blvd) was randomly selected from a probability distribution with 15 values.

Table B–3. Data columns simulated in APPLICANT table.

Column	No. values	Conditional upon	Note
applicant_id			1
applicant_term	8		
applicant_levl			
applicant_seriesno			
applicant_recruit_term			
applicant_college	2		
applicant_dorm_intent	3		
applicant_aid_intent	2		
applicant_type	5		
applicant_student_type			
applicant_datestamp			
applicant_degree	4	applicant_college	2
applicant_major	26	applicant_college	2
applicant_appldate	38	applicant_term	3
applicant_housingdate	15	applicant_term	3

Notes:

1. About 10% of the recruits were randomly selected as applicants for admission.
2. An applicant's anticipated degree and major depend on the college (business or liberal studies) to which he or she applied.
3. The date of application and the date the housing deposit is received depend on the term for which admissions is sought.

Table B–4. Data columns simulated in DECISION table.

Column	No. values	Conditional upon	Note
decision_id			
decision_applicant_seriesno			
decicion_applicant_term			
decision_seriesno			
decision_code	48	applicant_type	1
decision_date			
decision_datestamp			

Note:

1. Decision codes depend on the type of application submitted. Decision codes for early decision applicants differ from those in the regular decision pool. Decision codes were simulated as a single string of decisions based on a probability distribution. For example, the simulated string SRACPD gets parsed to produce three decisions: SR (second reading), AC (accept) and PD (paid enrollment deposit).

Table B–5. Data columns simulated in DOCUMENT table.

Column	No. values	Conditional upon	Note
document_id			
document_applicant_seriesno			
document_applicant_term			
document_code	6		
document_required			
document_receivedate	26		1
document_datestamp			

Note:

1. Year and month were selected using a probability distribution; the days were randomly selected.

Table B–6. Data columns simulated in MAIL table.

Column	No. values	Conditional upon	Note
mail_id			
mail_code	11	applicant_id	1
		decision_code	
mail_date	30		2
mail_datestamp			

Notes:

1. Some materials get sent only to applicants; others only to accepted applicants; and others only to accepts who've paid an enrollment deposit.
2. Year and month were selected using a probability distribution; days were randomly selected.

Table B–7. Data columns simulated in NAME table.

Column	No. values	Conditional upon	Note
name_id			
name_seriesno			
name_last	379	visa_type	1
name_datestamp			
name_first	690	visa_type	2
		person_sex	2
name_middle	350	visa_type	2
		person_sex	2

Notes:

1. Last names depend on whether an applicant is a U.S. or foreign citizen.
2. First and middle names depend on whether an applicant is a U.S. or foreign citizen, and on the applicant's gender.

Table B–8. Data columns simulated in PERSON table.

Column	No. values	Conditional upon	Note
person_id			
person_birthdate	19		1
person_ethnic	8		
person_gender	3		
person_datestamp			

Note:

1. Year of birth was generated from a probability distribution. Day and month were randomly selected.

Table B–9. Data columns simulated in PHONE table.

Column	No. values	Conditional upon	Note
phone_id			
phone_seriesno			
phone_type		address_type	1
phone_status	2		
phone_area			
phone_number			
phone_address_type			
phone_address_seriesno			
phone_datestamp			

Note:

1. The type of phone depends on the type of address. For example, a residential phone was permitted at home addresses but not at business addresses.

Table B–10. Data columns simulated in RECRUIT table.

Column	No. values	Conditional upon	Note
recruit_id			
recruit_term	10		
recruit_level	2		
recruit_datestamp			
recruit_degree	5	recruit_level	1
recruit_student_type	4	recruit_level	1
recruit_recruiterid	6	recruit_level	1
recruit_major	29	recruit_level	1
recruit_datein	56	recruit_term	2

Notes:

1. A recruit's anticipated degree, student type (freshman, etc.), anticipated major, and staff contact all depend on the whether the level is undergraduate or graduate.
2. The date a recruit record is first created depends on the recruit term. The year and month were selected using a probability distribution; the days were generated randomly.

Table B–11. Data columns simulated in TEST table.

Column	No. values	Conditional upon	Note
test_id		applicant_id	1
test_type	19		
test_date	49		2
test_datestamp			
test_score	587	test_type	3

Notes:

1. The probability that an applicant has submitted standardized admissions test scores is considerably higher than for recruits.
2. Year and month of test dates were selected using a probability distribution; days were randomly generated.
3. Test scores depend on the type of test. For example, SAT scores may range between 200 and 800 while scores for the Test of Standard Written English range from 20 to 80.

Table B–12. Data columns simulated in VISA table.

Column	No. values	Conditional upon	Note
visa_id			
visa_type	7		
visa_seriesno			
visa_citizen	57		
visa_datestamp			

Appendix C

SQL Operators and Functions

Table C–1. SQL operators.

Operator	Action	General form
ARITHMETIC		
*	Multiplication	a * b
/	Division	a / b
+	Addition	a + b
-	Subtraction	a - b
( )	Control order of actions	(a + b)/c differs from a + b/c
CHARACTER		
||	Concatenate strings	a || b
COMPARISON		
=	Equal	a = b
!= or <>	Not equal	a != b
>	Greater than	a > b
<	Less than	a < b
>=	Greater than or equal to	a >= b
<=	Less than or equal to	a <= b
in	Equals any member	in (list); e.g. in (a,b,c)
not in	Not equal any member	not in (list); e.g. not in (a,b,c,d)
between	Equal to or between	between a and b means >= a and <= b
not between	Less than or greater than	not between a and b means < a or > b
like	Match pattern	like 'a%' matches any string beginning with 'a'
not like	Does not match pattern	not like 'a%' returns any string not beginning with 'a'
is null	Data value does not exist	y is null means a row contains no data in column y
is not null	Data value does exist	data value does exist in column y for selected row
any	Compare value to list	y = any (a,b,c) if y = a or y = b or y = c
all	Compare value to list	y > all (a,b,c) if y > a and y > b and y > c
exists	True if subquery returns row	where exists (subquery select)
not exists	True if no row from subquery	where not exists (subquery select)
LOGICAL		
and	Expression true if both are true	a and b
or	Expression true if either is true	a or b
not	Reverses result	see examples under comparison operators
( )	Control order of actions	(a=b or c=d) and e=f differs from a=b or c=d and e=f

Table C–1. SQL operators.

Operator	Action	General form
SET		
intersect	Return rows in both queries	select ... intersect select ...
minus	Return rows in query 1 but not 2	select ... minus select ...
union	Return rows in either query	select ... union select ...
OTHERS		
(+)	Outer join two table columns	where table1.columnX(+) = table2.columnX
*	Select all columns from a table	select * from tablename;
all	Return all rows even if duplicate	select all ... from ...
distinct	Remove duplicate rows	select distinct ... from ...

Table C–2. SQL character and numeric functions.

Function	Action	General form	Example
CHARACTER			
ascii	Collating sequence number of first char	ascii(string)	ascii('example') = ascii('e') = 101
chr	Character having ascii value n	chr(n)	chr(101) = 'e'
initcap	Capitalizes initial letter	init(string)	init('ok') = 'Ok'
instr	Position of one string in a second	instr(s1,s2,n,m) where n = start and m = occurrence	instr('oklahoma is ok','ok',1,2) = 13
length	Number of characters	length(string)	length('ok') = 2
lower	All letters lowercase	lower(string)	lower('OK') = 'ok'
lpad	Left pads a string	lpad(s1,n,s2) left pads s1 to length n with s2	lpad('ok',5,'*') = '***ok'
ltrim	Trims characters from left	ltrim(s1, s2) trims s2 from the left side of s1	ltrim(' ok',' ') = 'ok'
replace	Replace one substring with another	replace(string,s1,s2) replaces each s1 in string with s2	replace('**ok**', '**', '-') = '-ok-'
rpad	Right pads a string	rpad(s1,n,s2) right pads s1 to length n with s2	rpad('ok',5,'*') = 'ok***'
rtrim	Trim characters from right	rtrim(s1,s2) trims s2 from the right side of s1	rtrim('ok ', ' ') = 'ok'
soundex	Find words that sound alike	soundex(string)	soundex('night') includes 'knight'
substr	Returns a sub-string	substr(s,m,n) returns a substring of length n starting at character m	substr('***ok',4,2) = 'ok'
translate	Replace one character with another	translate(string,c1,c2)	translate('**ok**', '*', '#') = '##ok##'
upper	All letters uppercase	upper(string)	upper('ok') = 'OK'
NUMBER			
abs	Absolute value	abs(n)	abs(-1) = 1
ceil	Smallest integer >= n	ceil(n)	ceil(12.56) = 13
floor	Largest integer <= n	floor(n)	floor(12.56) = 12
mod	Remainder of m divided by n	mod(m,n)	mod(3,2) = 1
power	Raise number to nth power	power(m,n)	power(2,4) = 16
round	Round number m places from decimal	round(n,m)	round(12.56,1) = 12.6 round(12.56,0) = 13
sign	Distinguish negative from positive	sign(n)	sign(7) = 1; sign(-7) = -1; sign(0) = 0
sqrt	Square root of n	sqrt(n)	sqrt(49) = 7
trunc	Truncate a number to m decimal places	trunc(m,n)	trunc(12.56,1) = 12.5 trunc(12.56,0) = 12

Note: ORACLE v7 includes trigonometric functions (SIN, COS, TAN, SINH, COSH, TANH), logarithmic functions (LOG and LN), and the exponential EXP.

Table C–3. SQL date and conversion functions.

Function	Action	General form	Example
DATE			
add_months	Returns date plus n months	add_months(date, n)	add_months('15-DEC-94',2) = '15-FEB-95' add_months('31-DEC-94',2) = '28-FEB-95'
last_day	Last day of month	last_day(date)	last_day('15-DEC-94') = '31-DEC-94'
months_between	Number of months between two dates	months_between(date1, date2)	months_between('19-APR-95','15-DEC-94') = 4.129
new_time	Convert date and time between time zones	new_time(date,t1,t2)	if EST is 10am, then GMT = '15:00' = to_char(new_time(to_date('10:00','hh24:mi'),'EST','GMT'),'hh24:mi')
next_day	Date of next week day after specified date	next_day(date1,day)	next_day('15-DEC-94', 'SATURDAY') = '17-DEC-94'
round	Rounds date and time using format	round(date,format)	if date = 20-DEC-94 then round(date,'MON') = 01-JAN-95'
sysdate	Current date and time	sysdate	
trunc	Truncates date and time using format	trunc(date,format)	if date = 20-DEC-94, trunc (date,'MON') = 01-DEC-94'
CONVERSION			
to_char	Convert number to character	to_char(n,format)	to_char(12000,'$99,999') = $12,000
to_char	Convert date to character	to_char(date,format)	if d = 15-DEC-94 to_char(d,'MM/DD/YY') = 12/15/94
to_date	Convert character date to date	to_date(char,format)	if c='2/9/95' to_date(c,'DD-MON-YY') = 02-FEB-95
to_number	Convert character to number	to_number(char)	if char = '15' then 2*(to_number(char)) = 30

Notes:

1. Other conversion functions include chartorowid, convert, hextoraw, rawtohex, and rowidtochar. These are seldom used for ad hoc reporting.
2. The time zone abbreviations in new_time are listed in Table C–7.
3. Formats available for use in the round and trunc date functions are listed in Table C–6.

Table C–4. Group and miscellaneous row function.

Function	Action	General form	Example
OTHER ROW			
decode	Compare two values and return a third	decode(val,comp1,result1, comp2,result2,default)	if val = 'OK' then decode(val,'ok',1,'OK',2,'Ok',3,9) = 2 if val = 'oK' then decode(val,'ok',1,'OK',2,'Ok',3,9) = 9
greatest	Returns greatest in a list of values	greatest(val1, val2, ...)	greatest('first','last') = 'last' greatest(10,1) = 10
least	Returns least in a list of values	least(val1, val2, ...)	least('first','last') = 'first'
nvl	If value is null, return a replacement	nvl(data column, replacement)	if age is null, then nvl(age, 'unknown') = 'unknown'
user	Username of current ORACLE user	user	e.g., returns OPS$GLEWIS
GROUP			assume 4 ages = 15, 20, 25, unknown
avg	Group average ignoring nulls	avg(data column)	avg(age) = 20
count	Count of rows except when value is null	count(data column)	count(age) = 3
count(*)	Count of rows including nulls	count(*)	count(*) = 4
min	Group minimum ignoring nulls	min(data column)	min(age) = 15
max	Group maximum ignoring nulls	max(data column)	max(age) = 25
stddev	Standard deviation	stddev(data column)	stddev(age) = 5
sum	Sum of values for group, ignoring nulls	sum(data column)	sum(age) = 60
variance	Variance	variance(data column)	variance(age) = 25

Note: Other row functions include dump, uid, userenv, and vsize. These are seldom used for ad hoc reporting.

Table C–5. Number formats used in *to_char(number, format)* and SQL*PLUS ***column*** command.

Element	Action	Example	Number	Result
9	Display width determined by number of 9s	9999	123	123
0	Leading zeroes displayed	0999	123	0123
$	Dollar signed prefixed to number	$999	123	$123
B	Zero values displayed as blanks	B999	0	
E	Scientific notation (use four Es)	9.99EEEE	123	1.23E+02
MI	Minus (-) displayed after negative numbers	999MI	-123	123-
PR	Negative numbers in <> brackets	999PR	-123	<123>
V	Number times 10n, where n = number of 9s after the V	9999V9	123	1230
comma	Place comma	9,999	1234	1,234
period	Place decimal point	999.99	123	123.00

Table C–6. Date formats used in *to_char(date, format)* and *to_date(char, format)*

Element		Action	Result (assume 2:15 pm 15-DEC-94)
DDD	*	Day of year	349
DD	*	Day of month	15
D	*	Day of week	5
DAY	*	Name of day (9 characters with blanks)	THURSDAY
DY	*	Name of day (3 character abbreviation)	THU
MM	*	Number of month	12
MONTH	*	Name of month (9 characters with blanks)	DECEMBER
MON	*	Name of month (3 character abbreviation)	DEC
YYYY or SYYYY	*	Year in 4-digits; "-" prefix on BC date if SYYYY	1994
YYY	*	Last 3 digits of year	994
YY	*	Last 2 digits of year	94
Y	*	Last 1 digit of year	4
YEAR	*	Year spelled out	NINETEEN-NINETY-FOUR
SYEAR	*	Year spelled out; BC date prefixed with "-"	NINETEEN-NINETY-FOUR
WW	*	Week of year (week 1 = days 1 - 7 of year)	50
W	*	Week of month (week 1 = days 1 - 7)	3
Q	*	Quarter of year	4
CC or SCC	*	Century; if SCC then "-" prefixes BC date	20
BC or AD		BC or AD indicator	15-DEC-94 AD if 'DD-MON-YY AD'
B.C. or A.D.		B.C. or A.D. indicator	15-DEC-94 A.D. if 'DD-MON-YY A.D.'
J	*	Julian date (days since Jan 1, 4712 BC)	2449702
/ or : or etc		Punctuation included in result	12/15/94 if 'MM/DD/YY'
"..."		String included in result	Dec 15 of 1994 if 'Mon DD "of" YYYY'
FM		Suppresses blank padding or leading zeroes	15-DEC-94 if 'fmMonth DD, YYYY'
HH or HH12	*	Hour of day (1-12)	02
HH24	*	Hour of day (0-23)	14
MI	*	Minutes	14:15 if 'hh24:mi'
SS		Seconds	14:15:00 if 'hh24:mi:ss'
SSSSS		Seconds since midnight	51300
AM or PM		AM or PM indicator	02:15 pm if 'hh:mi am'
A.M. or P.M.		A.M. or P.M. indicator	02:15 p.m. if 'hh:mi a.m.'

Notes:

1. Capitalization can be changed on appropriate formats by using variations of the elements listed. For example, if the month is December then 'MON' = 'DEC', 'Mon' = 'Dec', and 'mon' = 'dec'.
2. Elements marked with "*" can be used as formats in the *round* or *trunc* date functions.

Table C–7. Time zone abbreviations used in *new_time* function.

Element	Description
ADT	Atlantic Daylight Time
AST	Atlantic Standard Time
BDT	Bering Daylight Time
BST	Bering Standard Time
CDT	Central Daylight Time
CST	Central Standard Time
EDT	Eastern Daylight Time
EST	Eastern Standard Time
GMT	Greenwich Mean Time
HDT	Alaska-Hawaii Daylight Time
HST	Alaska-Hawaii Standard Time
MDT	Mountain Daylight Time
MST	Mountain Standard Time
NST	Newfoundland Standard Time
PDT	Pacific Daylight Time
PST	Pacific Standard Time
YDT	Yukon Daylight Time
YST	Yukon Standard Time

Appendix D

Scripts for Reporting Tools

Owners

overview.sql

```
/*
        sql:    overview.sql
        date:   22-mar-1994
        author: glewis
        purpose: database tables by owner
*/
set termout off
start &&object_dir\clears
start &&object_dir\hpprintr
start &&object_dir\date
start &&object_dir\time
start &&object_dir\owncol
start &&object_dir\escape
ttitle left xEscape skip 1-
        'Database tables and views by owner' -
        right 'Report name: overview.lis' skip 1 -
        left 'Date: ' xDate '     Time: ' xTime -
        right 'Page: ' format 999 sql.pno skip 2;

spool overview.lis
        start xover
        start &&object_dir\reset
spool off

start &&object_dir\clears
start &&object_dir\screen
```

xover.sql

```
/*
        sql:    xover.sql
        date:   17-apr-1994
        author: glewis
        purpose: sub-program for overview.sql
*/
break on report
compute sum of count on report
select
        owner,
        count(*) "count"
from
        all_catalog
where
        table_type in ('TABLE','VIEW')
group by owner
order by 1;
```

Tables

tables.sql

```
/*
        sql:    tables.sql
        date:   22-mar-1994
        author: glewis
        purpose: list of tables for a specified owner
*/
set termout off
start &&object_dir.\clears
start &&object_dir.\hpprintr
start &&object_dir.\date
start &&object_dir.\time
start &&object_dir.\owncol
start &&object_dir.\escape

start getowner
start definvar

ttitle left xEscape skip 1 -
        'Tables for owner: ' xOwner -
        right 'Page: ' format 999 sql.pno skip 1 -
        left 'Date: ' xDate '     Time: ' xTime -
        right 'Report name: ' xReport skip 1 -
        right 'SQL name:     tables.sql' skip 2;

spool &&xReport
        start xtables
        start &&object_dir.\reset
```

```
spool off

start &&object_dir.\clears
start &&object_dir.\screen
```

xtables.sql

```
column comments format a85 word_wrap
select
        t.table_name "name",
        t.table_type "type",
        t.owner "owner",
        c.comments "comments"
from
        all_tab_comments c,
        all_catalog t
where
        t.owner = '&&xOwner'
        and c.owner = t.owner
                and c.table_name = t.table_name
                and c.table_type = t.table_type
order by 1;
```

getowner.sql

```
set verify off
set termout on
accept Owner prompt 'Enter owner of tables (eg, KOMENDA): '
set termout off
```

definvar.sql

```
set feedback off
set heading off
column NextLine newline
ttitle off
set linesize 300
spool defines.sql
        select 'define xOwner =', upper('&&Owner'),
                'define xReport =' NextLine, '&&Owner'||'.lis'
        from dual;
spool off
start defines
set linesize 160
ttitle on
set heading on
set feedback on
```

Data dictionaries

dic.sql

```
set termout off
/*
        sql:     dictionary.sql
        date:    21-mar-1994
        author:  glewis
        purpose: produce a dictionary of data columns in a table
*/
set termout off
start &&object_dir\clears
start &&object_dir\hpprintr
start &&object_dir\date
start &&object_dir\time
start &&object_dir\owncol
start &&object_dir\escape

set verify off
set termout on
accept table_name prompt 'Table or view name (eg, RECRUIT): '
accept owner_name prompt 'Owner (eg, KOMENDA): '
set termout off

set feedback off
set heading off
column NextLine newline
ttitle off
set linesize 300
spool defines.sql
        select 'define xTable = ', upper('&&table_name'),
               'define xOwner = ' NextLine, upper('&&owner_name'),
                'define xReport = ' NextLine, '&&table_name'||'.dic'
        from dual;
        select 'define xTable_comment = ',
                decode(comments, null, 'No_description_available',
                        translate(comments,' ','_')),
               'define xType = ' NextLine, table_type
        from all_tab_comments
        where
                owner = upper('&&owner_name')
                and table_name = upper('&&table_name');
spool off
set linesize 160

ttitle on
start defines
define xLine =
'=====================================================================================
================================================================'
```

```
ttitle  left xEscape skip 1 -
left 'Date: ' xDate '      Time: ' xTime -
center xType ': ' xTable -
right 'Page: ' format 999 sql.pno skip 1 -
left 'Report name: ' xReport -
center 'Owner: ' xOwner -
right 'SQL name: dic.sql' skip 1 -
center xTable_comment skip 2 -
left 'Column Name                      Type    Width   Scale    Nulls' -
'    Column comments' skip 1 -
left xLine skip 1;

set recsep off
spool &&xReport
   start xdiction
   start &&object_dir\reset
spool off

set heading on
set feedback on
start &&object_dir\clears
start &&object_dir\screen
```

xdiction.sql

```
column name format a31
column type format a6
column width format 99999
column scale format 99999
column nulls format a9
column comments format a90 word_wrap
select
        t.column_name "name",
        t.data_type "type",
        decode(t.data_type, 'NUMBER', t.data_precision, t.data_length) "width",
        t.data_scale "scale",
        decode(t.nullable, 'N', 'NOT NULL', 'Y', 'NULL') "nulls",
        c.comments "comments"
from
        all_col_comments c,
        all_tab_columns t
where
        t.owner = '&&xOwner'
        and t.table_name = '&&xTable'
        and c.owner = t.owner
        and c.table_name = t.table_name
        and c.column_name = t.column_name
order by column_id;
```

Indexes

indexes.sql

```
/*
        sql:    indexes.sql
        date:   13-jul-1994
        author: glewis
        purpose: report of all indexes for tables with given owner
*/
set termout off
start &&object_dir\clears
start &&object_dir\hpprintr
start &&object_dir\date
start &&object_dir\time
start &&object_dir\owncol
start &&object_dir\escape

set verify off
set termout on
accept owner_name prompt 'Owner (eg, KOMENDA): '
set termout off

set feedback off
set heading off
column NextLine newline
ttitle off
set linesize 300
spool defines.sql
        select 'define xOwner = ' NextLine, upper('&&owner_name')
        from dual;
spool off
set linesize 160
ttitle on
set heading on
set feedback on
start defines

ttitle left xEscape skip 1-
        'Indexes on tables owned by: ' xOwner -
        right 'Page: ' format 999 sql.pno skip 1 -
        left 'Date: ' xDate '     Time: ' xTime -
        right 'Report name: indexes.lis' skip 1 -
        right 'SQL name:    indexes.sql' skip 2;

spool indexes.lis
        start xindexes
        start &&object_dir\reset
spool off

start &&object_dir\clears
start &&object_dir\screen
```

xindexes.sql

```
column uniqueness format a10
break on table on index on uniqueness skip 1
select
        a.table_name "table",
        a.index_name "index",
        b.uniqueness "uniqueness",
        a.column_name "column",
        a.column_position "position"
from
        all_ind_columns a,
        all_indexes b
where
        b.table_owner = '&&xOwner'
        and a.index_owner = b.owner
                and a.index_name = b.index_name
                and a.table_owner = b.table_owner
                and a.table_name = b.table_name
order by 1, 2, 5;
```

Utility programs

clears.sql

```
/*
        sql:    clears.sql
        date:   08-mar-1994
        author: glewis
        purpose: to reset breaks, computes and columns
*/
clear breaks
clear computes
clear columns
```

date.sql

```
/*
        sql:    date.sql
        date:   08-mar-1994
        author: glewis
        purpose: to capture today's date for use in report titles
*/
break on today
column today new_value xDate
select to_char(sysdate, 'dd-MON-yyyy') today from dual;
clear breaks
```

escape.sql

```
define xEscape = ECEEC&l1OEC(s16.66HEC&a10l176M
define xReset = ECE
```

hpprintr.sql

```
/*
        sql:    hpprinter.sql
        date:   08-mar-1994
        author: glewis
        purpose: to set parameters for spooling to HP Laserjet
*/

set pause off
set pagesize 45
set linesize 160
set echo off
set timing off
set escape #
set feedback on
set ttitle on
```

login.sql

```
set termout off
/*
        sql:    login.sql
        date:   18-apr-1994
        author: glewis
        purpose: to customize sql*plus environment at time of each login
*/
define object_dir = c:\oracle6\metasql\objects
define _editor = me
start &&object_dir\screen
set termout on
```

owncol.sql

```
/*
        sql:    owncol.sql
        date:   08-mar-1994
        author: glewis
        purpose: to set column formats for report printing
*/

/* ACADEMIC */
column academic_id heading 'id' format 99999
column academic_instcode heading 'inst|code'
column academic_degree heading 'degree'
column academic_degreedate heading 'degree|date'
column academic_sizeclass heading 'size|class' format 99990
column academic_rankclass heading 'rank|class' format 99990
column academic_gpa heading 'gpa'
column academic_seriesno heading 'inst|seriesno'

/* ADDRESS */
column address_id heading 'id' format 99999
column address_type heading 'addr|type' format a4
column address_seriesno heading 'address|seriesno'
```

```
column address_begindate heading 'begin|date'
column address_enddate heading 'end|date'
column address_city heading 'city'
column address_state heading 'state' format a5
column address_zip heading 'zip'
column address_nation heading 'nation' format a6
column address_street1 heading 'street1'
column address_street2 heading 'street2'
column address_datestamp heading 'datestamp'

/* APPLICANT */
column applicant_id heading 'id' format 99999
column applicant_term heading 'term'
column applicant_seriesno heading 'no.' format 999
column applicant_level heading 'level' format a5
column applicant_recruit_term heading 'recruit|term' format a7
column applicant_college heading coll format a4
column applicant_dorm_intent heading 'dorm|intent' format a6
column applicant_aid_intent heading 'aid|intent' format a6
column applicant_type heading 'appl|type' format a4
column applicant_student_type heading 'student|type' format a7
column applicant_degree heading 'appl|degree'
column applicant_major heading 'appl|major' format a5
column applicant_appldate heading 'appl|date'
column applicant_housingdate heading 'housing|date'

/* DECISION */
column decision_id heading 'id' format 99999
column decision_applicant_term heading 'appl|term'
column decision_code heading 'decsn|code' format a5
column decision_date heading 'decision|date'
column decision_applicant_seriesno heading 'applicant|seriesno'
column decision_seriesno heading 'decision|seriesno'
column decision_datestamp heading 'datestamp'

/* DOCUMENT */
column document_id heading 'id' format 99999
column document_applicant_term heading 'appl|term'
column document_code heading 'doc|code'
column document_required heading 'required' format a8
column document_receivedate heading 'receive|date'

/* MAIL */
column mail_id heading 'id' format 99999
column mail_code heading 'mail|code'
column mail_date heading 'mail|date'

/* NAME */
column name_id heading 'id' format 99999
column name_last heading 'last'
column name_first heading 'first'
column name_middle heading 'middle'

/* PERSON */
column person_id heading 'id' format 99999
column person_birthdate heading 'birth|date'
```

```
column person_ethnic heading 'ethnic' format a6
column person_gender heading 'sex' format a3

/* PHONE */
column phone_id heading 'id' format 99999
column phone_type heading 'phone|type' format a5
column phone_status heading 'status' format a6
column phone_area heading 'area' format a4
column phone_number heading 'number'
column phone_address_type heading 'phone|address|type' format a7
column phone_seriesno heading 'phone|seriesno'
column phone_address_seriesno heading 'phone|address|seriesno'
column phone_datestamp heading 'datestamp'

/* RECRUIT */
column recruit_id heading 'id' format 99999
column recruit_term heading 'term'
column recruit_level heading 'level' format a5
column recruit_degree heading 'recr|degree' format a6
column recruit_student_type heading 'student|type' format a7
column recruit_recruiterid heading 'recruiter' format a9
column recruit_major heading 'recr|major' format a5
column recruit_datein heading 'date|recruit'

/* TEST */
column test_id heading 'id' format 99999
column test_type heading 'test|type'
column test_date heading 'test|date'
column test_score heading 'test|score'
column test_datestamp heading 'datestamp'

/* VISA */
column visa_id heading 'id' format 99999
column visa_type heading 'visa|type' format a4
column visa_citizen heading 'citizen' format a7

/* cdecision code table */
column cdecision_code heading 'decision|code' format a8
column cdecision_translation heading 'decision'
column cdecision_accept_ind heading 'accept|ind' format a6
column cdecision_cancel_ind heading 'cancel|ind' format a6
column cdecision_enrl_ind heading 'enrl|ind' format a6
column cdecision_datestamp heading 'datestamp'

/* cdocument code table */
column cdocument_code heading 'doc|code' format a4
column cdocument_translation heading 'document'
column cdocument_datestamp heading 'datestamp'
```

```
/* cinst code table */
column cinst_name heading 'inst_name'
column cinst_street heading 'inst_street'
column cinst_city heading 'inst_city'
column cinst_state heading 'inst|state' format a5
column cinst_zip heading 'inst|zip'
column cinst_nation heading 'nation' format a6

/* clevel code table */
column clevel_code heading 'level|code' format a5
column clevel_translation heading 'level'
column clevel_datestamp heading 'datestamp'

/* cmail code table */
column cmail_code heading 'mail|code' format a6
column cmail_translation heading 'mail'
column cmail_date heading 'mail_date'

/* cterm code table */
column cterm_code heading 'term|code'
column cterm_translation heading 'term'
column cterm_datestamp heading 'datestamp'

/* cvisa code table */
column cvisa_code heading 'visa|code' format a4
column cvisa_translation heading 'visa'
column cvisa_datestamp heading 'datestamp'

/* caddress code table */
column caddress_code heading 'address|code' format a7
column caddress_translation heading 'address'
column caddress_datestamp heading 'datestamp'

/* cethn code table */
column cethn_code heading 'ethnic|code' format a6
column cethn_translation heading 'ethnic status'
column cethn_datestamp heading 'datestamp'

/* cphone code table */
column cphone_code heading 'phone|code' format a5
column cphone_translation heading 'phone'
column cphone_datestamp heading 'datestamp'

/* ctest code table */
column ctest_code heading 'test|code'
column ctest_translation heading 'test'
column ctest_datestamp heading 'datestamp'

/* savelist table */
column savelist_id heading 'id'
column savelist_rownum heading 'rownum'

/* constructed */
column sort_name format a25
column age format 999
column pctrank heading 'pct|rank' format 99999
```

```
column cszn format a30
column intl format a4
column initials_name format a25
column reminder1 heading 'reminder|monday|appl+1mon'
column reminder2 heading 'reminder|7wks|appldate'
column testcat heading 'test|range' format a8
column satc format 99999
column majorcat heading 'major|dept' format a10
```

reset.sql

```
ttitle left xReset;
column xCol noprint
set feedback off
select 'x' "xCol" from dual;
```

screen.sql

```
/*
        sql:    screen.sql
        date:   17-apr-1994
        author: glewis
        purpose: to set various screen characteristics when reporting to
                 monitor
*/
set pause "ENTER to continue ..."
set pause on
set linesize 80
set pagesize 24
set newpage 1
ttitle off
set escape off
set termout on
set echo on
```

time.sql

```
/*
        sql:    time.sql
        date:   08-mar-1994
        author: glewis
        purpose: to capture present time for use in report titles
*/
break on now
column now new_value xTime
select to_char(sysdate, 'hh24:mi') now from dual;
clear breaks
```

Appendix E

SQL*PLUS Commands and Options

Table E–1. Summary of SQL*PLUS commands.

Command	General form	Effect
@	@filename	Runs the command file "filename"
/	/	Runs the SQL command currently in the buffer
ACCEPT	ACCEPT variable options	Stores input in a user defined variable
APPEND	APPEND text	Adds "text" to end of current buffer line
BREAK	BREAK ON element actions	Determines report formatting when "element" changes
BTITLE	BTITLE print_specs options	Specifies title appearing at bottom of each report page
CHANGE	CHANGE /old/new	Changes "old" text to "new" text in current buffer line
CLEAR	CLEAR options	Resets current value for options (breaks, columns, etc.)
COLUMN	COLUMN name options	Specifies report column characteristics
COMPUTE	COMPUTE function OF element1 ON element2	Computes summary (eg, average) of "element1" breaking on "element2"
CONNECT	CONNECT username/password @db_specs	Connects a username to ORACLE database
COPY	COPY options	Copies results of a query to a table
DEFINE	DEFINE variable = text	Creates a user defined variable with a CHAR value of "text"
DEL	DEL	Deletes current buffer line
DESCRIBE	DESCRIBE owner.name	Lists data columns in table or view called "name" and owned by "owner"
DISCONNECT	DISCONNECT	Disconnects user from Oracle but does not exit SQL*PLUS
EDIT	EDIT filename	Calls default operating system editor and loads "filename"
EXIT	EXIT	Exit from SQL*PLUS environment
GET	GET filename	Loads a file called "filename" into the SQL buffer
HOST	HOST command	Executes a host operating system command from within SQL*PLUS
INPUT	INPUT text	Adds one or more lines of "text" after the current buffer line
LIST	LIST [n m]	Lists buffer lines n to m. Lists all lines if n and m are omitted
PAUSE	PAUSE text	Pauses, prompts the user with "text," and awaits a Return to continue
PROMPT	PROMPT text	Sends "text" to user's screen
REMARK	REMARK text	Denotes a comment line in a command file
RUN	RUN	Executes the SQL command in the buffer
RUNFORM	RUNFORM form_name	Executes a SQL*FORMS application from within SQL*PLUS
SAVE	SAVE filename options	Saves SQL command in the buffer to a file called "filename"

Table E–1. Summary of SQL*PLUS commands.

Command	General form	Effect
SET	SET system_variable value	Changes SQL*PLUS environment characteristics
SHOW	SHOW option	Lists the setting of an SQL*PLUS environment variable
SPOOL	SPOOL filename options	Stores report output in a file called "filename"
SQLPLUS	SQLPLUS options	Starts SQL*PLUS from the operating system
START	START filename arguments	Executes a command file, passing data values to parameters in the file
TIMING	TIMING START name/STOP/SHOW	Creates, stops, or displays timing area with performance data
TTITLE	TTITLE print_specs options	Specifies title appearing at top of each report page
UNDEFINE	UNDEFINE variable	Deletes a user-defined variable created with DEFINE

Table E–2. Options available for common SQL*PLUS commands.

Command/Options	Values	Effect
ACCEPT variable options		
NUMBER/CHAR	NUMBER	Variable must be a number
	CHAR	Variable must be a character datatype
PROMPT text/NOPROMPT	PROMPT text	Displays "text" before accepting user input for variable
	NOPROMPT	No prompting message displayed (the default)
HIDE	HIDE	User input for variable not displayed on screen
BREAK ON element actions		
element	column_name	Performs action whenever value of the data column changes
	expression	Performs action whenever the value of a user-defined *select* expression changes. Most conveniently used by giving the expression an alias in the *select* clause
	ROW	Performs an action after each report row; "break on row skip 1" double-spaces a report
	REPORT	Used with the ***compute*** command to print summaries at the end of a report
SKIP n/PAGE	n	Skip n lines before printing
	PAGE	Skip to a new page before printing

(Continued)

Table E–2. Options available for common SQL*PLUS commands.

Command/Options	Values	Effect
BREAK ON element actions		
NODUP/DUP	NODUP	Does not print break column value if it is identical to the value in the preceeding row. This is the default
	DUP	Prints the break column value for each report row
BTITLE (or TTITLE) print_specs options		
print_specs (one or more)	COL n	Indents to print at position n
	SKIP n	Skips to the start of a new line n times
	TAB n	Skips forward or backward n spaces
	LEFT	Left align in current line of title
	CENTER	Center in current line of title
	RIGHT	Right align in current line of title
	BOLD	Bold print
	FORMAT format	Sets a format model for title elements (e.g., page numbers)
text	text	Text of title, in single quotes
variable	user	Displays user defined variable in title
	SQL.LNO	Displays current line number
	SQL.PNO	Displays current page number
	SQL.USER	Displays current username
ON/OFF	ON	Turns on display of title (the default)
	OFF	Suppresses display of title
CLEAR options		
Any combination of values	BREAKS	Clears breaks set with the ***break*** command
	BUFFER	Clears the SQL buffer
	COLUMNS	Resets column display characteristics set with ***column*** command
	COMPUTES	Clears all computes set with the ***compute*** command
	SCREEN	Clears the monitor screen
	SQL	Clears the SQL buffer
	TIMING	Deletes timining areas set with the ***timing*** command

Table E–2. Options available for common SQL*PLUS commands.

Command/Options	Values	Effect
COLUMN name options		
name	column_name	Specifies the data column
	expression	Specifies the expression
	alias	Specifies an alias
Any combination of values	ALIAS alias	Assigns the column an alias named "alias"
	CLEAR	Resets column display attributes to the default values
	FOLD_AFTER n	Inserts a carriage return after each row in the column
	FOLD_BEFORE n	Inserts a carriage return before each row in the column
	FORMAT format	Determines the display format for the column
	HEADING text	Specifies the column heading. Enclose in single quotes
	NEWLINE	Identical to FOLD_BEFORE n
	NEW_VALUE var	Specifies a variable containing the data column value. Useful for displaying column values in top title
	NULL char	Specifies text to print when null values occur
	OLD_VALUE var	Specifies a variable containing the data column value. Useful for displaying column values in bottom title
JUSTIFY L/C/R	LEFT	Left align column heading
	CENTER	Center column heading
	RIGHT	Right align column heading
PRINT/NOPRINT	PRINT	Print the column. This is the default
	NOPRINT	Suppresses printing the column
ON/OFF	ON	Sets column display attributes on. This is the default
	OFF	Turns off the column display attributes without resetting
WRAP/WORD/TRUN	WRAPPED	Wraps CHAR string to next line if longer than column width
	WORD	Wraps CHAR string at word breaks
	TRUNCATED	Truncates a CHAR string at end of the column width

(Continued)

Table E–2. Options available for common SQL*PLUS commands.

Command/Options	Values	Effect
COMPUTE function OF element1 ON element2		
One or more function	AVG	Average of non-null NUMBER values
	COUNT	Counts non-null values of all datatypes
	MAXIMUM	Maximum of non-null NUMBER or CHAR values
	MINIMUM	Minimum of non-null NUMBER or CHAR values
	NUMBER	Count of rows, including null values, for all datatypes
	STD	Standard deviation of non-null NUMBER values
	SUM	Sum of non-null NUMBER values
	VARIANCE	Variance of non-null NUMBER values
OF elements	column_name	Specifies the data column to use in the computation The data column must appear in the *select* clause
	expression	Specifies an expression to use in the computation Most conveniently referenced with an alias given to the expression in the *select* clause
ON elements	column_name	The computation is printed whenever the value of the specified data column changes
	expression	Prints the computation whenever the expression breaks
	alias	Prints the computation whenever an alias breaks
	ROW	Prints the computation for each row
	REPORT	Prints the computation at the end of the report
SAVE filename options		
CRE/REP/APP	CREATE	Creates a file with buffer contents
	REPLACE	Replaces an existing file with buffer contents
	APPEND	Appends buffer contents to end of existing file
SHOW option		
Any combination of values	system_var	Current value of system variable set with ***set*** command
	ALL	List all settings
	BTITLE	Current btitle definition

Table E–2. Options available for common SQL*PLUS commands.

Command/Options	Values	Effect
SHOW option *(continued)*		
	LNO	Current line number in display or spooled output
	PNO	Current page number
	RELEASE	Release number of ORACLE RDMS
	SPOOL	Shows if output is being spooled
	TTITLE	Current ttitle definition
	USER	Current username used to access SQL*PLUS
SPOOL filename options		
OFF/OUT	OFF	Stops spooling
	OUT	Stops spooling and prints output at default printer

Table E–3. Common system variables used in the ***set*** command.

General form: SET system_variable value

System variable	Default	Optional values	Effect
CONCAT	on .	on/off, ./c	Defines end of substitution variable in a string (e.g., &y is substitution var in "&y.more")
DEFINE	on &	on/off, &/c	Character prefixing substitution variables
ECHO	off	on/off	Lists commands in ***start*** file as executed
EMBEDDED	off	on/off	"Off" forces each report to start on a new page
ESCAPE	off \	on/off, \ or c	Used in front of a substitution character if it validly appears as an ordinary char in a string
FEEDBACK	on	on/off	Displays number of rows returned in a query
HEADING	on	on/off	"On" prints column headings in a report
HEADSEP	on |	on/off, | or c	Divides column headings into two or more lines
LINESIZE	80	n	Maximum display characters on a line

Table E–3. Common system variables used in the ***set*** command.

General form: SET system_variable value

System variable	Default	Optional values	Effect
NEWPAGE	1	n	Blank lines printed before top title on each page ("0" sends a formfeed between pages)
NULL	"" (blank)	text	Display when ***select*** returns null value
NUMFORMAT	""	format	Default format for displaying numbers
NUMWIDTH	10	n	Width for displaying numbers
PAGESIZE	14	n	Number of lines from top title to page bottom
PAUSE	off none	on/off, text/none	Controls scrolling of terminal
RECSEP	wrap	wrap/each/off	Displays a line of RECSEPCHAR ("wrap" displays only after wrapped lines)
RECSEPCHAR	' ' (space)	space/c	Character used with RECSEP
SHOWMODE	on	on/off	"Off" suppresses display of changes made to system variables
SPACE	1	n	Number of spaces between report columns
SQLCASE	mixed	mix/lower/upper	Converts case of commands before execution.
SQLPROMPT	SQL>	text	SQL*PLUS command prompt
SQLTERMINATOR	on ;	on/off, ;/c	Character used to end and execute SQL
SUFFIX	sql	sql/text	Default file suffix
TAB		on/off	"On" uses the TAB character (default is system dependent)
TERMOUT	on	on/off	"Off" suppresses output display from start file
TIME	off	on/off	"On" displays current time at SQL prompt
TIMING	off	on/off	Controls display of timing statistics
TRIMOUT	on	on/off	"On" if trailing blanks allowed on display line
UNDERLINE	on -	on/off, -/c	Character used to underline column headings
VERIFY	on	on/off	"On" shows command with substitution variable replaced with a value
WRAP	on	on/off	"On" wraps data value to next line if too large for display column

Note: "/" means "or" (e.g., "on/off" means "on or off"), "c" means a character, and "n" a number.

References and Additional Reading

References

Much of the material in *ORACLE Reporting* originated in the ad hoc queries made by administrative end-users at Bentley College—queries in which the author was privileged to participate. During the preparation of this book, however, several sources were consulted regarding specific points of information. A listing of those sources appears below.

Carter, John. *Programming in SQL with ORACLE, INGRES, and dBASE IV.* Englewood Cliffs, NJ: PTR Prentice-Hall, 1993.

Corrigan, Peter and Gurry, Mark. *ORACLE Performance Tuning.* Sebastopol, CA: O'Reilly & Associates, Inc., 1993.

Ek, Torsten. "Working with Objects." *ORACLE Magazine* 8:40-44.

Koch, George. *ORACLE: The Complete Reference.* Berkeley, CA: Osborne McGraw-Hill, 1993.

Oracle Corporation. *SQL*PLUS User's Guide and Reference.* Redwood City, CA: Oracle Corporation, various editions.

Oracle Corporation. *SQL Language Reference Manual.* Redwood City, CA: Oracle Corporation, various editions.

Additional Reading

Several fine books on SQL*PLUS, SQL, and ORACLE are available. While not exhaustive, those listed below provide variety in breadth and depth of topics covered.

Carter, John. *Programming in SQL with ORACLE, INGRES, and dBASE IV*. Englewood Cliffs, NJ: PTR Prentice-Hall, 1993.

Corrigan, Peter and Gurry, Mark. *ORACLE Performance Tuning*. Sebastopol, CA: O'Reilly & Associates, Inc., 1993.

Hartley, Tim and Martyn, Tim. *ORACLE/SQL: A Professional Programmer's Guide*. New York: McGraw-Hill, Inc., 1992.

Hursch, Jack L. and Hursch, Carolyn J. *Working with ORACLE*. Windcrest Books, 1989.

Koch, George. *ORACLE: The Complete Reference*. Berkeley, CA: Osborne McGraw-Hill, 1993.

Sayles, Jonathan S. *How to Use ORACLE SQL*PLUS*. Wellesley, MA: QED Information Sciences, Inc., 1991.

van der Lans, Rick F. *The SQL Guide to ORACLE*. Wokingham, England: Addision-Wesley Publishing Company, 1992.

Wellesley Software. *Learning Advanced SQL*. Englewood Cliffs, NJ: Prentice-Hall, 1992.

Index

Symbol

Numeric

A

B

About the Author

When it comes to organizational databases, Gary Lewis considers himself an end-user—someone concerned about wringing useful information from the data. For nearly twenty years he's practiced this craft doing policy research in colleges and universities. He presently works at Bentley College where he's fielded thousands of ad hoc queries on operational, policy, and strategic issues. He currently designs and develops information systems used by college decision-makers. He has a doctorate in educational research and planning, has written books and articles on educational research methods, and has served on the faculties at the Harvard Graduate School of Education and SUNY/Albany. He also spent two years teaching mathematics and science at Komenda Teacher Training College in Komenda, Ghana. He firmly believes that organizational databases must become easier to use, so that people without programming background can interact almost conversationally with them.

Colophon

Text and figures in the manuscript were prepared using Microsoft Word 6.0 for Windows. Pages were composed using Ventura Publisher 4.2 with Minion as the text type, Stone Sans as the display type, and Letter Gothic Bold as the computer text type in the figures. The book was delivered to the printer as electronic prepress files. Pages were imposed electronically and plate-ready film was output.

Book designer and Compositor: Debra Marvin, Illuminator Desktop Publishing
Copy editor: Julie Sullivan
Cover designer: Rodelinde Albrecht
Cover printer: New England Book Components, Inc.
Indexer: Gary Lewis
Interior illustrator: Heather Lewis
Printer: Braun-Brumfield, Inc.

A Ghanaian theme runs through much of the book design. The brightly colored textured material on the cover was scanned from kente cloth, originally the cloth of Asante kings but now widely worn for ceremonial occasions. The symbols on the cover and in each chapter are adinkra symbols. They, too, commonly appear on cloth worn by Ghanaians for special events. The symbols are imprinted using a crafted wooden die dipped in ink and hand-pressed to the cloth. Each adinkra symbol has a name and a meaning. The following is a list of the symbols used in this book:

Cover: Aya (ay YAH). The fern, a symbol of independence, defiance, and fearlessness.

Preface: A star, taken from the proverb “A child of the Supreme Being, I do not depend on myself. My illumination is only a reflection of His.”

Chapter 1: Dweninimu aben (jen nee nee MOO AH bay). The ram’s horns, from the proverb “It is the heart and not the horns that leads a ram to bully.”

Chapter 2: Kojo Baiden (koh JOH BAY den). Symbol of the universe, combining the rays of the sun, the crescent moon, and the Asante stool.

Chapter 3: Binkabi (been KAH bee). Symbol of unity, from the proverb “Bite not one another.”

Chapter 4: Mmra Krado (mm RAH KRAH doh). The seal of law and order, a symbol of the authority of the Asante court.

Chapter 5: Sunsum (SOON SOOM). Symbol of the soul, implying purity and spirituality.

Chapter 6: Gyawn Atiko (JOW en ah TEEK koh). The hairstyle of Gyawu, a warrior chief of the Asante; symbol of courage and determination.

Chapter 7: Duafe (dee AH fih). Symbol of the wooden comb, representing several positive qualities of women: patience, fondness, and caring.

Chapter 8: Adinkrahene (a DINK krah HAY nay). "Chief of adinkra," or, the most important adinkra.

Chapter 9: Afuntun mmireku Denkyem mmireku (ah FOON toon mir eh KOO den CHEM mir eh KOO). Two crocodiles share the same stomach—a symbol of unity between different groups of people.

Chapter 10: Gye Nyame (jee nyah MAY). A symbol of the power of God.

Chapter 11: Fihankra (fee HAHN krah). A compound house, symbol of security and togetherness.

Chapter 12: Musuyidie (moo soo EE DEE YEH). Symbol of a charm that removes evil or promotes good luck.

Chapter 13: Epa (eh PAH). Handcuffs, the symbol of slavery, indicating that the law does not always respect people.

Chapter 14: Osram (OS ram). The moon—symbol of the positive female qualities of love and kindness.

Appendix A: Aya (ay YAH). The fern, a symbol of independence, defiance, and fearlessness.

Appendix B: The symbol of forgiveness.

Appendix C: Kuntinkantan (Koon tin KAHN TAHN). A symbol from the proverb, "Do not boast, do not be arrogant."

Appendix D: A symbol for the proverb "You can always undo your mistakes."

Appendix E: Symbol of knowledge and wisdom.

References: Kyekye ko aware. The star gets married to the moon, a symbol of faithfulness, love, kindness, marriage, and togetherness.

For more information about adinkra symbols, see Bartók, Mira and Christine Ronan. *Ancient and Living Cultures Series Stencils. West Africa Ghana.* Glenview, IL: GoodYearBooks, 1993.

Komenda Publishing Company

ORDER FORM

To Order:

Return this form with your payment to Komenda Publishing Company, P.O. Box 38-1395, Cambridge, MA 02238-1395

Ordered by:

Name ______________________

Address ______________________

City ______________________

State/Prov. ______________________

Zip/Postal Code ______________________

Country ______________________

Ship to: (only if different)

Name ______________________

Address ______________________

City ______________________

State/Prov. ______________________

Zip/Postal Code ______________________

Country ______________________

ISBN	Description	Price Each	Quantity	Price Total
0-9644912-3-0	ORACLE Reporting	$36.00		
			Subtotal (books)	
			Delivery in MA, add 5% Sales Tax	
			Add shipping and handling (from chart)	
			TOTAL	

Shipping, packing, and handling	U.S.	International
First book	$4.00	$6.00
Each additional book	$2.00	$3.00

Method of Payment:

All prices stated in U.S. dollars.

☐ Check enclosed, payable to Komenda Publishing Company

Thank You!

OR695

SOLOMON R. BAKER LIBRARY
3 1725 00363 0840